Between Past and Future

Quebec Education in Transition

Norman Henchey
Donald A. Burgess

Detselig Enterprises Limited
Calgary, Alberta

Norman Henchey
Donald A. Burgess
McGill University

Canadian Cataloguing in Publication Data

Henchey, Norman.   Between past and future

Bibliography: p.
Includes index.
ISBN: 0-920490-72-7

1. Education – Quebec (Province) – 1965- 2. Educa-
tion – Quebec (Province) – History.   I. Burgess,
Donald A.   II. Title.
 LA418.Q7H453   1987   370'.9714   C87-091237-2

© 1987 Detselig Enterprises Ltd.
P.O. Box G 399
Calgary, Alberta T3A 2G3

Printed in Canada   SAN 115-0324   ISBN 0-920490-72-7

Preface

The Quiet Revolution of the 1960s represented an important turning point in the evolution of Quebec society. A significant component of this Quiet Revolution was in the field of education which, in the process, underwent a transformation of major proportions.

The relationship between education and culture has always been of prime importance in Quebec, so much so that the Province's education system is subjected to continuous close scrutiny by the politicians, the press and the public. Changes, proposed changes, and even the hint of changes to Quebec's system of education almost always result in heated debate from virtually all sectors of society.

In spite of this detailed and almost daily attention to education and although there are many fine works dealing with the history of education in Quebec, we are unaware of any work that attempts to be comprehensive in its treatment, contemporary in the issues it engages, and both descriptive and analytical in its approach. These are our goals in writing this book.

We have taken as our primary concern the period beginning in 1960 with the Quiet Revolution and ending in the mid-1980s, a turbulent quarter-century in Quebec's educational development. We see Quebec through the eyes of English-speaking Quebecers, one born in the Province, one not; but what we are trying to see is the basic structure and spirit of Quebec education in its entirety, not just as it touches our own linguistic community. If this book is by English Quebecers, it is, nevertheless, about Quebec education as a whole, not only English-language education.

The book is addressed to our fellow Quebecers, English and French alike, and to those outside of Quebec who sometimes have considerable difficulty in keeping *au courant* with the changing vista of the Quebec educational scene. Although we do not claim to have turned our attention to every single aspect of Quebec education, we have attempted to treat our subject from a broad and comprehensive perspective – but without cluttering the view; and we have endeavoured to place these events in a context between Quebec's past, dominated by history and tradition, and its tentative future.

The first three chapters establish the specific contexts: the social, economic, political and cultural environments (Chapter 1); the historical traditions which have shaped contemporary education (Chapter 2); and the legal and political structures which provide the framework for education (Chapter 3). The next three chapters examine the three broad categories of the education system: the compulsory elementary-secondary sector (Chapter 4); the post-secondary sector of colleges and universities (Chapter 5); and the formal and non-formal patterns of adult education (Chapter 6). The next two chapters examine the major resources devoted to Quebec education: the human and intellectual resources of teachers and the general field of educational research (Chapter 7); and the financial resources which represent the investment of Quebec society in its learning commitments (Chapter 8). The last two chapters bring together the main policy issues: those rooted in the past (Chapter 9), and those which emerge in present trends and future possibilities (Chapter 10). Finally, in an *Afterword*, we could not resist the temptation to offer our own assessment of the present state of education in Quebec.

Throughout the text we have attempted to provide both a description of events, structures, and trends as well as an analysis of their meaning, significance, and implications. There are obvious risks to such an approach. We recognize that even description is far from objective and that analysis is of its nature problematic. In both description and analysis, we have tried to balance being fair with being stimulating, We trust that this approach will help to demystify what is, as we quickly discovered, a complicated subject and will provide a basis for appraisal and critical discussion.

For those who require more detail or wish to explore a particular aspect in depth, we have provided several appendices and a detailed bibliography of some of the more important source documents. As the language of this book is English and the majority of our sources are French, we also thought it wise to include a glossary of some of the terms and expressions that are widely used in Quebec education, but are little known outside of that milieu. Wherever possible, we have translated into English many terms, expressions and titles for which the French versions are in everyday use in Quebec, even within the English-speaking community. In some cases, we have taken liberty with the law, translating titles such as *Ministère de l'Education* and *Gouvernement du Quebec* in order to preserve a smooth flow in the text. This decision on behalf of style is not intended as a political statement.

Finally, we wish to thank McGill University, the Faculty of Education and the Department of Administration and Policy Studies for granting us sabbatic leaves so that we might research background information and begin the writing process. We also wish to thank our friends and colleagues at McGill and elsewhere who have provided resource materials or assisted in providing critical commentary during the book's preparation: Morton Bain, Joan Bénéteau, Réal Boulianne, Roger Magnuson, and Ronald Tali of McGill University, Robert Lavery of Dawson College, Gerald Brown of the Quebec Ministry of Education, and Jean-R. Deronzier and Jacques de Lorimier of the Superior Council of Education. In spite of their invaluable assistance, the views expressed and the responsibility for what follows are exclusively our own.

Norman Henchey
Donald Burgess

Montreal, August 1987

Contents

Detselig Enterprises Ltd. appreciates the financial
assistance for its 1987 publishing program from

Alberta Foundation for the Literary Arts
Canada Council
Department of Communications
Alberta Culture

1

Quebec Today: Society and Education

Many people view Quebec with a combination of fascination and apprehension. Those who live outside Quebec are often drawn by its distinctive style and European charm, its different language and customs, its fine cuisine and artistic originality. However, they are sometimes apprehensive of a "foreign" language and an unfamiliar culture and they may be disturbed or threatened by the political assertiveness – sometimes strident – with which Quebec has expressed its identity and its aspirations in recent decades. Those who live within Quebec are also fascinated by their unique society, but they too are apprehensive when they think of the past, and they are anxious about the survival of Quebec and its future development.

Quebec is not a simple reality, easily studied and understood. It is complex, varied, and spiced with ambiguities, contradictions and tensions. Any attempt to appreciate the contemporary realities of Quebec must weigh these tensions:

1. Quebec has historical, political and economic ties with the rest of Canada and economic and social ties with the Unitied States. Also, Quebec is a distinctive society that is dominantly French in language and culture and is served by institutions that arise from different historical traditions than those in English North America. It is drawn by a social vision that seems different from those of other provinces.

2. Quebec is a political unit, one of ten Canadian provinces that comprise the federal structure of the nation. Quebec is the home of one of the two founding peoples of Canada. It is an integral society in its own right, a political partner, and equal in importance, it believes, with English-speaking Canada.

3. Quebec places great emphasis on history and tradition, in some ways tending to be conservative and elitist. It is also a revolutionary society that has undergone profound social, cultural and economic transformations in the past twenty-five years to become increasingly dynamic, pluralistic, innovative and egalitarian.

4. The French of Quebec are more secure in their strong majority status in the province, but are still anxious about the survival of their language and culture in an English-speaking continental culture. The English of Quebec are insecure in their minority status in Quebec and anxious about the future of their communities and institutions, but are reassured by being part of the North American majority.

5. Issues of language, culture, philosophy, structure, the "collectivity" and constitutional rights are priorities on the social agenda of Quebec. Also on the agenda are issues of economic growth, technological advance, jobs, lifestyles, and individual freedom.

6. Quebec tends to be inward-looking, preoccupied with its own goals and needs and devising its own institutions and structures. Yet Quebec is forging close and varied links with France and the world French-language community, with other provinces, with various regions of the United States, and increasingly with the Far East.

Part of the dynamics of contemporary Quebec arises from the ambiguities of its existence and its aspirations: French society or multicultural society? Cultural and linguistic priorities or political and social ones? Political independence or economic interdependence? Centralized institutions to provide equality of opportunity or decentralized structures to encourage participation and differentiation? Respect for traditions or adaptation to a high-technology post-industrial future? Individual rights or collective responsibilities? Coherent planning or pragmatic action?

In its goals, structures, institutions and policies, Quebec is trying to find its own way. In this ongoing endeavour, education is at once the photograph of Quebec's past, the mirror of its present, and the screen on which it is projecting its future.

The People of Quebec

In terms of geographic size, Quebec is the largest province in Canada with 16% of the total territory. In terms of population, 6.5 million people were living in Quebec in the mid-1980s making it the province with the second largest population, after Ontario (8.9 million). One Canadian in four lives in Quebec.

Quebec's population density (the number of people per square kilometer) is half that of Ontario (the province with which it is most frequently compared). The pattern of distribution of the Quebec population shows a marked contrast between high concentration in the Montreal region and thin diffusion through the rest of the province. (See Table 1.1).

The growth of the Quebec population has not been keeping pace with that of the rest of Canada. In 1966, the Quebec population was almost 29% of Canada; by 1981, it had slipped to 26% and, given the trends, it will be around

Table 1.1

Population Distribution by Administrative Region
Quebec, 1983

Administrative Region	Number	%
Bas-Saint-Laurent – Gaspésie	236 700	3.6
Saguenay – Lac-Saint-Jean	304 800	4.7
Québec	1 045 100	16.0
Trois Rivie`res	448 500	6.9
Estrie	240 800	3.7
Montréal	3 677 200	56.5
Ile-Montréal	*(1 760 100)*	*(27.0)*
Nord et Sud	*(1 917 400)*	*(29.5)*
Outaouais	274 700	4.2
Abitibi-Témiscamingue (N.W.)	154 800	2.4
Côte-Nord	115 100	1.8
Nouveau Québec	18 300	0.3
Total	6 516 100	100

Adapted from: *Le Quebec statistique, Edition 1985-86,* Tableau 3, p. 88.

24% in the year 2000. In recent years, Quebec's growth rate has been approximately half that of the Canadian average.

This decrease in Quebec's share of the population is the result of three factors: the number of immigrants coming into Quebec, the number of Quebecers leaving the province, and the fertility rate within Quebec. Between 1976 and 1981, 100,000 more people left the province then entered it. A smaller proportion of recent immigrants from other countries were settling in Quebec and the province was also losing more of its people to other provinces than it was receiving from them, though the patterns of inter-provincial migration vary considerably from one year to another. At the same time, the fertility rate in Quebec (or the number of children per woman of child-bearing age) has dropped dramatically in the last 20 years, from 3.8 in 1961 to 2.0 in 1971 (slightly below zero population growth) to only 1.5 in 1983; it is now the third lowest in the world after West Germany and Denmark. This decline of population growth through migration and a birth rate below replacement levels is a subject of considerable concern because it has serious implications for the influence of Quebec within Canada, for the future of the French language and culture in the province, and for the evolution of the education system.

At the same time, the Quebec population is aging. In 1971, the median age was 25.6; in 1984, it was 31.0, a rapid rise. An aging population raises a number of questions about the ability of a smaller work force to support a larger dependent population of older citizens in the decades to come, about changes that need to be made in the priorities and resources for education and other social services, as well as about the political and economic vitality of the society at the beginning of the next century.[1]

Another important feature of the Quebec population is its linguistic and ethnic composition. There are important differences in this regard between Quebec and Ontario, as we can see in Table 1.2. The dominant group is stronger in Quebec than in Ontario and so is the second language group (English in Quebec). The linguistic diversity of Ontario, however, is greater than that of Quebec.

Table 1.2

Population Distribution by Mother Tongue, Quebec and Ontario

	Quebec	Ontario
French	82%	6%
English	11%	77%
Other	7%	17%
Total	100%	100%

Source: Statistics Canada, 1981 census.

While Quebec is unquestionably a French society in language and culture, there are one million Quebecers whose mother tongue is other than French, the largest linguistic minorities being the English, Italians and native peoples.

The English-language community does not represent a unified group. Over the years, the English and Scots have been joined by successive waves of American, Irish, Jewish, European, East Indian, West Indian, and other peoples. The community is also divided by religion, with different educational, social, and cultural institutions for Catholics, Protestants, Jews, and other groups. During this century, the English-language community has been declining in size and is becoming more concentrated in the Montreal area; these trends have been accentuated since the 1960s.[2]

A Post-Industrial Economy

The structure of the Quebec economy is an important context for the study of Quebec education. First, the economy provides the resources from which the society must draw for its investments in education. Second, the economy determines the job market which the majority of young Quebecers and many adults are preparing to enter after completing their education.

A popular image of Quebec's economy is one that is based on farming, pulp and paper, and mining, but the reality is quite different. Primary industries such as agriculture, forestry, fishing and mining account for under 4% of the gross provincial product (the value of all the goods and services produced in Quebec in a year). Secondary industries, such as manufacturing and construction, account for around 25%, and contrary to the popular image, over 70% of Quebec's wealth comes from tertiary industries: transportation, communications, energy, commerce, finance, services, and public administration.

The trends are clear if we look at the past 15 years (Table 1.3). Quebec has an advanced industrial economy and is moving into a post-industrial economy which is based largely on such services as information, communication, education, research, and consulting.

Table 1.3

Major Economic Trends

Sector	1969	1979	1983
Primary	5.3%	4.9%	3.9%
Secondary	33.3%	28.2%	25.4%
Tertiary	61.4%	66.2%	70.7%

Source: *Le Québec statistique, Édition 1985-1986, p. 137.*

As Quebec moves into the late 1980s, its economy is undergoing substantial restructuring as a result of increasing global competition, changing patterns of demand, concerns about the public debt and the cost of government, and the impact of the new technologies which are reshaping the economies of most developed regions. Changing styles and values are affecting the demand for goods and services, reducing some markets and expanding others. Job opportunities in the public sector (the civil service) and the parapublic sector (health, social welfare, education) are likely to be limited as attempts are made to control the cost of government. Computers, entertainment, and communication technologies are having a profound effect on the direction of economic development.

These developments are affecting the kinds and numbers of jobs being created, the relative importance of different industries, as well as the lifestyle of

Quebecers. For example, much of the wealth of the province is being generated by large-scale enterprises such as hydro-electric projects, yet most of the new jobs are being created by small and medium-size companies.[3]

The Politics of Identity

The political life of Quebec usually has different preoccupations from politics in other provinces. Prior to the 1960s, there were three major priorities of Quebec politics: first, the preservation of existing social patterns, especially those of language, religion and culture; second, the maintenance of a delicate balance among various forces, notably Church and state, French and English, politics and business, the elite and the masses; and third, the defence of provincial rights guaranteed in the Canadian constitution and established through custom.

During the Quiet Revolution, the political priority of preserving social patterns was transformed into a critical examination of existing structures and the development of policies that sought to modernize Quebec. The balance of forces was disturbed: the Church withdrew from its traditional position of political and social influence; the French majority sought to take charge of the economy; and Quebec's leadership moved to establish a more integrated social, political, and economic structure. The government took a more assertive posture in its dealings with Ottawa and the other provinces arguing that Quebec was not a province *comme les autres*, that it had to have the opportunity to define its own priorities, that its government must be able to ensure the dominance of French in Quebec, and that the province needed to broaden the scope of its influence.

Through the sixties and early seventies, the political preoccupations of Quebec were primarily the modernization and strengthening of the political structures of government, the secularization of social services, the transformation of public education, and the expansion of its influence in such fields as communications, economic policy and external relations.

While successive Quebec governments generally pursued these goals within the framework of the Canadian federal system, a second body of opinion developed in the province. This held that Quebec could never achieve its political, social and economic goals to become a mature society while remaining within Canada. They argued that there would be continuing frustration in Quebec and ongoing conflict between Quebec and the rest of Canada unless their province became an independent nation. The Parti Québécois arose from this conviction, and the FLQ and the War Measures Act of 1970 clearly underscored the point.

The Parti Québécois under the leadership of René Lévesque came to power in 1976, and governed for a decade. This government was committed to continuing the policies of modernization, social integration, and enhancing its international profile. It pursued these goals with less emphasis on economic development than on cultural and social aims: expanding government influence; regulating and promoting the French language in education, business and public signs (Bill 101); and encouraging the integration of minorities into the Quebec culture. Other goals included promoting Quebec culture in other countries and struggling with the federal government over the political control of Quebec.

By the mid-1980s, the emphasis shifted once again, from cultural and political issues to economic concerns. The rejection of the "sovereignty-association" option in the referendum of May 1980, the Canada Bill of 1982 (which patriated the constitution over the objection of Quebec and established a national Charter of Rights and Freedoms), and a series of Court decisions striking down certain provisions of Bill 101 all weakened the political momentum towards some form of independence. At the same time, the economic recession of the early 1980s, continuing concerns about job creation and economic development, and the impact of communications technologies raised economic issues to a higher priority on the political agenda.

This economic shift continued with the return to power of Robert Bourassa and the Liberal Party in 1985. Quebec, like many other societies, is undergoing a general movement towards political conservatism, a reduction of the role of government, and a greater emphasis on the private sector.

There are three political challenges now facing Quebec. The first is the continuing modernization of structures in the light of rapid economic, social and technological change – while preserving both the unique tradition and culture of the society and the system of social services which has been developed. The second challenge is the ongoing task of balancing the need for social integration with the requirements of a pluralistic society with different value systems, aspirations, and languages. The third includes the restoration of Quebec's particular status in the Canadian constitution, the strengthening of Quebec's influence on its future development, and the expansion of its international relations, especially with the community of French-language societies.[4]

Social and Cultural Development

Quebec society has undergone profound changes during the past twenty-five years. Social institutions have shifted from religious to secular control, family structures have altered, the role of women has changed substantially, and leisure activities have become more important. The traditional mosaic of French Quebecers, English Quebecers and Quebecers who come from other language and cultural groups has altered. The cultural and language policies of Quebec governments, which reinforced the French culture and language, have prompted some Quebecers to move elsewhere, changing the traditional patterns of migration. Strong homogenizing and Americanizing forces are at work on Quebec culture, a result of the increasing levels of schooling and urbanization of the population, the wider distribution of wealth, and especially the influence of the media.

In recent decades, Quebec's artistic community has undergone a renaissance that is characterized by great energy and creativity in music, visual arts, design, literature, theatre, dance and cinema. Quebec's culture has become enlivened by the contributions of different ethnic communities within its midst. Cultural development was supported by government aid, by a thriving publishing industry, and by the development of libraries, museums, and art galleries. Expo '67, the Olympic Games, world class art exhibitions, film and music festivals, a celebrated symphony orchestra and other such initiatives created a showcase for Quebec cultural achievements and provided an opportunity for Quebecers to share in the cultural experiences of other nations.

The period since 1960 was also one of intellectual accomplishment. Universities expanded dramatically between the 1960s and the 1980s. An important part of this expansion was in pure and applied research; significant research was also undertaken in corporations such as Hydro-Quebec, in government agencies, and in specialized research institutes. Another index of this activity is that, in 1983, an estimated 4,000 books and over 2,000 short works were published in Quebec.

The artistic and intellectual life of Quebec is also interrelated with that of other countries, especially the United States. Imports such as rock videos, cable television systems, VCR's, computer games, fast-food franchises, American films, magazines, and newspapers, and designer clothes, together with vacations in Maine and Florida, are all moving Quebec in the direction of a North American consumer society.

A remarkable social development has been the rapid and thorough secularization of the social structure. The parish has ceased to be the basic social unit; unions and professional associations are no longer Catholic; most health, social service and educational institutions have severed their formal affiliation with the Church. Thousands of priests and nuns have left their religious vocations, though many remain in their professions as teachers and social workers.

No less dramatic have been the changes in the Quebec family. The number of marriages has declined and, at the same time, divorces have increased from 6% of marriages in 1969 to 57% in 1982. One family in five is headed by a single parent, usually the mother, and often living in poverty. The decline in birth rate has already been noted.

A closely related trend is the changing role of women in Quebec society. Women's child-bearing responsibilities have decreased; their schooling has improved; their traditional roles as full-time wives and mothers have changed; the opportunities and choices open to them have expanded. In recent years, Quebec women are benefitting from reformed legal systems, improved maternity leave and daycare facilities, and a greater range of supportive organizations and networks. Though women are still underrepresented in politics, senior management, scientific professions and graduate programs, their influence as professionals, workers, volunteers and citizens is changing the face of Quebec society.

A last major trend is the growing importance of leisure in Quebec society. While Quebecers do not pursue "lifestyle" with the intensity of people in California and British Columbia, leisure activities are increasingly important as many Quebecers enjoy shorter work weeks, earlier retirement, longer lives, and longer vacations. Unemployment or underemployment also influences the need for leisure activities.

All of these social trends – cultural transformation, American consumerism, secularization, changing family structures, the new role of women, and the increasing importance of leisure – affect education. Some of these trends such as culture and leisure have implications for curriculum; some such as secularization put pressure on education structures. Changing family patterns and roles for women have implications for the role of the school in society. The general consumer or "pop" culture is the environment in which education functions and with which it must compete. Social and cultural cohesion is not easily achieved or preserved in such a pluralistic and changing environment.[5]

Quebec Education Today

The learning enterprise in Quebec is large, complex and expensive. In the broadest sense, the education system includes preschool programs, a compulsory elementary and secondary school system, a post-secondary structure of colleges and universities, and a variety of formal and non-formal learning activities for adults of all ages.

One Quebecer in three is involved in formal learning activities as a student, teacher, administrator, professional specialist or other worker. There are over 1.5 million students in formal programs from kindergarten to graduate studies, who study in 3,000 institutions under the guidance of 100,000 teachers and other professionals. This educational enterprise costs around $9 billion a year or $2,700 for every working person in the province.

The legal structure of Quebec education is like that of other provinces. It is based on the Canadian Constitution and is governed by a comprehensive Education Act which is regularly amended. Specialized acts deal with colleges, universities, private schools and other issues. Within this framework of school legislation, authority is exercised through over thirty regulations or orders-in-council of the provincial cabinet and hundreds of directives of the Ministry of Education.

Two government departments are primarily responsible for education: a Ministry of Education and a Ministry of Higher Education and Science. There are also a number of advisory bodies established to deal with various aspects of educational policy. The Ministry of Education has responsibility for the overall coordination of preschool, elementary, secondary, and some adult education. The Ministry of Higher Education and Science is responsible for colleges, universities, research, and science policy.

The local administration of preschool, elementary, secondary and some adult education is the responsibility of 234 school boards (1986 figures), divided along religious lines: 201 boards for Catholics (largely French), 29 for Protestants (largely English), and 4 multi-confessional boards (largely for native peoples).

The general structure of the education system is outlined in Figure 1.1. At the preschool level, there is a half-day kindergarten program available for 5-year-olds, a special program for 4-year-olds who are living in economically deprived areas or who have recently arrived in Quebec and must attend French schools. The elementary program normally lasts 6 years. Children are grouped according to age, 6-year-olds in the first year. Exceptionally able children may move to secondary school after five years. Pupils not ready for secondary school after the sixth year may stay a seventh (around 4% do so).

The secondary program lasts for five years and is divided into two cycles. Most courses are obligatory in the first cycle while there is a mix of required and elective courses in the second. Courses in vocational subjects are generally deferred to the last years of secondary school. There is a sixth year for those who wish to complete their program or take technical courses.

Slightly more than one-half of students finishing secondary school go on to further study in one of Quebec's 47 colleges (*colle`ges d'enseignement ge´ne´ral et professionnel,* or CEGEPs). These institutions are public and free and they offer two kinds of programs; three-year technical or career programs and two-year pre-university programs. There is no direct passage from high school to university in Quebec.

Around 20% of college students go on to undergraduate programs in one of Quebec's 7 universities. Undergraduate (first cycle) programs are usually three years or 90 credits in length and lead to a bachelor's degree. The patterns of master's, doctoral and advanced professional programs are very much like those of other provinces.

In addition to the public system, there is a network of private institutions offering programs at preschool, elementary, secondary or college levels. Many of these institutions receive government grants at the level of 60% or 80% of operating costs. In general, private elementary and secondary schools follow the same curriculum as the public schools.

The field of adult education includes a wide range of formal adult education courses offered by school boards, colleges, and universities. As well, adult education encompasses an even wider range of non-formal learning activities provided by business and industry, cultural institutions such as museums and libraries, the resources of the print and electronic media. Others are services offered by governments and by professional and voluntary organizations.

The teaching profession in Quebec is unionized and organized in local organizations at the school board level and in three provincial associations, one

Age		Year	Level	Division
17+	22+		University	Graduate
16	21	3		Undergraduate
15	20	2		
14	19	1		
(14)	19	(3)	College	
13	18	2		
12	17	1		
(12)	17	(6)	Secondary	Cycle Two
11	16	5		
10	15	4		
9	14	3		
8	13	2		Cycle One
7	12	1		
(7)	12	(7)	Elementary	Cycle Two
6	11	6		
5	10	5		
4	9	4		
3	8	3		Cycle One
2	7	2		
1	6	1		
–	5	K	Preschool	Kindergarten
–	4	P		Pre-Kindergarten

Figure 1. Structure of the Quebec Education System

for French teachers and certain other employees working for Catholic boards, one for English Catholic teachers and one for teachers employed by Protestant school boards There is a basic collective agreement for all teachers in Quebec covering salaries, classification, working conditions and grievance procedures. Most teachers at college and university levels are also unionized and covered by collective agreements.

Curriculum at the preschool, elementary, and secondary levels is established by the Ministry of Education. There is a formal curriculum structure (*régime pédagogique*) and there are detailed programs of study, lists of approved materials, and some official examinations. A curriculum framework and program guides also exist at the college level, though with more variation in content than at the secondary level. University programs are prepared by the institutions, but they must be approved by a committee of the association of universities and by the Council of Universities before they are formally recognized and funded.

The financing of the overall system of education in Quebec is highly centralized. The provincial government contributes 86% of the funds for education through grants to school boards and to private and post-secondary institutions, through student aid, and through the operation of the Ministries of Education and Higher Education. Local school boards and other forms of local government provide 2% of total revenues through local school taxes and payment for services. The federal government contributes 6% through manpower training programs, federal schools for native peoples, scholarships, and research grants. A final 6% of funds come from tuition, foundations, and private donations.[6]

Patterns

The general pattern of enrolments in Quebec is given in Table 1.4.

Enrolments have been falling in most areas of the public preschool, elementary, and secondary education sectors. This decline has been going on for some time, but many now be levelling out. Declines are serious in secondary school, especially in vocational programs and in the English sector. In contrast to the falling public school enrolments, private school enrolments have increased. College enrolments have increased slightly but university enrolments have continued to increase substantially. One striking characteristic of Quebec university enrolment is the large number of part-time students, equal in number to the full-time students and representing about 40% of the equivalent of full-time students. The enrolment estimate for adult education represents individuals following courses during 1983. It is hard to arrive at a reliable estimate of the number of adults taking courses because there is overlap among categories and because the programs vary in length.

In 1985-1986, students were being served by 2,542 public and 267 private elementary and secondary schools, 10 schools operated directly by the Quebec government and 30 schools under the jurisdiction of the federal government. At the post-secondary level, there were 47 public colleges (CEGEPS), 30 private colleges and 7 universities.

Almost 88,000 people worked in this elementary and secondary school system including 61,000 teachers and 6,000 administrators. This is an overall decline in personnel of 7.5% since 1981.

In 1985-1986, there were 123,000 pupils receiving elementary and secondary education in English. This represented about 11% of the school population and is largely concentrated (80%) in the Montreal area. Another 27,000 students were studying in the one private and four public English-language colleges and there were 37,000 students in the three English-language universities.

Table 1.4

Quebec Enrolment Patterns, 1981-82 and 1985-86

Level	1981-82	1985-86	% change
Preschool, Elementary, Secondary			
Preschool (4 years)	7 300	6 400	−12
Preschool (5 years)	90 300	94 700	+ 5
Elementary	554 800	568 600	+ 2
Secondary (General)	450 200	418 500	− 7
Secondary (Vocational)	81 100	50 200	−38
Total	1 183 700	1 138 400	− 4
Special Groups (included in above)			
Private Schools	87 600	95 300	+ 9
Learning Difficulties	93 100	110 500	+19
Special French	4 900	4 500	− 7
Lang. of Instruction: English	155 600	123 000	−21
French	1 027 100	1 013 400	− 1
Native	800	2 100	+252
Mother Tongue: English	120 300	102 400	−16
French	989 700	962 200	− 3
Other	73 500	73 900	+0.5
College (Full-Time)			
Pre-university	72 200	79 700	+10
Career (Technical)	69 100	77 100	+12
Total	141 300	156 800	+11
University (Full-time)			
Undergraduate	79 500	93 400	+17
Graduate	14 100	18 300	+30
Total	93 600	111 700	+19
University (part-time Registrations)			
Undergraduate and Certificate	83 100	97 400	+17
Graduate	12 100	13 500	+11
Total	95 200	110 900	+17
Adult Education (Estimate, 1983) ...	800 000		

Adapted from the following sources: Québec, *Statistiques de l'éducation: Préscolaire, primaire, secondaire* (Québec, Direction générale de la recherche et de la prospective, 1985), p. 15; Statistics Canada, *Advance Statistics of Education, 1985-1986*, p. 24-25; Québec, MEQ, *Rapport annuel 1985-1986* (Québec, 1986), p. 47-52; Statistics Canada, *One in Every Five.* (Ottawa, 1985).

The cost of the total system of education was $9 billion in 1985-1986. Quebec is currently devoting a larger share of its resources to education than Ontario; in 1985, Quebec spent 8.4% of its gross provincial product on education, compared to 6.5% for Ontario. In terms of income, the average Quebecer is spending $1 out of every $10 on education.[7]

There are a number of patterns which emerge from this picture:

1. Education in Quebec is an enormous social project, one that touches two million people, or one Quebecer in three, as a young student, adult learner, educator or other worker in the education system.

2. Education must be seen as a total system, from preschool services for young children to advanced post-secondary training, with the system including both formal institutions like schools and non-formal learning activities in a variety of contexts.

3. Private schools form a second system of considerable size and importance.

4. There is a complete English sector, from preschool to university and adult education.

5. Enrolments have been declining since 1981 in secondary education, in vocational programs, and in English-language education; they have been increasing at the elementary level, in programs of special education, programs for native peoples, and at the post-secondary level.

6. Quebec invests a great deal of money in education, both in absolute dollars and as a proportion to its overall wealth.

Policy Issues

There have been three major policy issues in Quebec education over the past two decades.

Expansion and Contraction

One of the priorities of the educational reforms of the 1960s was the expansion of educational opportunities for all Quebecers and a reduction of disparities in attainment among groups. A good deal of energy and money have been devoted to this goal and, so far, the results have been a qualified success.

Significant advances have been made in the level of schooling since 1971. Disparities still remain in the education system: between men and women and among ethnic groups. English-speaking people have the highest educational attainment of any group in Quebec, while French-speaking Quebecers remain behind English-speaking Quebecers in secondary school attainment and in university attendance access.

Yet the success of the policy is shown in the young population, 15 to 24 years of age. Quebec is now above the Canadian average in most categories of schooling and the gap between Quebec and Ontario has narrowed.

Two other measures indicate the success of the policy of expanding educational services and improving the retention rate of elementary and secondary schools. Between 1978 and 1984, the number of drop-outs was reduced by over 50%, and the number of young people returning to school after having dropped out has increased five-fold.[8]

If the trend towards increasing the level of schooling of the Quebec population has been in the form of pressure towards enlarging the system, a second trend has been a decline in enrolments, especially at the elementary and secondary levels. This is a result of migration patterns and especially of declining birth rates.

French public elementary and secondary enrolments declined by 15% between 1976 and 1982 and have almost levelled off since 1982; between 1976 and 1982, the English public school enrolments have declined by 38% and have fallen another 20% since 1982. Declining enrolments have had serious effects. The demand for teachers tied by fixed ratios to enrolments, dropped by 16% between 1976 and 1984. As a result, many teachers have left the profession or have been placed in the category of surplus teachers. Over 200 schools have been closed, often weakening the ties between school and the local community and requiring pupils to travel greater distances. The education support system of counselors, psychologists, consultants and specialists has been reduced by 20%. The reduction in staff, however, was not followed by a reduction in the operating expenses of school boards. These expenses rose from $2.8 billion in 1976 to $4.4 billion in 1984, an increase of 60%, mostly due to inflation.[9]

Centralization and Decentralization

As the system was undergoing conflicting trends of expansion and contraction, a second set of opposing trends pulled the structure of power and authority in two directions: one towards greater centralization and integration, the other towards greater decentralization and differentiation.

Since the beginning of the Quiet Revolution in 1960, a continuous and dramatic shift of power has occurred, away from local authorities and the Church to the government. In education, specifically, power has shifted to the Ministry of Education which was established in 1964. The Ministry assumed vigorous leadership in implementing the reforms of the Parent Report, in establishing new structures, in providing new funds for the development of the system, and in unifying different sectors and levels into a more coherent structure.

This impetus to expand the power and prestige of the Ministry of Education was supported by a number of factors: the pressure to control rapidly growing expenditures, the political status of the Quebec government as the major political institution able to modernize Quebec, an ethic of equality of opportunity, and a belief in the rationality of general systems theory. Over the two decades between the mid-1960s and the mid-1980s, the MEQ assumed control over negotiations with the teaching profession, exercised increasingly precise supervision over planning and budgets in all parts of the system and intervened more directly in private education. The MEQ also increased the standardization, precision, and control of curriculum, exercised powerful influence over the public colleges (CEGEPs), drew the universities more closely into a single post-secondary network, and became the dominant source of funds for all public education from preschool through university.

This concentration of power in the Ministry has had three effects. First, power was strengthened in other provincial structures because it forced groups such as teachers, parents, school boards, minority groups and universities to organize on a provincial basis. Second, local school boards experienced ongoing erosion of their power to raise taxes, control budget priorities, hire and utilize teachers, or determine curriculum. Third, Quebec education moved towards a bewildering and complex bureaucracy with floods of directives, massive documentation, intricate and complicated collective agreements and operating procedures. These trends reached a climax in the implementation of new curriculum guidelines, the *régimes pédagogiques,* of the early 1980s and through a series of attempts (ultimately unsuccessful) to produce what was to be a new education act with a completely reorganized structure of school boards (Bills 40 and 3).

As may be expected, this trend towards centralization did not go unopposed. Major challenges came from the English Protestant community, the school boards, and from within the government itself. The Protestant educational community saw its size diminishing, its independence challenged, and its distinctiveness compromised. It moved to mobilize its forces and to stand on the constitutional protections of Protestant education. School boards fought to preserve their taxations rights, preserve their role as locally elected and responsible government, and to oppose legal attempts to alter their traditional powers.

A third decentralizing force arose from a series of government proposals over the past twenty-five years to emphasize the freedom and autonomy of the individual school and to involve parents in the development of educational policy. Yet the processes of decentralization appeared feeble, even illusory, in the face of the structures and resources supporting centralization. An uneasy, shifting and unstable balance of forces is being maintained, between ministry and school boards, institutions and structures, majority and minority, public and private bodies, management and employees, and parents and professionals.

Resources and Quality

By almost every measure and criterion, Quebec has an advanced education system. Many administrators have training in management sciences. Teachers have a combination of higher qualifications, more experience, better salaries and job security, and lighter workloads than their colleagues in many other places in North America. Physical facilities are impressive thanks to massive building programs in the sixties and seventies. A whole set of new programs for every subject from kindergarten to the end of secondary school has been developed and is being implemented. Teaching materials, the professional services of specialists, counselors, animators, and psychologists support teaching and learning. Microcomputers are being introduced into schools and classrooms with impressive speed and at substantial costs. Hundreds of thousands of pages of briefs, consultations, studies, working papers, policy statements and guidelines have been produced to regulate and guide the quality of education. Thousands and thousands of serious, competent, and hardworking professionals are trying to provide quality learning services to young people.

Yet there is ample evidence of dissatisfaction with the quality of education in Quebec. A lead editorial in *Le Devoir* begins: "For a number of years now the malaise has been apparent: our education system needs to be brought up to date and reexamined in terms of the needs of the decades ahead." An Estates General on education, organized by teachers, school boards, the Ministry and parents, speaks of the urgency to improve the quality of education. Between 1980 and 1984, the success rate in government examinations at the end of secondary school was 60% with only 42% of pupils in the largest school board, the Montreal Catholic School Commission, succeeding in all their examinations. A series of articles called "*Rapport sur l'école*" in *L'Actualite* takes this as its theme: "Twenty years after the educational reform, dissatisfaction is general and profound." A Sorecom opinion poll in January 1986 reports that 58% of Quebecers believe that, considering the cost, the education system could be achieving better results. In a national Reid poll in August 1986, the question was asked: "Overall, do you think children in public schools today are getting a better education than they would have 25 years ago?" In other parts of the country, between 20% and 30% believe the quality of education has deteriorated, but in Quebec 59% believe the quality of education has deteriorated. A government report on writing skills among French-language pupils in 1986 indicates that the average grade-eleven pupil makes one mistake in every ten words.[10]

Many issues enter the debate about the quality of education in Quebec: competence in reading and expressing oneself in one's mother tongue, ability in a second language, importance of traditional values of responsibility and respect, and relevance of training for the job market. Rigidity and complexity of the system, poor quality of labor relations and costs of operating the system are other concerns, as well as the level of performance of secondary school graduates, insufficient attention to pupils above or below the average, and the ability of the system to meet the challenges of the new technologies.

The educational reforms of the sixties raised Quebecers' expectations that high quality learning services could be made available for everyone. The political, social, technological and economic climate of the eighties makes these expectations no less pressing, and no less difficult to realize.

Conclusion

Quebec is a distinctive society – in tradition, language, culture, and sense of self – but this distinctiveness is fragile, shaped as much by events outside its boundaries as by those within. The population of Quebec is growing more slowly than that of Canada and it is aging. Quebec society has undergone profound transformations in recent years. Its political priorities have been shifting somewhat from linguistic and cultural issues to economic ones as its economy is transformed into a post-industrial, information-based structure.

In this complex and constantly evolving context, education struggles to bridge a distinctive past with an uncertain and compelling future. Educational policy must try to establish a framework for dealing with learning in society, preserving continuity with its past and yet responding in a creative manner to the challenges of the present and future.

Education in Quebec has not yet been able to establish widely accepted policies for some of the key issues inherited from the past: the relationship between French and English linguistic and cultural communities, the place of religious and moral values in public education, the participation of various stakeholders in shaping educational policy and practice, and the equilibrium between quality of learning and equality of opportunity to learn.

To these historical issues are added the ongoing challenge of the present and day-to-day management of a large, complex and diversified system which has been undergoing the turbulence of expansion and contraction, conflict among different groups, and criticism about the quality of education and its relevance for the needs of Quebec and Quebecers.

Of its very nature, education is also preparation for the future. Educational policy in Quebec must therefore look at the trends and choices which appear to be shaping its future: the changing patterns of the population, the impact of communication technology on its social and economic structure, the lessening power of government to shape events, growing cultural pluralism, a general climate of economic competition, the changing and complex role of knowledge in society, and new and converging patterns of work, learning, and leisure.

This agenda of issues from the past, in the present and for the future suggests the need for rethinking some fundamental educational policies. This implies three things: an understanding of what is taking place in Quebec education, an analysis of causes, patterns, and implications of what is taking place, and an exploration of what this may mean for the future of education in Quebec. It is to these that we now turn our attention.

Notes

1. Serge Courville, "Le développement québécois de l'ère pionnière aux conquêtes postindustrielles," *Le Québec statistique, Edition 1985-1986* (Québec: Bureau de las statistique du Québec, 1985), especially p. 51-56; Louis Duchesne, "L'évolution démographique du Québec, 1980-1984," Ibid., p. 75-111; Ibid., Chapter 4, "Population," p. 267-324; Québec, Bureau de la statistique du Québec, *L'avenir démographique du Quebec*, (Québec: BSQ, 1985); " Perspectives démographiques régionales, 1981-2006" (Québec: BSQ, 1984).

2. Gary Caldwell and Eric Waddell (eds.), *The English of Quebec: From Majority to Minority Status* (Québec: Institut québéois de recherche sur la culture, 1982), especially Eric Waddell, "Place and People" (p.27-56), Gary Caldwell, " People and Society" (p. 57-72), and David Rome, "Jews in anglophone Quebec" (p.161-175); Sheila McLeod Arnopoulos and Dominique Clift, *The English Fact in Quebec* (Montreal: McGill-Queen's Press, 1980); Ronald Rudin, *The Forgotten Quebecers: History of English-Speaking Quebec 1759-1980* (Québec: Institut québécois de recherche sur la culture, 1985).

3. Pierre Gouin, "L'économie du Québec au début des années quatre-vingt," *Le Quebec statistique*, p. 129-142; Ibid., Chapters 9, 15, 20, 21; Québec, Bureau de la statistique du Québec, *La situation économique du Quebec: 1984 et 1er semestre 1985* (Québec: 1985).

4. See: Léon Dion, *Quebec: The Unfinished Revolution* (Montreal: McGill-Queen's Press, 1976); Dale Thompson (Ed.), *Quebec: Society and Politics – Views from the Inside* (Toronto: McClelland and Stewart, 1973); Dale Postgate and Kenneth McRoberts, *Quebec: Social Change and Political Crisis,* (Toronto: McClelland and Stewart, 1976).

5. Marcel Fourneir, "L'évolution socio-culturelle du Québec de la Second Guerre Mondiale à aujourd'hui," *Le Québec statistique,* p. 113-128; Ibid., Chapter 8 "Culture and 20 Communications," Québec, Standing Committee on Social Development, *For Quebec Families: A Working Paper on Family Policy* (Québec: Government of Quebec, 1984), especially p. 15-29.

6. Québec, Ministère de l'Education, *Rapport annuel 1985-1986* (Québec: MEQ, (1986), Québec, Conseil supérieur de l'éducation, *Rapport annuel 1984-85* (Québec: CSE, *1985), Québec Statistique,* Chapter 7, p. 417-457, *Québec Statistiques Préśolaire, primaire, secondaire* (Québec 1985); Statistics Canada, *Advance Statistics of Education, 1985-86* (Ottawa, 1985).

7. Québec, Ministère de l'Education, *Rapport annuel 1985-86* (Québec: MEQ, 1986), p. 47-52; Québec Conseil supérieur de l'éducation, *Rapport annuel 1984-85* (Québec, CSE, 1985), Annexe 1; Québec MEQ, *Repertoire des organismes et des etablissements d'enseignement, Edition 1984-85* (Québec: MEQ,1984); *Le Quebec statistique,* Chapter 7, p. 417-457; Québec *Statistiques de l'education: Préścolaire, primaire, secondaire* (Québec, 1985); Québec, *Indicateurs sur la situation de l'enseignement primaire et secondaire* (Québec, 1986); Statistics Canada, *Advance Statistics of Education, 1985-86* (Ottawa, 1985).

8. Daniel Maisonneuve, *L'etat de scolarisation de la population québecoise* (Québec. MEQ, 1984); Québec, MEQ, "La situation linguistique dans les établissements d'enseignement" (Québec: MEQ, 1983); Québec, *Statistiques de l'éducation: Prescolaire, primaire, secondaire,* (Québec, 1985).

9. Québec, *Statistiques de l'éducation: Prescolaire, primaire, secondaire* (Québec, 1985); *Indicateurs sur la situation de l'enseignement primaire et secondaire* (Québec, 1986); Québec, MEQ, "La situation linguistique dans les établissements de'enseignement" (Québec: MEQ, 1983).

10. Albert Juneau, *"L'ecole de demain," Le Devoir,* 3 avril 1986 *Le Devoir* 2 avril 1986; Jean Blouin et Jacques Dufresne, "Rapport sur l'école," *L'Actualite,'* 11-4 (avril 1986), 34-44; *Le Devoir,* 9 janvier, 1986; Angus Reid Associates Inc., "The National Reid Poll – August 1986)," 15 p. (mimeographed), Table 7.

2

Roots in the Past:
The Influence of History and Tradition

The distinctiveness of contemporary society in Quebec has its roots in history and tradition; many of its contemporary issues, therefore, can only be understood in terms of their historical roots. An historical perspective is essential, then, for an understanding of Quebec's current educational structures, institutions, policies and problems. As this book is primarily concerned with events in Quebec education that have taken place within the past twenty-five years, a comprehensive and systematic review of Quebec educational history is clearly beyond its scope and purpose. However, the reader who would like to know more about the history of Quebec education can refer to several excellent historical texts.[1]

The overall purpose of this chapter is twofold and it is therefore presented in two parts: first, a brief summary of the major chronological stages in the historical evolution of Quebec education in order to provide the background for more contemporary events; and second, the identification of certain significant characteristics and themes related to Quebec educational issues and of their development through the past. These characteristics and themes have been specifically selected not only for their historical significance, but because they continue to exist as major influences and therefore contribute to our understanding of contemporary events.

Historical Stages in the Development of Quebec Education

1. The French Régime (1608-1760)

The first historical stage took place under the French régime and was characterized above all else by the influence of the Roman Catholic Church. As in most other countries during this period, including France and England, schools that did exist were usually the result of private charity or religious enterprise. In Quebec, or in New France as it was then known, the first schools were established by the Jesuits, Recollects, Sulpicians, Ursulines, the Congregation of Notre Dame and the Frères Charon. The original intent was not so much to provide schooling for the few colonists, but rather to bring Christianity to the native Indians. While this endeavour was far from successful since the Indians were generally reluctant to adopt the ways of the white man, the priests, brothers and nuns of the various religious orders were successful in establishing a number of elementary and trade schools in the colony. Schools in New France did not differ significantly from those available in France at the time. One major accomplishment was the Jesuit establishment of a college and seminary (now Laval University) in 1635, a year before the founding of Harvard College in the Massachusetts Bay Colony. This college was modelled on those the Jesuits were operating in France at the time, and thus it was the beginning of a tradition of classical education in Quebec that was to continue until the latter half of the 1960s, long after these institutions had been abolished in France. The major influences that can be traced from the French régime through to the present time include the role of the Catholic Church in educational affairs and the long tradition of private schools, many of which have a religious foundation.

In spite of Church initiatives, general conditions in the young colony did not encourage much interest in education and schooling. The early preoccupation with the fur trade, the harsh environment and the lack of significant numbers of settlers caused the Catholic colony of New France to grow far more slowly than the Protestant colonies of New England to the south. The French were numerically incapable of either monopolizing the fur trade or of holding on to the vast tracts of territory in North America to which they had laid claim. This situation eventually led to the military defeat of the French in the Seven Years' War in 1759 and then to the eventual disappearance of France as a major colonizing power in North America. The consequences for the French-speaking population settled along the banks of the St. Lawrence river were extremely serious. Cut off from effective communication with France and with most of its leaders displaced, the French-speaking and Catholic *habitants* of Quebec had to face a new colonial power that was both English-speaking and Protestant.

2. The British Régime (1760-1867)

The British conquest of the French at Quebec in 1760 had profound political, social and educational implications for the young colony. As Mason Wade, an historian of French Canada, has observed:

> The position of the French Canadians was indeed desperate ... The New France which had been so utterly dependent upon the mother country throughout its existence was now separated and isolated from the France which had supplied its rulers, its apostles, its educators, its ideas, and its books. If the French Canadians were to remain French under the aegis of a foreign power whose language, religion, laws and customs were very different, they would have to do so on the strength of their own resources.[2]

One resource to which they turned was the Catholic Church, virtually the only organized institution that the British permitted to remain in the colony. During the years following the conquest, the Church gradually assumed a predominant role in providing social and educational services to the French-speaking population. But the Catholic Church was also faced with a competitor and a rival, the Anglican Church of the conquerors – and thus there came about a dualism between Catholicism and Protestantism that has continued to characterize Quebec education to the present day. A number of attempts were made to form a centralized school system, common to all; but with the exception of a structure called the Royal Institution for the Advancement of Learning (1801) that enjoyed some limited success particularly among English-speaking Protestants, all of these efforts failed. The Catholic clergy feared that a common school system, dominantly controlled by English-speaking and Protestant authorities, would inevitably lead to the assimilation and "Protestantization" of the French Catholic population.

Beginning in 1824, however, school legislation was conceived in a new spirit. The government sought to use, or to create, local rather than central bodies which would be given the responsibility for building, maintaining and managing schools. The first such attempt was the Fabriques Act of 1824 which authorized the *fabriques* (Catholic parish corporations or vestries) to devote up to a quarter of their budgets to the foundation and maintenance of schools in each parish. By investing parishes with powers in the educational field, the House of Assembly established the first local agency with official authority over schools. The Act granted considerable autonomy to the *fabriques*, but primarily because of local apathy and the absence of financial aid from the government, the legislation yielded few results. The Act was significant, however, in that it offered an alternative to the predominantly English Protestant "Royal" schools by permitting the establishment of a system to serve only Catholics. Thus, the groundwork had been laid for a dual education system based on religious and linguistic differences.

The most successful school legislation of the period was the Syndics Act of 1829. This legislation provided a board of commissioners composed of five members elected by property owners for each town or parish. They were to provide "the sole direction, control, management and administration of the Schools established by virtue of this Act." This was the forerunner of the present-day school boards in which schools are placed under the direct control of locally elected lay persons rather than ecclesiastic authorities. By 1834, there were reported to be over 1500 schools in the colony; although the majority of these were public common schools managed by elected commissioners, there were also schools of the Royal Institution, *fabrique* schools, and private schools operated by various religious orders. Unfortunately, this expansion of the school system in Lower Canada (Quebec) was interrupted by a political crisis in 1836, followed by the rebellion in 1837-38. In the absence of subsidies from the House of Assembly during this period, most of the public schools soon withered away as quickly as they had been established, but the basic design on which school organization in Quebec could be built had been drafted and tested. It gradually became clear that any system of public education for Quebec would have to incorporate the right of both French Catholics and English Protestants to co-exist.

When the crisis of the 1830s was over and after Quebec was united (1841) with Ontario (Upper Canada), Quebec had been without the legal framework of a school system for five years. Following the passage of an Education Act in 1841 that was designed to serve the two Canadas, it was gradually realized that political union could not conceal the major religious and cultural differences that existed in the two provinces. School laws suitable for Ontario were not always appropriate in Quebec and school laws suitable for Quebec were not always appropriate in Ontario. As a result, Quebec was granted a school law of its own in 1845. An important revision of the 1845 law was made in 1846, and eventually it was this Education Act of 1846 that provided the fundamental basis on which all succeeding educational law in Quebec was to be built. Because some of the structures and rights which this 1846 law established were enshrined in the British North America Act of 1867, many of its provisions continue to be in force today.

Among the more important components of the law were the establishment of both Catholic and Protestant school boards in Montreal and Quebec City and, beyond these two cities, the right of Catholic and Protestant minorities to dissent from the system of common schools in order to establish separate denominational school boards, known in Quebec as dissentient boards. As the majority of common school boards served a predominantly Catholic population and since the majority of dissentient school boards served the Protestants, the whole system quickly assumed a religious character. A Council of Public Instruction, composed of eleven Catholics and four Protestants, was appointed in 1859 with a mandate to serve the whole system; but as Confederation approached, it became clear that the interests of both Catholics and Protestants would be best served by preserving two separate systems.

As a result, the rights and privileges afforded to Catholics and Protestants by the existing laws, essentially the Education Act of 1846, were written into the Canadian constitution as Section 93 of the British North American Act. After stating that only the provincial legislature "may exclusively make Laws in relation to Education," Section 93 went on to declare that: "Nothing in any such Law shall prejudicially affect any Right or Privilege with respect to Denominational Schools which any Class of Persons have by Law in the Province at the Union." In other words, the constitution of Canada offered protection to the then existing legal educational rights of Catholics and Protestants (see Appendix C for the full wording of Section 93).

3. Consolidation of the System (1867-1900)

One of the chief characteristics of this period – and one that stood in marked contrast to developments elsewhere in Canada – was the lack of direct involvement of the state in the affairs of education. The Catholic Church was opposed to governmental participation in education because it feared that mixing politics and education would lead to secularization. The Protestants, on the other hand, were fearful that a French Catholic majority in the Legislative Assembly might eventually abolish the educational privileges granted to the English Protestant minority. For different reasons, then, both major religious groups supported a dual denominational school system divorced from the authority of the state.

The Catholic bishops during this period were sufficiently powerful to influence the government of the day to defer to their wishes insofar as educational matters were concerned. In 1869 the government divided the Council of Public Instruction into two separate committees, one Catholic and the other Protestant, permitting them to meet separately to deal with their different interests. This eventually led to the consolidation of two systems of education, one Catholic and other Protestant, with little communication and few common links between them.

This separation of the two major religious and linguistic groups in the province was further reinforced in 1875. In the face of pressure from the Catholic Church, the government abolished its short-lived Ministry of Public Instruction (1867-1875) and then granted seats on the Council of Public Instruction to all the Catholic bishops whose dioceses lay in whole or in part within the province. These measures were to place the authority for public education not with a duly elected government but with the Council of Public Instruction, or, more particularly with its Catholic and Protestant committees. This placement of authority reinforced the religious character and dualism of Quebec education, increased the separation of the Catholic and Protestant systems, and assured the virtual independence of the Catholic and Protestant systems from the political influence of the state.

Until the reforms of the 1960s, the Catholic and Protestant committees, acting for the most part independently of each other, determined the policy and direction of the two systems of public education. Not surprisingly, the larger Catholic system was greatly influenced by the Church which promoted an education system quite different from that of the Protestant system.

A major structural difference between the two education systems was that secondary education was given in public schools in the Protestant system whereas Catholic secondary education was provided almost exclusively by the private sector in the classical colleges operated primarily by the clergy and religious orders. These arrangements led to different programs and structures at the post-secondary level and resulted in little opportunity for the exchange of ideas or for cooperation between the two major cultural and linguistic communities in Quebec.

In the Catholic sector, classical colleges were virtually the only route to university education. This arrangement had several important consequences. The classical colleges were accused of being elitist since they were private institutions that tended to restrict enrolments to those few who could afford to pay the fees or those sponsored by scholarships. Second, the prestigious classical curriculum offered in these colleges changed little over the years and although it provided excellent training in literature, philosophy, culture and expression, there was little emphasis on technology, commerce or the applied sciences. Third, for many years classical colleges were available only to males.

Except for the convents and later on some classical colleges, few higher education opportunities existed for females in Quebec (see Chapter 5).

4. Modernization (1900-1960)

At the beginning of the twentieth century, Quebec exhibited many of the characteristics of a traditional rural society. By the early 1930s, however, Quebec was being transformed into a completely different society that was becoming both urban and industrial. The impact of this economic development, much of it financed and controlled by English-speaking interests, was to significantly alter the province's population distribution. For example, approximately 60 percent of the population lived in rural areas in 1901. By 1931, the situation had almost reversed with over 63 percent living in the urban areas.

Although the industrial revolution had clearly arrived, it had little immediate impact on Quebec's social, political, or cultural institutions. The traditional leaders of Quebec society, especially the Church, were primarily concerned with the dangers that industrialization and urbanization were bringing in its wake. "That is why," wrote Pierre Trudeau, "against an environment that was English, Protestant, democratic, materialistic, commercial, and later industrial, our nationalism developed a system of defence dominated by the opposite forces– the French language, Catholicism, authoritarianism, idealism, rural life, and later the return to the soil."[3]

Another serious threat to traditional values during this period was the increasing pluralism of the population. When the dual education system had been devised in the mid-nineteenth century almost the whole population of Quebec could have been classified as either French Catholic or English Protestant. But this situation was soon to change, first with the arrival of English-speaking Catholics from Ireland, and then with successive waves of Jewish immigrants from central Europe in the first half of the twentieth century. Both groups were faced with an education system that was designed primarily for others (French Catholics or English Protestants), and both groups had considerable difficulty in finding some form of accommodation with the existing system.

The English Catholics eventually won the right to send their children to English Catholic schools, but these schools were administered by predominantly French Catholic school boards. English-speaking Catholics were never granted school boards in their own right. The Jews, as non-Christians seeking to enter a Christian school system, were faced with even greater problems. With considerable difficulty and after much legal wrangling, the Jews eventually found accommodation within the English Protestant system although the problem of Jewish representation on Protestant school boards continued to be a matter for dispute.[4] The arrival of English-speaking Catholics from Ireland and of Jewish immigrants from continental Europe indicated that Quebec's educational structures were not designed to easily adjust to pluralism. This problem was to intensify with the arrival of other immigrants of various ethnic and religious backgrounds in the period following the Second World War.

By the end of the 1950s, many Quebecers believed that their education system was not well suited to a changing and modern Quebec. Pressure from many sources, including some from within the Church itself, demanded urgent reform; and during the 1960s, following many years of benign neglect, the government eventually acted to modernize and reform the province's educational system.

5. Quiet Revolution (1960-1970)

The reforms of the 1960s, generally referred to as the Quiet Revolution, affected virtually every aspect of Quebec's society. A new sense of identity emerged – secular and humanist, pluralist and urban, economic and technocratic – markedly more in line with the realities of a modern industrial state. This new French Quebec of the 1960s was also increasingly nationalistic. Evidence of major sociological change was to be found in the fact that Quebec's birthrate, traditionally the highest in Canada, had dropped to the lowest by 1961. But perhaps the most important change during this decade was the decline in the role of the Catholic Church and the subsequent transfer of moral and institutional leadership from the Church to the provincial government. In a very real sense, the state replaced the Church as the defender of Quebec's primary interests.

Many of these changes in Quebec society were to be reflected in the transformation of the education system. At the beginning of the 1960s, the government had set up a Royal Commission of Inquiry to examine the education system in its totality, from kindergarten to graduate studies and from local school taxation to central structures. Most of the education reforms during this period stemmed directly from the report of this Commission (the Parent Report). In 1964, a Ministry of Education was established to replace the Council of Public Instruction and its Catholic and Protestant committees as the official authority for all education policy in the province. A new body – the Superior Council of Education – was formed to give advice to the Minister and the government. Regional school boards were created throughout the province to provide universal and comprehensive secondary education; the classical colleges were replaced by a new network of post-secondary colleges known as *Collèges d'enseignement géhéral et professionel* (CEGEPs); teacher training was reorganized and upgraded; and the number of university places was increased. The degree programs in both English and French universities were revised and given a common structure and the Ministry issued a series of regulations changing the organization and content of elementary and secondary education. In sum, these reforms completely changed the face of education in Quebec and resulted in a spectacular increase in the proportion of the provincial budget devoted to education services. In a somewhat different development, the decade of the 1960s also witnessed a major transformation in the size and organization of the Quebec teaching profession (see Chapter 7 on Teachers).

The Royal Commission in the final volume of its report in 1966 recommended major changes to the basic confessional structures of Quebec's school boards, but there were a number of reasons, primarily political, why the structures were not altered during this period. There was a feeling in some quarters that perhaps the pace of reform was too rapid. In spite of this, the historic separation between the Catholic and Protestant education systems began to break down. This was brought about partly because the powers of the Catholic and Protestant committees had been sharply reduced, but also because the new Ministry of Education acted as a unified body. The Ministry's regulations regarding school and college organization applied to both Catholics and Protestants and for the first time without differentiation.

As the somewhat tumultuous decade of the sixties drew to a close, language rather than religion had clearly become a major issue in Quebec politics and in Quebec education. The language issue first came to public attention in the Montreal suburb of St. Léonard in 1968 when the local Catholic school board decided to phase out its English-language schools. Immigrant parents, especially those of Italian origin, reacted vigorously; their protests became headlines in newspapers across the nation. The Quebec Superior Court refused to intervene on the grounds that there were no laws in Quebec that guaranteed instruction in English. This indeed was the case, as educational rights for the minority were based primarily on tradition and on the constitutional rights afforded to Protestants in section 93 of the British North America Act. Section 93 contained no mention of linguistic rights, only denominational rights (see Appendix C).

The government meanwhile enacted Bill 63: "An Act to promote the French language in Quebec." For the first time in Quebec history, the law granted to all parents the legal right to have their children educated in the language of their choice, French or English. Predictably, this law assuaged the Italians and other immigrants in the province who wanted their children to learn English but did absolutely nothing to appease the concerns of French nationalists, many of whom interpreted the new law as a serious threat to the survival of their language and culture. As the 1960s drew to a close amidst mass demonstrations against the government and its language policies, Quebec's traditional nationalism had clearly found a new focus. by the state.

6. 1970 – Present

The decade of the 1970s began with the political upheaval created by the "Front de libération québécois" (FLQ) and culminated in the October Crisis of 1970: the British Trade Commissioner was kidnapped, the Quebec Minister of Labour murdered, and the War Measures Act imposed by the Federal Government. The decade also witnessed the growing popularity and subsequent election of the separatist *Parti Québécois*. Political debate was concerned with by the possible separation of Quebec from the rest of Canada. In the field of education, the decade was dominated primarily by linguistic nationalism and with the question of who should have access to English-language schools. Both the Gendron Commission in Quebec (1972) and the Federal government's report on Bilingualism and Biculturalism (1968-1969) had drawn attention to the relative weakness of the French language in Quebec and Canada. In Quebec, the declining birthrate in the French community had dropped to less than replacement level. The vast majority of immigrant children (85%) were attending English schools and more than 75,000 francophone children were also reported to be attending English schools.

It will be recalled that Bill 63 granting freedom of choice in the language of education had been greeted with considerable opposition in the French community. The Liberal Party led by Robert Bourassa was under considerable pressure to introduce new language legislation that would go much further than its predecessor to protect and promote the French language. The outcome was the Official Language Act (1974), or Bill 22 as it was more commonly known. Bill 22 repealed Bill 63 and went on to declare French to be the sole official language of Quebec. In addition, the Bill established French as the official working language of the public administration, public utilities, and professional corporations and it required that French be used "at every level of business activity, especially in corporate management and in firm names, on public signs ... and in consumer contracts." The section of the law on education rights (see Appendix D) subsequently developed into one of the more controversial aspects of the legislation and is believed to have contributed to the electoral defeat of Bourassa and the Liberal government in 1976.

In attempting to restrict the access of immigrants (and also, incidentally, of French-speaking Quebecers) to English-language schools, Bill 22 required that only those with a " sufficient knowledge" of the English language would be permitted to receive their instruction in English. In order to ascertain which children possessed "sufficient knowledge" the Minister of Education was empowered to develop language tests to be administered by the school boards. The complicated and controversial administration of language tests to young children, most of whom were only of kindergarten age, provoked fierce opposition from the English and immigrant communities.

The education section of Bill 22 pleased neither of the two major linguistic communities in Quebec. The English community was opposed to the law because of the tests and because the law was viewed as both discriminating against immigrants and as violating basic human rights. The French community, on the other hand, was upset by the difficulties in administering the tests, the vagueness of "sufficient knowledge" and the subsequent ease with which many immigrants were seen to circumvent the intention of the law. It was evident to all that Bill 22 had not resolved the language problem.

The first major piece of legislation passed by the Parti Québécois government (elected 1976) was Bill 101 or the Charter of the French Language (1977). Bill 101 was a comprehensive law dealing with all aspects of language policy: the language of government and the courts, business and work, signs and posters, professions and institutions and, not least, of education.

Considerably more precise than its predecessor, Bill 22, it has resulted in French becoming the official language in virtually all areas of Quebec life. In spite of proposed changes and the fact that several sections have been modified as the result of court decisions, and that various other sections are under appeal, the Charter of the French Language (Bill 101) continues to be the official legal structure for language policy in Quebec.

Insofar as access to English schools is concerned, Bill 101 (see Appendix E) is considerably more restrictive than its predecessor. It limits access to those who have at least one parent who attended English-language elementary school in Quebec. In effect, this restricts English education to children whose parents are English-speaking native Quebecers; it requires all others, regardless of language or place of origin, to receive their instruction in French, though some exceptions are made for those living temporarily in Quebec, for handicapped children and for native peoples. Bill 101 thus succeeded where Bill 22 had failed: to ensure that immigrants receive their education in French.

Although some would claim that Bill 101 has brought a degree of linguistic peace to Quebec there continued to be resistance to certain aspects of the law: a number of immigrant children, the so-called illegals, attended English schools in defiance of the law; and there have been a number of court challenges to the constitutionality of the law especially since the new Canadian Charter of Rights and Freedoms was proclaimed in 1982.

Although the language question was the dominant educational issue in Quebec during the 1970s, it was not the only development of note during the period. In 1971 and 1972, by two separate pieces of legislation, the number of school boards on the Island of Montreal and elsewhere was reduced from 1100 to approximately their present numbers: 8 on the Island of Montreal and 226 in the rest of the province. The same legislation extended the right to vote in school board elections to all citizens aged 18 years and older. A School Council for the Island of Montreal was established to coordinate some of the activities of the 8 island school boards, and consultative parent committees were set up at the level of each school and school board. In 1979, the government restricted the right of school boards to raise revenue from local taxes and, in effect, limited the school boards' taxation powers to a ceiling of 6 percent of their net expenses and parents were granted the right to direct representation on school boards. The decade was marked also by continuing and often bitter conflict between the teacher unions and the government over a variety of issues including job security, workloads and salaries.

The period from 1981 to 1985 was also dominated by several attempts to transform the basic structures of Quebec's traditional confessional school board system. In the summer of 1981, the government announced its intention to bring in legislation that was designed, in the words of the Minister of Education, Dr. Camille Laurin, "to complete the unfinished business of the Quiet Revolution." As recommended in the 1966 report of the Royal Commission, the proposal was to abolish confessional boards and elections by universal suffrage and to replace them with unified boards to be elected and managed by parents. The full intentions of the government were revealed in 1982 with the publication of a White Paper, *The Quebec school: a responsible force in the community*, which proposed not only the dismantling of the confessional school board structures as such, but also the virtual elimination of traditional school board functions.

Following a year of heated discussions, demonstrations and debate, the government tabled Bill 40 to implement these measures (1983) but soon after the Parliamentary Committee hearings on Bill 40 were completed in the spring of 1984, the Premier announced a cabinet shuffle in which the controversial Minister of Education was reassigned to another portfolio. Bill 40 was withdrawn and new legislation, Bill 3, containing further modifications to the overall plan, was tabled in the National Assembly in the fall of 1984. The bill was passed in December, but as soon as the government began to implement its provisions, the Protestant school boards – acting in concert with the Montreal Catholic School Commission – appealed to the Quebec Superior Court to disallow Bill 3 on the grounds that the Bill was unconstitutional. In June 1985, the court ruled that crucial aspects of the Bill were indeed unconstitutional since they impinged upon the rights and privileges of Catholics and Protestants as set down in Section 93 of the B.N.A. Act. The court then issued a permanent injunction preventing the government from implementing the law and, as a result, the structural reform movement was brought to a sudden and dramatic halt.

Finally, it should be noted that the early and mid 1980s were a period of severe budgetary restraint in Quebec education. Budget cuts were demanded of all sectors, and rigid collective agreements, including salary roll-backs, were imposed on the teaching profession. This period of financial retrenchment corresponded to severe enrolment declines in the elementary and secondary schools, leading directly to younger teachers being placed on surplus, fewer job and promotion opportunities, and an aging teaching profession. On a more optimistic note, the mid-1980s witnessed the emergence of a new spirit of cooperation among various partners involved in education. In the spring of 1986, the province's Catholic and Protestant school boards together with the teacher unions and the Ministry of Education called for the holding of a joint conference (the Estates General) to discuss the quality of education in Quebec's schools. A more equitable and simplified system of financing school boards was developed jointly by the Ministry and the school boards for implementation in the 1986-87 school year: Bill 24, adopted in 1986, reinstated the right of religious minorities to vote and be elected in school board elections; Bill 58

(1986) finally granted amnesty to the so-called illegal students; and a long-awaited government policy statement concerning technical-vocational education at the secondary level was unveiled in June 1986. In spite of continuing severe budgetary restraints, these measures indicated that after twenty-five years of change and turmoil in Quebec education a new era of relative stability might now be at hand.

Characteristics and Themes in the Evolution of Quebec Education

Another way of looking at the influence of history and tradition in the evolution of Quebec education is through an analysis of significant characteristics and themes that have emerged from the past. Some of these have been mentioned in the chronological account, but the major purpose of this second part of the chapter is to explore these characteristics and themes in greater depth, so as to provide a basis for understanding specific contemporary events.

1. Survival and Identity

Perhaps the most basic and fundamental theme underlying any study of Quebec is that of the survival of a minority culture on the North American continent. Cut off at an early stage from its roots and traditions in France, competing with other groups who were more numerous and more powerful, French Quebec staunchly refused to be assimilated into an Anglo-American world. There can be little doubt that the original intent of the British authorities after the conquest of New France was to anglicize the *Canadiens*; the Royal Proclamation of 1763 stated as much.

That assimilation did not occur is due to many factors, not the least of which was the presence in the colony of an organized Catholic hierarchy with which the British authorities soon reached an understanding. In return for the freedom to practice Catholicism, a religion that at that time was banned in England, the Church, in effect, guaranteed the loyalty of the people to the British crown. This is why French Quebec rebuffed overtures to participate in both the American and then the French revolutions. The arrangement between the British authorities and the Catholic Church suited both parties well, for the British obtained a ready-made system of administrative control and virtually complete freedom from competition in the fields of trade and commerce, while the Church obtained control in the fields of religion, education, and social and cultural affairs. Thus, in the wake of defeat and surrender, the Church and the local population found themselves thrown together in an alliance that was to last for almost two hundred years and was to provide the French language and culture with a protected and separate existence in a hostile New World.

Differentiated by language and by religion, and cut off from communication with France, French Quebec entered into a period of almost complete isolation from outside contemporary developments. Unlike other Western societies of the era which became increasingly interdependent, industrial, urban and secular, French Quebec chose (or was forced, depending on one's interpretation of history) to rely on its own limited resources and became characterized as homogeneous, self-sufficient, agrarian, rural, and Catholic. In this manner, but at the cost of economic progress and development, it was able to insulate itself from the influence of an alien Anglo-Saxon culture and thereby avoid the dangers of assimilation that industrialization and modernization might well have brought about.

French Quebec assured its survival as a distinct society by isolation; but at the same time, it also survived by sheer force of numbers. Directly encouraged by the Church, the Catholic population of Quebec effectively doubled every twenty-five years between 1760 and 1850 and, in the decade after the conquest, the birthrate was such that it was reported to be the highest ever recorded for a people of European origin. This population explosion, the "revenge of the cradle," not only assured the survival of a French presence in Canada, but eventually would lead to overpopulation in the somewhat limited areas suitable for agriculture. This resulted in a major migration from the land and into the towns and cities which, in turn, contributed to the eventual breakdown of Quebec's traditional isolationism and rural economy.

But French Quebec could not isolate itself forever from outside influences. Quebec possessed abundant resources – forests, water power, and mineral wealth – and it was not long before the combined forces of Anglo-American capital and technical knowhow began to make inroads into the very fortress of conservative French Quebec. As Pierre Trudeau has pointed out: "faithfulness to one's language and native soil cannot long withstand urgent economic pressure."[5] By the late 1930s Quebec had become a predominately industrial and urban state, a development that was to be accentuated by the Second World War. The influence of industrialization and urbanization resulted in the eventual breakdown of Quebec's traditional policies of survival: isolationism and natural population increase. The influx of immigrants into towns and cities during the first half of the twentieth century and the declining birthrate encouraged Quebecers to find new policies to ensure their survival in an English-speaking North America. These new policies, formulated this time by the state rather than the Church, eventually found expression in the various language laws passed in the 1970s.

The existence of the French language in a North American environment is in itself indicative of a distinct identity. But Quebec's distinctiveness does not depend on language alone: its different European roots, together with its own history and traditions, provide it with characteristics and institutions that are often quite different from those found elsewhere in North America. These are not only the result of its distinct history and tradition; they, in part, also reflect the wish of a people to continue to remain different.

In recent years, the traditional minority and survival mentality of Quebec has experienced an added dimension. Quebec, in reality, has two distinct minorities: the French as a minority within Canada and North America and the English as a minority within Quebec. In the past the English viewed themselves as an integral part of the larger English-speaking North American continent and have not been overly concerned about their minority status, their identity, or their survival. Since the enactment of language legislation in the 1970s, however, this has begun to change. For the first time in history, the English-speaking community has felt the need to attempt to define its identity and to form organizations such as the Council of Quebec Minorities and Alliance Quebec, in order to promote its own specific interests. The issues of language, survival, and identity are still important elements in Quebec society and as the recent discussions on bilingual signs have demonstrated, are likely to remain so.

2. Confessionality, Religion and the Church

While it is true that religion, and especially the Catholic and Protestant faiths, have been of major importance in the historical evolution of Quebec education, it would be a mistake to think that education in Quebec is exclusively religious in character. School structures in Quebec, as mentioned previously, were originally devised in the mid-nineteenth century to serve the needs of two distinct communities: French-speaking Catholics and English-speaking Protestants. The important point is that religion rather that language was used by each group to distinguish it from the other; the rights and privileges constitutionally protected in Section 93 of the British North American Act were likewise defined in terms of religion rather than of language. Confessionality – a word meaning the profession of a religious belief – also occurs in various forms at other levels of the system including the Ministry of Education, the Superior Council of Education, the school boards, and the schools themselves.

At the level of the Ministry of Education and under the authority of the Minister and Deputy Minister, two Associate Deputy Ministers – one of the Catholic faith and one of the Protestant faith – were established in law when the Ministry of Education was first formed in 1964. This apparent anachronism in an otherwise unified and secular Ministry of Education is perhaps best explained in the words of the Parent Report (1963):

> The strict division which has always existed between Protestant and Roman Catholic education has not always been to the advantage of pupils or of the community as a whole; in some respects it has delayed progress and prevented a fruitful exchange of ideas. Yet, even if it has been carried to an extreme, there is no reason why we should fall into the opposite error and seek unification at all costs, without regard for differences in belief, in outlook, language and culture.[6]

Confessionality also plays a role in the Superior Council which has two standing committees, a Catholic Committee and a Protestant Committee. Each has the power to recognize schools officially as Catholic or Protestant (see Appendices H and I) and to make regulations concerning all matters affecting moral and religious education in these schools.

Confessionality exits at the level of school boards in Quebec, although the precise legal status of many of these boards is often confusing. In strictly legal terms, only the Catholic and Protestant school boards in Montreal and Quebec City, and the few "dissentient" boards in other parts of the province are confessional or denominational boards. The vast majority of boards, therefore, are legally nonconfessional, open to all pupils regardless of religious affiliation or lack of affiliation. In practice, however, most of these boards have assumed a confessional character and status. They are referred to officially as school boards "for Protestants" or as school boards "for Catholics." Many are publicly identified as Catholic or Protestant boards, and they have schools that have been legally recognized as Catholic or Protestant by the relevant confessional committee of the Superior Council. In 1985-86 there were 201 school boards for Catholics, 29 for Protestants, and 4 designated for both Catholics and Protestants which primarily served native peoples. There have been several attempts over the past twenty years to alter the confessional basis of Quebec's school boards and to rearrange them on a linguistic or unified basis. To date, none of these attempts has been successful (see Chapter 3.)

At the present time, almost all the elementary and secondary schools in Quebec are legally recognized as either Catholic or Protestant. This came about in 1974 and 1975, when the Catholic and Protestant Committees of the Superior Council issued a blanket recognition of the respective confessional status to all existing schools within the school boards. Private schools and public colleges are legally nonconfessional, although private institutions may seek legal recognition if they wish. It is technically possible for individual schools to seek to have their confessional status revoked and therefore to become nonconfessional or neutral schools, but very few have opted or have been able to do so. In one recent and celebrated case, the parents of Notre Dame des Neiges school in Montreal requested neutral status which was granted by the Catholic Committee. But this was subsequently overturned by the courts on the grounds that the school belonged to the Montreal Catholic School Commission established prior to confederation and protected by the B.N.A. Act. According to the courts, all the schools in this board are legally Catholic and only a change of the constitution can alter that state of affairs.

A school in Quebec may be Catholic or Protestant in a variety of ways; there is no single type or model. In some cases, the school is Catholic or Protestant in name only; in other cases, the religious influence extends throughout the curriculum and is an intregal part of the general philosophy or ethos of the school. The majority of Catholic schools normally offer formal courses of Catholic religious instruction, although all students have the right to be exempted from this instruction and to substitute in its place a course in moral education.

Protestant schools, in contrast, have traditionally served a more diverse clientele – Protestants of various sects and denominations, Jews, Greek Orthodox, members of other religions including Catholics, and those who profess no religious belief at all. Consequently, Protestant schools have not usually offered formal courses in religious instruction; instead, they have tended to depend more on the implicit teaching of the Judeo-Christian heritage or have offered courses in Bible study or comparative religion.

In the Catholic system there has been pressure for some years to provide a course in moral education as an alternative to religious instruction. This may indicate less interest in religious values but may also indicate the more varied composition of the school population. In contrast, there is a reverse trend in some Protestant schools to reinstate courses in religious instruction. According to a recent poll of the Canadian population, 83% of respondents (88% in Quebec) want the public schools to impart moral values to students.[7] Quebec's school system, however, is the only public system in North America that mandates the compulsory teaching of religion or morals at all grade levels.

The role of the Catholic Church in Quebec has clearly changed in the past twenty-five years. Prior to the Quiet Revolution, the importance of the Church in preserving social cohesion and cultural identity within the French community cannot be questioned. It was able to accomplish this through its power, its leadership, and its control of much of the public and private educational networks. The Quiet Revolution, however, witnessed a transfer of power and moral authority from the Church to the state, a change that was welcomed or viewed as inevitable by nearly all sectors of society. Although there is no question of a return to the past, there is concern that the state acquired too much power in this transfer of authority and that the state is not the appropriate body to exercise moral leadership. In the vacuum thus created, the majority of parents expect the schools of Quebec to inculcate their children with appropriate religious and moral values. Within an increasingly pluralistic society, however, and with a variety of religious and moral values in evidence, this is no easy task.

Although Quebec is now divided more by language than by religion, the question of confessionality and religion is likely to continue to be an important theme in Quebec education in the foreseeable future.

3. Dualism and Pluralism

Another major factor in the evolution of education in Quebec, at least since 1760, has been the presence of a minority English-speaking population in a predominantly French-speaking milieu. An important theme running throughout Quebec's history since the conquest has been the relationship between these two communities and the accommodations that have been necessary to permit both communities to coexist. Dualism (the presence of two distinct groups) is therefore an important characteristic of education and society in Quebec and one that continues to exercise considerable influence. In recent years, however, the traditional version of dualism has been altered by the increasing pluralism of peoples, ideas, and values, in both the English-speaking and French-speaking communities.

At the time of the passage of the Quebec Act in 1774, there were fewer than 2000 English residents in Canada compared to 150,000 French. The linguistic and demographic map of Canada was soon to be profoundly altered: first by the arrival of the United Empire Loyalists fleeing the newly independent United States of America, and then by increasing numbers of English-speaking immigrants from the Old World. The French community, for its part, was homogeneous in both its ethnic origin and its Catholic religion. In contrast, the English community was diversified in ethnic origins, including not only Anglo-Saxons but also Scots and later Irish. While the community was largely Protestant, it included a wide range of religious adherents including Anglicans, Presbyterians, Methodists, Wesleyans, Congregationalists, Baptists, Universalists, and, not least, Catholics.

For many years after the conquest, French society tended to be isolated, rural, agrarian, and poor; it looked to a leadership elite of priests, doctors and lawyers who were trained in a classical, theological and literary tradition. English society, however, was more concentrated in urban areas and tended to be more pragmatic. In contrast to the French, English society generally looked to a leadership elite of business men and merchants who had shown their competence in the practical affairs of trade, commerce and manufacturing.

In the light of these differences in ethnic background, cultural assumptions, economic status, and religious persuasion, it should not be surprising that the two major communities in Quebec had very different views about education. French society viewed education largely in terms of cultural survival, religious formation, and for the elite, classical training. The French had a profound distrust of government intrusion in the field of education, fearing political interference and secularization, and stressing instead the rights of Church and family as the prime educators. English society, on the other hand, was more prepared to use government structures to promote and advance education. The English were influenced by the Presbyterian Scots who supported the right of all persons, regardless of social class, to have full educational opportunities, and by the New England example of local self-government and of non-sectarian and essentially secular common schools. It is not surprising, then, that the Catholic Church opposed all attempts by the government to establish a common school system in Quebec and that it insisted, instead, on Church-controlled Catholic schools. These differences in outlook of the two communities help to explain not only the eventual emergence of two distinct systems of education in Quebec, each one reflecting the social and cultural aspirations of its own community, but also the differences that developed over the years in school organization and curriculum.

The dual educational system not only reflected the notion of the "two solitudes," it also served to reinforce it by contributing to the relative isolation of the two communities. In recent years, however, the lines delineating the two communities have become considerably more obscure. The French community can no longer be stereotyped as isolated, monolithic, homogeneous and exclusively Catholic, and the English community can no longer be thought of as essentially Protestant, Anglo-Saxon and rich. Due in part to French immersion programs in the schools, many in the English community have become bilingual. Because of Bill 101, the French language and culture are now considered by many to be more secure in Quebec; and the traditional dualism based on religious differences is no longer as important as it once was. Linguistic, ethnic and cultural differences rather than religious affiliation tend to distinguish the various populations groups in Quebec.

To a large extent, the traditional dualism based on the over-simplified polarity of French-English relations has disappeared. In its place is the reality that Quebec has become a society of minorities. The most populous French-speaking group is, of course, very conscious of its minority status in Canada and North America. The English-speaking community, united more by a common language than by ethnic origin or a common culture, is acutely aware of its minority status in Quebec, even though it sees itself as part of the mainstream majority on the continent. Within the English group, in addition to the Anglo-Saxons, there are numerous ethnic communities including the Jews, Italians, Greeks, Poles, Germans, Portuguese, Ukrainians, East Indians, West Indians, Chinese, and many others. Certain other minority groups, such as the Haitians, Vietnamese, and Latin Americans, have tended to orientate themselves to the French community. In addition, the native peoples of Quebec including the various Indian groups and the Inuit, are increasingly concerned about their own identities and rights.

Perhaps the most significant change in the past twenty-five years is that the traditional composition of Quebec's French-speaking community is itself undergoing profound transformation. No longer can it be thought of as a homogeneous population descended essentially from the few settlers from northwest France who arrived in New France during the 17th and 18th centuries. Today, and especially in the more urban areas, the French-speaking community is increasingly pluralistic, composed of people with various racial, ethnic and religious backgrounds. It is estimated, for example, that by the year 2000 over half the children in school in Quebec will be the children of immigrants, and that within the metropolitan area of Montreal, ethnic minorities who already make up 25 percent of the school population will increase to 50 percent by the end of the decade. Formerly the majority of immigrant children attended English schools; today they attend French schools.

This influx of immigrants is a relatively new phenomenon for the French Catholic schools, and one that is already creating problems of adjustment and redefinition in a system that previously had been characterized by its ethnocentric homogeneity. These changes, together with a quite pronounced move away from isolationism, are creating a situation in which French Quebec is in process of having to redefine its own identity.

In a very real sense, then, Quebec is becoming a society characterized by pluralism rather than dualism. This is increasingly true not only in terms of the numerous ethnic groups, but also in terms of cultural assumptions, moral values, and religious persuasions. If the major challenge to educational policy in the past was to develop structures and programs that were responsive to the needs of a dualistic society, then perhaps the major challenge for the future will be to develop programs and structures that respond best to the needs of a pluralistic society.

Summary

The major themes that have characterized Quebec society in the past have been the French concern for identity and cultural survival in a predominantly English-speaking continent that eventually led to isolationism and ruralism; the dominant influence of the Church rather than the state in social and cultural affairs that served to preserve social cohesion and cultural identity; and the evolution of social, cultural, and institutional dualism based originally on religious differences that served to protect the interests of both French Catholics and English Protestants but also led to the two solitudes.

These characteristics were challenged by modernization and especially by the twin forces of industrialization and urbanization. Traditional values began to break down even if many institutions remained the same. The challenges posed by modernization were accelerated by the Second World War, a decline in Church influence, a falling birthrate, an increasingly pluralistic population, important changes within the realm of ideas and moral values, and the movement to obtain more economic and political power. Others are the increased demand for universal and better public service, new manifestations of nationalism, and by what can only be described as a revolution of expectations.

These challenges to traditional values and to traditional institutions eventually found expression in the period know as the Quiet Revolution. Quebec's traditional elite, dominated by the Church, gave way to a new elite of cabinet ministers, civil servants and business leaders. The state replaced the Church as the dominant authority in Quebec society. The government moved rapidly in the field of economic development and in the expansion of public services; and as a secular institution itself, it tended to emphasize integration rather than the dualism brought about by religious differences. Finally, after many years of benign neglect, the government granted a new priority to education as the primary instrument of social improvement, cultural development, and economic progress.

In terms of education, the key events of the past twenty-five years have been the Parent Report (1963-66) that presented a set of recommendations designed to deal with immediate problems and offered a vision of the future, the establishment of a Ministry of Education (1964) that has developed policy and provided most of the resources for education, and the new institutions and programs at all levels of the system. Others are the introduction, for the first time, of legislated linguistic policies, several unsuccessful attempts to reform the confessional structures in the system and, more recently, renewed economic priorities including proposals for decentralization, stricter budgetary controls, a return to the basics, and, finally, more emphasis on technology. In essence, the priorities of Quebec education in the past have tended to reflect the priorities of society as a whole and as society's priorities have shifted over time, so have those of education. This study of contemporary Quebec education offers, then, an insight into Quebec society as it has evolved during the past twenty-five years, a period of rapid and unprecedented social change.

Notes

1. Perhaps the best source, in English, is: Roger Magnuson, *A Brief History of Quebec Education*. Montreal: Harvest House, 1980. There is also an excellent historical summary contained in Volume 1 of the Parent Report: *Report of the Royal Commission of Inquiry on Education in the Province of Quebec*, 5 vols. Quebec: The Quebec Official Publisher, 1963-1966. For historical studies of Quebec education in the French language, the reader is referred to the voluminous works of Quebec's best know educational historian, Louis-Phillippe Audet, including *Le système scolaire de la province de Québec*, 6 vols. Québec: Les Presses Universitaires Laval, 1951-1956, and *Histoire de l'enseignement au Québec*. Montreal: Holt, Rinehart and Winston, 1971.

2. Mason Wade, M. *The French-Canadian Outlook.* Toronto: McClelland and Stewart, 1964. p. 16.

3. Trudeau, P.E. *The Asbestos Strike.* (trans. by James Boake), Toronto: James Lewis and Samuel, 1974. p. 12.

4. There are numerous books and studies, in English, concerning the problem of the Jewish community in Quebec education including Rexford, Elson I. *Our Educational Problem: The Jewish Population and the Protestant Schools*. Montreal: Renouf Publishing Co., 1924.

5. Pierre Elliot Trudeau. "*Federalism and the French Canadians*. New York, St. Martin's Press, 1968, p. 10.

6. Report of the Royal Commission of Inquiry on Education in the Province of Quebec (Parent Report), Government of Quebec, The Québec Official Publisher, Vol. 1, 1963, p. 95.

7. Angus Reid Associates Inc. "Back to School Poll," September 6, 1986, p. 15. Selected parts of this poll were published in the Montreal *Gazette* and in other newspapers across Canada on Saturday, September 6, 1986.

3

The Governance of Education
Authority, Power and Participation

The governance of education in democratic societies today is the result of a complicated interplay among those who exercise authority (the right to make decisions), those who exercise power (the capacity to influence decisions), and those whose lives and interests are affected by this authority and power. In order to understand and to participate more effectively in this complicated process, it is important to know who exercises authority and power and how these are utilized. It is also interesting to see how attempts have been made to renegotiate the traditional distribution of educational authority and power in Quebec.

The Legal Framework

On the face of it, the constitutional framework for education in Canada is clear and unambiguous: education is an undisputed provincial responsibility. Section 93 of the Canada Constitution Act of 1867 (British North America Act) makes this clear when it states: "In and for each Province the Legislature may exclusively make Laws in relation to Education." However, this exclusive authority in the field of education is, in practice, limited by certain important safeguards concerning Protestant and Catholic minorities. Section 93 therefore goes on to state that the rights and privileges of these two minorities, as specified in law at the time of Confederation, may not be removed or prejudiced by any subsequent law of the provincial legislature (see Appendix C for the full text of Section 93). In fact, there is a specific clause in Section 93 that permits the federal government to overturn any provincial legislation that is judged to be prejudicial to the rights of these two religious minorities, although this power has been rarely exercised.

It is moreover evident that the federal government in Canada has no direct constitutional jurisdiction in provincial systems of education. In Canada there is no central Ministry or Department of Education as there is, for example, in England, France, and the United States. Nevertheless, the federal government in Canada has an important role in education, including a) fiscal transfers to the provinces for post-secondary education, b) jurisdiction for the education of native peoples on reservations and in the North, c) schooling in federal prisons and military bases, d) manpower and occupational training programs for adults, e) the teaching of official languages, and f) research contracts, grants and fellowships. In addition, the federal government's jurisdiction in areas such as culture and communications, manpower and immigration, and in the transfer of resources to the provinces has serious implications for all provincial education systems. Some of these activities and especially those that directly affect education and cultural affairs are often viewed in Quebec as federal intrusions into an area of provincial jurisdiction.

Education policy at the national level in Canada is not formally developed by a federal government department as such, but by a number of national organizations, some of which are independent voluntary bodies such as the Canadian Education Association, the Canadian Teachers' Federation, the Canadian School Trustees' Association, the Association of Universities and Colleges of Canada, whereas others are federally funded bodies such as the Canada Council and the National Research Council. There is also the Council of Ministers of Education, Canada, which brings together the various provincial Ministers of Education in order to discuss common concerns, but this body tends to have some difficulty in reconciling the tensions that exist between divergent provincial and national priorities.

With the important exception of minority rights, the legal process and the courts have not played a major role in Canadian education as they have elsewhere. Instead, problems have usually been resolved through the political and legislative processes. The arrival of the Canadian Charter of Rights and Freedoms in 1982, however, suggests that litigation in the courts will increase in the years ahead – particularly perhaps in the field of equality of access to education services. The individual rights of teachers and students as well as those of the handicapped and special interest groups are likely to be more fully tested in the light of the Charter. As in the United States, there is also the possibility of education malpractice suits being brought by dissatisfied parents and students against individual schools, school boards, colleges and universities. Because the ultimate legal recourse in Canada is the federal Supreme Court, it is not unreasonable to anticipate an augmentation of the federal presence in provincial education systems. This may well have important and far-reaching consequences for the traditional role of education in Quebec.

The primary source of legal authority in the field of education in Canada is the Constitution Act of 1867. This grants legal authority to the provinces. The provinces exercise their authority through the provincial legislatures so that each province has its own Education Act and various other specialized Acts dealing with different aspects of the provincial education system. These Acts grant authority to the provincial government or Ministry, and these bodies exercise their authority respectively by means of orders-in-council or Ministry directives which are then applied by the various school boards, colleges and universities.

The Location of Authority in Quebec

In every province, the provincial legislature has the exclusive right to pass laws in regard to education. In Quebec this right is exercised by the National Assembly. This does not mean that the myriad of rules, regulations and directives concerning the day-to-day operation of education in Quebec are all debated and approved in the National Assembly. In fact, the majority of legal instruments concerning education, whether these are curriculum regulations, budgetary rules, requirements for teaching certificates, teachers' salary scales, and so on, are rarely debated in the National Assembly. The primary function of the National Assembly is to make laws, and the laws that it does approve usually contain provisions whereby the authority vested in the National Assembly is delegated to other bodies, such as the Ministry of Education or the cabinet. These bodies draw up the details concerning the application of the law. The details are subsequently published as rules, regulations, or orders-in-council, all of which carry the full weight of the law. In Quebec, the cabinet is usually referred to as the Council of Ministers and has the power to approve orders-in-council on a variety of matters including education. When the orders-in-council have been signed by the Lieutenant-Governor of the Province, these then become legal documents. They usually come into effect as soon as they have been published in the *Quebec Official Gazette.*

In addition, a number of other legal statutes directly or indirectly concern education. These include the *Quebec Charter of Human Rights and Freedoms* concerning freedom of religion and conscience for teachers and students, the *Quebec Labour Code* on union organization and the right to strike, the *Charter of the French Language* on the use of English and access to English schools, and the *Election Act* concerning school board elections. A different type of legal instrument with considerable impact on the day-to-day operation of the education system is the set of collective agreements that are negotiated between teachers and other school personnel and their employers. In Quebec, all public institutions including schools, colleges, and most of the universities have such collective agreements. These are usually extensive documents that set out in precise detail the various legal rights and obligations of the contractual parties (see Chapter 7).

In spite of appearances to the contrary, the actual number of laws in Quebec education are relatively few. Although various Bills are presented in the National Assembly, many of these do not become separate laws but are really amendments to existing laws, such as the *Education Act.* Prior to the reforms of the Quiet Revolution, the major law in Quebec concerning education was the *Public Education Act* which delegated considerable authority to the Council of Public Instruction and to its two confessional committees. In 1964 the government approved two new laws, the *Education Department Act* and the *Superior Council of Education Act,* jointly referred to as Bill 60. The new laws radically altered the central structures and created a Ministry of Education and Superior Council. These two new Acts, together with the large, comprehensive, and much amended *Public Education Act*, define the major structures, powers, rights and responsibilities of the various elements of Quebec's public school system. The *Private Education Act* (1968) establishes the rules and regulations for the recognition and funding of institutions outside the public sector, and the *General and Vocational Colleges Act* (1967) concerns the colleges. With the exception of the universities, these five laws essentially define all the major education structures in Quebec.

Central Structures

The most visible of the central structures in Quebec education is the Ministry of Education, established in 1964, and sometimes referred to as the Department of Education or more briefly as the MEQ. This Ministry, the largest provincial education ministry in Canada, was divided in 1985 into two ministries: a Ministry of Education and a Ministry of Higher Education, Science and Technology. For a short time in 1985, these ministries were headed by two separate Ministers but at the time of writing, both portfolios are directed by the same Minister. Currently, the field of Technology, but not Science, has been included in a different portfolio. The two ministries, Education and Higher Education and Science, exist as separate administrative entities each with its own deputy minister. A number of other provinces have a similar division of responsibilities.

The two education ministries are responsible for the implementation of the various laws and regulations, for policy making, and for the supervision, coordination, administration, and financing of the education system from preschool to the university level. Although the right to control the universities is open to some question, as is the right to determine the curriculum in confessional school boards, the two ministries can and do exercise considerable power over all aspects of education in Quebec.

The Ministry of Education is primarily responsible for the preschool, elementary and secondary sectors. It formulates policies for education goals and priorities, issues directives concerning management, curriculum and budgets, and produces curriculum guidelines and teachers' guides for all subjects in the elementary and secondary programs. The Ministry also specifies the administrative and budgetary rules for school boards and schools, issues and directs the marking of examinations for the Provincial School Leaving Certificates, establishes rules for the certification and classification of teachers, evaluates the qualifications of teachers and issues all teaching permits and diplomas, and provides the operating funds to school boards and the majority of private schools. The Ministry is also responsible for the overall quality of the system and must ensure that the values transmitted by the schools are in accordance with the aspirations of the Quebec population.[1]

As can be seen from the organizational chart of the Ministry of Education there is a large bureaucracy with a great many *Directions générales, Directions,* and *Services.* Under the political leadership of the minister, the chief administrative officer of the Ministry is the deputy-minister (*Sous-ministre*) who is a civil servant, as are all the other permanent staff in the Ministry. As indicated in the previous chapter, there are two associate deputy-ministers, one Catholic and one Protestant, and there are also four assistant deputy-ministers. These four assistant deputy-ministers are responsible respectively for the four major sectors of the Ministry: administration, labour relations, service to the elementary and secondary network, planning and pedagogical development.

In general terms, the four major functions of the Ministry of Education are as follows:[2]

1. *Pedagogy*: the definition and general organization of educational services for the population at large; the approval of programs; the listing of approved teaching materials, of optional courses, and of specialized technical programs; the criteria for granting equivalences; and the granting of certificates and diplomas.

2. *Human resources*: the definition of general working conditions throughout the school system; the establishment of a system of teacher classification and qualifications; the establishment of a general policy for teacher training, professional development, and the evaluation of personnel; and, in cooperation with the school boards, the negotiation of collective agreements.

3. *Material resources and finance*: the establishment each year of the budgetary rules for the distribution of funds granted by the National Assembly; the establishment of regulations concerning the financial management and auditing of educational institutions; the authorization of loans and capital building projects.

4. *Information*: the collection, processing, availability, and security of information necessary to the management of the education system; and the timely availability of appropriate data to facilitate decision making.

The 1984-1985 annual report of the Ministry of Education provides considerable information as to the number of employees and of their distribution by sector within the Ministry.[3] An analysis of this information together with the appropriate sectorial budgets provides an interesting insight into the various functions and responsibilities of the Ministry.

In addition to the Ministry of Education itself, located in Quebec City, the Ministry has a network of regional offices to serve the 11 administrative regions of Quebec. These are: (1) Lower St. Lawrence - Gaspésie, (2) Saguenay - Lac Saint-Jean, (3) Quebec region, (4) Trois-Rivières region, (5) Eastern Townships (Estrie), (6.1) Laval-Laurentian region, (6.2) Montreal South Shore region, (6.3) Montreal Island, (7) Outaouais Valley region (Hull), (8) Abitibi-Témiscamingue region, and (9) North Shore region.

This information reveals that the unified Ministry of Education employed 1720 personnel in 1984-1985 at a cost of over $103 million. In 1985-1986 the

Table 3.1
Number of Employees and Sectorial Budgets:
Ministry of Education, 1984-85

1) **Preschool, Elementary and Secondary**	**Employees**	**Budget**
Relations with school boards and regions	361	15 163 700
Pedagogical development	137	8 637 300
Material resources and finance	95	3 451 700
Adult education	30	1 141 100
Planning and data collection	26	1 065 700
Total	649	29 459 500
2) Labour Relations		
Relations with school boards and their personnel, teacher classification and probation	84	4 523 900
Appeals and tribunals	15	1 199 500
Total	99	5 723 400
3) Intersectorial Services		
Adult education	78	2 681 000
Private education	26	998,500
Teaching materials	81	10 858 400
Total	185	14 537 900
4) Planning		
Research	12	798 600
Economic and demographic studies	23	796 400
Policy and plans	64	3 727 100
Status of women	5	320 000
Secretariat	4	217 500
Total	108	5 787 800
5) Internal Administration and and Information Services		
Human resource management	63	3 742 200
Financial and material resource management	60	4 423 300
Communications	82	9 035 400
Administrative secretariat	26	1 259 500
Informational services	207	14 768 100
Computer services to network	122	6 825 800
Total	560	40 054 300
6) Ministry Central Services		
The office of Minister (Cabinet)	–	1 218 600
The office of deputy ministers	34	2 232 000
Coordination of Catholic education	12	738 800
Coordination of Protestant education	3	131 900
Internal audit and verification	7	304 100
Public relations and external affairs	16	728 500
Amerindian and Inuit education	3	118 800
Secretariat	11	344 200
Total	86	5 816 900

7) Superior Council of Education

Total	33	1 956 600

"new" Ministry of Education employed 1276 personnel at a cost of $86.6 million. Unfortunately, the relevant statistics from the Ministry of Higher Education and Science were not available at the time of writing, although it is known that 555 personnel were transferred from the "old" MEQ to the new Ministry of Higher Education and Science. In recent years there has been criticism that the central bureaucracy has become too large, too intrusive, too bureaucratic, too unwieldy and too expensive. There is a strong feeling in some quarters that some of the many responsibilities now exercised by the two ministries could perhaps be better delegated to other levels.

The Superior Council of Education, as briefly discussed in Chapter 2, is the chief advisory body to the Ministry of Education and was established in 1964. The Council's 24 members include 16 Catholics, 4 Protestants, and one member who is usually Jewish. The government appoints 22 members and the other two places are filled by the president of the Catholic Committee and the president of the Protestant Committee. The deputy minister of education and the two associate deputy-ministers are ex-officio members, but without the right to vote.

The mandate of the Superior Council contains three major elements. First, the Council must advise the Minister on all education regulations before these are finally approved; second, the Council must advise the Minister on any matter which the Minister submits to it for consideration; and third, the Council must submit to the National Assembly an annual report on the state and needs of education in Quebec. In addition, the Council may conduct public inquiries and seek opinions on any matter concerning education, subsequently submitting its findings and recommendations to the relevant Minister.

Associated with the Council are two confessional committees and four permanent commissions. Both the Catholic Committee and the Protestant Committee are composed of 15 members, including representation from religious authorities, parents and educators. The two confessional committees, unlike the Council and its commissions, have the authority to make regulations concerning the recognition of Catholic and Protestant institutions, the qualification of teachers of religion, and the curriculum concerning religious and moral instruction. From the viewpoint of religion and morals, but in these areas only, the two committees also have the right to submit advice directly to the Minister concerned. Although associated with the Superior Council in a structural sense, the Catholic and Protestant Committees are to a large extent independent of the Council and autonomous within the fields of their jurisdiction. Unlike the powerful confessional committees that existed prior to 1964, the jurisdiction of the present confessional committees is strictly limited to areas related to religion and morals. The four permanent commissions of the Council are concerned respectively with elementary education, secondary education, the education of adults, and higher education. The commissions, each of which has from 9 to 15 members, are appointed by and report directly to the Council.

In addition to the two education ministries and the Superior Council, two other central bodies with functions somewhat similar to the Superior Council are the Council of Colleges and the Council of Universities. These two bodies submit their recommendations directly to the Minister of Higher Education and Science. Unlike the Superior Council, they also have some supervisory and coordinating functions (see Chapter 5 for further details).

Intermediate Structures: The School Boards

Within the hierarchy of educational authority in Quebec and situated between the Ministry of Education and the elementary and secondary schools are the intermediate authorities known as school commissions or school boards. A school board is the basic unit for the provision of kindergarten, elementary, secondary, and some adult education services within a specific geographic territory. They are the legal corporate bodies that own the school buildings and property; they have the right to raise revenue from local school taxes; and they are the legal employers of the teachers, administrators, and other professional and nonprofessional staff. They also supervise the management and educational and financial activities of the schools within their territories.

School boards obtain their authority and power from two sources. First, the responsibility for providing schooling in Quebec was originally accorded to school boards by the Legislative Assembly prior to confederation and, over the years, these responsibilities have been codified into law and form part of the Public Education Act. Consequently, part of the authority of the school boards stems from the powers delegated to them by the Legislature. Second, school boards obtain authority by the fact that they are elected bodies and, as such, receive a mandate from the population of the territory over which they have jurisdiction. Originally, only property owners had the right to vote for school commissioners but, by amendments to the Education Act in 1971 and 1972, this right was extended to all citizens eighteen years of age or older, residing in the territory of the school board.

In the last analysis, the authority and power of school boards are derived directly from the powers vested in them by the provincial Legislature. Thus, the authority granted to school boards can only be withdrawn or modified by an act of the National Assembly. However, some confessional and dissentient school boards claim that they possessed certain rights and privileges in law prior to Confederation and that these were protected in Section 93 of the Canada Constitution Act of 1867. If this is the case then it would appear that the National Assembly cannot withdraw or substantially modify the rights and privileges of certain school boards without contravening the constitution. This issue again raises the question of whether or not the Province of Quebec has exclusive jurisdiction in the field of education.

There are at present 234 school boards in Quebec divided on religious lines: 201 school boards for Catholics, 29 for Protestants, and 4 for both

Catholics and Protestants. These last four multi-confessional boards are relatively recent; they were created primarily to serve the native peoples living in the north of Quebec. From a strictly legal point of view, however, there are three types of school boards in Quebec: Catholic and Protestant *confessional* school boards in Montreal and Quebec City; *common* school boards in the rest of the province; and *dissentient* school boards for the Catholic and Protestant religious minorities living outside Montreal and Quebec City. There are at present only five small *dissentient* school boards: three Protestant boards in Rouyn, Baie-Comeau, and Laurentienne, and two Catholic boards in Greenfield Park and Portage-du-Fort. Table 3.2 shows the number of these boards by confessionality and instructional level during the period of 1974-1985. Only five school boards had student numbers of 20,000 or more, whereas approximately two-thirds of the Protestant boards and more than one-third of the Catholic boards had enrolments of less than 2,000 students. Within the past two years,

Table 3.2

Number of School Boards 1974-1986

	1974-75	1984-85	1985-86
School Boards for Catholics			
Elementary (Local)	162	138	
Secondary (Regional)	46	38	
Elementary & Secondary (Integrated)	15	35	
Total	223	211	201
School Boards for Protestants			
Elementary (Local)	21	17	
Secondary (Regional)	8	7	
Elementary & Secondary (Integrated)	3	7	
Total	32	31	29
School Boards for Catholics & Protestants			
Elementary & Secondary (Integrated)	1	4	4
Total: School Boards Quebec			
Elementary (Local)	183	155	131
Secondary (Regional)	54	45	37
Elementary & Secondary (Integrated)	19	46	66
Total	256	246	234

Source: Gouvernement du Québec, *Statistiques de l'Education (Préscolaire, Primaire, Secondaire)*, Ministère de l'Education, Edition de Septembre, 1985 et 1986.

and specifically since the failure of Bill 3, there have been a number of voluntary amalgamations of school boards, resulting in a decline of the number of local and regional boards and an increase in the number of of integrated boards.

School board structures on the Island of Montreal are somewhat different from those in the rest of the province, primarily because the Montreal region is where the majority of the non-Catholic and non-francophone populations are concentrated. As a result, problems concerning religious, linguistic and minority rights have been more acute and have generated more heated debate on the Island than in the rest of the province. After several unsuccessful attempts to restructure the Montreal school boards in the late 1960s and early 1970s, the government eventually introduced legislation (Bill 71) in 1972 that reduced the number of boards from 33 to the present number of 8: six for Catholics and two for Protestants (See Table 3.3). At the same time, certain administrative functions, primarily financial, were placed under the jurisdiction of another type of intermediate body known as the School Council of the Montreal of Montreal.

The School Council is composed of representatives of the eight Montreal school boards and representatives of the Quebec government. Its original purpose was to recommend new school board structures for the Island; however, the Council has been unable to reach a consensus on this matter. The Council also has jurisdiction concerning the use of school buildings, the raising of loans, the preparation of the budget, and the provision of services to underprivileged areas. Specifically, it sets the school tax rates for the Island and distributes the budget to its member boards. As a result of recent court actions, the two confessional boards on the Island have been permitted to withdraw from the financial control of the Council.

Table 3.3

Enrolment in Montreal Island School Boards: 1985-1986

School Board	1985-86 Enrolment
Jérome -Le Royer (Catholic)	20 602
Montreal Catholic School Commission	100 163
Sainte-Croix (Catholic)	8 970
Verdun (Catholic)	5 627
Sault-Saint-Louis (Catholic)	12 398
Baldwin-Cartier (Catholic)	16 895
Protestant School Board of Greater Montreal	32 072
Lakeshore (Protestant)	11 639
Total	208 366

Source. Conseil scolaire de l'île de Montréal, "Résumé" Meeting of December 16, 1985.

In the majority of boards at the present time, the number of commissioners varies from 9 to 19 according to the number of students enrolled in the board. The commissioners are elected on the basis of universal suffrage for three-year terms. In addition to these elected commissioners, school boards in Quebec now have one or two appointed parent-commissioners. The commissioners elect one of their number to be president or chairman of the board. The chief administrative officer of the board, appointed by and responsible to the commissioners, is the director general, a position with similar responsibilities to those elsewhere of a Superintendent of Schools or Director of Education. The director general is responsible for the day-to-day administration of the school board and the management of its resources. In the larger school boards there is usually an assistant director general and a staff of professionals and administrators who are responsible to the director general for the operation of activities such as personnel, budget, pupil transportation, buildings and equipment, purchasing, curriculum and instructional services, and adult education. Within the field of curriculum and instructional services, the largest school boards also have a staff of consultants and professionals to assist teachers in curricular and pedagogical matters and to provide services and resources to the schools.

Traditionally, school boards in Quebec have enjoyed considerable administrative, educational, and financial autonomy. They had the right to determine the school tax rate based on the evaluation of property within their territories; they had the right to appoint, pay, and dismiss teachers; and they had the right to "regulate" the courses of study. Within the past twenty years, however, many of these traditional powers of school boards have been severely curtailed. In 1967, Bill 25 established a province-wide salary scale for all teachers in the public sector and created a structure whereby collective bargaining primarily took place on the provincial rather than the individual school board level. While this had the advantage of abolishing the disparities in salaries that existed between men and women teachers, and between rural and urban school boards, it also meant that school boards were no longer able to negotiate salaries and workloads directly with their employees. The detailed clauses of the various collective agreements signed by the teachers' associations and the employers have permitted the school boards only limited management of their personnel; and the ability of school boards to hire, transfer, or dismiss teachers has been severely restricted.

In terms of financial control, the school boards suffered a major reduction in their traditional powers when the government introduced a new method of financing school boards in 1979. Bill 57 transferred the majority of revenues generated by local school taxation to the municipalities in exchange for sales tax revenues. The school boards' ability to raise revenue from local school taxation was limited to a ceiling of 6 per cent of net expenses, or to 0.25 cents per $100 of real estate valuation, whichever was the lower. As a result, the government became the major source of revenue accounting for approximately 90 per cent of the school boards' expenses. A number of school boards believe that this restriction on their right to tax is unconstitutional as it contravenes Section 93 of the 1867 Constitution Act. As the result of a Supreme Court decision in 1984, the confessional school boards in the cities of Montreal and Quebec, but not the other boards, have now been exempted from the taxation limitations imposed by Bill 57.

Finally, the school boards' power to regulate the curriculum has been considerably restricted by the curriculum regulations (*régimes pédagogiques*) that were introduced by means of an amendment to the Education Act in 1979. All of these measure have resulted in a considerable reduction in the powers traditionally exercised by the province's school boards.

Local Structures: the Schools

Elementary and secondary schools are the third level of authority in Quebec's public school system. The school is generally the only structure with which the public has direct contact and in the everyday lives of students, teachers and parents, it is viewed as the most significant institution. Yet it is probably the structure with the least authority. The individual school is legally owned by the school board; its educational policies are largely determined by the school board; it is managed according to criteria established by the school board; and it is staffed entirely by employees appointed and paid for by the school board. In terms of the industrial model, it is possible to think of the school as a "branch plant" of the school board.

Nevertheless, in recent years and specifically at the request of parent groups, several attempts have been made to redistribute authority between the schools and school boards so as to provide the school with more power. The first major step in this direction was taken in 1979 when the government approved Bill 71. For the first time in Quebec law, the school was defined and given a legal status: "A school is an institutional entity under the authority of a principal, designed to provide education to pupils in an organized manner, in whose activities the pupils, teachers, other members of the staff and parents participate "(Bill 71, Clause 32.1). Defining the school in this manner did not grant it any more authority. According to the same bill: "A school is established by the school board in accordance with the conditions determined by the board " (Bill 71, Clause 32.2).

Bill 71 also defined the responsibilities of the school principal (or the head teacher in the case of smaller schools). It was made clear that the principal functioned "under the authority of the director general of the school board" and "in accordance with the policies and regulations of the school board." Specifically, the law defined the responsibilities of the school principal in the following terms:

Under the authority of the director general of the school board, the principal or the person in charge of a school is responsible for defining its orientation and activities, seeing that it runs smoothly and attains the objectives set for it, and shall apply the policies, regulations and instructions concerning the school, and give an accounting of his administration (Bill 71, Clause 32.3).

Bill 71 in effect confirmed that the school and its principal operated almost exclusively under the authority and control of the school board.

Most schools have a school council composed of teachers. These school councils advise the principal on educational matters such as timetables, the requisition and allocation of textbooks and teaching materials, the grouping and classification of pupils, the teaching of moral and religious instruction, the use of pedagogical days, evaluation and grading procedures, and extra-curricular activities. In some schools, especially some secondary schools, there are also student councils elected by the students. The specific functions of student councils vary considerably from school to school, but are generally quite limited.

The Role of the Parents in the Schools

Parents have been serving on school committees and participating in parent-teacher associations for years; although until 1960, this form of participation was almost exclusively confined to the Protestant sector. The first local home and school association in Quebec was established in 1919. Local associations were eventually established in most Protestant schools and together they formed the Quebec Federation of Protestant Home and School Associations in 1944. Over the years the Federation has made numerous representations to various bodies on matters of interest to Quebec parents. Although the Federation has now dropped the word "Protestant" from its title, it is viewed as an organization primarily representing English Protestants.

In the last few years, a new organization known as The English Speaking Parents' Network has attempted to bring English-speaking parents together from both the Catholic and Protestant sectors. These voluntary organizations are not unlike those found in other provinces or the United States. In Quebec, however, these organizations have been found primarily within the English-speaking community. The French-speaking majority has a different history and tradition.

Prior to the Quiet Revolution, the role of the Church in Quebec education was such that there were few opportunities for French-speaking parents to become actively involved in school affairs. The Royal Commission report of 1966 had recommended a major change in school board structures in which parents would have been a key element at the level of both the school and the school board, but these recommendations were not implemented. A series of somewhat ad hoc arrangements for parental involvement in the Catholic schools, such as consultative committees and educational workshops, had been tried during the period 1965-1970, but none of those had proved entirely satisfactory.

Eventually, ln 1971, the government tabled two pieces of legislation in the National Assembly designed to ameliorate some of the more important weaknesses in the educational system and to provide a formal means by which parents could participate. To parents, the effects of Bill 27 and Bill 71 were essentially the same since they established a legal framework for the participation of parents within the system both at the level of the individual school and at the level of the school board. Although the mandates have changed over the years, the basic structural arrangements for parent participation in Quebec remain as established by these two laws.

The legislation required that a school committee composed of local parents be established in every school controlled by a public school board. The principal and one representative (designated by the teachers in the school) were to be ex-officio members of the committee, but they were not entitled to vote. School board commissioners (trustees) were specifically excluded from being members of the school committees. At the level of the school board, a parents' committee was required to be established for every public school board in the province, and was to be composed of the president, that is a parent, from each of the board's constituent school committees.

The function of the local school committee was to stimulate the participation of parents, to help improve school services, and to make recommendations to the school's administration concerning the quality of teaching and of school life. The function of the parents' committee was to coordinate the work of the local school committees, to encourage the participation of parents, to transmit recommendations from the school committees to the board, and to propose improvements in the administration and management of the board's schools.

A significant step was undertaken in 1975 with the formation of the Fédération des comités des parents de la province du Québec, an organization which brings together representatives from all the province's parents' committees and which has evolved as an important political pressure group.

Following the consultations on the Green Paper (1977) the government devised legislation that would strengthen the roles of the existing school and parents' committees, would require that consultation with parents on certain subjects be made compulsory, and would guarantee direct representation of parents both on the school board and on its executive committee. The legislation would also establish orientation councils in which parents would be permitted to participate, plan, and implement an educational project for each school. Accordingly, two laws were passed in 1979 to give effect to these intentions: Bill 30 and Bill 71 (not to be confused with Bill 71 of 1972).

Bill 30, passed in June 1979, gave parents the right to be directly represented on school boards and on the boards' executive committees. In the case of a local elementary board or of a regional secondary board, the parents' committee was to elect one of its members to serve as parent commissioner. In the case of an integrated board that offered both elementary and secondary levels of instruction, the parents' committee was to elect two parent commissioners – one to represent elementary schools and the other, secondary schools. These parent commissioners were to exercise all the rights and powers of elected commissioners, except that of voting. The primary intent of these measures was not so much to permit parents to participate in the administration and management of the school boards as such, but to ensure that parents would have access to all the information and policy decisions of the school board concerned. The parent commissioners would thus be in a position to report back to the parents' committee which, in turn, would report back to the individual school committees and to the parents at large.

Bill 71 included provisions whereby parents could participate in a process of defining the local school as a community school (see Chapter 4 on the Educational Project) and could have it withdrawn to a large extent from the control and supervision of the local school board. In principle, the parents could play a major role in determining the specific orientation or ethos of the school. This could come about by means of an orientation or "ways and means" committee.[4] The orientation committee was to be composed of the school principal as chairman, three parents appointed by the school committee, two members of the teaching staff elected by the teachers of the school, one commissioner or additional parent appointed by the school board and, in the case of secondary schools, two senior students elected by all the students in the school. Unlike the more or less homogeneous committees composed of teachers, parents or students, the composition of the orientation committee was different because it was designed to bring together all the principal agents involved in the day-to-day operation of the school. Bill 71 also stated that the school board was obligated to establish an orientation committee when requested to do so jointly by the school principal, a teacher and a parent.

Once established, the orientation committee was to have the following functions:
1. to determine the specific orientation(s) of the school;
2. to participate in the preparation of the school's educational project, follow the carrying out of that project, evaluate it and draw up a report on it;
3. to make by-laws respecting the conduct of the pupils of the school;
4. to make by-laws for the use of school premises;
5. to make recommendations to the school board on the introduction of new curricula;
6. to make recommendations to the school board on the implementation of school daycare services;
7. to prepare and submit its budget to the school board for approval and see to its administration.[5]

The new law thus envisaged that the orientation committees would assume a number of responsibilities formerly exercised by the school boards. For a variety of reasons, a number of boards instructed their school principals to have nothing to do with this new creature. Some of the teachers' associations instructed their teachers likewise (contract negotiations were going on at the time). As orientation committees could only be established at the specific request of principals, teachers, and parents acting in concert, it is not surprising perhaps that very few orientation committees were ever established. The parents tended to be those most disappointed. This legislative attempt on the part of the government to grant more authority to the local school can only be described as a failure.

The reasons for this failure go a long way to explain the far more radical proposals that were to come later in the White Paper. The government appeared to be convinced that somehow or other, local public schools should be granted more authority and power and that parents should be given a more meaningful role within these schools. It is obvious, however, that any increased authority for the schools and parents would have to come at the expense of those who currently exercised that authority, namely the school boards and the teachers.

Provincial Groups and Associations

In any discussion of Quebec education it is important to realize that the exercise of power and influence is not restricted to the three levels of the structure as enumerated above. The Ministry of Education, the school boards, and the schools are perhaps the most visible structures, but by no means do these possess a monopoly on power and influence. Among the more influential groups are the associations that correspond to the two basic types of school boards in the province: the Quebec Association of Protestant School Boards (QAPSB) and the Federation of Catholic School Boards (Fédération des commissions scolaires catholiques du Québec) or FCSCQ. On behalf of their membership, these two associations exist to negotiate with their employees and are important and powerful pressure groups concerned with promoting and protecting the rights of the school boards in general.

A similar observation can be made of the teachers' associations. Although it might be logical to expect there to be two such associations, as there are with their employers, there are in fact three. These three associations reflect the reality of Quebec education rather than the structural duality. First and foremost, because of its size and influence, is the Centrale de l'enseignement du Québec (CEQ) which represents employees in the French sector of the Catholic school boards. Representing teachers employed in the Protestant school boards is the Provincial Association of Protestant Teachers (PAPT) and representing teachers employed in the English schools of Catholic school boards is the Provincial Association of Catholic Teachers (PACT). Occasionally, all three of these associations join forces with other unions in the public sector to bargain collectively or to confront the government (see Chapter

7 for further details on teacher unions). There are also a number of subject oriented teachers' associations concerned with the promotion of individual subject disciplines.

Because of the high profile that usually accompanies teacher negotiations in Quebec, the three teacher associations and two associations of school boards receive considerable publicity and are therefore relatively well known. There are, however, a number of other groups both in the public and private sectors which are perhaps less well known, but nevertheless function effectively at the provincial level. Within their respective fields of expertise these other groups occasionally influence government's and school boards' policy to their point of view. These include the groups representing the interest of private schools and the various parent associations of which the Fédération des comités de parents de la province du Québec (FCPPQ), the Federation of Quebec Home and School Associations and the English Speaking Parents' Network are perhaps the most well known.

Within the field of school board administration, there are a number of associations that represent senior administrators. The two largest associations are the Association des directeurs généraux des commissions scolaires (ADI-GECS) which represents all the directors general, the Association des cadres scolaires du Québec (ACSQ) and the Fédération québécoise des directeurs d'école (FQDE) which represent the senior administrators and school principals respectively within the French Catholic sector. The English sector is represented by equivalent but considerably smaller associations in both the Protestant and Catholic networks.

Outside of the formal education network, there are a number of other organizations that function as influential pressure groups in the matter of establishing education policy. Although it is impossible to mention all of these by name, they include religious groups such as the Quebec Assembly of Catholic Bishops, business and commercial groups such as the Conseil du Patronat and the Chambre de Commerce, and various cultural groups such as the Societé de St. Jean Baptiste and Alliance Quebec. The media is also an important influence especially *Le Devoir* and *La Presse* newspapers and the magazine *L'Actualite.* In general, it would be true to state that there is more public debate on educational policy in Quebec than there is in most other provinces.

Proposals for Change

In the final volume of the Parent Report published in 1966, the commissioners had discussed the dual confessional school board structure in Quebec and had concluded that it was inappropriate for modern times. They recommended its abolition and its replacement by a unified secular school board structure that would have permitted the existence of both confessional and non-confessional schools operating in either French or English. This proposal was not favourably received at the time, particularly in the more traditional and rural areas of the Province, and it was never implemented.

Subsequent attempts to alter the confessional board structures on the Island of Montreal, most notably the recommendations of the Pagé Commission in 1968 and of Bill 62 in 1969, also met with considerable opposition and had therefore been rejected or withdrawn. In the 1970s the School Council of the Island of Montreal likewise failed to reach consensus on the matter of structural reform for school boards on the Island of Montreal. It was evident that no consensus existed as to the nature or even the necessity for structural reform. In its election platform of 1976, however, the Parti Québécois had indicated its intention to tackle this thorny problem once and for all; and in June 1982, under the political leadership of the Minister of Education, Dr. Camille Laurin, the government released a White Paper entitled: *The Québec School: a responsible force in the community.*[6]

The proposed structural changes announced in the White Paper had two dimensions: first, the abolition of the traditional dual confessional school board structures in favour of a linguistic system on the Island of Montreal and of a unified school board system elsewhere in which all schools would be public and common; and second, a redistribution of traditional powers at the intermediate and local levels in favour of the schools rather than the school boards. A number of arguments were advanced in the White Paper in favour of these proposals: the problems caused by increased pluralism especially with regard to religious exemptions in the schools and the right of all citizens to exercise freedoms of conscience and of religious expression; the duplication and excessive number of school boards particularly at a time of declining enrolments; the number of immigrants receiving their French language instruction in Protestant schools. Other arguments were the excessive bureaucratization, politicization, and insensitivity of school boards and the problems experienced by parents in participating in school affairs.

In the summer of 1983, after a year of intense and sometimes impassioned debate, Bill 40, *An Act respecting public elementary and secondary education,* was tabled in the National Assembly by the Minister of Education. Its scope was impressive. After defining the various forms of educational services to be made available and listing the rights of pupils, the Bill went on to enumerate, in detail, a new distribution of power and authority in Quebec's public school structures. As anticipated, the Bill gave legal expression to the thrust of the ideas proposed in the White Paper; and although some of the criticism leveled at the initial proposal had been partially rectified in Bill 40, there were still many areas that concerned a number of groups.

The lack of consensus about the direction of the reform, particularly among various Protestant groups, became very clear to the public during the course of the Parliamentary Committee hearings on Bill 40 held in early 1984. Not only was it clear that there was no consensus about the Bill, it was increasingly obvious that the Minister and the government itself were in serious political trouble on the matter. Soon after the conclusion of the hearings the Premier announced a cabinet shuffle in which Dr. Laurin was replaced as Minister of

Education by M. Yves Bérubé.

The new Minister announced that his specific mandate was to rescue the reform package by attempting to identify those areas in which a consensus could be found. After a series of consultations with the major groups involved during the summer of 1984, the government withdrew Bill 40, and in November the Minister tabled Bill 3, *An Act Respecting Public Elementary and Secondary Education,* in the National Assembly.

The major provisions of Bill 3 were as follows:

1. Some limited autonomy was to be granted to individual schools, although the proposal to grant a legal corporate status to the school had been withdrawn. The school was to remain as "an institutional entity under the authority of a principal" as had previously been the case (Bill 71, 1979). The school would remain the property of the school board, and the school board would continue to appoint the principal and staff. In terms of the relationship between boards and schools, it was clear that the school board was back in control. Clause 111 of Bill 3 stated that: "Each school board has jurisdiction over every elementary and secondary school to which it issues a deed of establishment." The school, however, would have the authority to determine its educational project and its religious orientation and it could "integrate the religious beliefs and values of a particular denomination or of several denominations into its educational plan." In essence, the Bill reinstituted a form of governance for schools that was very similar to that envisaged for the unsuccessful orientation committees authorized by Bill 71 in 1979.

2. Parents were to become more involved in decision making at the level both of the school and the school board. At the level of the school, parents were to form a majority on the school council. At the level of the board, instead of having one commissioner per school as had been proposed in the White Paper and Bill 40, the new law proposed a compromise in which school boards would have from 8 to 16 members according to its enrolment, approximately two-thirds of whom would be elected by universal suffrage on a ward basis and the other one-third would be parent-commissioners elected by the members of school councils. All commissioners, including the elected parents, would have the right to vote; however, only those elected on the basis of universal suffrage could vote in the matter of establishing the school tax rate.

3. The mandate of the school was to be expanded to include the promotion of the social and cultural interests of the community it served. The proposition that the school could keep any fee or rental income from these activities was, however, withdrawn.

4. School board territories throughout Quebec, rather than only those on the Island of Montreal, were to be on a linguistic basis. This change reflected a year or more of intense lobbying on the part of certain elements within the English-speaking community. School boards and not individual schools

were to be legally responsible for the provision of educational services.

5. The the the two confessional school boards in the city of Montreal and two in Quebec City were to be reduced in size to the territories that existed in 1867, an area that included very few schools. These and the five small dissentient boards would be permitted to continue operation under the provisions of the previously existing Education Act.

6. The right of the population to educational services, the rights of students, and the powers of the Minister and of the government in the field of education were enumerated in detail.

7. A commission under the authority of the Minister would be established to begin implementing the law during the 1984-1985 school year.

A number of groups urged the government to submit Bill 3 to the courts for a ruling on its constitutionality before enacting it into legislation, but the government chose to ignore this advice and quickly passed the law in December 1984.

As soon as the government attempted to implement the new law in 1985, the Quebec Association of Protestant School Boards acting in concert with the Montreal Catholic School Commission petitioned the Quebec Superior Court to disallow Bill 3 on the grounds that it was unconstitutional and trespassed upon their rights and privileges as set out in section 93 of the Constitution Act of 1867. In June 1985, the court ruled that Bill 3 was indeed unconstitutional and issued a permanent injunction preventing the government from implementing the law. Bill 3 and the structural reform movement were therefore terminated. Although this represented a considerable victory for the confessional school boards, it also meant that other aspects of the law about which there had been little disagreement, such as new arrangements for school board elections or the integration of elementary and secondary school boards, would also not be implemented.

Although the Parti Québécois government indicated an intention to appeal this decision to higher courts, the Liberal government (elected in 1985) announced through its Minister of Education, M. Claude Ryan, that it would not proceed with the appeal and that it would not propose further major structural reform until a more solid consensus was reached. The new Liberal government passed Bill 24 in May 1986 facilitating the fusion or annexation of school boards on a voluntary basis and authorizing new arrangements for school board elections, but the confessional basis of Quebec's educational structures remained essentially the same as originally established in the 1840s.

Conclusion

From the time of the Quiet Revolution, the province of Quebec has moved rapidly and effectively to modernize its public education system. Its schools, colleges, and universities are now arguably equal, if not superior, to those elsewhere in Canada. In terms of parent participation, its legislation is unequalled in North America. Yet its school system continues to maintain basic structures that were originally designed in the first half of the nineteenth century. Several attempts have been made to effect a fundamental change in these structures, but all have met with failure. The fact remains that changing circumstances have made these structures considerably less appropriate than they once were. Some of the current problems are as follows:

1. The division into local elementary school boards and regional secondary boards, outside the Montreal area, results in the duplication of some services and creates problems of coordination between two levels of instruction.

2. School boards in Quebec currently number 234. Because of declining enrolments, a reduction in this number is becoming a practical economic necessity, if only to ensure that a minimum level of services is available to all children.

3. Within the English-speaking community particularly rapid declining enrolments are seriously jeapardizing the viability of both English-Catholic and English-Protestant schools and of their respective support systems. If these schools are to survive, then some form of consolidation is urgently required.

4. English-speaking Catholics who send their children to Protestant schools have been effectively disenfranchised for many years. A court case launched in March 1986 is attempting to clarify the rights of English Catholics in the light of the Constitution Acts of 1867 and of 1982. It is likely that groups such as English Catholics, French Protestants, other religious groups, and those without religious affiliations will increasingly turn to the courts for a clarification of their educational rights. A structure designed essentially for two religious groups is likely to be increasingly under pressure, especially in the light of provisions of the Canadian and Quebec Charters of Rights and Freedoms.

5. The current structures are evidently unable (or perhaps unwilling) to provide non-confessional schools for those who desire them. Attempts by parent groups to have some schools declared pluralist or neutral have met with failure. The increasing pluralism in Quebec schools, especially in the Montreal area, will almost certainly create more pressure in support of non-confessional schools. On the other hand, many traditional Catholics and fundamentalist Protestants are concerned that increased pluralism is leading to indifference to religious values in many so-called Catholic and Protestant schools.

6. The recent and continuing growth of enrolments in the French-Protestant sector, due primarily to the effects of Bill 101, is creating some interesting problems. Protestant school boards are having to close English schools to make room for this growth; as a result, a traditional bastion of the English language and culture in Quebec is becoming increasingly French. It is also

ironic, if not a little bizarre, that the French language, if not the French culture, is being promoted in school boards managed primarily by the English-speaking community. A number of French Catholic boards, faced themselves with the problem of declining enrolments, view the expansion of the French Protestant sector as a potential threat to their own survival.

7. In a pluralistic and rapidly changing society, it is beginning to appear that a more reasonable way of defining the appropriate roles of different groups is necessary. In the past, it was quite clear that the Church was primarily responsible for the education system. The debates of the last few years have involved numerous groups: political leaders, civil servants in the Ministry and regional offices, school board commissioners, school board and school administrators, teachers and their associations, parent groups, religious groups, and special interest groups. If only one group has dominant control, then the other groups will feel excluded and become increasingly resentful and uncooperative.

8. Parents in some areas are dissatisfied with their limited role and are demanding a greater say in school affairs. They are particularly outspoken when declining enrolments force school boards to close local schools. Major disputes between school boards and parents have become quite common.

9. Dissatisfaction with the quality of education in the public schools has persuaded many parents to enrol their children in the private sector. As a result, private school enrolments in Quebec have been increasing and have augmented the already serious decline in public school enrolments. The flourishing private sector, heavily supported by government subsidies, is viewed as a threat by both school boards and teacher unions.

10. The evidence of the past five years would suggest that there has to be a balance between the powers exercised at the different levels of the structure. If the balance is shifted too far in the direction of local control or of central control, a counter movement tends to occur. It now appears clear that the population supports the retention of competent bodies at the local and intermediate levels in order to offset the dominant influence of the Ministry of Education. A better balance is also required between centrally developed policies to ensure equality of opportunity for all children on the one hand, and of polices designed to permit the expression of local needs and values on the other.

The experiences of the past twenty-five years suggest that for fundamental structural reform to be successful in Quebec, at least three preconditions must be met. The first is the creation of a broad consensus, if not about the details of the reform, then at least about the necessity for reform and the general direction that this should take. This consensus can only come about in a climate of mutual trust and when care has been taken in advance to consult all the major parties concerned. The somewhat arrogant approach of announcing policies and plans prior to consultation seems to lead only to confrontation.

Second, it is important that legislation be clear and precise. Legislation that attempts to change too many things at once tends to run into trouble either because people do not understand its complexity and therefore distrust it, or because various interest groups can manipulate public opinion against it, or because different groups object to different parts. If the legislation attempts to change too many things at once, it runs the risk of antagonizing nearly all the vested interests.

Third, it now appears that the courts intend to take a broad and generous view of the protections granted to minorities (confessional and linguistic) in the Canadian constitution. Legislation must therefore be sensitive to the rights of minorities. If there is a broad consensus in favour of basic structural change, reform can only come about in one of two ways: either as a result of direct negotiations and subsequent agreement between parties involved, and/or as a result of changes to Section 93 of the Canada Constitution Act of 1867. As the amending formulas are not at all easy to achieve, it would appear that direct negotiations are likely to be more productive.

Ultimately, there is the question of how important the structures are in effecting quality education, and how much time, money, and intelligence Quebec can afford to invest in structural debate. The current concern is not so much towards the building of better structures but with the possibility of simplifying and deregulating what already exists. The challenge in the years to come will be to make the structures, whatever form these may take, operate effectively in the interests of quality education for all Quebecers.

Notes

1. Gouvernement du Québec, Ministère de l'Education, *Rapport annuel 1984-1985.* Québec, 1985, p. 9.

2. *Rapport annuel 1984-1985, p. 9.*

3. *Rapport annuel 1985-1985*, p. 17-39.

4. The term "Orientation Council" was used in the Green Paper (1977); "Ways and Means Committee" in the Orange Paper (Plan of Action, 1979); and "Orientation Committee" in Bill 71 (1979).

5. Gouvernement du Québec, Ministère de l'Education, *The School's Orientation Committee What? Why? How?* Direction générale des réseau, 1980, 32 p.

6. Gouvernement du Québec, Ministère de l'Education, *The Quebec School: a Responsible Force in the Community,* (White Paper), 1982, 95 p.

Elementary and Secondary Education Structures and Programs

The public elementary and secondary schools in Quebec have undergone dramatic changes within the past twenty-five years. In spite of these changes, or perhaps because of them, the education provided in the elementary and secondary schools is a matter for considerable debate and public discussion. There are two major factors that account for this. First, as it is primarily in the schools that a society's culture, values, and future socio-economic development are nurtured and shaped, and because of the special importance attached to these matters in the province of Quebec, the schools have an important role in influencing the type of society that Quebec will become. Second, as education is perhaps the most important field in which the provincial government has exclusive jurisdiction, the relationship between politics and schooling in Quebec is particularly acute. In purely quantitative terms moreover, the elementary and secondary levels are by far the most important sector in Quebec education. Together, the elementary and secondary schools number almost 3,000; they are attended by over 1 million full-time students; they offer employment to some 88,000 full-time employees of whom 61,000 are teachers; and they account for about 80 per cent of all public expenditures on education.[1] The elementary and secondary sector is thus one of Quebec's most important and most costly social services, but it also represents a major and perhaps crucial investment in the future of Quebec society.

In order to illustrate some of the important changes that have taken place in the past twenty-five years, it is interesting to compare the schools of today with those that existed in the early 1960s, prior to the changes with which this chapter is primarily concerned. Among the more obvious changes have been the construction of large comprehensive schools throughout the province, the increased level of schooling of the population at large, the enhanced role for parents, and the emergence of a more highly qualified and unionized teacher workforce. But the most dramatic changes have been within the schools and classrooms themselves and, in particular, in the type of education that children receive and the overall approach and methods that teachers use.

Prior to the important reforms of the 1960s, the type and style of education provided in many of the classrooms of elementary and secondary schools were the subject of considerable criticism. In his best-selling book, *The Impertinences of Brother Anonymous* (1960) Jean-Paul Desbiens (Frère Untel) poked irreverent fun at both the ecclesiastic authorities who were then primarily responsible for public education and the old-fashioned and religious-oriented curriculum then in vogue in many schools. "We are a hundred and fifty years ahead of all other countries as to the essential thing (which is Heaven)," he wrote, but "by the American clock, we are at the time of the Middle Ages."[2] The Parent Report commissioners, writing somewhat less passionately in 1963, were particularly critical of the type of education provided in many French Catholic schools. They described it as anaemic, authoritarian, textbook-ridden, and distorted by an overemphasis on religion leading to mental malnutrition.[3] They painted a generalized picture of the elementary school in the early 1960s in none too flattering terms:

> The result of this system has been a book-ridden education dominated by concern for examination results and by fear ... Too often the existing atmosphere of the elementary school locks the child within himself, warps his natural growth ... The pupil was not given a chance to search, to feel his way, to put to use his intellectual faculties. He had to absorb everything in predigested form and, during long hours in the classroom, he had to sit through a succession of irksome exercises and endless reviews. Here was a sure way to kill intellectual curiosity, to atrophy the mind, to produce passivity ... To promote this kind of accomplishment, discipline stressed keeping silence and sitting still to the point that they became the ultimate academic virtues.[4]

Such has been the pace of change, that some twenty-five years later, this generalized and somewhat stereotyped picture of a Quebec elementary school in the early 1960s no longer exists. Inspired by the teachings of modern psychology, especially those of Jean Piaget, and staffed by better qualified teachers, a Quebec elementary school today offers a type and style of education that bears little resemblance to the old stereotype. The elementary school is no longer a terminal institution that prepares many children directly for work, but rather a foundation stage of schooling that prepares all children for secondary level education. Its function is not necessarily to dispense the greatest possible knowledge in the greatest number of subjects but rather to provide a sound basic "formation" in the skills required for further study. The methods most commonly used by the teachers are no longer as rule-bound, formal and authoritarian as they once were but are more individualized, "child-centred," and "activist."

At the secondary school level, the changes have been equally dramatic, but of a somewhat different nature. Twenty-five years ago, Catholic secondary education in Quebec was offered in a variety of different institutions, mostly private and in a variety of different formats. These included trade schools, classical colleges, family institutes, apprenticeship centres, agricultural schools, and various other types of public and private institutions. Most of the programs were terminal; and although some provided access to the *Ecole Polytechnique*, only the elite classical colleges, offering an eight-year program primarily for boys, provided direct access to the more prestigious faculties in the French-language universities. There were also major differences, at all levels of the system, in the type of facilities and programs offered to English-speaking and French-speaking students. With inadequate facilities, a poorly qualified teaching force, strictly enforced examination hurdles and too many "dead end" programs, numerous children simply dropped out of school altogether. The Parent Commission, writing in 1964, described this situation as follows:

> When he leaves the elementary grades, the student has public schools, classical colleges, trade schools and private specialized schools available to him. The public school programme alone offers six courses of study to boys and and five to girls ... Classical instruction in the public school system is in its infancy, especially for girls; the trade and vocational school system cares for only a small fraction of the pupils it should properly enrol. Moreover, this division of secondary education among institutions of various kinds and the organization of the public secondary course into over-rigid compartments force students into a choice of courses which is often premature.[5]

Today, nearly all of these institutions and programs have disappeared, and in their place is a province-wide system of public secondary schools, most of them comprehensive and open to all, irrespective of geographical location or financial resources. The major structural differences between English and French or Protestant and Catholic institutions have likewise disappeared so that all students now follow essentially the same pattern of secondary education. Instead of a multiplicity of programs and strict grade levels, there is now a common program for all students in the first two or three years at the secondary level, only limited course options thereafter, and a system of subject promotion rather than grade-level promotion to account for individual differences. Instead of general classroom teachers offering all subjects to a specific grade level, most secondary teachers are subject specialists teaching a range of grade levels. While some of these changes continue to be controversial and some doubt their efficacy, there can be little argument that secondary education in Quebec today is very different from what it was only a few years ago.

These then are some of the more outstanding changes that have taken place during the past twenty-five years. There have been others, of course, such as the extension of kindergarten for all who desire it, the enhanced role for parents, the introduction of immersion programs for the teaching of French, and a drastic revision of the curriculum – to name but a few. The major purpose of what follows in this chapter is to describe the system with particular reference to its distinctive features, to outline some of the many changes that have taken place in elementary and secondary education in Quebec during the past twenty-five years, and to discuss some of the major problems and policy issues that have arisen during this period.

The Organization of Schooling in Quebec

The basic pattern for school organization in Quebec is fairly straightforward. Unlike England, for example, which has a threefold division into infant, junior, and secondary levels, or certain other jurisdictions that include a middle school or junior high school sector, the basic pattern in Quebec is a simple twofold division into elementary and secondary levels. The majority of students spend one year on a half-time basis in kindergarten, followed by six years at the elementary level and five years at the secondary level. This pattern differs from most other jurisdictions in North America in that full-time schooling extends for only 11 rather than 12 years.

The kindergarten program, although it differs from the elementary program in that it is not compulsory, is usually located in the local elementary school building. At the present time, it is a half-day program in the majority of schools and is only funded as such by the government, but there is some pressure from parent groups to extend it to a full-time basis. In areas which are officially classified as economically disadvantaged, kindergarten classes are offered for four-year olds. The legal age of admission to the kindergarten is five years before October 1st and the legal age for admission to the elementary school is six years before October 1st. The minimum school leaving age is the end of the school year in which the student attains the age of fifteen years. The secondary school program therefore normally extends two years beyond the official age for compulsory education with most students graduating from secondary school at the age of seventeen years.

In comparison to the elementary school, the secondary school is larger and has a considerably more complex organization. The five-year program is divided into two sections: grades 7 and 8 are known as 1st cycle; grades 9,10, 11 as 2nd cycle. While grade levels are used extensively in the elementary school, it is more normal in the secondary school to refer to the grade levels as Secondary I (for grade 7) through to Secondary V (for grade 11). The majority of secondary-level students follow the *general* program which is normally completed in five years. There is also a *short* vocational program that is completed in Secondary IV, and a *long* vocational program that is completed in Secondary V, but may sometimes extend into Secondary VI, depending on the specialty. In 1984, 5 percent of the high school graduates were in the *short* vocational program, 21 percent in the *long* vocational program, and 74 percent in the *general* program. Approximately 70 percent of the relevant age group obtained a high school leaving diploma, general or vocational, and approximately 56 percent proceeded to the college level.

Elementary and secondary schools in Quebec may be classified as in either the *public* sector or the *private* sector. In 1985-86 there were a total of 2,542 elementary and secondary schools in the public sector. The private sector accounted for a total of 267 schools, the majority of which were secondary schools. All private schools must be approved by the Ministry of Education and are classified according to one of three categories: (1) those declared to be in the *public interest* which receive government subsidies that account for approximately 80 percent of their operating expenses; (2) those *recognized* for the purpose of subsidies which receive government grants amounting to approximately 60 percent of their operating expenses; and (3) those with a *permit* which are legal recognized private schools in receipt of no government subsidies. An interesting feature of education in Quebec is that just over 8 percent of the elementary and secondary students attend private schools This is a considerably higher rate than is found in the other provinces of Canada and requires some comment.

Private schooling in Quebec, particularly that provided by the Church, has a long tradition extending for over 350 years, For many of those years, private schools provided the only type of education available in Quebec, thus helping to keep the French-Canadian heritage alive; and until the institution of a Ministry of Education in 1964, the Church continued to be responsible for the provision of a variety of private educational institutions especially at the secondary and post-secondary levels. During the reforms of the 1960s, when many private institutions disappeared and the influence of the Church declined, the important role of the private sector was reaffirmed by its specific inclusion in educational legislation (see the Preamble to Bill 60: Appendix G) as was its right to receive financial assistance from the state. Subsequently, a Private Education Act, concerning the establishment, recognition, regulation and financing of private schools was adopted in 1968. While these measures served to ensure that subsidized private schooling could continue to exist and even to flourish in Quebec, there has also been a certain amount of opposition to private schooling. Some school boards and teacher unions, faced with the twin problems of declining enrolments and surplus teachers, view the private sector as a potential threat to their own existence, particularly as enrolments in private schools continue to increase. There are also those who believe that private schools are an elitist and a divisive element in society and should therefore be abolished, while others are prepared to accept the existence of private schools – but not as institutions subsidized by the state. There is also the criticism that the private sector tends to "cream off" some of the more able students from the public sector and that comparisons of the public and private systems, especially the comparison of examination results, are not therefore valid. In the face of this opposition to private schooling, the role of private education in Quebec continues to be a controversial issue.

In addition to the division of schools into the public or private sectors, the organization of schooling in Quebec is distinguished by two further factors, namely confessionality and language. While schools in the private sector may or may not be affiliated with a particular religious denomination (Catholic, Anglican, Jewish, Pentecostal and so on), and there is in fact a network of approximately 30 private schools specifically serving the Jewish community, all schools in the public sector are classified as either Catholic or Protestant or both, depending on the type of school board that manages them.

Elementary and secondary schools in Quebec, Catholic and Protestant, are also classified according to the language of instruction. An interesting feature that complicates the situation further is that within an institution that is officially and legally described as an English school, it is possible to find instructional programs that are given almost exclusively in French. These schools are those that offer French immersion programs of various types and cater to those eligible for instruction in English but who choose to receive the major part of it in French. Because of the legal restrictions in Bill 101 and the *régimes pédagogiques* there are no English immersion programs in French schools.

Major Reforms in the 1960s

The most important education reforms in Quebec were those that took place in the early 1960s as part of the Quiet Revolution. These reforms changed the character and structures of elementary and secondary education and were designed both to modernize the system and to improve accessibility so that secondary schooling was made available to all children irrespective of socio-economic background or geographical location. The first set of reforms took place in 1961, before the Parent Commission issued its report. The second set stemmed directly from the recommendations contained in the Parent Report and were implemented by the newly established Ministry of Education in the period of 1964-1969.

The measures undertaken in 1961, known collective as the *Magna Charta of Education*, raised the school-leaving age from 14 to 15 years, abolished public secondary school fees, granted to parents the right to vote in school board elections, and increased government spending at all levels of the system. A major provision of the law was that public school boards be required to provide schooling up to and including grade 11 for all children within their jurisdictions. The overall effect of this measure was to force many of the 1500 school boards, the majority of which in the more rural areas then offered only elementary level education, to consider how they could provide facilities for secondary education.

In the rural areas, few school boards had sufficient children to even contemplate providing secondary education themselves. An experimental program of regionalization had been tried in Chambly County, south of Montreal, in 1958 in which a number of local elementary Catholic schools boards had voluntarily pooled their resources in order to provide a secondary school. It was upon this experiment that a plan for providing regional secondary schools was based. *Opération 55* was officially launched by the newly instituted Ministry of Education in 1964 and, on a more or less voluntary basis, involved the grouping of elementary boards to create 55 regional secondary school boards under Catholic direction across the province. Later, nine regional boards under Protestant direction were added for a total of 64 regional boards. The specific responsibility of these regional boards was to build, manage, and operate public secondary schools on behalf of the elementary boards in the region. As a result of these measures, a number of large comprehensive secondary schools were built throughout Quebec during the course of the 1960s, the majority of them in rural areas. Unlike the situation in many other jurisdictions, some of the largest secondary schools in Quebec are to be found outside the major urban areas.

Other than the "bricks and mortar" (or more accurately the glass and concrete) that came about as a result of *Opération 55*, the organizational, curricular and pedagogical reforms in the elementary and secondary schools took place as a result of the recommendations contained in Volume 2 of the Parent Report published in 1964. These basic reforms were implemented by means of a series of regulations issued by the Ministry of Education, of which the regulations known as Number 1 and Number 7 were by far the most important for the elementary and secondary sector. Regulation 1 issued in 1965 established the basic structures: a half-day kindergarten program available, but not compulsory, to all pupils aged 5 years; a 6-year elementary level divided into two cycles; a 5-year secondary level also divided into two cycles; and automatic promotion between the two levels at the age of 13 years. All public schools, irrespective of confessional or linguistic status, were to follow this basic unified pattern with the result that some of the more obvious structural variations between the Protestant and Catholic systems rapidly disappeared.

Elementary Education

At the elementary level, the reforms of the 1960s were more concerned with processes than with structures. In order to understand what took place and why, it is necessary to appreciate the general characteristics of elementary education in Quebec prior to the Quiet Revolution. Public education at the elementary level was the specific responsibility of the two confessional committees of the Council of Public Instruction and, as a result, there were two quite separate systems, one Catholic and the other Protestant, each inspired by different philosophies of education. The Parent Report commissioners were opposed to this notion of a dual system and were particularly critical of the French Catholic elementary schools.

> Whatever may have been the merits or deficiencies of our elementary education in the past, the need for its reform in depth is now beyond question. Today's society is so radically different from yesterday's, and tomorrow's gives promise of being so exacting in its demands on man, that the necessity for the school to make fundamental changes suited to a new era is acknowledged everywhere. The elementary school whose sole task was to teach enough reading, writing and arithmetic to enable people to deal with life's simpler problems is outmoded.[6]

Inspired by the teachings of modern psychology and by the examples that the commissioners themselves had witnessed in England, Germany and Switzerland, the Parent Report recommended a six-year, co-educational, "activist" elementary school in which the educational programs would be child-centred rather than program-centred. Elementary education lays the foundations; it supplies the tools to the child's future development," stated the Parent Report, "hence 'formation' more than 'information' is the goal which the elementary school must set for itself."[7] This notion of a dynamic activist school was based on a two-fold fundamental principle of child psychology: that the child is essentially an active being and that the child's capacity and personality develops through active participation. The activist school model as recommended by the Parent commissioners depended primarily on the natural curiosity of the child and could thus be regarded as the best realization of a genuinely child-centred education.

As far as teaching was concerned, the Parent Report suggested more latitude be made available to individual teachers: in preparing their lesson material, in teaching methods, and in giving test and examinations. The report also recommended that the formal evaluation of teachers by superiors and by Department of Education inspectors should be eliminated and that pedagogical directives, as much as possible, should not be mandatory. In terms of what should be taught in the elementary schools, the Parent Report recommended in effect that this should be left up to the teachers and the school boards to determine. In place of an "inventory" type program in which learning objectives were spelled out in precise detail, the Parent Report recommended a "general framework" program in which the teacher was encouraged to adapt the program in a more personal manner to the individual needs of the pupils.[8]

The overall result of all these measures, it was hoped, would be to free the elementary schools from the somewhat narrow and strict formality that had been all too common in many Quebec schools. Such educational movements, often referred to as "liberal," "progressive," or "humanistic" were widespread in many Western countries during this period and, in most instances, were reactions to the somewhat authoritarian and teacher-centred elementary schools that had existed previously.

Following the publication of Regulation 1, the Ministry of Education issued *The Cooperative School: Comprehensiveness and Continuous Progress*[9] in 1966 which served both as a commentary on the meaning of the Regulation and as a guide to both educators and parents as to how the Regulation could be implemented in practice within the schools. *The Cooperative School* made it clear that the fundamental thrust of the regulation was to place the emphasis on the individual child. "The academic reorganization of our educational system is entirely based on the child. The main purpose of all the measures proposed is to ensure a balanced education for each child by enabling him to progress at a rate which best suits his aptitudes and personality."[10] In essence, *The Cooperative School* suggested a flexible and ongoing regrouping of pupils rather than strict grade levels, continuous progress in individual subjects rather than promotion by grade, a general framework-type program rather than a detailed and rigid inventory-type program, and emphasis on the team-teacher rather than the general classroom teacher. The overall effect of these measures was to free the elementary school from excessive external restrictions and supervision; but at the same time, it placed prime responsibility for the quality of the program at the local level and specifically on the teaching staff at the school.

Secondary Education

At the heart of the secondary school reforms of the 1960s was the extension of secondary education from four to five years (that is, commencing in grade 7 rather than grade 8), the abolition of secondary-level tuition fees, the belief in a unified program structure for all Quebec schools whether English or French, Catholic or Protestant, the elimination of separate programs in favour of a core program with electives for all, and the decision to endorse the principle of a comprehensive rather than a differentiated model in which all secondary education would be offered in one institution. This last was a major departure from the traditional model in French Quebec, although it was fairly common throughout the rest of North America. Most secondary level educational facilities in Quebec had been strictly differentiated into academic and vocational institutions with virtually no possibility of transfer between them. The institutions offering the classical program were the most prestigious, but there were also many other institutions, both public and private, offering general, commercial, scientific, technical and trade programs. The decision to endorse the comprehensive model meant that all students could sample a mix of both academic and vocational courses before committing themselves to a future career. An important contributing factor in the decision to endorse the comprehensive principle was the fact that the federal government was prepared to make substantial building and equipment grants to provinces that wished to invest in technical and vocational manpower-training programs. Unlike previous Quebec governments, which had refused to accept federal funding for education, the new government in Quebec was prepared to do so. It made good financial sense, therefore, to include technical and vocational training programs in both the new comprehensive secondary schools and in the colleges that were soon to follow. In this manner, substantial amounts of federal funding for education expansion were quickly made available to Quebec.

Associated with the decision to endorse the comprehensive principle was the intention that students within the comprehensive school would be able to choose for themselves the type of program that was best suited to their aptitudes and abilities.[11] This led to a number of important implications for the structure and organization of Quebec's new comprehensive secondary schools. If the school was to offer a full range of academic and vocational courses in order to cater to all tastes, the school must of necessity be a large one. This was so not only because of the number of specialized courses and staff that would be required but because of the number of students required to form economical class groups and in order to make optimum use of expensive facilities. Clearly, a secondary school wishing to offer some or most of the courses would have to have a large student enrolment. The Parent commissioners were of the opinion that the ideal enrolment in such a school would be in the range of 1,000-1,200 students. However, many of the comprehensive schools built in Quebec during the 1960s were often considerably larger than this, some of them with enrolments of more than 3,000. These factors of efficiency and economy of scale in very large measure determined the learning environment of these schools which in turn subsequently led to the charge that they had often become little more than teaching factories.

Another important element was the question of the division of time and of emphasis between basic or "general" education on the one hand and vocational or "specialized" education on the other. A related question was concerned with how much of the program should be compulsory and common to all students and how much should be optional and a matter of student choice. In response to these questions, the Parent Report commissioners recommended a number of measures concerning options and electives that were subsequently implemented by means of Regulation 1 and *The Cooperative School*. Most of these measures, listed below, continued to be characteristic of Quebec's secondary schools until the changes brought about by the new curriculum regulations in the 1980s:

1. All students, irrespective of linguistic or confessional differences, should be exposed to the same type of basic education. As *The Cooperative School* pointed out: "The secondary school must thus try by all possible means to assure *for all young people* a training which will prepare them either to proceed to more advanced studies or to the practice of some occupation in the working world."[12] "In the future, pupils leaving the elementary school will no longer be divided into sections or dispersed in schools providing a particular programme. They will all come together at the secondary school to obtain there, in common, a general education which will gradually become diversified under a system of electives."[13]

2. A system of electives, the so-called "cafeteria" model, was to be instituted for about half of the program in which students could decided for themselves which courses to take.

3. The secondary school was to be divided into two cycles in which the first cycle (grades 7 and 8) would offer the general basic courses common to all, and the second cycle (grades 9-11) would offer most of the electives.

4. Subject promotion would be instituted in order to permit students to move forward at different speeds for the different subjects in the curriculum.

5. Grouping or streaming would be encouraged so that each core subject could be offered at three levels of difficulty: the regular course, the basic minimum course and the enriched course. "Stated in another way, each subject in the school programme of the secondary school will offer an opportunity for personal choice on the part of the pupil. The school programme of the comprehensive secondary school will thus be a programme with *options*."[14]

With the benefit of hindsight, it is now possible to see that many of these measures, although progressive and designed at the time to remedy serious deficiencies in the system, also contained the seeds of future difficulties. There was an almost immediate negative reaction on the part of some parents to the large size and impersonal character of many of these comprehensive schools, especially those located in rural areas. The contrast between the small local school, where everyone was known, and the large, impersonal and often distant comprehensive school was indeed a major one. In addition, the system of electives, options, subject promotion and streaming created major difficulties within the schools themselves. Some of these difficulties were of an administrative nature, such as devising individual timetables for every student, but there were also problems of a more personal sort. In such a large organization, with students in different groups for different subjects, it was often difficult for the students themselves to relate personally to any of the teachers or even to their own peers. These difficulties eventually led to the charge that the comprehensive schools lacked adequate supervision and had become too impersonal and anonymous.

It should be noted that these reforms were being instituted within the context of three broad social trends. First, there was the general background of the social climate of the 1960s with its emphasis on personal freedom, individualism, and choice. The comprehensive school model merely reflected these trends. Second, there was a reaction in Quebec to the authoritarianism that had been a major characteristic of the Duplessis era and of a school system dominated by the Church. Third, the province was faced with the challenge posed by the increased numbers and rising expectations of the post-war baby boom. In large measure, the convergence of these three social trends served to shape the general thrust of the 1960s education reform movement.

In spite of the problems, there can be little doubt that the reforms of the 1960s were largely successful in achieving their primary objectives. The system was modernized and made more democratic, and free secondary education was made available to all children irrespective of socio-economic background or place of residence. According to Ministry of Education Statistics, the rate of access at the kindergarten level which was 52 percent in 1961, had risen to 73 percent in 1966, and to 97 percent in 1978, even though kindergarten-level instruction in Quebec was and is not compulsory. At the secondary level the number of 15-year-olds attending school increased from 75 percent (1961) to 97 percent (1977), and approximately 56 percent of secondary level students now go on to some form of higher education.[15] The reforms of the 1960s therefore denote a major educational and social accomplishment.

In terms of curriculum and teaching methods, the reforms of the period left a great deal of latitude to individual school boards, schools, and teachers. There was therefore considerable variation in the interpretation of objectives, the selection of content, the choice of teaching materials, and the procedures of evaluation. Towards the end of the 1970s, there was mounting public criticism of education, and a new trend was emerging with proposals for more centralized control of objectives and content, more detailed programs, and more systematic evaluation of learning outcomes.

The Green Paper (1977)

In September 1977, some ten years or so after the reforms of the Quiet Revolution had been implemented, the Ministry of Education released a Green Paper entitled: *Primary and Secondary Education in Québec.[16]* This discussion document was issued in response to mounting criticism from the public about the quality of elementary and secondary education, a general criticism that was being heard throughout North America at the time. The introduction to this document, signed by the Minister of Education, M. Jacques-Yvan Morin, provided an interesting insight into the overall nature of the problems that were then perceived to be afflicting Quebec's elementary and secondary schools:

> Over the past fifteen years the population of Québec has resolutely attempted to improve its schools. Considerable sums of money have been devoted to the opening up of the educational system to the greatest number of pupils, particularly at the secondary level. Quebecers wanted to modernize both programmes and methods so that young people may be better prepared for life in contemporary society. Why do all these efforts appear to have achieved so few results? ... People complain that many secondary schools have degenerated into teaching factories, that they have become depersonalized. ... People claim that widespread and continuous experimentation, absence of detailed programmes and progress reports on pupils have created impromptu teaching to the detriment of any sort of learning process. ... People complain that the school and the teachers demand too little of the pupils, that in some institutions there is a lack of rules of discipline and of the work ethic. ... In short, many parents and educators feel that our schools have no coherent educational plan and that the training of our children is deteriorating.[17]

The intention of a Green Paper is to outline the nature of a given problem and to provoke discussion rather than to offer a specific solution. The authors of the Green Paper admitted that the original reforms of the Quiet Revolution had been more concerned with physical expansion, the problems of "brick and mortar," than with the more educational aspects of schooling. In order to help resolve the pedagogical and administrative difficulties then perceived to be afflicting the schools, the Green Paper offered for public consideration some 68 hypotheses concerning possible changes. Included among the solutions to the various problems at the elementary level were the following:

1. Specified learning objectives for each subject;
2. Uniform content and time allotment for all schools throughout Quebec;
3. More detailed programs;
4. More stress on language and writing skills;
5. More study work at home;

6. More emphasis on the evaluation of learning outcomes;
7. Instead of two 3-year cycles, there could be three 2-year cycles with formal evaluation procedures at the end of each cycle.

At the secondary level, the Green Paper had the following suggestions for public discussion:

1. Precise objectives for each subject with a minimum time allocation for each;
2. Cycle 1 for three years rather than two, with few electives, stable class groupings, and team teaching;
3. Cycle 2 for two or three years with fewer options and only limited specialization;
4. A vocational program extended to grade 12 (Secondary VI);
5. Uniform and precise curriculum for all secondary-level subjects;
6. Formal evaluation at the end of each of the two secondary-level cycles.

In addition to the question of the teaching programs at the elementary and secondary levels, the Green Paper was concerned with three other important issues. These were school organization, parent involvement, and school administration. Whereas the general approach of the Green Paper was for more centralization and uniformity in the field of curriculum and teaching methods, it went on to suggest greater decentralization and even diversity in the areas concerned with administration, school organization and parent involvement.

Following publication of the Green Paper and during the course of the year 1978, the Ministry of Education launched a massive operation to consult the population on their reactions to its proposals. The results of this consultation exercise were subsequently published by the Ministry of Education in seven volumes of which one summarized the reaction of the English-speaking community.[18] It is of some interest to note that English-speaking groups did not participate very actively in this consultation exercise; perhaps, they were of the opinion that the problems were predominately in the French sector and therefore did not directly concern the English schools. However, an appreciation of the results of this consultation is essential for a full understanding of subsequent events, as the government frequently used these results to justify future policy initiatives. The active involvement of French-speaking parent groups and of the major teacher unions was particularly significant. There were, however, only a few areas in which a solid consensus was reached. A number of critics also pointed out that it was illogical to promote the notion of administrative decentralization through an individualized educational project for each school while at the same time suggesting a more uniform and centralized program of studies. In a similar vein, it was illogical to focus the school on the individual creativity of the child, which had been the major focus of Regulation 1 and *The Cooperative School*, while at the same time suggesting a strict and uniform curriculum that all students would be obliged to follow. To many who had endorsed the progressive view of education as espoused in the Parent Report, the Green Paper proposals represented a major step backwards. In spite of these criticisms, the results of the Green Paper consultations demonstrated some general, if largely unfocused, support for change.

Policy Statement and Plan of Action

In February 1979, the Minister of Education released another document entitled *The Schools of Quebec: Policy Satement and Plan of Action*,[19] sometimes referred to as the Orange Paper. It outlined the policies that the government had adopted following the Green Paper consultations and explained how the Ministry of Education intended to implement its plans. The proposals contained in the Orange Paper can be divided into two distinct categories: those concerned with curriculum and pedagogical matters, and those concerned with organization and structures such as school management, parent participation, and decentralization. In both categories, the Orange Paper announced changes of major importance that were to lead to a system of education very different to the one resulting from the Parent Report.

In the fields of teaching and curriculum, the Orange Paper announced the government's intention to introduce new regulations that would call for the Ministry of Education to develop new courses of study and new teaching guides throughout the school curriculum, which would specify minimum learning objectives in all subjects, and would introduce new and more precise criteria for evaluation and school-leaving certification. The streaming of children into different courses was to be abolished, and children with learning difficulties or physical handicaps were to be integrated (mainstreamed) into regular classrooms as much as possible. Within the category of structure and administrative organization, the Orange Paper announced that legislation would soon be introduced whereby parents would be permitted direct representation on school boards, and principals would have to consult parents on matters related to school objectives and procedures. Orientation committees – composed of parents, teachers, the school principal, and others – would be permitted to develop a distinctive educational project for each school. In June 1979, Bill 30 authorized the direct representation of parents on school boards, and in December 1979, Bill 71 provided for the establishment of orientation committees and granted to the Minister the right to establish a pedagogical system (*régime pédagogique*) in the schools.

Curriculum and the régimes pédagogiques

At the heart of any education system is the curriculum, a plan that determines the learning objectives to be achieved, the content of teaching and learning, the procedures for instruction and evaluation, and the framework or context within which this teaching and learning is to take place.

From a strictly historical perspective there have been three broad stages in the development of curriculum in Quebec's elementary and secondary schools. Prior to the reforms of the Quiet Revolution, curriculum matters came under the jurisdiction of the confessional committees of the Council of Public Instruction. These two committees developed quite separate curricula inspired respectively by Catholic and Protestant social, cultural and educational philosophies. Both curricula, however, were developed centrally and were strictly controlled by the school boards and Education Department inspectors. The second stage in the evolution of curriculum in Quebec came from the recommendations contained in the Parent Commission report. These reforms, implemented by means of Regulation 1 and *The Cooperative School*, were of a progressive nature and left a good deal of initiative to school boards, local schools and to individual teachers. Although the curriculum was only loosely controlled by the Ministry of Education during this period, for the first time in Quebec's history it applied equally to both Catholic and Protestant schools. The third stage in the historical development of Quebec's curriculum originated with the public consultations concerning the *Green Paper* (1977). It was clear that there was a considerable degree of public dissatisfaction with the curriculum as then established. This eventually resulted in proposals for a much more structured curriculum as announced in the *Policy Statement and Plan Action* (Orange Paper 1979). In contrast to the decentralized *modus operandi* then in vogue, the new curriculum policy was to be considerably more precise, detailed, controlled and centralized.

The first step in implementing this third stage of curriculum reform was the appearance in Bill 71 (1979) of a short, but significant amendment to the *Education Act*. By means of this amendment, the government reinforced its right to make regulations "for the establishment of the pedagogical system (*régime pédagogique*) in the schools placed under the control of school commissioners or trustees."[20] Soon after, the Ministry of Education circulated two draft regulations, one for kindergarten and elementary schools, the other for secondary schools, for consultation by educators and parents. Prior to submitting the regulations for Cabinet approval, the Minister (as required by law) formally sought the advice of the Superior Council of Education which, on the whole, was favourable. The two regulations were then officially approved by the Cabinet in February 1981 and came into effect in July 1981 with provisions for the gradual implementation of various articles between that date and July 1986. The two regulations, better known in Quebec as the *régimes pédagogiques*,[21] largely replaced Regulation 2 concerning tests and examinations, Regulation 6 concerning the teaching of French, and Regulations 1 and 7 concerning school organization.

In contrast to the general curriculum framework of Regulation 1, the two new regulations imposed a uniform pattern of school organization and curriculum. The two *régimes* are carefully-worded and detailed documents that establish the rules for virtually every aspect of the day-to-day operation of the province's elementary and secondary schools. As these regulations are now officially in force in all the schools of Quebec, their key elements are described in some detail:

1. *General Structure*: The *preschool* level includes an optional program for 4-year-old children who have learning handicaps or who live in areas classified as economically disadvantaged. The regular kindergarten program for those aged 5 years before October 1st remains optional for parents who wish it. The *elementary* level, as in Regulation 1, is divided into two three-year cycles. The *secondary* level also includes two cycles: Cycle 1 consisting of two years (Secondary I and II) and Cycle 2 which is is of three years duration for the general program, but may be two, three, or four years for vocational programs.

2. *Quality of Language*: The quality of written and spoken language, French or English, is the responsibility of all teachers at every level and not just the sole responsibility of specialist language teachers.

3. *Programs*: All programs and courses are prescribed or approved by the Minister of Education. The courses contain both compulsory objectives which every pupil must attain and optional objectives which may be adapted to meet the special priorities of the area. School boards may design special programs for their own needs but these must first be approved by the Minister. School boards and the Ministry are to be involved in the continuing evaluation of programs.

4. *Textbooks*: Every pupil must have at least one textbook for each course. These textbooks and other teaching material must be approved by the Minister. Unauthorized textbooks and materials are not permitted.

5. *Pupil Evaluation*: It is the responsibility of school boards to evaluate the extent to which pupils meet the objectives of the programs. At the end of the secondary program, official Ministry examinations evaluate performance in subjects designated by the Ministry. These subjects normally include those required for school leaving certificates. Where there are official examinations, 50 percent of the final mark is determined by the local school board and 50 percent by the Ministry. For each course taken by a pupil at the secondary level, the passing mark is raised from 50 percent to 60 percent.

6. *Information to Parents*: At the beginning of each school year, parents must receive (a) a summary of the educational program for their child and a list of textbooks; (b) a copy of the general regulations of the school; and (c) the names of all the teachers instructing their child. Written evaluations of the child's progress and behaviour must be sent to parents at least 5 times per year, four of which must be formal report cards as prescribed by the Minister. The first evaluation must be sent not later than the end of October. For children with learning disabilities, reports must be sent at least once a month.

7. *School Records*: School records are confidential and only the following have access to them: the pupil, the parents, administrators and teachers

concerned with the pupil, and representatives of the Minister. These records are to be kept until the person involved attains 75 years of age.

8. *Pupil Services*: It is the responsibility of the school board to provide each pupil with psychological, pastoral, health, and social services as needed. School boards must also provide pupils with auxiliary services which develop their self-reliance, which provide them with appropriate supervision in school at all times, and which encourage them to participate in student activities. The school board is further responsible for providing special services to pupils with learning disabilities and to those from economically disadvantaged areas. As far as possible, children with learning disabilities are to be integrated into regular school activities (mainstreaming).

9. *Services for pupils who do not speak French*: Introductory classes (*classes d'accueil*) are to be offered for children who are not French-speaking provided that (a) they are not eligible for English instruction, or (b) their parents have been less than five years in Quebec. French schools may also offer special classes in remedial French (*classes de francisation*) for pupils who need to improve their basic skills in the language.

10. *School Calendar*: The school year consists of 200 days, of which at least 180 days are to be used for instructional purposes.

11. *Teaching Time*: At the preschool level, including kindergarten, pupils receive five half-days or 11 1/2 hours of instruction per week. Pupils receive five days or a total of 23 hours of instruction per week at the elementary level and five days or a total of 25 hours of instruction per week at the secondary level. The regulations also specify that at the elementary and secondary levels, pupils are to have a minimum of 50 minutes for lunch.

12. *Elementary School Program*: The breakdown of subjects at the elementary level is shown in Table 4.1.

13. *Secondary School Program*: The secondary school program consists of two Cycles: Cycle 1 composed of Secondary I and II and Cycle 2 composed of Secondary III, IV, V (and VI). In each year there are compulsory courses to be taken by all students and usually some optional courses. Generally speaking, there are no options in Secondary I and II, one option in Secondary III, two in Secondary IV, and three in Secondary V. Each course is assigned a credit weighting. One credit is the equivalent of 25 hours of instruction or one 50 minute period in a six-day cycle, though some variation in time is permitted. The complete program of studies is composed of 176 credits, of which 152 credits are compulsory and 24 are optional. The breakdown of courses and the assigned credit weighting is as shown in Table 4.2.

14. *Certification.* There are two kinds of high school leaving diplomas: a Diploma of Secondary Studies (*Diplome d'études secondaires*) and a Diploma of Vocational Studies (*Diplome d'études professionnelles*). A successful student may obtain either one or both. All courses completed

Table 4.1
Subjects in the Elementary School Curriculum

Subject	Grades 1-3 First Cycle hrs/week	Grades 4-6 Second Cycle hrs/week
Mother Tongue (French or English)	7	7
Mathematics	5	4
Moral *or* Religious Instruction	2	2
Physical Education	2	2
Arts (music, dance, drama, art)	2	2
Social Studies	2	2
Natural Science	1	1.5
French as a Second Language *or*	2	2
(English as a Second Language)	–	(2)
Manual Activities	–	0.5
Total Hours Per Week	23	23

It should be noted that pupils have the right to choose between religious instruction (Catholic or Protestant) or moral instruction. English as a Second Language begins in the 2nd Cycle in French schools whereas French as a Second Language begins in the 1st year in English schools. In English schools, French may also be used as the language of instruction for other subjects (as in immersion programs).

since the beginning of secondary school, including the compulsory and optional courses, are recorded. To qualify for the Diploma of Secondary Studies, a student must pass at least 130 of the possible 176 credits, including 40 compulsory credits: (See Table 4.3).

It is now clear that the *régimes pédagogiques* represent a major change in direction. Whereas the curriculum reforms stemming from the Parent Report in the 1960s indicated a shift from centralization and control towards a system that was characterized by freedom, individuality and choice, the *régimes* represent a marked shift in the opposite direction. Freedom was replaced by control, individuality was replaced by the need for equality, and choice was replaced by restriction, all undertaken in the name of improving the quality of education.

Although the Ministry was responsible for the overall planning and development of the new programs, considerably less attention was given to appropriate implementation strategies. As a result, teachers' guides, textbooks, evaluation materials and the inservice training of teachers have all been behind schedule and the planned timetable for the introduction of new programs has been delayed. The delay in the production of English-language translations led

Table 4.2

Distribution of Credits at the Secondary Level

Subject	Cycle One		Cycle Two		
	I	II	III	IV	V
Mother Tongue (French or English)	6	6	6	6	6
Second Language (English or French)	4	4	4	4	4
Mathcmatics	6	6	4	4	4
Moral *or* Religious Instruction	2	2	2	2	2
Physical Education	2	2	2	2	2
Personal and Social Training	1	1	1	1	1
Career Guidance	1	1	1	1	1
General Geography	4				
General History		4			
Geography of Quebec and Canada			4		
History of Quebec and Canada				4	
Arts (one of art, music, dance, drama)	4	4			
Ecology	4				
Home Economics		4			
Introduction to Technology			4		
Human Biology			4		
Science (Chemistry or Physics)				4	
Economics					4
Total Required Credits	34	34	32	28	24
Optional Credits	(2)	(2)	4	8	12
Total Number of Credits (176)	34	34	36	36	36

to the official postponement by two years of the application of the new regulations in English schools. The introduction of new compulsory courses such as ecology, home economics, introduction to technology, and economics meant that many teachers had to be reassigned, often into areas for which they were not trained. Other problems at the secondary level included the lack of sufficient physical science courses and a general uncertainty about the role, if any, of vocational education in the new curriculum. While it is still too early to evaluate the full implications of the new regulations, it is not too early to be concerned about some of the important issues:

1. Although curriculum committees of selected teachers were at work developing the new programs and teachers' guides, the general framework of the curriculum and the specific approval of programs were under the direct control of government officials in the Ministry of Education. They determined the assumptions, objectives, and structure of the new pro-

Table 4.3
Credits Required for Secondary School Certification

Number of Credits	Subject	Secondary Year
12	Mother Tongue (French/English)	IV and V
8	Second Language (English/French)	IV and V
4	Mathematics	IV
2	Moral *or* Religious Instruction	IV or V
2	Physical Education *or* Personal and Social Training *or* Career Guidance	IV or V
4	Chemistry *or* Physics	IV
8	Geography of Quebec and Canada, History of Quebec and Canada, Economics	III, IV or V

grams, the procedures for evaluation, and also approved the textbooks and teaching materials. There are those who argue that this placed too much authority at the central level and enabled the government rather than the school boards and teachers to decide what should be taught in the schools.

2. All programs are uniform for all schools throughout Quebec, English or French, Catholic or Protestant, urban or rural. Such uniformity stands in marked contrast to the increased pluralism that is now characteristic of much of Quebec society. Critics suggest that as democratically elected school boards are more responsive to local needs than the somewhat distant and bureaucratic Ministry of Education, there should be more room for local initiatives to reflect these local needs. In particular, some confessional boards believe that they, rather than the government, have the right to determine the curriculum and that this right is protected in the constitution.

3. The basic philosophy of the programs is that of a competency model and associated behavioural objectives, with a shopping list of general, terminal and intermediate objectives established for every subject, from art to physics. It is questionable whether all subjects lend themselves to this type of technocratic approach, particularly in those subjects where creativity normally plays an important role. In any event, it is argued, can the educational process itself be reduced to a set of precise objectives which are appropriate for all children in all circumstances? Where are the individual differences, about which a great deal of lip-service is paid, to be taken into account?

4. Similarly, as streaming is removed in favour of one program for all children, there is a trend away from adapting the program to the needs of the

pupil in favour of adapting the pupils to the needs of the program.

5. There is a heavy emphasis in the new curriculum on general education, especially on those studies that supposedly contribute to the cultural integration of society. Such subjects include, for example, general and Quebec history and geography, personal and social training, moral and religious instruction, human biology, ecology, and economics. In comparison, there is relatively little emphasis on the pure sciences or in new subjects such as computer science and technology.

6. It is unclear whether the new programs will lead to a higher failure rate among less talented students or whether these will lead to a weakening of the education provided for the talented or more serious student. The abolition of streaming, the postponement of vocational education, the large proportion of compulsory subjects, the more systematic evaluation procedures, and the raising of the pass mark from 50% to 60%, might lead to higher standards for some but it might also lead to a higher failure rate (and drop-out rate) for others. On the other hand, the reduced number of electives and advanced courses, the fact that all students must take essentially the same program, and the absence of emphasis on the sciences, might not challenge the more able and ambitious student. There is, in fact, a distinct possibility that as the program is aimed at the so-called average or normal student, students at both extremes of the ability range might tend to be neglected.

7. There is no clear indication in the regulations of a well thought out and articulated philosophy inspiring the pattern and content of the curriculum, a philosophy that would prepare young people for the post-industrial world of the 21st century. There is little, if any, acknowledgement of the importance of the new technologies (microcomputers, for example), of new conceptions of knowledge arising from the physical sciences, or of new possibilities for social structures. Rather than a progressive curriculum, the traditional concept of subject disciplines represents a definite step in the direction of "back-to-basics." This may be what the public says it wants, but it should be pointed out that it is also possible for a curriculum to be both rigorous and forward-looking.

8. There are few new ideas in the curriculum about how to teach creative and logical thinking, new skills for using modern information technologies to find and reduce the quantity of information now increasingly available to all, or new values of simplicity, balance and interdependence that may be required for survival in the decades to come. Instead, traditional disciplines are patched together with more or less traditional content.

9. Given the increased pluralism of Quebec society today, it should not be surprising if controversy develops about the prescribed content of certain required courses, particularly in sensitive areas such as sex education, moral and religious instruction, economics, history, and personal and social training. Different interest groups will almost certainly object to

specific content, as has already happened with the sex education program, and there are as yet no procedures to deal with this kind of problem. A related question concerns the teaching of English as a second language in French elementary schools. According to the regulations, this should not commence until grade 4. A number of French-speaking parent groups, and some school commissions, have been demanding that it start in grade 1, when the teaching of French as a second language begins in English schools.

10. There is concern among teacher groups that the detailed programs leave little leeway for pedagogical innovation. Of particular concern is the trend toward seeing the teacher more as a technician providing a service rather than as an autonomous professional. With little, if any, control over the curriculum and content, the *régimes* tend to reinforce the role of the teacher as a direct agent of the state.

11. There is the danger that the long catalogues of general, intermediate, and terminal objectives will themselves tend to become the complete program rather than the minimum content to be expected of all pupils. If this happens, the "minimum" might soon become the "maximum" and the overall standard of education could well decline.

12. Finally, the centralized framework for the evaluation of both programs and students will tend to "set" the policies for individual boards, schools and teachers, and thus inevitably lead to uniformity and standardization.

In the summer of 1986, the Minister of Education proposed a number of changes to the *régimes pédagogiques*. At the elementary level, the most significant change was a proposal to permit the teaching of English in French schools as early as grade 1, provided that the quality of French was deemed satisfactory. At the secondary level, the most important proposal was for the introduction of an additional compulsory 4-credit course in the physical sciences to be included at the Secondary II level. However, in order to make room in the timetable for this course, it was clear that some of the other compulsory credits would have to be deleted. The Minister therefore proposed an overall reduction in the number of credits assigned to personal and social training and to career guidance. In December 1986, the Government of Quebec approved several changes to the *régimes pédagogiques* including the insertion of a new compulsory course in physical sciences at the secondary II level and two new programs in vocational education. The government did not approve the proposal to permit the teaching of English as a second language from grade 1 in French schools. These changes were announced in the Quebec Official Gazette in January, 1987.

Program Variations

Within the general framework of the *régimes pégogiques* are a number of major variations that deserve attention and raise important issues. These variations include a) vocational education, b) special education, c) French language immersion programs, and d) alternative schools.

a) Vocational Education

The *régimes pédagogiques* of 1981 dealt only incidentally with the issue of vocational education. They were concerned with general education only, but it was indicated that new policies in the vocational area would be forthcoming. The general intention was to eliminate early specialization in vocational education by delaying it to the end of secondary school. In 1982, the Ministry of Education issued a special document on the subject entitled: *Technical and Vocational Education for Young People: Proposals for Revival and Renewal.*[22] Although this document stressed the value of technical and manual work it also proposed that more emphasis should be placed on the general rather than the specialized education of youth in preparing them for the world of work. The justification for this attitude was that technological change in the modern world is so rapid that many specialized programs soon become outdated and many youngsters who had received vocational training in the schools could not find work in their areas of skill. The report recommended, then, that vocational training should normally begin after Secondary V, in a concentrated Secondary VI (grade 12) program, and only after students had completed a sound general education. In this manner all students would possess the basic skills that would enable them to adapt to a changing labour market. The report suggested, however, that some optional courses in vocational education could begin before Secondary V for certain students, but that the *short-vocational* program, seen as a "dead-end" program and sometimes as a "dumping ground" for children with behavioural problems or handicaps, should be eliminated.

Although the postponement of vocational education to the Secondary VI level in favour of a more general education for all students has considerable support, there are those who argue that without vocational education earlier on in the secondary school certain students will not be attracted by the general program and will therefore tend to drop out of school. A related problem is the question of what would happen to all the technical-vocational teachers while these changes were taking place. As a result of these difficulties, the full implementation of the concentrated Secondary VI vocational program was postponed for several years, pending a new policy statement from the Ministry.

In June 1986, the Minister of Education, Claude Ryan, released a new policy statement on vocational education entitled: *La formation professionnelle au secondaire: plan d'action.*[23] This new plan called for the elimination of both the *short* and *long* vocational programs and proposed the introduction of two new levels of certification. The first, leading to a *Diploma of Professional*

Studies, would be open to students of 17 years of age who had obtained, as a minimum, credits in the Mother Tongue, Second Language, Mathematics and Religious or Moral Instruction at the Secondary IV level. The program would require between 36 and 72 credits, according to specialization, and would be exclusively in the field of that specialization. The second level of certification, leading to a *Certificate of Professional Studies* would also only be available to students who had reached 17 years of age. In this case, a student would have to obtain, as a minimum pre-requisite, credits in Mother Tongue, Second Language, and Mathematics at the Secondary III level. This program would require completion of 72 credits, normally in Secondary IV and V, of which 12 credits in each year would be general and 24 credits vocational. The *Diploma* program was designed to give access to skilled trades, while the *Certificate* program was oriented more towards trades involving manual labour and skills. The Minister requested that school boards and other interested parties submit their comments on these new proposals so that a new policy could be implemented at the beginning of the 1987-88 school year. In January 1987, the government published changes to the *régime pédagogique* approving these two new vocational programs, although the age restriction was reduced from 17 to 16 years. Although these developments represent a certain compromise with the original intentions of the *régime*, early specialization prior to the age of 16 had been eliminated.

b) Special Education

One area where the public education system has changed dramatically in the past twenty-five years has been in its approach to the teaching of children with learning difficulties, a field sometimes referred to as special education. Prior to the reforms of the 1960s, children with mental or physical handicaps or with severe behavioural problems were rarely accepted into the public school system. There were some private facilities operated by religious orders, by parent associations and by charitable organizations. In 1961, for example, barely one-half of one per cent (0.5 percent) of children classified as special students attended classes in public schools, most of them in the Montreal and Quebec City areas. In contrast, by 1985-86, approximately 10 per cent of all children, or 110,453 students, were officially classified as "children with difficulties in learning and adaptation" and were enrolled in Quebec's public school system.

During the 1960s and 1970s, the most frequently used approach by the school boards to the organization of services for these students was the formation of special education classes. The majority of these classes were located within regular schools and taught by teachers with some training in special education, although some school boards concentrated these classes in *special schools* exclusively reserved for children with various forms of physical and mental handicaps. In 1976, however, a *Comité provincial de l'enfance inadaptée*, known as COPEX, issued a report that revealed many gaps in the services available to children with difficulties and was also critical of the tendency towards the segregation of such children.[24] As a direct result of the COPEX report and of the approval by the National Assembly in 1975 of the Quebec Charter of Human Rights and Freedoms and in 1978 of the *Loi assurant l'exercice des droits des personnes handicapées*, the Ministry of Education announced a completely new policy concerning special education in 1979.[25]

In essence, the new policy involved a *volte-face* in the previous practice of segregating children with difficulties into special education classes or special schools. Henceforth, the aim of the policy was "to ensure that children with special needs have access to quality educational services, appropriate to their needs, *within a regular school environment*, in order to enable them to function effectively in the community as adults."[26] "Thus, the public school will open wide its doors to physically or mentally handicapped children."[27] This new policy for the gradual integration of children in difficulty, whether mental, physical or behavioural, into regular classrooms in regular schools is known in North America as mainstreaming. Whatever may be the moral and judicial merits of this new policy, it nevertheless places a considerable burden on the regular classroom teachers, many of whom lack appropriate training for this new responsibility. There is also considerable criticism, from parents and from teachers, that many school boards simply do not have adequate financial resources at present to provide the quality of service that is required. Another interesting implication of the new policy is that, unlike the private sector that can select its clientele, the public school system is required by law to accept the "responsibility of responding adequately to the educational needs of all Québec children."[28] It is argued by some that given the generous subsidies provided to private schools in Quebec, the new policy might eventually contribute to an even wider disparity between the two systems in that the private schools will tend to cater to the talented and/or rich, whereas the public schools, required by law to accept everyone irrespective of ability, aptitude or handicap and offering most of the vocational programs, will become the depository for the rest.

c) French Immersion

The teaching of French in English schools has witnessed a remarkable surge in quality and effectiveness during the past twenty-five years. Much of this improvement is the direct result of the new importance afforded to the French language in Quebec, especially in the world of work, prompting parents to demand better quality French programs in English schools. The improvement has also been the result of two related factors, one involving staffing and the other teaching methods. Since the mid-1960s it has been possible for Protestant school boards to hire Catholic teachers, with the result that many French classes are now taught by native French-speaking Quebecers. The second factor has been the development of French immersion classes, first developed in the Montreal south shore community of St. Lambert. French immersion is a system of teaching in which most or all subjects are taught in the French language. Programs can begin in kindergarten or grade 1, in grades 3 or 6, or in grade 7; and they can extend for one year or for several years. There are, in fact, a number of patterns for French immersion in English schools, as there are also a number of patterns of post-immersion in which certain courses at the secondary level continue to be taught in French. The improvement in the quality of French teachers and the popularity of French immersion programs have together resulted in a significant qualitative improvement in the teaching of French as a second language.

It is an irony of the times, however, that the very success of French immersion programs has also resulted in major problems. First, English school boards, unlike their French counterparts, have assumed a commitment, with heavy financial costs and from which realistically they cannot now withdraw, to offer both the regular English program and a variety of French immersion and post-immersion programs. Second, as enrolment in the English sector has been declining at an even faster rate than in the French sector, many school boards are now financially unable to continue their "smorgasbord" of French immersion programs, even though the demand for such programs continues to increase. Indeed, in some rural areas, school boards have often found it impossible to start such programs, resulting in major discrepancies between the level of services provided to urban and rural children. Third, the success of French immersion has been dependent upon the recruitment of mother-tongue French teachers with the result that many English-speaking teachers have been placed on surplus. Given the popularity of French immersion programs among parents, it is now becoming difficult for some school boards to staff the regular English program. It is truly ironic that many Protestant school boards, popularly viewed as bastions of the English language and culture in Quebec, are in fact staffed by many French-speaking Quebecers and have become very successful promoters of the French language. Such is the popularity of the French programs in Protestant school boards, that these boards are attracting students from the Catholic sector and to some extent are now making good the shortfall in enrolment due to the decreasing English-speaking population.

The success of French immersion and of full-time French programs has changed the character of the Protestant education system, so that it can no longer be regarded as synonymous with English education. Furthermore, the success of French immersion has created a fragmentation within the system itself, with French immersion classes and schools being regarded as serving the most able students, and English language classes and schools sometimes regarded as the depository for those who cannot manage the greater challenges of the immersion program.

d) Alternative Schools

Another recent development that could also reinforce fragmentation is the introduction of alternative schooling within the public sector. Alternative schools are those that offer a specific curricular focus or pedagogical approach that appeals to a selective clientele with specific interests. Such schools are similar to the *target, lighthouse* or *magnet* schools that are found in some parts of the United States, although within Quebec, they are perhaps more directly comparable to private schools. Although alternative schools are not yet numerous in Quebec, they are to be found in both the Catholic and Protestant sectors and at the elementary and secondary levels. Some alternative schools cater to a specific type of clientele such as high school drop-outs or pregnant teenagers. At the elementary level, most of the alternative schools are within the French sector and feature a pedagogical approach based on open education.

It is at the secondary level, however, that the development of alternative schooling based on a particular curriculum focus poses the most serious problems. Although several such schools are to be found within the French sector, a number are also found within the English sector. Among these are FACES (Fine Arts Core Education School) operated by the Protestant School Board of Greater Montreal (PSBGM), and the Thomas d'Arcy McGee Centre for Fine and Performing Arts operated by the Montreal Catholic School Commission (MCSC). As their names suggest, these focus on Fine and Performing Arts, and students are drawn to the schools from all areas in the Montreal region. These schools are permitted to establish their own admission criteria and to be selective in their choice of students.

More recently, the PSBGM has approved the establishment of two other alternative secondary schools, one with a focus on French immersion and computer science and the other with a focus on academic achievement, discipline and personal fitness. The evident popularity and success of these schools raises important questions as to the future direction of secondary education in Quebec. If some schools are permitted to "cream off" the most talented or conscientious students, will this mean that the other schools will cater only to the less talented and less ambitious students? Does this create two broad categories of schools, selective on the one hand and community-based on the other, and with two broad classes of students? Does this mean that public schools will begin to compete with each other for clientele? What are the implications for an open and accessible education system and what does this imply for the philosophy of public education? Conversely, the success and popularity of the alternative schools give notice that the public sector can respond effectively to the needs of its clientele without recourse to the private sector. The development of alternative schools, however, raises important questions as to the very nature of public schooling, but no more so perhaps than the government's own promotion of the educational project.

The Educational Project

One distinctive and interesting measure, discussed first in the Green Paper of 1977 and then confirmed in the Orange Paper of 1979, was the proposal for each school to develop an educational project. The notion of each school becoming more autonomous and developing an individual character, philosophy or ethos, stood in marked contrast to the many centralizing tendencies that had otherwise characterized the system of education in Quebec since the 1970s. The proposal for each school to develop an educational project therefore deserves to be studied in some detail. Its genesis is to be found among the various hypotheses concerning school management that were proposed in the Green Paper. In that document, the government unequivocally stated that it intended to proceed with the administrative decentralization of the school system in one form or another.

According to government sources, the official definition of an educational project is expressed in the following manner:

> The educational project is the dynamic initiative by which a school, through the concerted will of the parents, the students, the administration and the staff, undertakes to implement a general plan of action.[29]

Other than the fact that it is a "dynamic initiative" organized collectively by the major partners within the school, the official definition does not clarify the matter particularly well. In general terms, the notion of an educational project implies that individual schools should reflect the diversity of their own communities and that each school should develop its own character, style, dominant values, and orientation. This could include, for example, the religious or moral character of the school, the kind of conduct that is promoted among pupils (and teachers), the way in which learning is approached and organized, the development of a curricular or extra-curricular focus, or a particular relationship between the school and its community.

Taken at face value, the notion of a decentralized public school system in which each school community "is responsible for its own salvation"[30] is a somewhat radical proposition because its logical development could lead to a major reorganization of the traditional pattern of educational decision-making in Quebec education and thus a realignment of the locus of power. It also suggest that the popularization, creation and development of educational projects, far from being complementary to existing structures, would in fact challenge those structures and lead to a new definition of the role of the school, and subsequently to a new pattern of relationships with school boards and the Ministry of Education. The consequences, then, of a system of schools with well articulated educational projects would be very different from the traditional structures found within the public sector of most of North America.

In 1979, and as announced in the Orange Paper, the government approved legislation (Bill 71: *An Act to again amend the Education Act*), for the purpose, *inter alia*, of "promoting the carrying out of an educational project in every school and ensuring the participation of the pupils, the parents, and the school and school board staff members. Every school may from now on assert its individuality by adopting a specific educational project ... The establishment of a school orientation committee constitutes a new means of ensuring the participation and concerted action of the various sectors of the milieu."[31] The failure of these orientation committees (see Chapter 3) and therefore of the educational project to operate as planned led to important consequences particularly in the legislation to reorganize schools and school boards that was to follow in the 1980s. There are, however, three issues that emerge from the educational project idea that deserve some attention. These issues point out some of the anomalies and paradoxes that surround the whole notion of the educational project. The first concerns the broad question as to whether or not educational individuality can be legislated. Given the nature of an educational project, it is self-evident that no single model could be imposed on all schools. The legislation was therefore more concerned with process than with product which in turn led to the realization that there was no clear definition or understanding of what an educational project really was. On the other hand, the legislation was primarily of an enabling character and left much to the wisdom and leadership qualities of the local participants. That these qualities did not easily emerge was not necessarily the fault of the legislation.

The second issue concerns the nature of the educational project itself. Was it really as radical as its supporters claimed? According to one analysis it was difficult to identify any differences between a school that adopted an educational project and one which, for reasons which had nothing to do with official formulations, respected differences, accommodated the needs of its participants, sought appropriate solutions to its problems, and consulted effectively with its members.[32]

The third issue revolves around the supposition that the educational project was nothing more than "an anomoly wrapped in illusions." The major thrust of the proposals in the Green Paper, the Orange Paper and the *régimes pédagogiques* had been in the direction of the scientific and technological management of education. This was the educational philosophy which valued the standardization of timetables, terminal behavioural objectives, detailed curriculum guidelines, and systematic and objective evaluation. It was a worldview based on rationality, coherence, consistency, and systems; it was an orientation not peculiar to Quebec, but one which reflected a general trend of back-to-basics, of increased accountability and of competency-based approaches to learning. In many ways, this philosophy can be thought of as a thoroughly modern and scientific system of education. Why, then, would the Ministry promoting such a philosophy at the same time also be promoting the notion of decentralization, individualization, and the educational project? To some, it was merely a paradox: illogical, inconsistent, and unworkable. To others, the educational project with its emphasis on participation and school initiative was nothing more than a natural extension of Regulation 1 and the subsequent development of the cooperative school. According to this interpretation, the educational project was simply a means by which schools could adapt regulations to their own style and go beyond them in order to address local needs. To those of a more Machiavellian turn of mind, however, the educational project was seen as an elaborate smokescreen cunningly designed by the Ministry to camouflage the centralizing, technocratic and statist character of the other reforms then underway.

Summary and Conclusion

Quebec's elementary and secondary schools have undergone many turbulent changes during the course of the past twenty-five years. The most dramatic occurred during the 1960s when the system not only underwent physical expansion to cater to the baby-boom population and increased societal expectations, but shifted direction to become more open, more democratic, and more progressive. In purely quantitative terms, these measures were successful and resulted in a considerably increased level of schooling of the Quebec population.

During the 1970s, while the instructional program did not change significantly, the schools of Quebec were faced with challenges of a different nature. Enrolments declined overall leading to surplus teachers and school closures; parents became more involved in school affairs; and the schools became frontline participants in the province's language debate. Increased pluralism, both of the population and in the realm of values and ideas, resulted in schools having continuously to adapt to changing demands and expectations. There was also a nagging and widespread belief in the minds of the public that the quality of schooling was not what it should be.

The first half of the 1980s were in many ways the most unsettling for the public education system. Faced with mounting criticism concerning the type of education given in the schools, the curriculum has undergone a major shift in direction, the overall effectiveness of which is far from clear. Teachers had their salaries reduced and workloads increased. The profession was aging, there was less mobility, and many teachers were on surplus. Teachers, parents, schools, and school boards expended considerable energy on the sometimes bitter debate on confessionality, linguistic rights and structures, the role of parents, and in the discussions surrounding the White Paper proposals and Bill 40.

Today, the schools are still unsettled. The new curriculum has yet to be fully implemented and, at the secondary level, the role of vocational education in the overall scheme of things has only recently been determined. In some areas, enrolments continue to decline leading to school closures, surplus teachers, and teachers transferred to new assignments. The average age of the teaching force continues to increase and there are at present few prospects for new teachers. To make matters worse, all of this is taking place at a time when budgetary restraint is adversely affecting all levels of the education system. A more positive note, however, is a temporary end to the rumours of major structural change; the problem of the illegal students has finally been resolved; there is a new system for financing school boards; and there is some evidence of a new spirit of cooperation among the various partners involved in the elementary and secondary sector. On balance, the inevitable conclusion to be drawn is that despite the successes which have not been inconsiderable, in spite of the enormous resources that have been allocated to education, in spite of the best efforts of a dynamic Ministry of Education, of dedicated teachers and of numerous school board administrators, and in spite of the voluminous reports, consultations and studies that have characterized Quebec education during the past twenty-five years, the elementary and secondary sector is nevertheless suffering from what appears to be a malingering malaise, clearly failing to live up to public expectations. Rightly or wrongly, the perception of the public in Quebec is that education today is not as effective as it was twenty-five years ago. In response to a question about public school education, the results of a recent public opinion poll[33] demonstrated that the rate of dissatisfaction in Quebec was almost twice as high as it was elsewhere in Canada.

"Overall do you think children in public schools today are getting a better education then they would have 25 years ago, a worse education, or about the same education as they would have 25 years ago?"

	Total	B.C.	Alberta	Man/Sask	Ontario	Québec	Atlantic
(Base)	(1675)	(171)	(304)	(122)	(535)	(403)	(140)
Better	42%	46%	53%	57%	45%	22%	60%
Worse	36%	30%	22%	22%	32%	59%	26%
Same	22%	25%	25%	21%	24%	19%	14%

According to this poll, almost twice as many Quebecers as other Canadians believe that the quality of education had declined during the past twenty-five years. Although 84 percent of Quebecers think that an education "is more important than ever for someone to do well," over 60 percent believe that the public schools are not doing a good job teaching the basics. Furthermore, 69 percent of Quebecers would prefer to send their children to private rather than to public schools.

Clearly, something is wrong. At the Estates General on the quality of education held at Montreal in April 1986, participants indicated "their substantial agreement with most of the basic structures and orientations of the present educational system" but they were also critical "about the specific operation of these structures and about the way in which these orientations are put into practice on a daily basis."[34] There were reports of incoherence, inadequacy, dysfunction, rigidity and inefficacy: complementary services to pupils "struggle along and are completely insufficient;" the new programs in the *régime* are good "but, in practice, they do not even respond to minimum needs" The final conclusion was that "almost everything in the system has gone wrong and the specific routes on which it is engaged are in need of major consolidations or rectifications to ensure that they will lead somewhere some day."[35]

But are the public schools of Quebec really as bad as they are perceived to be? Do Quebecers perhaps have shorter memories than others and romanticize the "good old days"? Does the education system advertize its successes or only its failures? Does the widespread discussion of educational issues in Quebec increase public expectations to unrealistic levels? Do Quebecers demand higher standards than others? There are, as yet, no clear answers to these questions but what is certain is that elementary and secondary schooling will continue to be a subject for debate and a major preoccupation in Quebec for the foreseeable future.

Notes

1. Québec, Ministère de l'Education. *L'Ecole: Les gens de l'avenir, Statistiques de l'éducation préscolaire et de l'enseignement primaire et secondaire au Quebec*. (Québec 1986).

2. Jean-Paul Desbiens (alias Brother Jérome, alias Frère Untel). *Les Insolences du Frère Untel*. (Montréal, Les Editions de l'Homme, 1960). Translated into English by Miriam Chapin as *The Impertinences of Brother Anonymous*, Montreal, Harvest House, 1962, p. 23-24, 35-36.

3. Quebec. *Report of the Royal Commission of Inquiry on Education in the Province of Quebec* (Parent Report), Vol.2, 1964, p. 89, 92, 97.

4. Parent Report, Vol.2, p. 95.

5. Parent Report, Vol.2, p. 126.

6. Parent Report, Vol.2, p. 89-90.

7. Parent Report, Vol.2, p. 100, 103

8. Parent Report, Vol.2, p. 101.

9. Quebec. *The Cooperative School: Comprehensiveness and Continuous Progress*. (A commentary on Regulation 1 of the Department of Education), Québec, Information Service, Department of Education, September 1966, p. 116.

10. *The Cooperative School*, p. 7.

11. Parent Report, Vol.2, p. 49.

12. *The Cooperative School*, p. 69.

13. *The Cooperative School*, p. 70.

14. *The Cooperative School*, p. 81.

15. Québec, Ministère de l'Education. *Statistiques de l'Education*. Direction générale de la recherche et de la prospective, (Québec 1985).

16. Québec. Ministère de l'Education. *Primary and Secondary Education in Quebec: Green Paper*. (French Version 1977) English version 1978, p. 147.

17. *Green Paper.* p. 9.

18. The seven volumes of reports, all published by the Ministère de l'Education, included: *Synthèse des résultats de la consultation (1978); Synthèse des audiences nationales (1978); Synthèse des audiences régionales (1978); Résultats d'un sondage (1978); L'enseignement primaire et secondaire: résultats d'un sondage (version abrégée)* (1978); *Synthèse des audiences anglophones* (1978), *Revue de presse sur le Livre vert de l'enseignement primaire et secondaire* (1978). In addition, the Superior Council of Education issued its *Avis sur le Livre vert de l'enseignement primaire et secondaire* in June, 1978.

19. Québec. Ministère de l'Education. *The Schools of Quebec: Policy Statement and Plan of Action.* (Québec 1979). p. 159.

20. Bill 71: *An Act to again amend the Education Act*, Article 3, (December 21, 1979).

21. Québec. *Regulation respecting the basis of elementary school and preschool organization* and *Regulation respecting the basis of secondary school organization.* Orders-in-Council. (February 25, 1981). Published in the *Gazette Officielle du Quebec* (April 15, 1981). Vol. 113, No. 15, p. 1213-1232. Also published with commentary, Ministère de l'Education. (Direction générale du développement pédagogique, 1983).

22. Québec. Ministère de l'Education. *Technical and Vocational Education for Young People: Proposals for Revival and Renewal. (Quebec 1982).*

23. Québec. Ministère de l'Education. *La formation professionnelle au secondaire: Plan d'action.* (Québec: 17 juin, 1986).

24. Québec. Ministère de l'Education. *L'Education de l'enfance en difficulté d'adaption et d'apprentissage au Quebec.* Report of the Comité provincial de l'enfance inadaptée (COPEX) (Québec: 1976). p. 693.

25. Québec. Ministère de l'Education. *The Schools of Quebec: Policy Statement and Plan of Action: Children with difficulties in learning and adaptation.* (Québec 1979). p.39.

26. *Children with difficulties*, p. 15.

27. *Children with difficulties*, p. 18.

28. *Children with difficulties*, p. 15.

29. *Plan of Action*, p. 35.

30. *Plan of Action*, p. 35.

31. Assemblée Nationale du Québec, *Bill 71: An Act to again amend the Education Act*, (1979), Explanatory Notes.

32. Gary Anderson & Janyne Rahming, "The Educational Project; From Policy to Practice," *McGill Journal of Education,* 18.2. (Spring 1983). p. 102.

33. Angus Reid Associates Inc. *Back to School Poll*, September 6, 1986, p. 15. Selected parts of this poll were published in the Montreal *Gazette* (p. A1

and A2) and in other newspapers across Canada on Saturday, September 6, 1986.

34. Comité des Etats Généraux. *Objective 100%: Proceedings of the Estates General on the Quality of Education: Summary of Workshops.* (Québec: 1986). p. 225.

35. *Summary of Workshops*, p. 225.

Post-Secondary Education:
Colleges and Universities

Quebec's structure of colleges and universities represents a break with traditions prior to 1960 and in many ways is without parallel in other provinces and states.

Quebec students wishing to pursue their studies beyond secondary school attend either a public college or a private institution offering equivalent programs. The public colleges are popularly referred to as CEGEPs, *collèges d'enseignement général et professionnel*, loosely translated as general and vocational colleges or as academic and technical colleges.

Colleges offer two basic types of programs: two-year programs leading to university entrance and three-year technical programs preparing students for direct entry to a career. All public colleges (CEGEPs) offer both types of programs, though private colleges may offer only certain academic or technical options. After completing a two-year pre-university program, students enter university and work towards a bachelor's degree in such fields as arts, science, commerce, engineering and education. Most bachelor's programs are 90 credits or three years in length, 30 credits or 10 semester courses constituting a normal full year of study. For students who live in Quebec, there is no direct passage from secondary school to university, but transfer programs are available in most university faculties for secondary school graduates from outside the province.

Evolution of the Colleges

When the members of the Parent Commission in the 1960s turned their attention to post-secondary education, they found a patchwork of institutions which offered limited access and limited opportunities, which were in many areas strongly elitist in character and traditional in spirit, and which showed dramatic differences between French and English structures.

On the French side, there were a variety of post-secondary institutions: classical colleges, affiliated with a university, offering four-year college studies leading to a baccalaureate; normal schools providing Bachelor of Pedagogy degrees and diploma programs for those wishing to become teachers; and institutes of technology, home economic institutes, and specialized institutions giving advanced training and certificates to secondary school leavers. In addition, there were three French-language universities, Laval, Montreal, and

Sherbrooke which offered academic and professional programs that normally required the classical college degree as a condition of admission. On the English side, there were two teachers colleges (the major one being the St. Joseph Teachers College in Montreal), two liberal arts colleges in the American tradition (Loyola, Marianopolis), and three universities, McGill, Bishop's, and the recently chartered Sir George Williams University. An example illustrates the differences between French and English structures. A French student wishing to obtain a Bachelor of Science degree would normally follow a four-year general arts program in a classical college and a three-year specialized program in university, a total of seven years after grade eleven; an English student would normally go directly from grade eleven to university and receive his B.Sc. in four years.

The problem facing the reformers of the Quiet Revolution had four facets: how to expand access to post-secondary education from public secondary schools; how to re-orient post-secondary training away from classical and general studies to the new priorities of science, commerce and technology; how to establish a coherent system of post-secondary education that would integrate the variety of institutions and remove the glaring disparities between French and English structures; and how to do all these without inviting chaos and conflict among the powerful vested interests of the Church, the universities, the English and the traditional French elites.

The solution proposed by the Parent Commission and adopted with some modification by the government was bold, imaginative and rational, with all the strengths and weaknesses which these characteristics bring to a public policy. New institutions (originally called Institutes) were to be established, between secondary school and university. They were to be the required route through which secondary students would pass before going to university; they would complete the general education of the students; they would be comprehensive (*polyvalent*), offering both pre-university and advanced technical programs within the same institution, bringing the two kinds of students and programs together; and they would be public and secular institutions, not associated with the Church or other interest group. These institutions would be free to all full-time students; they would open up access to post-secondary studies for all social groups who had never imagined the possibility of a university education and they would provide within one structure a high degree of equality of educational opportunity. Finally, they would link secondary and university levels, education and work, school and community, young and adult learners. Even before they were created, the colleges of Quebec carried a heavy burden of expectations and a rich strain of social idealism.[1]

In June 1967, the legislature passed Bill 21 which allowed for the creation of colleges (CEGEPs) as legally established public corporations. By September of the same year, 12 colleges had been established and, by a year later, there were 23 French colleges with 38,000 students. Within three years, there were over 40 of these institutions throughout Quebec. Most of the new colleges were "instant institutions" created out of an amalgamation of existing classical colleges, normal schools and institutes of technology. The stress of integrating administration, philosophy and staff of such diverse institutions, the press of rapidly increasing student numbers, and the public expectation and social idealism surrounding the new colleges made their survival precarious. The worldwide climate of student unrest in the late 1960s and anxiety about the number of places available in Quebec universities for college graduates added to the birth-pangs of the colleges and led in 1968 to a wave of demonstrations, strikes, and occupations which closed the institutions that had only recently been opened. When the orgy of self-examination had run its course and the colleges began functioning again, the ideals and structures of the colleges had survived – but their naiveté had certainly been tempered.[2]

The 1970s and early 1980s were a period of expansion, development, adjustment and analysis for college education in Quebec. Between 1967 and 1983, enrolment at the college level (the equivalent of grades 12 and 13), public and private, increased 150 percent.[3] In the decade 1972-1982, enrolments in pre-university programs in the public colleges doubled and those in technical programs tripled.[4] The colleges consolidated and expanded their regular programs by working in joint committees with secondary school personnel and with university admission officers. This was to smooth problems of articulation between the colleges and other levels. The colleges became heavily involved in programs of continuing education, community development and, recently, in programs of international cooperation with developing nations. By the early 1970s, competing programs had been sharply reduced by the integration or closing of normal schools, technical institutes, and most classical colleges, and by the withdrawal of universities from college-parallel programs (mainly the traditional freshman year in English universities). A number of private institutions continued to offer pre-university programs or specialized technical programs.

The seventies and eighties were also years of difficult adjustment for the colleges in their efforts to realized their social mission, and in their attempts to serve an increasing and diversified clientele. They were engaged in developing programs, in establishing an appropriate mode of internal administration and management, in developing their own identities (distinct from secondary schools and universities), and in establishing some distance between themselves and the government which was their sponsor, mentor, and major source of income.

Like their colleagues in elementary and secondary schools, college instructors were unionized; most were affiliated with a major Quebec labour union (CSN, Confédération des syndicaux nationales), others were affiliated with the chief teachers' union, the CEQ. Labour relations in the colleges shared the general turbulence of labour relations in the public sector during this period. In addition, there were many internal conflicts between administrators and teachers' associations over college policy, working conditions, and local issues.

The adjustments for English-language institutions were different but in some ways more difficult than for French institutions. First, there was the tradition of direct passage from secondary school to the English universities (as elsewhere in North America) and the creation of colleges was a seen by many as needless intrusion into a structure that was working well, forcing English-language education to accommodate itself to the French structure. Second, there were no institutions from which English colleges could be created; Loyola was to join with Sir George Williams to form Concordia University, and Marianopolis, directed by the Sisters of the Congregation Notre-Dame, became a private college. The first English public college or CEGEP, Dawson College, was established in 1969 in downtown Montreal and became the largest college in Quebec, French or English, with a number of campuses. It was followed by Vanier college in suburban St. Laurent, John Abbott on the West Island, and Champlain, a regional college with campuses in St. Lambert, Lennoxville, and Quebec City. At present, programs for English students are also offered in the French public colleges in Gaspé and Hull.[5]

This was also a time of periodic analysis of the colleges, their goals, successes, problems, and possibilities. Various proposals were made for their improvement and future development. In 1975, a committee of the Superior Council of Education produced a report on the college, generally referred to as the Nadeau Report. This report was followed by a working document of the Ministry of Education (the "GTX Report"), a government policy paper called *Les collèges du Quebec: Nouvelle etape* (1978), a revision of the law governing colleges and a new set of regulations for programs (both in 1984), and a policy statement of the Council of Colleges called *Le CEGEP de demain* in 1985.[6] All of these documents, despite their different source and purposes, shared a common faith in the importance and validity of the basic college concept, a satisfaction that the colleges had made post-secondary studies more accessible to the population – secondary graduates and adults alike – and a recognition that major problems continued to exist. There was agreement on major priorities for the future including improved institutional evaluation, new policies on technical education, improved labour relations in the colleges, and increased research activity. If the colleges began with a clearer image of what they were not, rather than what they were to be, they were developing a more positive understanding of their nature and role as they approached the end of their second decade.[7]

Structure and Programs of the Colleges

In 1983-84 there were 47 public colleges in Quebec including 7 English ones (4 institutions plus additional campuses) and there were 30 private institutions, offering an assortment of college-level programs.

The colleges varied in size. Twenty-two of the 47 public colleges had enrolments of over 3,000 students (Dawson College had over 5,000 students) and five of them had fewer than 1,000 students. In contrast, 25 of the 30 private colleges had fewer than 1,000 students.[8]

There were 157,000 students attending these colleges, 139,000 (89 percent) in public institutions. The enrolments were evenly divided between two-year pre-university programs and three-year career (technical) programs, though in private institutions two-thirds of the students were in pre-university programs. 27,000 students (17 percent) attended English-language programs but, unlike those in French colleges, fewer than 25 percent were in career programs. Table 5.1 shows the full-time enrolments in the major categories of pre-university and career programs.[9]

Table 5.1
Full-time Enrolment in Major College Programs, 1983-84

	Enrolment (1983-84)	%	Graduates (1983)	%
Pre-University (Academic) Programs				
Health, pure and applied sciences	27 900	18	7 700	21
Social sciences and commerce	40 300	25	12 700	35
Arts	4 800	3)		
Language and literature	4 400	3)	1 600	4
Other	1 200	1)		
Total	78 600	50	22 000	60
Career (Technical) Programs				
Biological technologies	13 600	9	2 900	8
Physical technologies	19 300	12	2 800	8
Social technologies	8 800	6	1 800	5
Administrative technologies	31 300	20	5 300	15
Applied arts	4 800	3	1 200	3
Language and literature	100	...		<1
Other	100	...		<1
Total	78 000	50	14 000	40
Grand Total	156 600	100	36 000	100

Adapted from: *Le Québec Statistique, Edition 1985-1986*, p. 440-443.

Twenty-five per cent of the students and 35 percent of the graduates were in programs leading to university faculties such as arts, commerce and education. A second important group, 18 percent of the students and 21 percent of the graduates were moving towards studies in medicine, dentistry, nursing, science and engineering. A third group consisting of 20 percent of the students and 15 percent of the graduates were in technical or career programs related to business and administration.

There are two basic types of programs: pre-university programs, consisting of 42 to 50 credits, normally lasting two years; and career (or technical) programs, consisting of 50-83 credits, normally lasting about three years which prepare students directly for the labour market. Both types of programs lead to a Diploma of College Studies (DEC, or *Diplôme d'études collégiales*), which is the entrance requirement for Quebec universities.

These programs consist of three kinds of courses: compulsory courses, courses in an area of pre-university concentration or career specialization, and complementary courses. Compulsory courses include 8 credits in language and literature (English in English colleges), 8 credits in humanities (in English college) or philosophy (in French colleges), and 2 2/3 credits in physical education. An area of pre-university concentration consists of 24 to 36 credits in one of the following: health science, pure and applied science, social science, commerce, creative arts, and language and literature. An area of career specialization consists of 32 to 65 credits in a field, and the following are a few examples: business administration, secretarial science, data processing, nursing, wildlife management, popular music, forestry, photography, dental hygiene, police work, computer programming, industrial automation, child care and airplane piloting. There are also 8 credits of complementary courses selected by the student outside the area of concentration or specialization. The majority of these courses are determined by the Ministry of Higher Education, the remainder selected by each college.

In addition to these basic programs, there are also programs leading to a Certificate of College Studies (CEC) consisting of between 32 and 65 credits in vocational training, and a Diploma of Advanced College Studies (DPEC) consisting of 10 to 30 credits. The basic framework for these programs is governed by a *Regulation Respecting the Basis of College Education*, approved by the government in 1984. The detailed program and course requirements are described in the Ministry's *Cahiers de l'enseignement collégial* which are published annually.[10]

The general structure and operation of these colleges and their programs are coordinated by three bodies at the provincial level, a department of the Ministry of Higher Education, a Council of Colleges, and a Federation of Colleges. Within the Ministry of Higher Education and Science, there is a directorate for college education (DGEC, Direction générale de l'enseignement collégial). It includes over 100 administrators, professionals, and support staff and a budget of over $6 million. Its mandate is the development of policies and regulations concerning curriculum, student life, personnel (including participation in negotiations), and resources, as well as the implementation and evaluation of programs.[11]

The Council of Colleges (*Conseil des collèges*) was established in 1979 as part of a revision of the Act governing the colleges. Its mandate is to advise the Minister and report on the state and needs of the colleges. It is composed of 18 members including a president, 8 representatives of the colleges, 3 from business, 1 parent, 1 representative each from secondary education, the universities and the government, and the presidents of the Council's two commissions. The law also calls for two commissions: a commission on evaluation to advise the council on policies of institutional evaluation and their application and to offer evaluation services to the colleges; and a commission on technical education (*l'enseignement professionnel*) to examine policies in this field and ensure liaison with other groups concerned with technical education.[12] The public colleges are grouped in an organization called *La Fédération des CEGEPs*, while the private colleges have formed *l'Association des Collèges du Quebec* (ACQ), to provide communication and cooperation among institutions and to develop policies on certain common issues.

Each public college is a legal corporation in terms of the civil code of Quebec and each has a Board of Governors consisting of 20 members appointed by the Minister of Higher Education. The board includes the senior administrators, personnel and students of the college, parents, and representatives of different groups in the region. Each college also has an academic council of about 20 members, a majority of whom are instructors. The council advises the college administration on matters related to the organization of programs, instruction. and certain academic appointments. The administrative head of the college has the title of *director general* and is assisted by an academic dean (director of pedagogical services), a director of student services, and other administrators such as directors, deans, and coordinators.[13]

Issues in College Education

As the college system of Quebec looks forward to the beginning of its third decade of existence, a number of important policy issues are on the agenda of planners, administrators, instructors and other educators in the colleges.

First there is the continuing question of the *identity* of the colleges and their links with other institutions. While the colleges have succeeded in both staking a territory between the secondary school and the university and in establishing bridges with these other levels, a good deal of uncertainty, and some suspicion, remains about what the colleges do, how they follow from the programs of secondary schools, and how they prepare students in both general education and specialized competence for university studies. From a comparative perspective, the Quebec colleges have features in common with junior and community colleges elsewhere in North America, with senior academic secondary programs in Europe such as the British Sixth Form and the French Lycée, and with post-secondary technical institutions in many countries. Yet, the colleges of Quebec are unique in their ideal of bringing together, in one framework, advanced technical preparation, general education, pre-university study, continuing education, and community service. Few planners, in either universities or colleges, have been very successful in seeing the post-secondary experience of students as a continuum from the first year of college to the end of the university. Nor has anyone been entirely convincing in demonstrating the success of the colleges in realizing their diverse and ambitious goals.

Second, there is the *balance* between the coherence of the college system as a whole – governed by consistent regulations, structures, and procedures under the guidance of a Ministry and Council – and the pluralism, initiative and pride of individual colleges in developing their own visions and creating their own enterprises. It may be that current inclinations to deregulate the colleges will continue or it may be that centralized structures of control and labour relations will inhibit the tendencies towards diversity.

Third, there are the complex *links* which colleges are establishing with other sectors of society, especially the local community they serve, business and industry, cultural groups, voluntary organizations and special-interest groups. Many colleges have been successful in winning the confidence of employers, especially for their technical programs, and many have also been appreciated for their efforts in community development and services to adults. There remain the dangers of overextension and unrealistic expectations, as well as the problem of balancing market pressures and social commitment with academic and institutional integrity.

Fourth, the internal *harmony* of the colleges is an important issue, focusing on the relationships between those in professional programs and those in academic programs, between administrators and instructors, and between conservative and radical ideologies. It remains an open question whether administrators and unions in the colleges will be able to adopt a more collaborative style of interaction in the years ahead or whether the conflicts of the first two decades will continue, tending to inhibit the creative development of the colleges.

Fifth, institutional *evaluation* is becoming a priority for many institutions including the colleges and with it issues of the selection of goals, criteria by which the quality of services can be measured, processes by which credible assessment of an institution can be made, and methods of making the institution responsible for quality control. The issue of evaluation will be particularly sensitive in relation to institutions like the colleges which have high and diverse expectations for academic preparation, social relevance, sensitivity to a volatile job market, teaching, adult education, and, increasingly, research activity.

Sixth, as the academic staff of the colleges stabilizes in composition and matures in qualifications and experience, inclinations and pressures for more *research* activity have been mounting, challenging the original conception of the colleges as primarily teaching rather than research institutions, and raising new questions about the recognition of research as part of job expectations. Many college teachers are scholars and researchers and the scholarly production of many of the colleges is becoming impressive. This may move colleges in the direction of a university ethos, a move that is unlikely to take place without some debate.

Finally, there is the general issue of *technical* education, matters of federal and provincial jurisdiction as well as different interests of various government departments. Technology is both an area of high priority for the economic development of Quebec and an unstable domain in the age of rapid developments in information and communication technologies, computer applications, and biotechnologies. The colleges will likely continue to be the educational institutions closest to the waves of technological change and the ones most in need of stabilizing influences in a period of ongoing turbulence.

It remains to be seen whether the original ideals of accessibility, comprehensiveness, and adaptability can be preserved in the demanding and fluid environment of the late eighties and the nineties. It may also be a time to rethink the realism of the Quebec college ideal and to ask if other models of advanced technical education, of general culture, and of access to university may be considered as alternatives to the present post-secondary structure.

The Universities of Quebec

Although it is possible to trace the roots of advanced education in Quebec to the Jesuit College and the Quebec Seminary – both founded in the middle of the 17th century – the first university in the modern sense was McGill, which received its royal charter in 1821. Its character was molded by its origins in the English merchant class of Montreal, the Scottish tradition, the broad-minded Anglican clergy and by the professional orientation of its first unit, a medical school. As McGill grew and developed over a century and a half, it acquired an international reputation for professional training, graduate studies, and research, for brilliant and sometimes eccentric academics, for the range of its programs and the confidence of its self-image. It benefited from the generosity of the Canadian business community and through the links provided by the many foreign students with McGill degrees who were to return to leadership positions around the world.

After the founding of McGill, two other universities were established, Laval in Quebec City in 1851 and Bishop's in Lennoxville in 1853. Laval grew out of the Quebec seminary and became the major French-language institution in Quebec. Through its professional faculties, Laval trained the political, legal, social and religious elite, the senior civil servants of the government, and many of the critics and reformers who were to challenge this elite in the 1950s and 1960s. Bishop's University represented both British and rural traditions in Quebec, maintaining a modest and sober presence and a steady leadership for the English-speaking community especially in the Eastern Townships.

A third stage in the evolution of Quebec universities was the development of a major French university in Montreal. The Ecole Polytechnique was established in 1873 for the training of engineers and the Ecole des Hautes Etudes Commerciales (HEC) in 1915 for business administration. These two institutions eventually joined with a branch of Laval University in Montreal to create the Université de Montréal in 1920. Since that time, the university (which is symbolically on the other side of the mountain from McGill) has developed into a major university with a comprehensive range of programs of professional training and research. However, the two schools Polytechnique and HEC have retained their identities as affiliated institutions. In 1954, the Université de Sherbrooke was founded to serve the increasing French-speaking population of the Eastern Townships (Estrie), offering, like Bishop's, university services outside of the metropolitan areas.

The next major initiative was a response of the government to the pressures of expansion and increasing expectations as a result of the post-war baby boom and the first wave of reforms of the 1960s. As graduates of the new colleges were beginning to seek university places, the government, following a model of the state university systems of New York and California, created the University of Quebec in 1968, a public provincial university with a central administration (but no campus) in Quebec city and constituent universities, first in Montreal (UQAM, Université du Québec à Montréal), Trois-Rivières (UQTR), Chicoutimi (UQAC), and Rimouski (UQAR). The government also established additional constituents: Institut national de recherche scientifique (INRS, 1969), Ecole nationale d'administration publique (ENAP, 1969) Hull (UQAH, 1972), Téle-Université (1972), Ecole de technologie supérieure (ETS, 1974) and Institut Armand Frappier (IAF, 1975). The University of Quebec is unique among the province's universities in its structure as a university system with constituent institutions, in its social mission to expand university services to the population, especially adults, in the regional leadership of many of its constituents, and in its academic organization based on modules (groups of students and professors following the same program) and departments (organization of professors in a discipline). In their vitality, diversity of character and often unconventional approaches to teaching, service and research, the universities of the UQ system have provided a stimulating complement to other institutions.

In 1974, Concordia University was established in Montreal, bringing together Loyola College and Sir George Williams University, one with a tradition as a Jesuit liberal arts college of university-level quality and aspirations, and the other with a downtown community and adult education orientation originally rooted in the Young Men's Christian Association (YMCA). Though this seemed to be an unlikely marriage, the two institutions have formed a university that offers an impressive balance of scholarship and community service, especially in adult education. Finally, in 1985, the government granted a charter to the Collège militaire royal de St. Jean (CMR) to allow it to award degrees to those cadets who follow university programs, mainly in science. Somewhat ironically given Quebec's traditions, the government in 1985 refused a charter to the Institut catholique, an organization sponsored by the Archdiocese of Montreal for the training of teachers of religion for Catholic schools.

Patterns of University Enrolment

We get a general picture of the patterns of enrolment in Quebec universities from the data presented in Table 5.2.

Table 5.2
Enrolment in Quebec Universities, 1984-85

Institutions	Undergraduate		Graduate		Total	
	Full Time	Part Time	Full Time	Part Time	Full Time	Part Time
UQ Total	23 240	46 166	1 581	2 885	24 821	49 051
Chicoutimi	2 388	4 345	117	158	2 505	4 503
Montréal	13 172	16 314	999	1 392	14 171	17 706
Rimouski	1 277	3 775	84	1 4	1 361	3 879
Trois-Rivières	4 128	5 164	211	502	4 339	5 666
Northwest	425	2 090	26	34	451	2 124
Hull	1 240	3 378	18	209	1 258	3 587
ITS	585	576	...	...	585	576
ENAP	...	48	...	397	...	445
INRS	...	...	...	50	...	50
IAF	...	14	...	39	...	53
Télé-Université	25	10 462	...	...	25	10 462
Laval	16 990	7 849	3 587	2 052	20 577	9 901
Montreal	13 601	18 821	3 925	4 096	17 526	22 917
Ec. Poly.	3 277	851	430	442	3 707	1 293
HEC	1 369	5 425	164	896	1 533	6 321
Sherbrooke	6 949	3 740	1 582	541	8 531	4 281
Bishop's	1 137	635	2	19	1 139	654
Thomas More Inst.	...	355	...	...	...	355
McGill	13 407	2 821	4 630	1 177	18 037	3 998
Concordia	10 802	11 543	1 727	1 467	12 530	13 010
CMR de St. Jean	255	...	...	...	255	...
Total	91 028	98 206	17 628	13 575	108 656	111 781

Source: Statistics Canada, *Universities: Enrolment and Degrees, 1984-85* (81-204), p. 8-9, 14-15.
Notes: (1) Part-time enrolments refer to individual students who may be following one course or a substantial proportion of a full program. Full-time equivalent

enrolments are not easily inferred from these figures. (2) Undergraduate enrolments include bachelor and certificate programs; graduate enrolments include master's and doctoral programs as well as graduate diplomas and medical residents. (3) UQ = Université du Québec; ITS = Institut de Technologie Supérieure; ENAP = Ecole Nationale d'Administration Publique; INRS = Institut National de Recherche Scientifique; IAF = Institut Armand Frappier (bio-medical research); Télé-Université = the distance education institute of Université du Québec; Ec. Poly. = Ecole Polytechnique, the engineering school affiliated with the Université de Montréal; HEC = Haute Etudes Commerciales, an institute of business administration affiliated with the Université de Montréal; Thomas More Institute = an independent adult education institution in Montreal affiliated for degree purposes with Bishop's University; CMR de St. Jean = Collège Militaire Royal de St. Jean, a military college operated by the Department of National Defence.

In terms of full-time enrolment, the largest universities are the Université du Québec system (23 percent of the total), Université de Montréal (21 percent), Laval (19 percent) and McGill (17 percent). On the other hand, using part-time enrolment as the measure, the UQ system is by far the largest with 44 percent of the total, followed by Montréal (27 percent) and Concordia (12 percent). On the basis of full-time students, the largest graduate program is at McGill which has over 25 percent of all full-time graduate students in Quebec, followed by Montréal and Laval. The Université de Montréal has the largest number of part-time graduate students (30 percent of the total for Quebec).

Another way of comparing Quebec universities is in terms of the number of certificates and degrees granted in a year. In 1983, Quebec universities conferred 22,000 bachelor's degrees, 3,600 master's degrees, 400 doctorates and 12,000 certificates or diplomas (normally following programs of the equivalent of one year of study).[14] The UQ system granted 25 percent of these bachelor degrees and 38 percent of the certificates. The Université de Montréal granted the largest number of master's degrees (29 percent) and the second largest number of certificates. At the doctoral level, the largest number of degrees were granted by McGill (1/3 of all doctorates granted in Quebec that year), followed by Montreal and Laval.

In summary, these figures indicate certain patterns: the UQ system mainly serves undergraduate (bachelor degree) students and part-time clientele in certificates and diplomas; Laval's major enrolments are at the undergraduate and master's level; Sherbrooke, Concordia and Bishops's are largely at the undergraduate level; the two institutions with the widest range of enrolments are Montréal and McGill, with Montréal much more heavily involved in certificate and diploma programs; within the UQ system, the Montreal campus (UQAM) accounts for about half of the enrolments and graduates at all levels.

It is also interesting to compare certain patterns of university graduates and enrolment between Quebec and Ontario. The following is the distribution of graduates by level in the two provinces for 1984:

	Quebec	Ontario
Bachelors	57.0%	80.3%
Undergraduate certificates	29.6%	4.3%
Master's	9.8%	13.1%
Doctorates	1.1%	1.7%
Graduate diplomas	2.5%	0.6%
Total	100.0%	100.0%

This is the distribution of full-time and part-time enrolment for 1984-85:

	Quebec	Ontario
Full-time	108 656	185 410
Part-time	111 781	95 830

This is the distribution by major fields of study:

	Quebec	Ontario
Education	23.1%	13.4%
Fine/applied arts	3.3%	2.6%
Humanities	10.2%	11.1%
Social sciences	39.2%	35.2%
Agriculture/biological sc.	3.6%	4.2%
Engineering/applied sc.	7.0%	9.4%
Health professions	6.6%	4.9%
Mathematics/physical sc.	5.0%	7.2%
Other	1.9%	12.0%

And this is the distribution of graduates by sex:

	Quebec	Ontario
Female	51.5%	50.1%
Male	48.5%	49.9%

Some comparisons may be made between the two provinces on the basis of this information. First, there are striking differences in the proportion of certificates and diplomas. These represent almost 1/3 of graduates in Quebec universities but under 5 percent in Ontario. Second, part-time enrolment is a substantial part of Quebec universities and much less so in Ontario where full-time study is the dominant pattern. Third, Quebec produces proportionally more graduates in education, fine arts, social sciences and health professions, with Ontario ahead in humanities, agriculture/biological sciences, engineering/applied sciences, and mathematics/physical sciences.

It is also worth noting that 12 percent of Ontario graduates are classified as "other" compared to 1.9 percent of Quebec graduates. This suggests another important difference in enrolment distributions between the two provinces. In Ontario, 27,000 full-time and 16,000 part-time students were registered in general undergraduate arts and science programs, compared to only 6,000 full-time and 4,000 part-time students in Quebec. Finally, the proportion of women graduates is higher in Quebec than in Ontario, though many of these women in Quebec are concentrated in part-time certificate programs and in certain areas of specialization, especially those related to teaching.[15]

The University System

Higher education in Quebec has undergone five major changes since the early 1960s. First, it has experienced dramatic growth in size; second, its institutional patterns have been changed by the arrival of colleges and the creation of the University of Quebec system; third, there have been strenuous attempts to coordinate and rationalize the traditionally independent universities into a network that reflects the growing financial dependence of universities on government grants. Fourth, curriculum changes have involved new programs, more specialized bachelor's degrees, many short certificate and diploma programs, and the integration of teacher education into the universities. Finally, there have been periodic analyses of the role of the university in society and the kinds of policies that would be appropriate for future university development.

Between 1961 and 1981, the post-secondary age population, 17-24, grew from 565,000 to 915,000, an increase of over 60 percent in 20 years. During the same period, the per cent of this population who were in full-time post-secondary programs (at college or university level) rose from 12 percent in 1962 to 26 percent in 1981. This meant that post-secondary enrolments in colleges and universities increased from 66,000 to 235,000, an overall increase of 250 percent. Another measure of the growth of the university population is in terms of full-time equivalent (FTE) students or calculating the proportion of a full program that a part-time student is taking. On this basis, university FTE enrolments went from 90,000 in 1973-73 to 144,000 in 1983-84, an increase of 60 percent in a decade.[16] Women were 32 percent of full-time undergraduate enrolment in 1970 and 46 percent in 1983.[17]

A second influence on universities involved the creation of colleges and the University of Quebec. The colleges assumed the responsibility for the first two years of post-secondary study after high school (12th and 13th years of schooling). This had two effects on universities: it shifted the task of advanced general education from universities to colleges, moving undergraduate programs towards a high degree of specialization, virtually eliminating the general B.A. and general B.Sc. programs; and second, it removed the freshman year from existing four-year undergraduate programs, reducing almost all bachelors programs to 3 years' (90 credits) duration. This made program design at the undergraduate level more compact and tightened course sequences, especially in the physical sciences. Thus, undergraduate programs became shorter, often more difficult, and generally more specialized.

The University of Quebec was a new player in the university league. It saw itself as more democratic, less elitist, more flexible than the traditional universities. It was committed to extending university education, both to different regions of the province though its various campuses, and also to different social and economic groups. In this objective, it relied on a diversity of programs, especially certificate programs, and a wide range of part-time courses. As a system within a system, the University of Quebec was different in structure, culture, and sometimes policy from other Quebec universities; its major constituent, UQAM in Montreal, has generally considered itself a "de facto" university in its own right and has periodically sought its independence from the UQ structure.

The general structure of the university system in some ways parallels that of the college system. There is a department in the Ministry of Higher Education and Science (and before 1985 in the Ministry of Education) dealing with university affairs, the Directorate of University Teaching and Research (Direction générale de l'enseignement et de la recherche universitaire). Its function is to promote university teaching and research within the framework of a network of services largely financed by the government. It works with the Council of Universities and the individual institutions to establish policies and priorities, it provides the funds to institutions and it coordinates services and programs. However, it does not, as yet, exercise the degree of control over institutions and programs that prevails at the college level.[18]

In addition to the Ministry of Higher Education and Science, an important element of the university structure is the Council of Universities which was established in 1968. This body has the general responsibility of coordinating university programs, sponsoring studies of the needs and services of university education, and advising the Ministry on university policy, especially matters dealing with the financing of teaching and research. The Council is composed of 12 members appointed by the government who represent the Ministry, the universities, and the broader community. There are two committees of the Council: one which approves new programs for recognition and funding, and one on finance. During the academic year 1984-85, the Council issued 21 documents advising the Minister on such subjects as new programs, funding, planning, research, and professional diplomas. The Council also sponsors sectorial studies in different fields such as applied science and education, examining the match among needs, programs and resources in a discipline or profession.[19]

Other provincial bodies which have an influence on universities are the following: the Conference of Rectors and Principals of Quebec Universities (CREPUQ, Conférence des recteurs et des principaux des universités du Québec), an association of university institutions; FAPUQ, the Fédération des associations des professeurs des universités du Québec, the body that brings together the associations of professors in each institutions, all of which are unionized except at McGill; the Office of Professions (Office des professions) which controls admission to a number of professions and through which certain professional programs are accredited.

These structures are all elements in the ongoing attempts to balance the traditional institutional autonomy of universities with the needs of coordination and accountability for public funds The Ministry and the Council of Universities are the major influences in stressing the provincial network; the individual institutions and their organization CREPUQ are the major defenders of diversity. Since the 1960s, there has been a clear movement in the direction of less institutional freedom and more system planning: extensive demands for information have been made on the institutions; the universities are all very dependent on government grants and their development is affected by the size of the total grant for universities, a policy decision that reflects political and economic pressures; and their development is also affected by the allocation which the government makes among the institutions, following a complex formula that is based on historical patterns and enrolment. The role of the Council of Universities in program approval and the role of the government in determining salaries for unionized employees in the education sector (including non-academic employees in universities) have all reduced the autonomy of the universities. On the other hand, the culture and tradition of each institution, including the individual constituents of the UQ system, provide counterbalancing influences in the direction of differentiation, independent initiative and resistance to government control.

In addition to growth, the creation of new institutions, and new organizational structures, a fourth trend in university education since the sixties has been the development of new programs. The creation of the colleges forced the universities to completely reorganize the structure of their existing undergraduate programs, changing them from a four-year or five-year pattern to one that was generally three years or 90 credits in length. At the same time, university programs became more specialized, on the assumption that general education was the task of the colleges; thus, bachelor's programs tended to follow the pattern of an honors degree in a field or that of a major and minor in two fields. Many programs were also developed in new areas or new specializations within existing fields: family medicine, communications, computer science, sexology, linguistics, environmental studies, human relations and many more. University programs during this period were also affected by the integration of teacher education into the university. This required a variety of academic and professional courses for new and practicing teachers, many of whom could only follow courses on a part-time basis.

Beginning with the Parent Commission report in 1964, a number of studies and policy statements have had direct implications for universities. The Parent Commission laid out the essential blueprint for university development in Quebec, a blueprint that was followed quite closely by policy makers; the major deviation was the rejection of the Parent proposal for the creation of a number of universities with limited charter, in favour of the framework of the University of Quebec.[20] In the early 1970s, the newly established Council of Universities produced a series of four planning documents on the general objectives of higher education and the orientations which the universities as a whole and institutions in particular should develop during the 1970s.[21]

The role of universities in cultural development, teaching and research was one of the topics raised in a government policy statement in 1978, *A Cultural Development Policy for Quebec.*[22] The question of research policy was tackled more directly by the Quebec government in a discussion paper in 1979 and a policy statement 1980.[23] At the same time, the economic context of university policy was studied in two major statements on economic policy in 1979 and 1982, the second underlining the need for reorienting the Quebec economy in the direction of the new information technologies.[24]

In 1979 there was a major study of Quebec universities published by a special commission, the Commission d'étude sur les universités (CEU). The Commission's report consisted of four volumes dealing with future trends, the place of the university in Quebec society, the organization of the university system, and the education of teachers. The recommendations of the CEU stressed the traditional roles of teaching and research, acknowledged the importance of the social responsibilities of universities, and supported the value of university autonomy.[25]

By the mid-1980s, Quebec universities, like their counterparts in other places, were feeling the pressures of budget restrictions and shifting enrolment patterns. University operating costs were high and not easily cut, yet the universities were vulnerable to government policies of budget compression. The result was an extended period in the late 1970s and early 1980s during which the universities were not only seriously underfunded but also had difficulties in basic financial planning due to the uncertainty in funding policies. At the same time, the priorities for programs leading to careers and professions and for research and development in the priority areas of information technologies were not always easily engaged at a time of little growth and financial constraint.

Policy Issues in University Education

In recent years, a number of important policy questions have been preoccupying planners, administrators and everyone else involved in university education in Quebec. While some of these issues are peculiar to Quebec, most are shared by universities in many other places. Each person and group has a favorite list of policy issues and a different ranking for items, but these are some of the key questions being asked.

(1) To what degree has the goal of greater accessibility to higher education been realized?

(2) Have Quebec universities been able to balance accessibility with excellence, quantity with quality?

(3) To what degree does the pattern of enrolment among disciplines reflect the needs and aspirations of Quebec society?

(4) Is there some general agreement about the major functions of the university – teaching, research, social criticism, consulting and other commercial

activities, and community service?

(5) Is there an appropriate balance between centralized government control and decentralized institutional autonomy?

(6) How effective is the internal administration of universities?

(7) Are the criteria and procedures for funding universities fair, adequate and balanced?

(8) How well does the university fit into a philosophy of continuing education, linking the universities with the colleges, professions, the international scholarly community and the labour market?

(9) How can universities assure the continuing renewal of personnel?

(10) Will the universities be able to exhibit the leadership traditionally associated with higher education?

Accessibility – If there has been an overriding goal for higher education in Quebec since 1960, it is to expand educational opportunities or to open access to university to all who can profit from it. This involved reducing or eliminating disparities between men and women, metropolitan centres and remote areas, French and English, rich and poor. While the system is far from perfect, a general trend towards greater accessibility to university study as well as towards the reduction of differences among groups has occurred. If upper and middle classes are still over-represented among university populations, the contrasts are less stark than they were in the 1950s. If people in remote areas have fewer facilities and programs, many are now served by the University of Quebec network and the programs of Télé-Université. Overall participation rates of men and women are roughly equal, though there are considerable variations among programs. On the other hand, in 1981-82 there continued to be considerable variation among language groups in global access rates to full-time studies: 18% French vs. 24% English. Participation was higher in part-time programs for French than English (18% vs. 10%) and for women than men (20% vs. 13%).[26] Quebec is clearly moving in the direction of equality of access, especially for French women; however, gaps still remain for other language groups, the poor, and the isolated.

Quantity and Quality – A second major goal of higher education has been to catch up with other places in North America (notably Ontario) in the proportion of the population with university degrees. In the mid-1970s new graduates with undergraduate degrees accounted for 23% of their age groups in Ontario compared to 15% in Quebec. By 1984, it is estimated that the per cent had changed to 21% in Ontario and 18% in Quebec. The per cent of the 27-year-old age group in 1981 with graduate degrees was 3% in Quebec and 5% in Ontario (and 8% in the United States).[27] Thus, there has been some success, but a significant gap still remains. Two further questions need to be asked: Is there some optimum per cent of an age group that should participate in university study? How is the quality of university education affected by increasing the number of students? It is not obvious that a continuous increase in university

participation is necessarily a good thing; it depends on the preparation and aptitude of those participating, on the alternatives to university education available,
on the quality and relevance of the programs, and on the ability of the society to
underwrite the high cost of university education. Much of the participation in
university in Quebec is in short-term, part-time undergraduate certificate programs (almost 30% of all university graduates in 1984), programs for which it
is difficult to ensure continuity and depth of study, adequate student services
and rigorous quality control. More generally, Quebec universities have
improved in the qualification of their academic staff, their resources and facilities, and in their research activity, and most institutions are engaged in ongoing
assessment of their programs. Yet a comprehensive, critical and credible
assessment of university education in Quebec remains to be undertaken.

Distribution – It is important to consider not only the total numbers of
graduates at different levels but also the distribution among major fields. Over
70% of Quebec graduates are in four fields (education, social sciences, health
professions and fine arts) compared to 55% in Ontario; 15% of Quebec graduates are in biological, pure, and applied sciences, compared to 21% in Ontario.
Behind these patterns is the question to what extent the distribution of graduates should match some image of social priorities (should there be more
engineers and fewer teachers?) and, if there is such an image, how can it be
translated into policy. The most popular full-time undergraduate programs in
Quebec are business (16,000), engineering (10,000) and education (10,000); in
Ontario, the leaders are general arts and science (27,000), business (17,000) and
engineering (15,000). If there is an invisible hand such as the labour market
guiding the choice of fields of study, its influence is harder to discern and harder
still to guide.[28]

Functions – The university is the only social institution that combines the
functions of teaching and research. The conservation of existing knowledge,
the generation of new knowledge and the interrelationship between them are at
the core of the nature of a modern university. There has been a good deal of
debate in Quebec, as elsewhere, about the relative importance of each, whether
one develops at the expense of the other or whether they are, in the real world as
well as in the ideal world, mutually supportive. Furthermore, there has been
considerable debate in Quebec about the other functions of the contemporary
university as a publicly supported social institution: its contribution to the
society and service to the common good; its critical function to examine and
debate important social issues; and its entrepreneurial function of providing
consulting services, contract research, resources such as computer facilities,
and products for profit. For some, universities need to be more conscious of
their social responsibilities; for others, the social responsibility of the university
is not something separate but rather a consequence of the quality of its primary
teaching and research activities. For some, the university should more faithfully
reflect the present society; for others, it should remain apart, providing a critical
perspective detached from current political and social currents. Some applaud
the initiative of universities and professors in engaging in profit-making

ventures, while others worry about the corruption of teaching and scholarship by the marketplace. The debate goes on and positions are based on the different conceptions of what a university is and should be.

Control – The ongoing debate over who should control universities –how much and by what means – tends to shift between two poles. At one pole there is a government system of public institutions of higher education controlled by a Ministry; at the other pole, there are autonomous institutions responsible for their vision of their mission and accountable in general for their resources. It is clear that centralizing tendencies have prevailed since the 1960s and that the Quebec government has assumed a more commanding presence in university policy than was previously the case, allocating resources, standardizing procedures, setting broad policy objectives and attempting to rationalize the university system in the interests of the common good. On the other hand, the universities resist attempts to view them as an integrated system or network, analogous to the public compulsory school system, and they vigorously defend the importance of institutional independence as an essential counterpoint to state control, bureaucratic trivia and political meddling. While continuing attempts have been made to mediate the various perceptions, and although the policy positions of both government and universities have varied over time, the debate is likely to continue, sharpened by the broader issue of the role of government as social engineer and of the value of deregulating public services.

Management – Universities face a basic contradiction in the style of their internal management. On the one hand, the nature of teaching and research and the long tradition of universities have favoured either a paternalistic system, an oligarchy of senior academics, or a broader collegial and participatory system of decision making and administration which involves all academics, members of the community on a board of governors or equivalent, and more recently students and non-academic staff as well. On the other hand, the rapid growth of the institutions, the rise of unions and collective bargaining within the universities, and closer relationships with the civil service of government have inclined university management in the direction of bureaucratic and business models. On some occasions, the administrations and the faculty are opposing and mutually suspicious camps; in some institutions, the paternalistic centralization of an earlier period was replaced by a bureaucratic centralization. In many institutions, there is the feeling that an inordinate amount of time and energy is devoted not to research and teaching, but to meetings and memoranda, procedures, reports and processes by which some people try to control the work of others. The layers of decision – from department to committees to faculties to more committees to senate to senior administrators and boards – form a mirror image of other layers of decision at the provincial level. The management of universities has become too heavy and is distracting from its prime functions, yet the road to simpler operations appears elusive.

Funding – As the financial support for the universities becomes more difficult to find in a competitive environment, critical questions are being asked: should the public or the users pay, how much money should be invested in university teaching and research in relation to other social and educational priorities, and how should this money be allocated to various institutions and programs? The major sources of the operating revenue of Quebec universities in 1979 were 9% from fees, 3% from foundations, gifts and revenue-producing activities, and 88% from the provincial government. In Ontario the figures were 13% from fees, 9% from other sources, and 78% from government. In the United States, they were 20% from fees, 29% from other sources, and 51% from government.[29] In Quebec, three factors are combined: low cost to the client in fees, a high level of participation in university study, and a major demand on pubic funds to support university cost. If universities are to preserve some distance from government, they may find it necessary to reduce their dependence on government funds. There is no easy answer to the question of how much money Quebec can or should be willing to invest in universities. This depends on the nature of its political, economic, and social priorities and on the current effectiveness of the university system. If major social projects involve a high demand for advanced expertise and if the evolving society needs a population with advanced learning, investments in universities must become a political priority and they must take a long-range perspective. Many institutions also question the dependence of existing formulas for funding institutions on enrolments and historical patterns, arguing that this discourages innovative research and advanced programs that are more expensive to operate, and that it works against institutions that have changed their operations since the ground rules were established over a decade ago. Yet it is not easy to devise a better system. There continues to be a good deal of reliance on crisis management and "ad-hocracy" in the financing of universities.

Continuing Education – In a period of rapid social change, economic turbulence, competition and political complexity, the concept of continuing education is an attractive one, linking initial training with recurrent patterns of retraining and further development. There has been some analysis in Quebec about what place the university should have in an overall system of continuing education, beyond the current efforts to offer part-time programs and courses, non-credit workshops, and special services for adults. One issue is the ties between colleges and universities, and the degree of articulation in programs. Another is the increasing importance of non-traditional clientele, adults and senior citizens in many programs, full-time as well as part time. A third issue is the ongoing responsibility of the university as a resource for professions and communities in the constant intellectual, cultural and vocational revitalization that is needed. Finally, there the international dimension of continuing education, the role of the university as a link between Quebec and intellectual communities elsewhere. The needs of continuing education are altering the "educational ecology" of universities.

Renewal – The major resource of a university is the intelligence, creativity and vigour of its academic and professionals staff and the vision of its administrators. As university enrolments level off, and as ongoing budget constraints limit opportunities for development, the academic staff is growing older, job mobility decreases, administrative positions become harder to fill with imaginative people, and job prospects for young academics are limited. In the early 1980s, 32% of professors were under 35 years of age and 16% were over 55; in the late 1980s, 24% will be under 35 and 25% over 55. After that, there will be increasing need to replace older professors who retire. Thus there is a combination of few openings for new graduates followed by rising demand. This has serious implications for ongoing staff renewal in the short term, recruitment of qualified staff in the longer term, and policies of continuity and transition between the two periods.[30]

Leadership – As in other societies, Quebec looks to universities for leadership: in setting the tone for the general quality of direction of other levels of public education; in stimulating the development of the society's professionals and elite groups; in providing the basic research and scholarship needed to enrich social, cultural, and economic development; and in addressing in an articulate and thoughtful way the major social, moral and intellectual issues of the day. To do all this, universities must be constantly renewing themselves. They must have at least some distance from the immediate pressures of the moment. They must have academic freedom to be both creative and critical, and they must enjoy the confidence of the society. As university personnel move in and out of senior positions in government, public corporations, business and professional bodies, universities exchange with society, offering theoretical expertise and receiving practical realism in return. Quebec needs leadership from the universities.

Post-secondary education in Quebec has come a long way since the 1950s. It is more extensive, more expensive, more varied, more important, more relevant, more contentious. If more is being invested in colleges and universities, more is being expected of them. And more questions are being asked about their future.

Notes

1. Quebec, *Report of the Royal Commission of Inquiry on Education in the Province of Quebec*, (Quebec, 1964), Vol. 2, Ch.6, "Pre-University and Vocational Education," p. 159-194; Quebec, Department of Education, *College Education and the General and Vocational Colleges*, Document Number 3 (Quebec, 1968).

2. N. Henchey, "Quebec Education: The Unfinished Revolution," *McGill Journal of Education*, 7,2 (Fall 1972); 108-109; J. Lipkin and A. Denis, "Quebec's CEPEGs: Promise and Reality," *Ibid*: 119-134.

3. Jeanne L. Blackburn, "Le premier défi des cégeps: Recevoir les milliers d'élèves qui n'y sont pas encore," *Le Devoir*, vendredi 27 janvier 1984, p. 15.

4. R. Morissette, "Portrait statistique: En 92, les cégeps recevront 25,000 étudiants de moins qu'en 82," *Ibid*, p. 16.

5. A.E. LeBlanc, "Les cégeps anglais: Un milieu qui a choisi de s'integrer aux institutions québécoises," and W. Tierney, "Des personnalités bien campées," *Ibid*, p. 27; D.A. Burgess, "The English-language CEGEP," *McGill Journal of*

Education, 6-1 (1971): 99-101.

6. Conseil supérieur de l'éducation, *Le collège: Rapport sur l'etat et les besoins de l'enseignement collégial*, (Rapport Nadeau), (Québec, 1975); "Le point de vue de la direction de l'enseignement collégial sur l'enseignement collégial," (Rapport "GTX"), (Québec: MEQ, 1975; *Les collèges du Québec: Nouvelle etape, (Québec: MEQ, 1978); Quebec, MEQ, Regulation Respecting the Basis of College Education (Quebec, 1984);* Conseil des collèges, *Le cegep de demain*, Québec, 1985).

7. See: Conseil des collèges, *Cinquième rapport annuel 1983-84 (Québec, 1984) and Sixème rapport annuel 1984-85*, (Québec, 1986).

8. Calculated from data in Quebec, Ministère de l'Education, *Repertoire des organisms et des etablissements d'enseignement: Statistiques de l'enseignement, Edition 1984-85* (Québec: MEQ, 1984, p. 12-15).

9. Québec, *Le Québec statistique: Edition 1985-1986*, (Québec: 1986); adapted from Tableau 7, p. 436-437, Tableau 10, p. 440, Tableau 13, p. 442-443.

10. Québec, Ministère de l'Education, *Regulation Respecting the Basis of College Organization* (Quebec, 1984).

11. Québec, Ministère de l'Education, *Rapport Annuel 1982-1983*, (Québec, 1983). p. 26-29.

12. Conseil des collèges, *Sixième rapport annuel 1984-1985* (Québec, 1986).

13. For a bibliography on college education in Quebec, see A.E. LeBlanc, "Collegial Education in Quebec – A Bibliography," *McGill Journal of Education"*, 20-3 (Fall 1985), p. 273-280.

14. Québec, *Le Québec Statistique, Edition 1985-1986*. (Québec, 1986), Tableau 14, p. 444-445.

15. Statistics Canada, *Universities: Enrolment and Degrees*, 1984-85 (81-204), Table 16, p.40.

16. Conférence des recteurs et des principaux des universités du Québec, *Reflections sur l'avenir de l'universite'au Québec,"* (Montréal: CREPUQ, 1985), Tableau 1, p. 40.

17. For part-time enrolments, see CREPUQ, *Ibid*, p. 36-38; for proportion of women students, see Statistics Canada, *Education in Canada, 1973*, Table 29, p. 424 and *Education in Canada, 1983* Table 24 p. 114.

18. Ministère de l'Education, *Rapport annuel, 1982-1983*, p. 30-32.

19. Conseil des universités, *Seizième rapport annuel, 1984-1985* and *Bulletin 2-4* (decembre 1985), p. 8.

20. Quebec, *Report of the Royal Commission of Inquiry on Education in the Province of Quebec*, (Quebec, 1964), Vol. 2, Chapter 7, "Higher Education," p. 195-260.

21. Conseil des universités, Cahier I, *L'évolution récente de l'enseignement supérieur au Quebec (1972); Cahier II, Objectifs genéraux de l'enseignement supérieur (1973); Cahier III, Les orientations de l'enseignement supérieur dans les annés 70 (1973); Cahier IV, Perspective 1976 des orientations de l'enseignement supérieur (1976).*

22. Quebec, *A Cultural Development Policy for Quebec* (Quebec, 1978).

23. Québec, *Pour une politique quebécois de la recherche scientifique,* (Québec, 1979); *Un projet collectif: Enoncé d'orientations et plan d'action pour la mise en oeuvre d'une politique quebécoise de la recherche scientifique,* (Québec, 1980).

24. Québec, *Batir le Quebec: Enoncé de politique economique, synthése, orientations et plan d'action* (Québec, 1979); *Le virage technologique: Batir le Québec, Phase 2: Programme d'action economique 1982-1986* (Québec, 1982).

25. Commission d'étude sur les universités, *Comité de coordination* (Vol. 1), *Comité d'etude sur l'universite' et la sociele' quebecoise* (Vol.2), *Comité d'etude sur l'organisation du système universitaire* (Vol.3), *Comité d'etude sur la formation et le perfectionnement des enseignants* (Vol.4), (Québec: CEU, 1979).

26. Conseil supérieur de l'éducation, *Apprendre pour de vrai: Rapport 1984-1985 sur l'elat et les besoins de l'eaucation* (Québec: CSE, 1986), Annexe I, p. 85. Based on a study by A. Lesperance, "L'accès à l'université au Québec: Mesure du phénomène selon le sex et la langue maternelle de 1978-1979 à 1981-1982," DEED, ministère de l'Education, 1984.

27. CREPUQ, Annexe 1, p. 29-30.

28. Statistics Canada, *Universities: Enrolment and Degrees, 1984-85* (81-204), Table 8, p. 22.

29. CREPUQ, p. 43-54.

30. Conseil supérieur de l'Education, *Pour le renouvellement et le ressourcement du personnel de l'enseignement,* (Quebec, 1985), p. 15-19.

6

Adult Education:
Continuing Learning

In addition to the formal structure of elementary and secondary schools, colleges, and universities directed primarily to the young, there is also a vast array of resources and services in Quebec intended primarily for the adult population. These include formal learning activities, those sponsored by an educational institution such as a college, and non-formal activities, those which take place within the framework of organizations and institutions that are not exclusively or even primarily educational in purpose.

The size and importance of adult education in Quebec can be judged by the following: in 1983, 800,000 adults, 18% of the population 17 years of age and over, followed at least one adult education course; 263,000 adult students were taking courses offered by school boards; 100,000 adults were registered for courses given by colleges (CEGEPs) which is almost 50% of their total registrations. In 1984, 75,000 adults 25 years of age or older were taking full-time or part-time undergraduate courses in university, 47% of undergraduate registrations. This represents less than half of the adult education activity; it does not include courses in private schools, those offered by employers, unions and professional groups, the programs of voluntary organizations, and the educational activities of the media and cultural institutions. Furthermore, there is every indication that the expectations for adult education will increase in the coming decades as the population structure of Quebec shifts towards adults and senior citizens, as people live longer, enjoy a better quality of life, and have more available leisure time.

Adult learning in Quebec is not a new phenomenon, but one that has roots well into the last century. At one time, adult learning services were mainly intended to compensate adults for the limitations of their initial schooling. These services were usually sponsored by private organizations and voluntary groups. Since the 1960s, adult education services have been continuing to address these basic needs, but they also have become increasingly preoccupied with the advanced learning needs of a modern, rapidly changing and complex society for which initial training cannot be expected to provide complete and lasting preparation. At the same time, these services have become more dependent on government support and coordination. In the past twenty-five years, there has also been growing recognition of the special learning needs of various adult groups within the population: young adults unable to find work, older workers displaced by a changing economy, women wishing to enter the labour force after years away from it, adults who are completely or functionally illiterate, the physically handicapped, native people, and older citizens who have retired. There is also greater sensitivity to the general intellectual and cultural needs of the population as a whole, including a wide range of topics in public health, legal rights, consumer education, community organization, environmental protection, effective participation in social and public life, self-expression, artistic appreciation, cultural enhancement, fitness, personal fulfillment, support in times of crisis, and leisure activities.

As these activities of adult learning have increased in scope and diversity, they have raised questions: How well are these education programs serving the needs of the adult population? What is the relative importance of learning services for adults and for the young? What should be the relationship between the formal school system and adult education, should they be integrated, coordinated, or kept separate? What are the best means of promoting and coordinating adult learning, especially for those who need it most and use it least? How does adult learning differ from school learning? Can all learning, for young and old alike, be integrated into a single framework of continuing, recurrent or lifelong education?

Adult Learners in Quebec

A first step in a study of adult education in Quebec is to look at the number and characteristics of the adults who follow learning programs, the types of programs they follow, and the institutions which offer these programs. Fortunately, there is a good deal of information available about adult learners. It comes from a survey of learning activities of adults across Canada for the year 1983 which was sponsored by the federal Secretary of State and Statistics Canada. The survey covered over 91,000 persons across the country, just under 18,000 in Quebec. An analysis was prepared by the Canadian Association for Adult Education (CAAE) and the data for Quebec were further analyzed by the Institut canadien d'éducation des adultes (ICEA), the Quebec Association for Adult Learning (QAAL) and in a special report of the Superior Council of Education.[1] From these and other sources we can sketch a general portrait of adult education in Quebec for the year 1983.

In 1983, over 800,000 Quebecers, 17 years of age and older, took at least one adult education course. This was a participation rate of 18%, making Quebec's rate the sixth highest among Canadian provinces. Across the country, the rate ranged from 9% in Newfoundland to 20% in Ontario to 25% in Alberta, In Quebec, over half of the adults participating in adult education were in the two metropolitan regions of Montreal and Quebec city.

More women than men took courses. The participation rate for women was 20% compared to 16% for men; the Canadian averages were 22% for women and 17% for men. There were other important differences. Over two-thirds of the women were following courses related to personal interests and hobbies and one-third were following courses that were academic or job-related; in contrast, only one-third of men were following personal interest and hobby courses while two-thirds took academic and job-related courses. For men 23% of the courses were offered by an employer, and 31% were paid by an employer, while for women the rates were much lower, 7% and 11%.

Younger adults were more inclined to take courses, 27% of the adults between 25 and 34 years of age and 24% of those between 35 and 44 were taking courses. Just under 12% of adults 55 years and over were participating in courses. All of these rates are below the corresponding Canadian averages.

Adults with a high degree of schooling were much more inclined to take courses than those with less schooling. Almost 30% of Quebec adults have eight years of school attendance or less, but only 5.5% of this group participated in adult education. At the other end of the scale, 12% of the adult population had a post-secondary diploma and 33% of these were following at least one course; 9% held a university degree and 40% of this group were participating.

Adults who were active in the labour force were more inclined to take courses than those outside: the participation rate was 24% for those employed, 18% for those unemployed and only 10% for those not part of the job market. The motivation for taking courses also varied. Just under 50% of employed and unemployed adults were motivated by career more than personal interest, yet fully 80% of those not active in the labour force were taking courses out of personal interest. The comparative figures also showed that career motivation was less important for Quebecers than for other Canadians; for example, 49.5% of unemployed Quebecers who were taking courses did so for career purposes, compared to 62.9% in Ontario and 58.9% for Canada as a whole.

The rate of participation of English Quebecers was slightly higher than that of French Quebecers, but only 9% of those with a mother tongue other than French or English were actively involved in adult education courses. While the French relied more on voluntary organizations and private schools, in the English community, universities and school boards were the major providers of courses. The English were more inclined than the French to take academic courses and less inclined to take recreation and personal interest courses.

There were significant patterns in the type of course being taken. 34% of Quebec participants were taking job-related courses, the lowest per of any region in Canada. In contrast, 29% of Quebec adults were following courses in the areas of personal development and general interest, the highest in Canada.

A number of patterns emerged in the analysis of the organizations and institutions which provide courses to adults. In Quebec, 20% of the courses were given by voluntary organizations, 19% by private schools, 14% each by employers and universities, 13% each by colleges and school boards, and 7% by unions and professional bodies. That is, the public school system (boards, colleges, university) provided 40% of the courses; private schools, voluntary organizations and employers/unions each provided about 20% of the courses. In Ontario, on the other hand, voluntary organizations provided only 13% of the courses; there, major providers were employers (20%), colleges (20%) and school boards (16%). While private schools in Quebec were offering 20% of the courses, in Ontario they accounted for only 10% of the courses. In general terms, universities, private schools, and voluntary organizations were more important in adult education in Quebec than elsewhere, while employers, unions, colleges and school boards were less important in Quebec.

From this information, there are a number of generalizations that deserve consideration. (1) Women, the young, the English, the employed and the well-educated are those who take most advantage of adult education services. (2) Men, especially those who have little schooling, are making less use of adult education. (3) The emphasis in adult education in Quebec is less on academic and career-orientated goals than in most other parts of Canada. (4) Quebec also differs from the rest of Canada in its strong reliance on voluntary organizations and private schools to provide adult education. (5) The public school system, boards and post-secondary institutions account for less than half of adult education courses offered in Quebec.

Formal Programs

Formal adult education programs are offered by school boards, colleges, universities and private schools. Some of these programs are designed primarily for adults, for those over a certain age and who have been away from school. Other programs are more general in nature, attracting adults as well as younger learners. Programs also differ in their goals and content: some are academic and lead to standard diplomas; some are orientated to training in a specific trade or career; some are cultural and recreational; and some are primarily intended for the personal development of the adult learner.

In 1983-84, Quebec school boards offered adult education services to over 263,000 students. 55% of these adults were following part-time academic programs or courses of a social and cultural nature; 37% were following full-time academic courses or vocational programs on either a full-time or part-time basis. These students were served by almost 4,000 teachers, administrators and support staff. The total cost of adult education in school boards for 1983-84 was almost $140 million.[2]

School boards offer a variety of programs: (1) Literacy programs for those unable to read and write at a satisfactory level, usually offered on a tutorial basis; (2) Academic programs leading to a high school leaving certificate; (3) Second language courses in English and French; (4) Full-time vocational courses in various trade, technical and commercial areas, offered in cooperation with the Canada Employment and Immigration Commission; (5) Part-time manpower courses which emphasize trades and occupations in which new skills are in demand; (6) Special programs on non-traditional work for women, in fields where women make up less than one-third of the work force;

(7) On-the-job training through a cooperative program sponsored by governments, school boards and private industry, designed to give young people on welfare a year's paid work and study experience; (8) "Preparation to work" programs that help people seek and apply for jobs (9) Remedial education for young adults on welfare, leading to a high school leaving certificate; (10) Transition to work, a job-search program for unemployed women; (11) Programs of social and vocational integration of youth, an extensive academic, vocational, and counseling program for unemployed high school drop-outs and (12) Non-credit social and cultural courses in such areas as arts, crafts, consumerism, fitness, financial planning, health, and retirement planning.[3] There are also correspondence courses offered directly by the Ministry of Education.

The colleges, or CEGEPs, are also serious in their commitment to adult education and often have a department of adult education. Their activities serve 100,000 students and are varied, including not only part-time programs leading to the diploma of college studies and individual courses in culture and recreation activities, but also intensive workshops and short-term certificate programs in a variety of fields such as languages, administration, running a small business, computer applications, and new industrial techniques.

Another groups of adult learners are those enrolled in formal university programs. In the fall of 1984, there were 31,000 adults, 25 years of age and older, enrolled in bachelor's programs in Quebec universities (29% of all undergraduate students) and another 44,000 enrolled in certificate and diploma programs, (83% of the total). Women represented slightly over half (50.7%) of new students in a first degree program in 1983 and 57.5% in certificate programs. Part-time students tended to be concentrated in such programs as administration (30%), education (26%) and social sciences (20%). Finally, 12% of new students in 1983, who entered bachelor's programs, were admitted on the basis of equivalent experience rather than the formal requirement of a diploma of college studies. Equivalent experience was the basis of admission for 63% of those entering certificate programs.[4]

Despite difficulties in defining who is an "adult student" at the university level, these figures suggest that (a) adults (25 years of age and older) form a significant part of undergraduate enrolments, (b) short-term part-time certificate programs attract a larger proportion of adult students, (c) women are present in greater proportions in part-time than in full-time programs, (d) three-quarters of the part-time clientele are concentrated in three major program areas (administration, education and social science), and (e) substantial number of new university students are admitted to programs on the basis of maturity and equivalent experience rather than normal academic qualifications.

There are five institutions of higher education in Quebec that have made special contributions to formal adult learning over the years. Sir George Williams University (now part of Concordia University) in Montreal began as part of the YMCA in 1926, granted its first bachelor's degrees in 1937 and became a university in 1959; as a college and university, Sir George Williams pioneered evening courses for adults in Quebec, at both secondary and college levels, and there are thousands of university graduates today who would never have received a university degree except for the services and resources offered by this institution. Second, the Thomas More Institute was founded by a group of English Catholics in 1945 and since that time has provided intellectual stimulation for many, and B.A.'s for some who wished them, based on a discussion format and a study of the Great Books in the tradition of Hutchins and Adler. Third, the University of Quebec campuses, established in the late 1960s and 1970s, have provided certificate and degree programs to many adults in different regions of the province who would have been unable to attend courses in the major urban centres. Fourth, the creation of the Faculty of Continuing Education of the University of Montreal in 1974 gave adult education a new status within the structure of a traditional university, and together with the department of adult learning (*andragogie*) in the Faculty of Education, it provided a focus for the study and practice of adult education. Fifth, the work of Macdonald College of McGill University in adult education should be acknowledged, especially for the rural and agricultural communities of Quebec.

In addition to the adult education programs and courses offered by the school boards, colleges, and universities, there are a large number of private institutions which serve the adult population, some funded in part by the Ministry of Education, many holding permits but receiving no support from public funds. These include such institutions as commercial colleges, secretarial schools, and specialized trade schools providing courses in everything from hairdressing and computer programming to bartending and real estate. There are schools of dance and music, institutes of yoga, fine arts, judo, soccer and hockey and as well as charm schools, ceramic workshops, language schools and fitness institutes. Some of these institutions have a short life span, riding the wave of a specific and transient fad, while others are more enduring, establishing a reputation and often diversifying their service beyond their original purpose. These private institutions bring diversity and choice to the landscape of adult education in Quebec.

Non-Formal Programs

Non-formal adult education includes learning services and resources provided by public or private organizations as secondary activities to their primary functions. These can be grouped into five broad categories: (1) Economic programs offered by business and industry, unions and professional organizations; (2) Cultural programs sponsored by libraries, museums, literary organizations and community centres; (3) Communications through print and electronic media and the new information networks and data bases; (4) Government and professional resources offered by various agencies and departments, professional corporations, social services, and political parties; (5) Voluntary organizations bringing together persons who share a common interest – women, religion, the environment, a local community, civil rights, and so on. There is enormous variety in these non-formal activities, in their objectives, structures, learning programs, services, and resources.

The first category of non-formal activities are those which are *economic* in orientation. This includes a wide range of training programs which major business and industrial enterprises have organized for their employees. Banks, Bell Canada, Hydro-Québec, Via Rail, and high-technology manufacturing and service enterprises have special training programs for the initiation of new staff, retraining programs to update current staff in new techniques, and programs for the training of managers and executives. Many companies also make use of contracts with independent consulting and training groups, such as International Correspondence Schools and Techart, which provide both courses and French-language materials, and with institutions like Lasalle College which is involved in many training programs in business and industry. Learning services are also offered by various small mangement consulting firms and university-based or college-based groups specializing in industrial relations, management skills, small business management, and the quality of working life. In some large companies, these activities have a permanent structure and staff and they account for a major investment of funds in the development of human resources.

Important adult education activities are involved when a company brings in management consultants to recommend improvements, when business enterprises must launch a new product or service or engage in major reorganization, expansion or contraction. Some manufacturers – especially those like Northern Telecom in high-technology fields – often provide training programs for customers of their products; other enterprises sponsor educational materials and learning services directed to the general public, dealing with issues like conservation, nutrition, safety or the creative use of leisure time.

Other adult education programs are sponsored by economic organizations such as the board of trade, the chamber of commerce, the advertizing and sales clubs, the stock exchange, investment brokers, and tax accountants. Labour unions have been offering training programs to their members and sponsoring adult education and research through structures such as the Canadian Labour College founded in 1963.

The cooperative movement is also active in adult education. The first credit unions (*caisses populaires*) were established in 1900 and the number and influence of banking, farmer, consumer and insurance cooperatives have grown dramatically over the years. In 1963, the Desjardins Cooperative Institute was created to provide programs for the training of managers of credit unions and cooperatives. The Desjardins cooperative movement is active in cooperative education programs for the public and in assisting developing nations in the establishment and organization of cooperatives. University programs in cooperative education are offered by the Universities of Montreal and Sherbrooke and by Télé-Université.

Cultural programs of adult education include those which are organized around certain cultural resources such as museums and libraries and some that are sponsored by cultural organizations or groups of performers. Although Quebec has been behind the rest of Canada in library facilities, over 80% of the population are now served by a network of 120 independent municipal libraries, 19 public libraries. and almost 650 municipal libraries affiliated with 11 central libraries. There are 172 bookstores in Quebec including 12 English and 14 bilingual ones. Most of the libraries and many of the bookstores sponsor discussions, exhibitions, and presentations.[5]

Quebec has over 800 cultural centres, including concert halls, cultural and artistic centres, and 124 museums, as well as summer theatre, archives, and exhibitions halls. Natural science facilities include 70 botanical gardens, zoos, bird sanctuaries, aquaria and experimental farms. There are 500 arts and crafts studios, 240 theatres, 170 dance studios, and 140 art studios for painting and sculpturing. Finally, there are over 2,000 locations for social events, community recreation centres and local halls.[6]

These facilities are used by over 570 groups; half of these are theatre groups, followed by music and dance groups and associations with a particular historical, religious or ethnic focus. There is probably a much larger number of groups, many of which have not sought government grants or otherwise come to public attention. Many of these groups take part in the 150 or so festivals which occur each year. These cultural activities are supported annually by over 20 Quebec government ministries and agencies to an extent of $251 million. The combination of cultural resources and active participants offers rich opportunities for adult education, not only for those directly involved but also for the audiences whom they reach with their work.[7]

Another important and exceedingly influential system of adult education is the network of *communication*, both print and electronic media. Quebecers are served by 12 daily newspapers, including two in English, with circulations ranging from under 7,000 to over 300,000. There are almost 200 weekly newspapers, 15 of them in English, about 90 general periodicals (26 in English or another language) and 140 specialized magazines, (60 in English or another language).[8]

Electronic media include 120 radio stations, and 30 television stations, not counting American radio and television stations that are available throughout much of Quebec.[9] A great deal of print has been produced and consumed about the educational potential of television, especially in the area of values and attitudes. For many people, radio, and especially television are the major source of adult learning in our society, intended and explicit or unintended and implicit. Since 1968, Radio-Quebec has been a major network for educational television and in a limited way parallel to TVOntario and Public Broadcasting in the U.S., both of which are also available in Quebec through cable television facilities.

The communications media, both print and electronic, have served to extend Quebecers' perceptions of the world and of themselves, to link remote parts of the province with the mainstream, and to shape political, economic and social attitudes. Newspapers and magazines, through regular features and special series, help Quebecers understand complex current events and increase the range of ideas and attitudes from which they may choose in shaping their own lives. Through radio and television, adults have powerful and attractive learning resources which often provide different role models, style and ideas to those commonly imported in regular commercial radio and television from the United States and other parts of Canada.

Two other communication systems are growing in importance and potential for adult education: video clubs and computer-based information networks. The educational potential of video-clubs has yet to be realised, especially when we learn that the films in greatest demand are horror and "adult" films. Recently, however, there has been an increasing number of educational videos on the market, especially in such fields as cooking and fitness.[10] With the increase in the number of home computers, the potential of data bases and information networks for increasing access to learning services is virtually unlimited.

A fourth source of adult education is found in the range of *government and professional* services offered to Quebecers. In the past two decades, all levels of government, federal, provincial and municipal, have been more generous in the materials which they have produced for general information – ranging from basic information about services and how to obtain access to them, data about Canada, Quebec, different regions and municipalities, to detailed guides to everything from safe driving to trout fishing, house insulation to fitness. Furthermore, political parties, beyond their activities of partisan and promotional nature, have contributed to public education through their engagement of major contemporary issues facing Quebecers. They stimulate public debate on such crucial and sensitive issues as cultural development, exploitation of natural resources, relations with other regions of the continent, language policy, minority rights, urban development, and the just distribution of wealth and opportunity. From time to time, professional corporations have also entered public debate on issues concerning their professional competence – the civil rights implications of impending legislation, public health hazards of pollution, the dangers of fad diets, the consequences of insensitive urban renewal, the plight of the homeless, the abused and the poor. Spokespersons for the churches, the bar association, and other professional bodies have brought a different perspective to the public awareness of current issues.

At the community level, the health, legal and social services provided by the CLSC's (Centres locaux de services communautaires) have been a major point of contact, reference and help for many persons, especially those experiencing a personal crisis. All of these resources and activities, of governments and professions, add an official and expert dimension to the adult education activities which are available and they should be included in any comprehensive treatment of adult education in Quebec.

A final group of non-formal resources and services are those sponsored by *voluntary organizations* throughout the province. There are about 1,000 voluntary associations recognized by the Ministry of Education as OVEP's (Organisations volontaires d'éducation populaire), not counting the many more that have not sought official recognition or funding. In 1985-86, grants of over $12 million were given to various organizations.[11] Some of these groups are provincial in scope; others are restricted to a specific area or urban district. Some are primarily educative in purpose, seeking the development of their members and/or the enlightenment of the general public on a certain issue; others are primarily political, directed to pressure and public action to further a particular cause.

Voluntary organizations in Quebec have roots that go back over 100 years to the founding of the Mechanics' Institute in 1828, the *Institut canadien* in 1844, and the YMCA in 1851. During the second half of the last century, many voluntary associations were formed, usually centred on a religious and cultural community such as the Jews, the Irish and the Scots; these associations usually had various purposes – social activities, charitable works, religious commitment, cultural conservation, and often athletic activities. Another type of voluntary organization arose in the rural areas, bringing together farmers to work for programs of common interest. There was an urban counterpart of these groups, a variety of private clubs and associations based in a common occupation, or a common social and economic status. Both secular and religious voluntary organizations expanded during this century and each changed in character as the nature of their clientele shifted and as other bodies entered the field.[12]

Two major developments took place in the 1960s which changed the role of voluntary organizations. The first was the creation of citizens' committees in Montreal which brought together people in a district or across districts to promote improvements in living conditions and quality of life, especially better and low-cost housing, improved health services, better schools, and more recreational facilities. Many of these groups were the inspiration for others which formed to promote literacy training for adults, assistance for the physically and mentally handicapped, defense of minority rights, environmental protection, consumer advocacy, and improvement in the quality of life and opportunities for women. All of these groups are to some extent on the boundaries of political and educational activities; their programs usually involve the raising of the consciousness of their members, making the public more sensitive to an issue (usually through public relations and the use of the media) as well as influencing policy makers in government or the private sector to respond to the objectives of the group. These groups are generally organized as networks, much in the pattern of similar movements in the United States.

A second major development in the 1960s was the entry of the provincial government into the field of voluntary organizations. The government assumed many roles: as the body seen to be in control of policy decisions to whom appeal must be made, as the sponsor of many activities in the education field formerly left to voluntary initiative, as a source of funding for voluntary groups, and as the authority seeking to coordinate and institutionalize adult education in the society. Many of the adult education groups came together to form a coalition to resist budget cuts for adult education in the early 1980s and to react to new government policy proposals in 1984.

The major associations whose primary mandate is adult education include the Institut canadien d'éducation des adultes (ICEA), which since 1970 has been the major catalyst for voluntary adult education in Quebec, and the Quebec Association for Adult Learning (QAAL), the major English group promoting adult learning. There are numerous other organizations bringing together workers in the field of adult education and community development, as well as other bodies such as labour unions, teachers' associations, some post-secondary institutions, and farmers' groups which are closely involved with the voluntary sector of adult education. White it is impossible to estimate with any confidence the number of adult Quebecers influenced by the work of voluntary organizations, or the nature of the influence they exert, this groups of organizations form an important part of adult education services in Quebec. If current trends to reduce the role of government in social life continue, the voluntary sector will likely take on a new significance.

The Vision of the Jean Commission

A major event in the development of adult education in Quebec began in 1980 when the government established a study commission on adult education, formally called the *Commission d'étude sur la formation professionnelle et socio-culturelle des adultes*, and commonly known as the Jean Commission after the chairperson, Michèle Jean. The commission's mandate was to prepare a comprehensive policy for the education of adults.

The commission consulted widely, held 20 regional sessions, received 276 briefs, published a 367-page working document in 1981, held a symposium attended by 400 persons, and in 1982 published a final report entitled *Learning: A Voluntary and Responsible Action*, a summary report, and 5 appendices. The report was divided into six parts: historical background of adult education in Quebec, basic education, accessibility to adult education, participation and structure. The report contains no fewer than 430 recommendations dealing with all areas of policy, structure, target populations, programs, finance, and strategy.[13]

The report began by establishing the context of adult education and developing the following principles: (a) society should enable individuals to develop their full potential; (b) adults should have a right to education without distinction of sex, age or occupation; (c) this right to education should be defined in a general law and should be at least the equivalent of 13 years of schooling; (d) adult education must be made more democratic, encouraging individuals and groups to assume responsibility for their learning. To respect these principles, adult education, structures and services must become more accessible, they must change their image and practices, and they must be more open to participation by the clients they serve.

Adult education should be centred on the basic education of all adults. This includes learning how to learn, relating to time and space, assuming social roles, introduction to science and technology, openness to the philosophical and spiritual aspects of life and to major ideological trends, understanding of the workings of the economy, familiarity with political institutions, knowledge of the working world, making decisions and working in groups, introduction to the arts, awareness of the body and of health, and occupying leisure time.

Special steps should be taken to improve accessibility to adult education, especially for certain target groups such as young unemployed adults, older persons who have retired, immigrants, women, handicapped persons, native people, adults in prison, and those who are completely or functionally illiterate. Inequalities of access to education should be reduced: first in schools by giving adult learners equal importance to young learners; second, in the workplace by opening up policies for study programs, through access to professional corporations and regulated trades, and in retraining programs following plant closings and mass layoffs; third in the cultural field of media, museums, conservatories, and recreation. Attention should also be given to reducing disparities in adult education among different regions of Quebec.

The images and practices of adult education have to be transformed by removing barriers between sectors and disciplines, by recognizing experience and achievement as equivalent to formal schooling, by encouraging "project learning" evaluated by "continuing education credits," by changing teaching practices to respect more fully the experience and maturity of the adults, and by deschooling learning structures. Other methods are improving the way academic institutions serve the public and the world of work, expanding the services of distance education, promoting self-education and educational research, and improving the sensitivity and professional competence of both adult educators and teachers working at all levels of the regular school system.

The participation of adults in the design and development of their learning programs should be encouraged. Public and private enterprises with more than 20 employees should be required to create training committees to determine training requirements and to prepare, implement, and evaluate training plans on an annual basis. Adult learners in educational institutions should have the right to participate in defining goals and developing procedures and they should also be adequately represented on policy-making bodies. The autonomy of voluntary community groups should be respected and they should be represented on bodies that allocate resources and establish policy. Schools and municipalities should cooperate in making their facilities widely available.

Changes should be made in the general administration and management of adult education in order to give greater priority to the planning and support of adult education. There should be a single agency in the Quebec government responsible for adult education. In the first phase, there should be a minister responsible for adult education to draft a general law, integrate the different adult education sectors in the Ministries of Education and Manpower, establish regional structures and negotiate control over federal job-related training programs. After three years, an Office of Adult Education should be created, responsible to a department such as the development of human resources, with a coordinating committee representative of interested ministries and a board of directors widely representative of both producers and consumers of adult education services. This body would be responsible for determining needs, planning, providing resources, coordinating activities, leadership, evaluation and research.

Administration at the regional level should be decentralized and Regional Centres for Adult Education should be established (CREA), (Centres regionaux d'éducation des adultes), one in each urban community and 15-25 for the rest of the province. Each centre should have a board of directors composed of local citizens and representatives of public institutions involved in adult education. Their function should be to identify regional needs, assess resources, develop plans, encourage participation, disseminate information and report on adult education activities in the region. The centres should offer educational "brokerage" services (SRAR, Services d'accueil et référence) to advise individuals and groups on programs.

The financing of adult education should include a system of loans and bursaries available to unemployed adults for academic and professional training of all types. Priority should be given to basic education, especially literacy programs. All companies should be required to allocate 1.5% of their total payroll to personnel training. Special funding programs should be established for community groups involved primarily in education and for education programs of unions. Educational institutions should be required to allocate at least 2% of their operating budgets to community services.

There is no doubt that the vision of the Commission on Adult Education was imaginative and daring. It was warmly received by most adult educators and by those who looked for a general policy that would support – in law – the rhetoric of continuing education that until then had seldom left the domain of pious intentions. It was supported by those who were frustrated with the patchwork of structures and jurisdictions and by those anxious about the financial vulnerability of existing programs. There was considerably less warmth in the reaction of the formal education system, the business sector, and cost accountants.

The essence of the recommendations was threefold: a new priority, visibility, and legal status for adult education on a par with other education sectors; the unification of provincial structures and coordination of effort, balanced by decentralization of specific policies and services; a broad commitment of many bodies including federal and provincial governments, educational institutions, private enterprise, and the diverse organizations and programs active in continuing education. It was an imaginative and ambitious plan with little chance of realization.

Structures, Priorities, and Jurisdiction

If the original mandate of the Jean Commission was framed at a time of economic growth and faith in grand plans, the final report came at a time when the economy was in recession, unemployment was high, resources were limited and the government had other things on its mind besides adult education. In 1984, two years after the report of the Jean Commission, the government issued *Continuing Education Program: Policy Statement and Plan of Action*, prepared under the joint authority of the Minister of Education, the Minister Responsible for the Status of Women, and the Minister of Manpower and Income Security.[14]

The policy statement (a) approved the general philosophy in the Jean Commission report, (b) adopted a structural and pragmatic approach to the issues, (c) transferred manpower training programs completely to the Ministry of Manpower and Income Security, (d) abolished the section on adult education in the Ministry of Education, (e) integrated adult education activities into school board and college operations, and (f) identified priority areas in basic education and vocational training.

The major challenge, according to the policy statement, was that while Quebec was attempting to develop an advanced economy and a high-technology society, in competition with other regions, 2 million Quebecers age 15 and over – almost half the 15+ population – were not in school and did not have a secondary diploma. Furthermore, almost 3/4 (1,300,000) of these had less than 9 years of schooling, and almost 300,000 of them (7% of the 15+ age group) had not completed 5 years of schooling. 15% of adult Quebecers (18+) were reading and writing rarely or never, including almost 200,000 who were for practical purposes illiterate.[15] Priority must be given to basic education and to "qualifying" training, programs that lead to formal diplomas or an equivalent social recognition.

The proposed government policy was based on twelve major objectives:

(1) to confirm the adult education mandate of the schools and training centres of various government departments;

(2) to urge various departments to define and publicize the objectives and methods of their programs;

(3) to give adults access to regular educational programs on the same conditions as the young;

(4) to promote an effective response to the educational needs of adults through (a) individualized structures, (b) diversified settings and educational practices, (c) a system of recognizing past educational achievements, (d) distance education and (e) the training of adult educators;

(5) to reinforce efforts to encourage people to continue their studies and to provide them, especially women, with adequate information on career choices;

(6) to confirm the mission of school boards and voluntary organizations to provide community education;

(7) to confirm the role of public education in manpower training and upgrading, especially in relation to programs, services, supervision and recognition of achievement;

(8) to recognize the mandate of the Ministry of Manpower and Income Security to supervise and implement manpower programs, and to transfer the funding of such programs from the MEQ to MMIC; in return, equipment and furnishing used by MMIC agencies in training will be transferred to the MEQ;

(9) to underline Quebec's demand for exclusive jurisdiction and control of funds allocated by the federal government for manpower development;

(10) to promote a partnership to improve the accessibility to and quality of on-the-job training, a partnership between workers and management, and between private enterprise and the education system;

(11) to promote new methods of apprenticeship and cooperative education;

(12) to decentralize the administration of manpower development programs to regional Vocational Training Commissions (CFP, commissions de la formation professionnelle).

The policy statement went on to propose the creation of an interdepartmental committee with representatives of five Ministries: Status of Women; Industry, Commerce and Tourism; Manpower and Income Security; Science and Technology; and Education. Its mandate was to recommend budgets and new directions. Other structural changes were to include better coordination between Ministries of Education and Manpower, better collaboration at the regional level between public education and the vocational training commissions (CFP), and the creation of integrated drop-in and referral services for adults.

The statement concluded with a set of priorities. In the education sector these involve better support for adults wishing to return to secondary or college studies, adapting services to the needs of adults, better support for daycare to aid women continuing their studies, and the development of vocational and technical training programs in the light of manpower policies. In the manpower sector, the priorities were to integrate women into non-traditional sectors, to train manpower in areas key to technological change, to respond to shortages in expanding areas, to prepare "free-enterprise" managers, retrain personnel in weak economic sectors, help employees to upgrade their training to retain their jobs, and improve the qualifications of the underprivileged. In the community education sector, priority was to be given to increasing funding to non-profit organizations working in community education, supporting community projects for underprivileged and unemployed young adults, providing basic training for the functionally illiterate, promoting both social and occupational integration of handicapped persons, and improving resources to help women return to school or work.

Needless to say, there were many who were distressed about the direction of this policy statement, believing that the spirit of the Jean Commission had been seriously undermined, first by dividing rather than by integrating government responsibility, second, by shifting power from the Ministry of Education to Manpower, third, by absorbing adult education within public education, a reversal of the normal spirit of continuing education, and fourth, by laying heavy stress on pragmatic, economic and manpower priorities.

One key area was that of structure and responsibility. Since 1966, there had been a section in the Ministry of Education, first called Continuing Education and 1973 renamed Adult Education (Direction générale d'éducation des adultes, DGEA). There had also been overlap, confusion and no little competition between the adult education activities of the Ministry of Education and the manpower programs under the jurisdiction of the Ministry of Manpower and Income Security.

Since 1969, Vocational Training Commissions had been established (Commissions de la formation professionnelle, CFP), with 11 formed by MMIS throughout the province on a regional basis. Their role was clearly defined in a manpower vocational training act of 1983. They had equal representation from employers and employees and they had the mandate to make agreements with educational institutions or to offer courses directly in apprenticeship, vocational training, upgrading, or retraining. The Ministry of Manpower was also responsible for agreements with the federal government on manpower training, the latest being *an Act to establish a national program for occupational training* passed by the federal government in 1982.

Despite much talk of the need for unity and coherence in blending academic, popular and vocational programs, the following were stark realities: (1) Economic development is priority number one in Quebec and, thus, vocational training has higher priority than programs of personal or cultural development; (2) Two-thirds of the Quebec adult education budget is in vocational training; (3) 80% of these funds for vocational training come from the federal government; (4) Funding is now primarily the responsibility of the Ministry of Manpower, nor Education; (5) The Ministry of Manpower "pays the piper and calls the tune," and the Ministry of Education interprets the music and plays the pipes.

Since the publication of the policy statement in 1984, the government has proceeded to implement the different proposals. Responsibility for vocational education was transferred from the Ministry of Education to the Ministry of Manpower and Income Security; the former section of adult education within the MEQ was closed down and most of the personnel transferred to the MMIS. A section on adult education was incorporated within the general structure of preschool, elementary and secondary education and the personnel in adult education in the MEQ dropped from 170 to 30.

The adult education activities of the Ministry of Education are now largely the following: (1) grants to voluntary organizations (OVEPs) and unions engaged in popular education; in 1984-85, almost $8 million was given to 961 organizations and 14 unions, an increase of $3 million from two years before (2) development of regional drop-in and referral services for adults (SRAR's) and coordination of adult education programs offered by universities, colleges and school boards in each regions; (3) establishment of an organization for distance education and the creation of new correspondence courses; (4) coordination with other ministries on organization and funding of vocational education, promotion of basic adult education, and encouragement of means of evaluating programs and granting academic recognition for experience.[16]

It is possible that some of the concern with the government response to the policy proposals of the Jean Commission was lessened when Michèle Jean was appointed deputy Minister of Manpower and Income Security.

Continuing Education, Continuing Challenge

Quebec's continuing education policies remain ambiguous. The UNESCO concept of "lifelong education and learning" as an "overall scheme aimed both at restructuring the existing education system and at developing the entire educational potential outside the education system" clearly appeals to Quebecers' inclination towards structures, coherence, logic and organizational elegance. So does UNESCO's view of continuing education as a scheme in which "men and women are the agents of their own education, through continual interaction between their thoughts and actions."[17] On the other hand, there is no doubt that such a philosophy, if taken seriously in policy, funding, and organization, would radically transform the present education structure and would also have profound effects on the learning activities that are taking place in the non-formal sector of voluntary organizations, cultural institutions, business, and other groups. It would be a challenge to the formal sector of elementary, secondary and post-secondary institutions to rethink their role, and their importance, as "the first stages" of ongoing learning services; it would be a challenge to the non-formal sector of organizations and institutions to rethink their role, and the freedom they enjoy, as they move into closer alignment with the formal sector and with a broader social policy for the development of Quebec's human resource potential. This is the challenge that continuing education offers to the existing formal and non-formal learning institutions of Quebec society.

Nevertheless, adult education, with or without a general policy of continuing education, is challenging and being challenged by the formal sector. The population is aging. The under 20 age group is becoming a less significant population. The learning needs of the adult population are increasing, in basic skills and advanced competence, and special groups – young adults, the unemployed, new managers, retired persons– are pressing their demands for learning services at a time when the demand for regular elementary, secondary, and soon post-secondary programs declines. The individual learning needs of adults are being reinforced by the social needs of Quebec society for trained workers and professionals in key economic sectors, for general as well as specialized skills, and for a broadly educated adult population. Yet it is not evident, based on the survey of adult education activities in 1983, that these individual and collective needs of Quebec are being adequately addressed or that present policies show promise of improving the situation. As the education system declines, adult education is becoming a growth area and one that is going to require more attention.

Adult education is Quebec is also an area that continues to be vulnerable, caught as it is in larger political agendas, a bargaining point between conflicting federal and provincial jurisdictions, dependent on yearly funding fluctuations, and staffed mainly by volunteers and part-time professionals. It is competing with powerful pressure groups of teachers' unions, school boards, private schools and post-secondary institutions, all naturally preoccupied with their own survival.

This formal sector is now moving into the field of adult education, seeing in adults both new clientele and new opportunities to maintain facilities and employ teachers. This is leading more in the direction of institutionalizing all learning than in the direction of "deschooling" and diversifying learning activities central to the concepts of continuing education and the learning society.

Notes

1. Canada, Secretary of Sate and Statistics Canada, *One in Every Five: A Survey of Adult Education in Canada.* (Ottawa, 1985); Canadian Association for Adult Education, *An Analysis of the Statistics Canada Adult Education Survey, January 1984* (Toronto: CAAE, 1985); Quebec Association for Adult Learning, "Adult Education in Quebec" (Montreal, QAAL, n.d.; Institut canadien d'éducation des adultes, "La participation à la formation des adultes au Québec en 1983," (Montreal: ICEA, 1985); Conseil supérieur de l'éducation, *L'Accessibilité du système d'éducation aux adultes* (Quebec, 1986).

2. Ministère de l'Education, *Statistiques de l'éducation: préscolaire, primaire, secondaire* (Québec, 1985), p. 59-66.

3. Provincial Organization of Continuing Education Directors – English, *A Guide to English Language Adult Education Services in Quebec, 1985-86).*

4. Conseil supérieur de l'éducation, *Les adultes dan les programmes reguliers de l'université: Des etudiants à part entière* (Québec, 1985), p. 6-12.

5. Québec, *Le Québec statistique, Edition 1985-86,* (Québec, 1986) p. 464, 473-475.

6. Ibid., p. 467-470.

7. Ibid., p. 486-488.

8. Ibid., p. 945, 952-953.

9. Ibid., p. 946-947, 953.

10. Ibid., p. 965, Tableau 19.

11. Québec, Ministère de l'éducation, *Rapport annuel 1984-1985*, p. 23.

12. For the history of adult education in Quebec, see: Commission d'étude sur la formation des adultes (CEFA), *L'éducation des adultes au Québec depuis 1850: Points de repère*, Annexe 1 of *Apprendre: Une action volontaire et responsable*, Report of the Jean Commission (Québec: CEFA, 1982).

13. Commission d'étude sur la formation des adultes, *Adult Education in Quebec: Possible Solutions. Work Document.* (Quebec: CEFA, 1981); *Apprendre: Une action volontaire et responsable*; *Learning: A Voluntary and Responsible Action – Summary Report*; *Annexe 1, L'éducation des adultes au Québec depuis 1850: Points de repère*; *Annexe 2, Sondage sur les adultes québécois et leurs activités éducatives*; *Annexe 3, Sondage sur les pratiques de formation en enterprise*; *Annexe 4, Recherches connexes de la Commission*; *Annexe 5, Bibliographie annoteé sur la formation des adultes*, (Québec: CEFA, 1982).

14. Quebec, *Continuing Education Program: Policy Statement and Plan of Action* (Quebec, 1984).

15. Ibid., p. 12-13.

16. Québec, Ministère de l'Education, *Rapport annuel,1984-1985*, p. 23-25, 27.

17. Quoted in CEFA, *Learning: A Voluntary and Responsible Action – Summary Report*, p. 7.

7

Teachers and Teaching:
Organization, Preparation, Research

Considering the major changes that have taken place in Quebec education over the past twenty-five years, it is not surprising that teachers and their profession have undergone a comparable transformation. They increased in number and in their academic and professional qualifications. Their professional organizations became more effectively organized and more powerful. Their working conditions have become more standardized and codified. Teachers have achieved improved legal status, lower pupil-teacher ratios, better security, more equitable renumeration, and a wider range of benefits. The state of the teaching profession has been the subject of numerous and extensive studies; policies related to their initial preparation and professional development have been debated almost continuously. The traditional stereotype of the Quebec teacher as a member of a religious order bound by vows of poverty, chastity, and obedience has changed into another stereotype, more secular, militant, ambitious, independent and middle class. The importance of the teachers in Quebec's educational reform and the dignity of their social mission have inspired a substantial body of rhetoric.

At the same time, teachers and their organizations have been under a variety of pressures during this period: to transform a traditional elementary and secondary system into a modern education structure, to adapt to new types of organization, to prepare new curricula, to adopt modern methods, and to improve their own qualifications. Their associations shifted emphasis from voluntary and vaguely professional priorities to organized activity that attempted to combine the demands of professional service with the requirements of a union working under the Labour Code and a complex collective agreement. At times, the associations assumed the characteristics of a political pressure group. Their rising confidence and expectations regularly brought them into conflict with the school boards that employed them and with the powerful provincial government that controlled resources. These conflicts were frequently accompanied by work interruptions (euphemistically called "study sessions", strikes, emergency legislation and imposed settlements. Teachers have had to cope with a rapid and enormous expansion in enrolments and then with precipitous decline leading to a climate of stress, insecurity, disillusionment, burn-out, and for many, career changes. Every criticism of the poor quality of education was laid at their classroom door. Since 1960, the teaching profession in Quebec has become stronger in some ways and in others weaker, with a status and image that remain essentially ambiguous.

143

Profile of Quebec Teachers

If we think of the teaching profession in its broadest terms, it encompasses almost 100,000 teachers in Quebec. This includes over 60,000 public elementary and secondary school teachers working for Catholic or Protestant school boards, 5,000 teachers in private elementary and secondary schools, 400 teachers working in special federal schools and in schools for the blind and deaf, 12,000 instructors in colleges (CEGEPs) and 8,000 professors in universities. To these must be added the many people working full-time or part-time in adult education courses, in training programs in business and industry, in public and private day-care centres, in the production of educational materials, print and electronic, as well as those working as educators for voluntary religious, cultural, public health, fitness, athletic, and community development organizations.

Yet we customarily think of the formal teaching profession as the group of legally certified teachers working in the field of public elementary and secondary education, members of a professional teachers' organization, and governed by the conditions of a provincially negotiated collective agreement. This group represents over two-thirds of the total and is the one group for whom we have the most complete information. A 1984 report of the Superior Council of Education on the condition of the teaching profession gives the following statistical profile of Quebec teachers in the year 1983-84.

- There were 67,000 public school teachers.
- 51% of teachers worked at the preschool and elementary levels and 49% at the secondary level.
- 2,700 teachers (1 teacher in 25) were on availability (surplus) list, and 4,500 (1 in 15) were on leave (maternity, pre-retirement, illness, etc.)
- Almost 2/3 of teachers (64%) were women. Women constituted 87% of preschool and elementary teachers but just under 40% of secondary teachers.
- The average age was just under 40 (compared to 38 years in 1978) and teachers had the following age distribution:
  7% were under 30 years old
  47% were between 30 and 40 years
  33% were between 40 and 50 years
  11% were between 50 and 60 years
  1% were over 60 years
- On the average, women teachers and those working at preschool and elementary levels were younger in comparison to men and those in secondary schools. Montreal teachers were generally older than those in other parts of the province.
- The average teaching experience was just over 17 years, and the distribution was like this:

17% had under 10 years experience
48% had between 10 and 20 years experience
29% had between 20 and 30 years experience
6% had over 30 years experience.

– The average number of years of academic and professional preparation (*scolarite*) was 16, with the following pattern:
21% had 14 years or fewer
13% had 15 years
20% had 16 years (usually a bachelor's degree)
22% had 17 years
13% had 18 years
11% had 19 years, or 20 years with a doctorate.

– 28% of elementary school teachers had minimum qualifications (14 years of education or fewer) compared to 14% of secondary teachers. On the other hand, 35% of secondary teachers had advanced qualifications (18 years or more of education) compared to 14% of elementary teachers.

– Major trends in the qualifications of teachers between 1974 and 1984 were: (a) a significant decline in the number of teachers with minimum qualifications (14 years or fewer) from 40% to 20%; (b) stability of those with middle-level qualifications (16 years) at about 20%; (c) an increasing proportion with advanced qualifications (18 years or more) from under 10% to over 20%.

– In 1983-84, teachers' salaries ranged from a minimum of $18,000 for a teacher with 14 years of education in the first year of teaching to a maximum of almost $42,000 for one with 20 years of education, a doctorate and 15 years of experience. In the category of 15 years of experience and 16 years of education (in general, a bachelor's degree), Quebec salary scales were 7th among the 10 provinces, above New Brunswick, Newfoundland and Prince Edward Island (Alberta was first, Ontario 6th).[1]

Another profile of Quebec teachers can be drawn from an extensive survey of teacher attitudes conducted in June 1978 by the research branch of the Ministry of Education. A questionnaire of 424 items was distributed to a sample of 4,000 teachers in Quebec, elementary and secondary, public and private, French and English. 70% of those contacted responded. The questions covered a wide range of issues and the results were published in nine volumes. The following is a small sample of some of the attitudes of Quebec teachers.

– 65% of married teachers had a spouse with a full-time job.

– 30% never or rarely attended religious exercises and another 35% attended services once a week.

– 80% of teachers expressed general satisfaction with their work and 75% said that, given a choice to do it over, they would still become teachers.

– The factors teachers thought most contributed to teaching success were classroom experience and personal effort in preparing and organizing work.

- Fewer than 1 teacher in 10 thought preservice programs helped them to relate to parents, assist children with learning problems, or understand changes introduced in schools; 93% of teachers called for a more practical pre-service program.

- 81% thought teaching had more stress than other professions, 77% that it required more human relations skill, and half that it was more tiring; only 46% felt it was more prestigious than other professions.

- 55% of teachers took no active part in union activities and another 19% considered themselves quite active; teachers were split on whether union militancy was a threat to professionalism: 34% agreed and 44% disagreed.

- 65% said they very often or always used the same content and pacing for the whole class, 16% used individualized methods and 12% had learning groups within the class;

- One-half of teachers felt they did not have adequate teaching materials, 41% believed that a good text was as effective as an instructor and 44% thought group instruction was preferable to individual instruction.

- Fewer than 40% were prepared to say that the three R's were more important than other things; 90% thought that teachers should develop all the talents of children, not mainly their intellectual abilities; over 80% worried that curriculum did not allow enough time for the less gifted pupils and felt that children should learn at their own rate even if they could not cover the whole curriculum.

- 82% of teachers believed that secondary school students were required to specialize too early and a substantial majority believed that students should spend more time with one teacher, even at the secondary level.

- Only 6% were in favour of the current confessional division of school boards but there was no general agreement on what would be better.

- 58% thought French as a second language should begin in grade one but only 47% thought the same about English as a second language.

- Only 13% described their schools as innovative though 80% cautioned that rapid change in schools should be avoided; almost 80% thought schools should have greater autonomy.

- 53% thought there were too many pupils who did not want to study, 51% thought that too often pupils were disinterested in their work and only 39% were satisfied with their pupils' motivation; 90% thought pupils were leaving school without acquiring much of a taste for reading.

- 57% of teachers thought that only a minimum of brilliant students could profit from university; almost 70% thought that the differences among pupils were the result of environmental factors rather than heredity.

- Only 42% believed they could rely on parents for help if there was a problem and 48% felt parents showed a general lack of understanding.

– 35% believed there were strained relations between younger and older teachers and 56% thought many teachers were not strict enough; 55% said that the teachers in their school preferred to work alone but 62% felt that teachers were generally interested in participating in decisions concerning the school's goals and policy.

– 73% said they used their intellectual abilities in their work, 79% felt they had a chance to be creative, 88% agreed that they had complete freedom in running their class.

– Only 44% believed a teacher could influence the way the school system was run and only 47% thought they could influence the way the school was run.

– 1 teacher in 5 would send his or her children to private elementary schools and over half would send them to private high schools, if they were able to do so.

– Almost 60% of teachers believed that schools conveyed the values of the dominant class in society, 64% thought teachers should refrain from discussing politics in class, and 50% said they never discussed political questions in class.

– Half of the teachers thought that the minimum level of schooling necessary for everyone was full secondary education; 87% agreed that young people should be taught discipline, determination and the meaning of work.

– 2 teachers in 5 considered the most important task of the school to be the training of the gifted for leadership.

– 54% thought that education was given too much importance in hiring and 89% felt that the possession of a diploma was far from being the best guarantee of competence in work.

– Over half felt that too much importance was being given to the search for new ways of teaching and fewer than half were of the opinion that changes in the previous 15 years had improved the quality of education.

– Half thought that school translated social inequalities into educational equalities and 44% believed that only a radical transformation of the economic and political system could solve the educational problems of the underprivileged.

– 38% were optimistic and 26% pessimistic about the future of the teaching profession; 38% said that life in school was so remote from the ideal that they despaired for the future and 35% felt that there was not much that could be done to solve major school problems.[2]

These results showed a profile of the teaching profession in 1978 that was divided in its opinion about basic educational values, pulled by conflicting conservative and progressive –even radical – inclinations, concerned about its place in society, and anxious about the quality of education. They also showed a thoughful and serious approach to educational issues. Given the slight turnover in the teaching profession in Quebec since the late 1970s, it is likely that many of these attitudes still prevail among teachers, with traditional inclinations perhaps etched more deeply and anxieties considerably intensified. Despite the power of education structures and the intentions of policy makers, the processes of formal education are filtered through what classroom teachers think, feel, and believe.

The Evolution of Teachers' Associations

There are three provincial teachers' associations in Quebec: the Centrale de l'enseignement du Québec (CEQ) which groups teachers and some other employees in French-language schools; the Provincial Association of Protestant Teachers (PAPT) whose members are teachers and other professionals working for Protestant school boards; and the Provincial Association of Catholic Teachers (PACT) for teachers working in Catholic schools where the language of instruction is English. Each of these provincial associations is made up of local teachers' associations ("syndical units") for teachers in a particular school board or region.

The PAPT has the distinction of being the oldest teachers' association in Canada, founded in 1864. At first it was a general education association including in its membership school commissioners, university professors, civil servants and church leaders, but over time it came to be restricted to certified teachers. Since 1945, membership has been automatic for all teachers in the Protestant school system. The CEQ began in 1946 as the *Corporation des instituteurs et institutrices catholiques du Quebec* (CIC), a professional organization of lay teachers in French Catholic and some English Catholic schools. It changed its name in 1967 to the *Corporation des enseignants du Quebec* (CEQ) and again in 1973 to the present *Centrale de l'enseignement du Quebec* (CEQ) because its membership also included other workers in education besides teachers. The third association, PACT, was founded in 1962 and received its charter in 1969. It serves the interests of teachers working in English-Catholic schools.

For the three associations, their local organizations, and their members, the period since 1960 has been one of turbulence, change, reorientation and conflict. Between 1963 and 1971 the number of teachers increased from 54,000 to 71,000 (+30%), the per cent of teachers with less than 15 years of training dropped from 83% to 44% and those with less than 5 years experience fell from 42% to 18%. These changes in size, qualifications and experience were accompanied by a rapid secularization of the profession in the Catholic system: in 1960, 38% of teachers were members of religious orders while in 1967 this had dropped to 14%.[3]

A second important development during the 1960s was the unionization of the profession. In 1959 only a few teachers' associations held labour certificates, but by 1972 almost all did. The first "modern" collective agreement was signed in 1960 between the Montreal Catholic School Commission (the largest in Quebec) and its English and French teachers. This included a variety of articles on salaries, working conditions, fringe benefits, teacher-pupil ratios, and union rights. In 1964, the Labour Code of Quebec was amended giving teachers and civil servants the right to strike, a right that teachers were to use freely; of the 26 teacher strikes in Canada during the 1960s, 21 were in Quebec[4].

Third, as negotiations between teachers and their employers expanded in scope and became more intense, the arena for negotiation and eventual agreement or legislated settlement shifted from local school boards to the provincial level. As the educational expansion in Quebec progressed, costs mounted sharply and so did the share paid for by the Government of Quebec. A crisis was reached in 1967. In October 1966, the Ministry of Education published guidelines for school boards in their negotiations with teachers. Between November 1966 and February 1967, over 13,000 teachers in the Catholic system went on strike, supported by Protestant colleagues who held "study sessions" and threatened mass resignations. On February 19th, the Assembly passed *An Act to Ensure for Children the Right to an Education,* commonly known as Bill 25, the first of what was to be a series of laws and decrees imposing settlements in labour disputes in the field of education.

Bill 25 did three things: (1) it ordered the teachers back to work, solving the immediate crisis; (2) it imposed a single salary scale for most teachers in the province, wiping out existing disparities among regions as well as differences between various types of teachers, male and female, elementary and secondary; (3) it set up machinery for bargaining at the provincial level between the three teachers' associations on the one hand (CEQ, PAPT, PACT) and two federations of school boards, Catholic (FCSCQ) and Protestant (QAPSB), and the Provincial government on the other.

The results of this Bill were the following: the government made a substantial advance in its goal to standardize educational structures and to strengthen its control over expenditures, at the expense of school board autonomy; the three provincial teachers' associations gained negotiating and political power at the expense of their local units; and the three associations were forced into a sometimes uneasy alliance in their dealings with school boards and government. It took almost three years following Bill 25 for the parties to sign a first collective agreement (November, 1969).[5]

Labour relations between teachers and government were equally turbulent during the 1970s and 1980s. Negotiations took place every three years and generally lasted from six months to a year. Study sessions, rotating strikes, full strikes, and a common front with other public sector employees punctuated educational development during the period. Collective agreements were imposed by government decree more often than they were arrived at by collective bargaining.

A number of factors made relations between government and teachers seriously strained: government awareness of its power as both employer and final arbiter of labour relations; the general power of the Ministry of Education and its inclination to extend and exert control; the growing militancy of teachers and their growing radicalism in social policy, especially in the French sector. Other factors were the frustration and anxiety among teachers about enrolments and job insecurity, pressure on the government from an economic recession and competing claims for financial resources, a complex structure of negotiations at the provincial level, and the cumulative effect of increasingly intricate and complicated collective agreements.

During the school year 1982-83, the government and school boards were unable to come to an agreement with their teachers, especially on matters of job security and salary. The problem was made more serious by the government's financial difficulties and its proposal to reduce teachers' salaries to ease the fiscal crisis. In response to teachers' strikes the National Assembly passed Bill 111 in February 1983. The bill (1) ordered teachers back to work, (2) removed the right to strike until December 31, 1985, (3) threatened to dismiss without further procedure any teacher who did not return to work, (4) made the teachers responsible for proving their own innocence, and (5) made unions responsible for making sure their members complied with the law. The Bill also specified penalties and fines for teachers who did not obey the law, and (6) suspended the application of the Quebec Charter of Rights as it might have applied to the issue.

Following the teachers' return to work and attempts at further negotiation and conciliation, a set of decrees defined new working conditions for teachers. The major features were: (1) new salary schedules implementing temporary reductions of about 17%, (2) a progressive increase over three years of the numbers of hours per week (subsequently modified through negotiations), (3) changes in the procedures for determining which teachers were to be declared surplus, and (4) reduction of salary and workload to 80% for teachers in their second and third years of surplus.

There can be little doubt that the periodic crises of negotiations and conflict have affected the climate and development of education during the period. It is easy to blame a rigid system, a domineering government, an indifferent public or an insatiable profession, but the matter is more complex than this. By the mid-1980s, however, there were some hopeful signs that the various partners in education were attempting to make their own positions more flexible, their expectations more realistic, and their relations less adversarial.

The major preoccupations of teachers and their associations at the present time include the following: job security in the face of declining enrolments; the rights of teachers to be involved in educational policy-making; support for adapting to curriculum change and serving pupils with learning difficulties; ways of reducing the stress which an aging teaching profession is experiencing; and means of improving the quality of educational services.

The decline in school enrolment during the 1970s and 1980s was in dramatic contrast to the rapid expansion of the 1960s. Between 1970 and 1983, elementary and secondary enrolments dropped from 1.6 million to 1 million, a decline of one-third. During the same period, the teaching force went from just under 70,000 to 64,000, a decline of 7% and the pupil-teacher ratio dropped from 22.9:1 to 16.5:1. In 1984-85, almost 1,600 teachers were on surplus, which means that they were paid salaries but were without a permanent teaching position. Different assignments from supply teaching to resource personnel were used to absorb most of these surplus teachers, but the situation remained serious. Even though global enrolments are expected to stabilize at just under the 1 million mark until the mid-1990s, some areas will be affected more than others, especially secondary education, vocational programs, Montreal schools, and English-language institutions. Enrolments in English-language schools on the Island of Montreal are expected to decline from 72,000 in 1983 to 53,500 in 1988, a drop of one-quarter in six years. This poses problems of reassigning teachers in their areas of teaching competence, it means there are few openings for new and younger teachers, and it presents a major challenge of maintaining staff morale and renewing an aging teaching force.[6]

Teachers have also been seeking rights to participate in decision making, both at the provincial level on issues of general policy and at the local level on matters affecting school board operations and school policy. While certain rights of consultation have been granted, the interpretation and limitations of consultation have sometimes resulted in disputes and in missed opportunities for cooperative ventures. At the same time, considerable ambiguity exists in the relative rights of government and school boards to develop policy, of administrators to apply policy, of parents and sometimes students to express their expectations as clients, and of teachers to employ their professional judgment.

Teachers have also had to cope with a comprehensive reorganization of the curriculum from kindergarten to the end of secondary school, with detailed programs, new teaching materials, and more systematic evaluation. Many teachers feel that the new programs have been implemented without sufficient preparation and too quickly; as a result, teachers have not been given sufficient assistance, materials, and resources to prepare for the new courses they are expected to teach. To some extent the same criticism is made about efforts to mainstream children with learning difficulties. In 1985, there were over 100,000 children with various learning disabilities and handicaps, over half of whom were integrated into regular classes. This was and is an added challenge for many teachers who often had neither the training nor adequate support services to cope with them.

It is not surprising, then, that many teachers are suffering the symptoms of stress and that the phenomenon of teacher burn-out is becoming common. All of this is occurring in a climate of continuing criticism about learning in public schools, the level of achievement of secondary school graduates, student mastery of the basics (especially language competence) and the development of serious habits of study. In the centre of all this turmoil is the teacher and the teaching profession facing a government anxious to reduce the public debt. The challenges facing the teaching profession show every indication of continuing into the future.[7]

Laws and Regulations

The teaching profession, unlike others, is not governed by a professional code which recognizes the right of a professional corporation to determine conditions of entry, professional conduct, discipline of members, and rules of serving the public. Instead, the teaching profession is governed by a series of laws and regulations, and by the provisions of a collective agreement signed by the three teachers' associations, the two federations of school boards, and the Quebec government.

In more precise terms, the legal status of teachers, their rights, and responsibilities, are determined by the following: (a) the Education Act of Quebec; (b) certain provisions of the Labour code of Canada; (c) certain provisions of the Civil Code of Quebec, the Criminal Code of Canada, and the Canadian and Quebec Charters of Rights and Freedoms; (d) Regulations 4 and 5 of the Ministry of Education dealing with the certification and classification of teachers; (e) the general curriculum regulations (*régimes pédagogiques*) governing preschool, elementary and secondary education; (f) certain articles of the Regulations of the Catholic Committee and the Protestant Committee; (g) the general Collective Agreement (*Entente*) determining working conditions for all public school teachers in Quebec; (h) special local agreements signed between a local teachers' association and an individual school board; and, finally, (i) a more or less extensive body of directives, operating procedures, policies and practices determined by a school board or an individual school, usually in consultation with the teachers and their associations. Thus, there is considerable uniformity in status and working conditions for all public school teachers in Quebec as well as some diversity in local policy and practice.

Although the *Education Act* is the basic framework of legislation for public education in Quebec, fewer than 20 of its over 700 articles deal with teachers or those "holding a pedagogical or educational position." These articles deal in very general terms with the following issues: a complaint to the minister against a teacher and the procedures to follow (Art. 18); cancellation of a teachers' contract by school commissioners (Art.190); the engagement and non-reengagement of teachers (Arts. 200-211); the right of boards to transfer teachers to another class, school or position (Art. 212); the duty of teachers to report pupil absences (Art. 278); and two forms, one for the engagement of teachers (Form 17) and one for informing teachers that their services are no longer required (Form 18). [8]

Bill 3 (1984) which was adopted in December 1984 to replace most of the existing Education Act, but which was subsequently judged unconstitutional by the Quebec Superior Court (1985), had a chapter on teachers which contained 29 articles. These made explicit the teachers' right to participate in formulating school policy, to enrich the program, to choose instructional methods and to refuse to give denominational religious or moral instruction. [9]

The *Labour Code* of Quebec includes teachers in its general provisions:

assuring the right of associations, the procedures for forming bargaining units, the rights of individuals and unions, the procedures of collective bargaining and dealing with grievances, and the conditions pertaining to a legal strike. The *Criminal Code* of Canada contains certain provisions governing the use of "reasonable force" by school teachers and other persons standing in the place of a parent, the criminal responsibility for the excessive use of force, as well as criminal negligence. The *Civil Code* of Quebec contains a number of relevant provisions dealing with the responsibility of persons for damage and the rights and duties of parents and guardians in respect to their children. There are also numerous other Acts of the Province of Quebec which have specific implications for teachers (Acts incorporating professional associations, special legislation in relation to collective agreements, etc.). The Canadian *Charter of Rights and Freedoms* and the parallel Quebec Charter protect teachers from discrimination and protect their rights as citizens..[10]

A second layer of the legal structures concerning the teaching profession is that of regulations or Orders-in-Council approved by the Council of Ministers (Cabinet) of the Quebec government. Two of these regulations deal specifically with teachers: Regulation No. 4 on teacher training and permits (1966) and Regulation No. 5 on teacher classification for salary purposes (1968). Regulation No. 4 provides for two kinds of teaching authorizations, a temporary permit valid for five years for those entering the profession and a permanent license (or certificate) issued to those who have held a permit and have complete two years of teaching deemed to be competent. The regulation also calls for the establishment of a Teacher Education Committee, but this was allowed to lapse a number of years ago. Regulation No. 5 outlines general policies for recognizing academic and professional studies for the purpose of determining salary categories (years of schooling). It defines a year of full-time study as the equivalent of 30 credits (1 credit = 45 hours of lectures, practical work, study, and assignments). It also provides guidelines for recognizing part-time studies and establishes certain principles for granting equivalences for studies taken outside Quebec.[11]

Two general curriculum regulations (*régimes pédagogiques*), one for preschool and elementary education and the other secondary education, provide detailed guidelines which define a teacher's roles and responsibilities. During the 1960s and 1970s, government guidelines for curriculum were general, brief, and open-ended – leaving to individual school boards, schools and teachers considerable latitude in interpreting goals, constructing programs, selecting teaching materials and adapting curriculum to the needs of their pupils. The curriculum regulations of the early 1980s and the individual subject programs developed in virtue of these regulations went a long way in centralizing and standardizing curriculum design across Quebec. They substantially reduced the role of the individual teacher in curriculum development. At the same time, program changes, combined with declining enrolments and delays in the production of supporting material, have all served to complicate staff assignments and increase the number of teachers who find themselves working with unfamiliar subjects, often with little preparation, advanced notice, or assurance that they will have the same assignment the following year. These problems are especially acute at the secondary school level and in small school boards.[12]

There are two other regulations which affect a certain aspect of the teacher's role: the regulations of the Catholic Committee and Protestant Committee dealing with religious and moral education. The regulation for Catholic schools requires that personnel in such a school "respect its confessional character" and they should be Catholic if possible, though non-Catholics may be hired. Teachers may ask to be exempted from religious instruction. The regulation of the Protestant Committee is less precise in terms of who may teach in Protestant schools, but the regulation also guarantees the freedom of teachers to be excused from religious instruction.[13]

The Collective Agreement

The basic document covering the rights and responsibilities of teachers is the *Collective Agreement* between the teachers' associations and the school boards. There are three such agreements, one for PAPT, one for CEQ, and one for PACT, although the general structure and major provisions of all three agreements are worked out in negotiations at the provincial level or imposed on all associations by government legislation. Some minor variations in procedures and school organization (such as dates for holidays) are established locally between teachers' associations and school boards.

The collective agreements are substantial documents. The Agreement for Protestant schools for the period 1983-1985, for example, contains 269 pages, 12 chapters and 27 appendices. The chapters deal with (1) definition of 43 terms; (2) field of application and recognition of unions, boards, and associations; (3) union prerogatives including communication, union delegates, released time for union activities, and deduction of dues; (4) procedures for consulting with teachers; (5) conditions of employment and fringe benefits, engagement and dismissal, leaves of absence, and pensions; (6) renumeration, classification, evaluation of years of schooling, and recognition of experience; (7) professional improvement; (8) workload, organization of classes, teaching time, and responsibilities; (9) procedures for settling grievances and arbitration; (10) general provisions concerning the agreement and its interpretation; (11) teachers in adult education, and (12) special provisions for teachers in remote regions. The appendices deal with various forms such as contracts and certain technical procedures.[14]

According to the agreement the general duty of the teachers is "to provide learning and educational activities to pupils and to participate in the development of student life." The teacher's "characteristic responsibilities" are listed in the following manner:

> "1-to prepare and present courses and lessons within the guidelines of the authorized programs;

2- to collaborate with the other teaching and non-teaching professionals of the school in view of taking the appropriate measures to meet the individual needs of pupils;

3- to organize and to supervise socio-cultural, sports and recreational activities;

4- to assume the responsibilities of a teacher-specialist in guidance for pupils;

5- to assume the responsibilities of a teacher-librarian for pupils;

6- to organize and supervise industrial training periods in collaboration with the companies of the community;

7- to assume the responsibilities of "encadrement" (advising, home room teacher) of a pupil or a group of pupils;

8- to evaluate the performance and progress of pupils for whom he is responsible and to so report to the school administration and to parents according to the system established after consultation with the appropriate body;

9- to supervise the conduct of the pupils for whom he is responsible and that of the other pupils when they are in his presence;

10- to monitor the late arrivals and the absences of his pupils and to so report to the school administration according to the system established after consultation with the appropriate body;

11- to participate in meetings relating to his work;

12- to perform other duties which may normally be assigned to the teaching personnel." (Art. 8-1.02)

The number of teachers that may be employed by a school board or assigned to a school is determined by a series of average and maximum group sizes for different categories of pupils. These are as follows:

Category	Average	Maximum
Preschool	15	18
Elementary (1-3)	25	27
Elementary (4-6)	27	29
Special classes	5-15	7-19
Secondary (gen.)	30	32
Secondary (voc.)	10-30	13-32

The average determines the total number of teachers that may be employed by a board. The maximum fixes the largest number of pupils that may be placed in a certain teaching group; under certain circumstances (e.g. lack of qualified personnel), these maxima may be exceeded but the teacher is compensated according to a fixed formula. (Art. 8-2.02, 8-2.03). Teachers are expected to be present in school for the equivalent of 27 hours per week and for 200 days per year. The teacher's workload ("services rendered directly to pupils") is 23 hours per week at the preschoool and elementary levels and 20 hours per week at the secondary level. (Art. 8-3.03, 8-4.02, 8-4.04).

Full-time teachers are engaged by a school board for a contract of one year; this contract is automatically renewed unless the teacher or board indicates otherwise. The contract of a teacher who is not legally qualified is automatically terminated on June 30th. A teacher who has two full years of continuous service with a board has tenure with that board and security of employment, even if the number of pupils decline and the teacher is declared surplus.

Teachers may be assigned to a school or transferred by a board within a 50-kilometer radius of their present school or residence. According to the collective agreement, the assignment of teachers must take into account the needs of the school system, the particular characteristics of the school or class, and the qualifications, experience and preferences of the teacher. In practice, a teacher meets these criteria if he has a specialized diploma or the equivalent of one year's teaching experience in the assigned area. Furthermore, for general preschool and elementary school subjects, for high school English, social science. or economics, or junior high school mathematics or science, a general teaching diploma is considered a qualification. (Art. 8-8.02, 8-8.03). Some teachers' unions feel that this gives too much arbitrary authority to school administrators; on the other hand, some critics are concerned that the conditions are too vague to ensure that the needs of schools and learners are served by teachers assigned to their fields of academic and professional competence.

A board may dismiss a teacher, that is, terminate his contract, for one of the following reasons: incapacity, negligence in the performance of his duties, insubordination, misconduct or immoral behavior (Art, 5-7.01). A board may decide not to re-engage a tenured teacher, that is, not renew his contract for another year, for any of the reasons mentioned above or because of a surplus of personnel. In both cases, dismissal and non-reengagement, there are provisions for appeal, filing a grievance and seeking arbitration. In fact, teachers are rarely dismissed, partly because of the difficulty of proving such causes as misconduct, negligence or incapacity, partly because effective policies of evaluating teachers are rare, and partly because of the length, cost, and complexity of the process.

A school board must determine its provisional staffing needs for the coming academic year before April 1st of each year. When an excess of teachers is anticipated in a particular teaching field, the teachers with the lowest seniority (continuous experience in the board) are declared to be "on availability." In general, a teacher's standing in a board or a school is determined by two factors: teaching field and seniority with the board. There are 6 teaching fields at the preschool and elementary level, 13 in general subjects at the secondary level, and 3 at combined elementary-secondary levels. Teaching fields in secondary vocational education are determined by the board and teachers' association In the collective agreement for teachers in the French sector, 34 teaching fields are identified.

For purposes of renumeration, teachers are classified according to two criteria: number of years of academic and professional education (minimum 14, maximum 20) and number of years of experience (maximum 15). The classification of teachers' schooling (*scolarite*) is determined by the Ministry of Education according to the principles enunciated in Regulation No. 5 and the current manual for evaluating years of schooling. There is a single salary scale for all Quebec elementary and secondary school teachers, regardless of location, level of teaching, sex or teaching specialty. In 1982-83, the structure of the salary scale for Quebec teachers included the following: 7 categories for years of schooling and 15 years for experience. Salaries range from approximately $18,000 (14 years of schooling, 1st year of teaching) to $42,000 (20 years of schooling and 15 years of experience). In addition to the basic salary, teachers have a number of fringe benefits including maternity and other leaves, sick leave, and a pension plan that offers a maximum of 70% of an average of the best five years' salary to teachers who reach a maximum of 35 years of teaching recognized by the Quebec government (no minimum age for those with 35 years).

These provisions of the collective agreement are supplemented by a number of local agreements between school boards and teachers' associations and by various policies at the level of the school board and school. These provide some degree of variation in teachers' working conditions from one place to another.

Because of this structure, teaching in Quebec may be regarded as an over-regulated profession with teachers working within concentric circles of rules, regulations and laws. A good deal of energy, time, money, and imagination is devoted to the elaboration of structures, their management, the negotiation of their alteration, and to finding ways of getting around them so that teaching and learning can proceed. There is a sense of fatalism and legalism among many teachers and administrators in relation to prospects for change, the pursuit of quality, and the value of initiative. There are clear lines drawn, and often adversarial relationships, between teachers who are unionized and administrators who are considered part of management and separate from teachers. The general instability in a system that has been declining has led to a climate of anxiety among teachers. The general instability in a system that has been declining has led to a climate of anxiety among teachers about their chances of having a permanent assignment, to patterns of "bumping" less senior teachers, and often to constant movement from one assignment to another.

After two decades of complex structures and turbulent relationships, it may be time to consider a new model for promoting the goal that all parties claim to espouse – improvement of the quality of learning service for children and young people.

The Preparation of Teachers

Since the beginning of the Quiet Revolution in education, one continuing preoccupation of educators and policy makers in Quebec has been the academic and professional education of teachers. Since 1964, there have been over 25 major studies and policy statements on teacher education by the Ministry of Education, various consultative councils, and professional associations, – not counting the hundreds of individual studies, conferences, colloquia, surveys, working documents and responses to other documents.

The preservice preparation and the inservice development of teachers constitute an important sector of the overall system. A study by the Council of Universities of education programs in Quebec for the academic year 1983-84, provides this picture of teacher education. In 1983-84, there were 28,000 students in teacher education programs, a drop of 4,000 from 1977 figures; they represented 12% of total university enrolment in Quebec. One-half of these students were enrolled in bachelor's programs and one-third in one-year certificate programs. There were also 3,000 master's students and 600 doctoral students. 60% of the students were enrolled in part-time programs. The same year, Quebec universities graduated 7,000 students in education, including 4,000 with bachelor's degrees and 2,600 with certificates, many leading to one of the 72 different teaching permits and diplomas issued by the Ministry of Education.

Twelve institutions offered 392 programs in the study of education, and over 650 professors had appointments in faculties, departments and schools of education. The largest teacher education programs were at UQAM (7,000 students registered), Montreal (4,000), Laval (3,500), Sherbrooke (2,800) and UQTR (2,400). For English education there were McGill (1,800), Concordia (1,200) and Bishop's (16). Students could choose from 112 certificate programs, 162 bachelor's programs, 10 graduate diplomas, 88 master's and 20 doctoral programs.[15]

Twenty years earlier, the structure of teacher education in Quebec was very different, sharing the general characteristics of Quebec education of that era: separation between Catholic and Protestant systems and Church control in the Catholic sector. In the Catholic system, most teachers were prepared in normal schools which offered certificate programs for secondary school graduates and, in some cases, a four-year Bachelor of Pedagogy program in affiliation with a university. In 1962-63, there were over 100 normal schools in Quebec; 11 of these were operated by the government including the St Joseph Teachers College, which prepared English-Catholic teachers. The remainder were operated by religious orders. In that year, there were 1,700 professors in these schools, 13,000 students, and 4,000 new teachers were graduated. Teachers for the Protestant system were trained in two institutions: McGill University's Institute of Education at Macdonald College, which had 38 professors, just under 700 students and about 275 graduates in 1962-63 and Bishop's University in Lennoxville which has one full-time professor and 18 students in a one-year program for university graduates. The French-language universities of

Laval and Montreal had no faculties of education, but they did have affiliated institutes (*Instituts pédagogiques* and *écoles normales supérieures*) which offered advanced degrees in education (counseling, administration, theory) and specialized programs for preparing teachers for secondary schools and classical colleges. Similar programs were offered in the Faculty of Education of the newly founded University of Sherbrooke.[16]

When the Parent Commission published Volume II of its Report in 1964, it made a number of recommendations about the reform of teacher education. It proposed that the universities assume responsibility for all teacher education; that the minimum entrance requirement for training programs be raised to 13 years of schooling (two years of college); that programs be of either one-year duration for university graduates or three-year duration leading to a bachelor degree; and that the practical component of student teaching be increased to an average of one month per year of training. Other recommendations were that teacher education be coordinated by a special committee established by the Minister of Education; and that a distinction be made between an interim permit granted at the end of an initial program and a permanent certificate granted after successful completion of a period of probation. Thus, the Parent Commission established the agenda for the transformation of teacher education, a process that was to wax and wane over the next two decades.[17]

In response to the recommendations of the Parent Commission, the new Ministry of Education produce a series of regulations in the mid-1960s including Regulation Number Four, "Respecting the Permit and the Licence to Teach," in March 1966. This regulation (a) established 13 years of schooling as the minimum level of admission to a training program; (b) determined that programs may vary but must include the equivalent of one year of professional studies, including psychology, teaching methods, and classroom practice; (c) created teaching permits, valid for five years, which would be granted by the Ministry to graduates of approved programs; (d) required a period of probation of two years before this permit could be converted into a permanent teaching license; and (e) called for the creation of a Teacher Education Committee to advise the Minister on such matters as the recognition of teacher education institutions, the definition of teaching competence, and the approval of training programs. Following this regulation, guideline were developed for programs and procedures for the supervision of teachers on probation. Despite initial efforts to organize probation for new teachers, the structure of probation did not work very well; there were variations from board to board in how seriously the procedures of assistance and evaluation were taken and there was also opposition on the part of some of the teachers' associations, especially the CEQ, to a policy of having some teachers evaluating other teachers. The teacher education committee was established, did some work, was reconstituted and then allowed to lapse, due in part to uncertainty about its mandate, reservations on the part of some of the participants, more pressing priorities facing the government, and a tendency to find specific means of dealing with particular issues affecting teacher education.[18]

One of these pressing matters was the process of integrating the existing normal schools into the universities. Between 1964 and 1968, the number of normal schools dropped from over 100 to 53 and, at the same time, the universities moved to establish faculties of education based on the model of the United States and English Canada, generally embracing initial teacher education, upgrading, and graduate studies within a single institution. During the same period, new colleges were created to provide public pre-university and technical programs after secondary school and the University of Quebec was founded with campuses in various parts of the province. Between 1968 and 1971, the normal schools disappeared: some were closed by the religious orders that ran them; some became secondary schools; some became integrated into a college. Others formed the nucleus of a constituent of the University of Quebec (such as at UQAM, the Université du Québec à Montréal) – usually in partnership with a classical college and an institute of technology, and a few were integrated into existing faculties of education (at Laval, for instance). The major English-language normal school, the St. Joseph Teachers College in Montreal, was amalgamated with the Faculty of Education of McGill and the new faculty was relocated on the main Montreal campus of McGill in 1970.

During the 1970s, teacher education institutions faced two major challenges: developing preservice and inservice programs to meet the needs of an expanding teaching profession and finding their appropriate place within the environment of a university. Following government guidelines which were elaborated in virtue of Regulation Number Four, faculties of education developed three-year bachelor of education programs for the preparation of elementary and secondary school teachers, the latter usually in cooperation with other university faculties. In some institutions, the patterns were concurrent, melding professional and academic studies; in others, students pursued academic studies in a major area and came for professional training towards the end of their program. In addition, universities developed a variety of part-time degree and certificate programs designed to assist practicing teachers adapt themselves to new tasks and to help them upgrade their academic and professional qualifications for salary purposes. Master's and doctoral programs began to develop in educational theory, and in such professional areas as guidance, special education, administration, and educational technology.

The transition of staff and programs from normal schools to universities was smoother in Quebec than in many other places where this kind of transfer took place. This was due to three factors: enlightened policies of the government which assisted normal school teachers to obtain advanced qualifications, mainly at the doctoral level, the flexibility with which the integration was managed in different institutions, and the rapid evolution of university institutions, especially the newly created University of Quebec, during this period.

Toward the end of the 1970s, problems developed in some areas. These included the sharing of responsibility for teacher education among government, universities, professional associations and school boards; discontent on the part of many teachers with the services of professional development they were receiving from the universities; the ineffectiveness of the probation system in achieving its original goals; lack of adequate and substantial practical components in many teacher education programs; and a certain ambiguity in the position which teacher education units occupied within the structure of universities.[19]

In 1977, the government created a commission to study the university system (Commission d'étude sur les universités). As part of its final report in 1979, one of its committees presented a report on teacher education and professional development. The committee examined various philosophical orientations of teacher education; the education of teachers in the context of continuing education; the various roles of Ministry, universities, and school boards; and educational research. The committee underlined the need for diversity in teacher education, made various suggestions for strengthening programs, supported the importance of teacher education units within universities, and called for closer liaison within universities and between universities and the school system.[20]

During this same period in the late 1970s, the Ministry was embarking on a massive reorganization of the curriculum of elementary and secondary schools and beginning to take steps to align teacher education programs with the competencies need to teach these programs. The Ministry published a series of "orientation documents" proposing guidelines for reorganizing teacher education programs for preschool and elementary school teachers (1977), and for special education, secondary and specialist teachers (arts, second language, physical education) (1980). These guidelines sought to move programs in the direction of broader areas of competence, emphasis on instructional techniques more than theory, skills in dealing with students who have learning difficulties and more time devoted to practical experience on campus and in schools. These documents raised some questions about the importance of specialized academic training and general professional skill, and about the responsibilities of universities and the government to determine needs and set objectives for teacher education programs. In general, however, teacher education programs in the universities were reorganized along these general lines[21]

The universities are responsible for the development, management and quality of teacher education programs. The Ministry of Higher Education, establishes general guidelines which programs must follow, approves individual programs for purposes of certification, and grants temporary teaching permits to those recommended by the universities.

There are three general categories of programs in education: initial programs of teacher education for those wishing to enter the profession, inservice programs for practicing teachers wishing to upgrade their qualifications or expand their range of competence, and graduate studies leading to master's and doctoral degrees. Initial teacher education programs are of two types: three-year programs leading to a Bachelor of Education degree for those who have completed collegial studies, and programs, one or one and one-half years in duration, for university graduates. Students in these programs normally select one of the following areas of specialization: preschool and early childhood education (kindergarten to grade three), elementary education (grades one through six), academic secondary education with concentrations in one or two subjects areas, vocational education in technical or business subjects, or specialist teaching in an area such as fine arts, second language, physical education, or teaching the handicapped and children with learning difficulties. All initial teacher education programs must normally include courses in psychology, child development, educational theory (philosophy or sociology of education), and knowledge of the Quebec school system. Also required are a course in teaching methods related to the area(s) of specialization and a course in adapting teaching to the needs of children with learning difficulties. The program must include the equivalent of 18 credits (more than one semester) of practical experience, usually in the form of an internship.

The universities offer a wide range of courses and programs for the continuing education of practicing teachers. Most of these are given on a part-time basis and lead to a bachelor's degree or to a certificate. Almost all certificate programs are the equivalent of 30 credits or one full year study. They offer training in such areas as special education, reading instruction, second language teaching, educational technology, and the teaching of individual subjects. Most universities offer various graduate programs leading to a master's degree in education administration, counseling and guidance, educational psychology, educational technology, theory (comparative education, philosophy of education, etc.) and elementary and secondary school teaching. These programs and those offered at the doctoral level are generally governed by the regulations of the university's Faculty of Graduate Studies and Research or its equivalent. Practicing teachers also have the opportunity to follow non-credit courses and workshops on practical teaching problems, sponsored usually by school boards and/or teachers' associations.

In 1983, the Ministry tabled yet another document on the planning of teacher education, "La formation et le perfectionnement des enseignants du primaire et du secondaire: vers des amenagements, Fiches de discussion" (June 1983). This document dealt with five major issues: the sharing of responsibility for teacher education among the Ministry, the universities, school boards and professional associations; the professional and practical components of teacher education; the probationary system; the legal right to teach and teaching permits; and inservice professional development. This document invited and received reaction from the Superior Council of Education and the Council of Universities, teachers' associations, and various universities.[22]

As we move into the second half of the 1980s, Quebec is still trying to come to grips with balanced and realistic policies to provide quality training for new teachers, and a system of professional support to help those in the profession adapt to rapidly changing demands. Also of concern is an appropriate sharing of responsibilities among the groups directly concerned with the quality of teachers – the government that provides resources and must guarantee competence, universities that must offer the programs and ensure quality, school boards that hire the teachers, and professional associations that must protect the interests of their members and clients.

Meanwhile, faculties and departments of education have seen their numbers drop in many programs in recent years and they have sometimes felt themselves neglected and underappreciated in their universities. They have been accused of being remote from the real needs of the teaching profession in the school system. In its 1986 report on education programs, the Council of Universities raised a number of critical issues. Programs are fragmented and often over-specialized; there is lack of coordination both within universities and among institutions; education professors are caught between the culture of their universities and the world of public schools. There are many programs with small enrolments, with 50% of education courses having fewer than 21 students with one-third with fewer than 11 students. There is no coordination among enrolments in initial programs for new teachers, inservice programs for practicing teachers, and policies for assigning teachers in the school system. Most popular programs are in areas where there are surplus teachers and there are few students in programs leading to areas needing qualified specialists (e.g. second language, mathematics and science). Universities have not included teacher education among their priorities.[23]

Despite the many studies concerning teacher education, confusion and ambiguity remain. Between 1979 and 1983, the universities have produced 15,000 new teachers while there have been only 6,000 openings for new teachers in public schools – 60% of them filled by experienced teachers. On the other hand, it is estimated that 50% of all Quebec teachers (32,000) will retire in the 15-year period between 1985 and 2000. No steps are being taken to increase the supply of qualified teachers in key areas such as second languages, mathematics and sciences. Concerns with the quality of public education are not clearly linked with policies for improving the quality of teachers, or with policies for evaluating quality. The proportion of initial teacher education programs devoted to practical experience are often very limited and in many institutions the quality of supervision is uneven. Some believe that teacher education programs are light and uninspiring in content, others that they should be lengthened because there is so much to be learned. Some favour more general preparation so that teachers will be more adaptable in periods of change, while others argue that academic specialization should be strengthened. Teacher education in Quebec faced one set of challenges in the 1960s and early 1970s; it is clearly facing another set of challenges for the 1980s and 1990s.

Educational Research

Like other aspects of education in Quebec, educational scholarship has evolved rapidly in recent decades, expanding in scope and becoming more diversified in content and method.

Prior to the 1960s, educational scholarship in Quebec was largely in the humanistic tradition, with many excellent historical and philosophical studies. The Parent Commission in the early 1960s was a catalyst for educational research, launching an era of sociological and political analysis of the educational system: comparative studies with other societies, analysis of demographic patterns and educational attainments of various social groups, and studies related to learning processes and teaching methods.

Throughout the sixties and seventies, educational research continued to expand because of a number of factors: the encouragement and support of the provincial government through grants and bursaries; a program of retraining normal school professors in doctoral studies, often outside of Quebec; the integration of normal schools into universities; and the expansion of graduate programs in education in Quebec universities which trained a new generation of educators in research skills. Many of these graduates found careers as consultants in school boards, professors in colleges, and researchers in government and in various educational organizations. Educational research also benefitted from two important structures which the government specifically created to foster research. The first was a structure created in 1970 to distribute research funds to university scholars and graduate students engaged in research projects (FCAC, Formation de cherchers et à l'action concertée, now called FCAR). The second project was the founding of INRS (Institut national de la recherche scientifique) in 1972 as an affiliated institute of the Université du Québec; this institute established a separate section for educational research in 1975 which continued until 1986 when it was dissolved.[24]

At the present time, there are important research activities taking place throughout the system. First, there is the research work of the Ministry of Education and the Ministry of Higher Education and Science. The Ministry of Education has a planning and development section with a directorate for research and development (Direction générale de la recherche et du dévelopment) In 1986-87, this directorate had a budget of just under $2.6 million and a staff of 56. In 1985-86, the research and development unit analyzed the financing of school boards and did forecasts of enrolments. It also engaged in studies of performance indicators, values of youth, policy analysis and program evaluation. The branch maintains a computerized data base of research studies called EDUC and information on careers. In the field of adult education, studies were done on literacy, the recognition of experience, training programs for adult educators, and study leave. The second major activity of the government is the support of educational research through the funding of professors and students in the FCAR (formerly FCAC) program and other specialized programs, operated by the Ministry of Higher Education.[25]

Educational research is also conducted by a number of public councils and institutes such as the Superior Council of Education, the Council of Colleges, and the Council of Universities. Each year, the Superior Council publishes an annual report on the state and needs of education as well as a dozen briefs and studies of specific topics such as alternative schools, teacher education, student needs, adult education and curriculum. These are usually based on existing studies, surveys, interviews and visits. From time to time the Council has also sponsored major studies on such subjects as the participation of parents in school, the teaching profession, values, and equality of educational opportunity. The two councils for colleges and universities commission conducted studies related to post-secondary education.

Major participants in research in education are the faculty members and students of the province's colleges and universities. In 1983-84, grants and contracts for educational research in faculties and departments of education amounted to $7.3 million. Major sources of funding were the Quebec government (64%), federal government (19%), school boards and other educational institutions (11%), foundations (4%), non-Canadian sources (2%). The most important source of research funds from the Quebec government were: first, two specialized programs of the Ministry of Education (one for teachers of French, first language and one for teachers of vocational areas) and the research grants program administered by the Ministry of Higher Education (FCAR). MEQ and FCAR grants for educational research are roughly equal in size. Most of the educational research support from the federal government comes through funding agencies in science and engineering (in the area of physical education) and the Social Sciences and Humanities Research Council (SSHRC). The most important research projects of the FCAR program are for team research involving professors and graduate students. Funded research only represents one part of scholarly activity in education and does not include much of the theoretical and applied work by individuals and groups or many of the publications, for which financial support has not been sought.

Just under half of the funded research deals with teaching, including 38% on specific teaching methods. The remaining projects cover a wide range of topics. There appears to be little research activity in analysis of the school system, in second languages, the teaching of mathematics, sciences and the arts, multicultural education and history of education. Despite a common impression to the contrary, most of the educational research in Quebec is practical and applied, rather than theoretical.[26]

This research activity has led to over 2,000 master's theses and doctoral dissertations. Articles are published in such scholarly publications as *La Revue des sciences de l'éducation, Canadian Journal of Education*, and *Prospectives*. It has been disseminated in scholarly conferences such as those of the Canadian Society for the Study of Education (CSSE) and l'Association canadienne-française pour l'avancement des sciences (ACFAS) which is the French-language equivalent of the Canadian Learned Societies. It has also led to over 600 books and monographs in education printed in 1983 alone, including textbooks and government documents, a substantial production considering the size of the scholarly community in Quebec in the field of educational studies.[27]

Educational research in Quebec is distinctive for three reasons. First, comprehensive research is fairly recent compared to other societies and the field is largely occupied by the first generation of researchers. Second, the provincial government has been a far more powerful influence as the producer, consumer, and resource for research than governments in other provinces or American states. Third, the particular character of Quebec as both a French-language and a North American society has made Quebec scholars and policy-makers hesitant about borrowing heavily from research findings or using learning materials produced elsewhere. This has led to an attempt to "cover the ground" of research. Quebec's preoccupation with its unique education-society interrelationships, its concerns with the cultural and economic functions of schooling, and its policy of developing curriculum in its own style have led to heavy demands on scholars to produce information and analysis needed for policy decisions and the materials such as textbooks needed for curricula at all levels of Quebec education. On the other hand, language barriers have sometimes prevented the effective communication of research activity in Quebec to scholars elsewhere on the continent. Thus, Quebec faces a challenge of matching its research needs with the expertise and funding necessary to meet these needs.

These expectations are even more demanding as we move into the information age with the increasing cultural and linguistic pressure of North American communications technology, the need to prepare French-language software for the educational market of Quebec, and the constraints on the research and development funds in a climate of stiff economic competition. There is also an urgent need, in Quebec as elsewhere, to communicate research findings to those who may be in a position to use them, policy makers in government and teachers in classrooms.

Notes

1. Quebec, Conseil supérieur de l'Education, *La condition enseignante.* (Québec, 1984), p. 11-20, 208-210.

2. R. Cormier, C. Lessard, P. Valois, *Les enseignantes et enseignants du Québec: Une étude socio-pédagogique,* (Québec: MEQ, Service de la recherche, 1979), Vol. 1, Appendix F.

3. R.E. Lavery, "Changes in the Teaching Profession," *McGill Journal of Education,* 7,2 (Fall 1972): 167-168.

4. Ibid., p. 169.

5. N. Henchey, "Quebec Education: The Unfinished Revolution," *McGill Journal of Education,* 7,2 (Fall 1972): 106-108.

6. Conseil supérieur de l'Education, *La condition enseignante,* Chapter 2; CSE, *Pour le renouvellement de le ressourcement du personnel de l'enseignement* (Québec, 1985), p. 1-6.

7. Conseil supérieur de l'Education, *La condition enseignante,* Chapter 3 "La tâche éducative." Also N. Henchey, "Alternatives to Decay: Prospects for the Teaching Profession in the Eighties," in *Canadian Education in the 1980's,* J.D. Wilson, editor (Calgary: Detselig, 1981), p. 233-250.

8. Quebec, *Education Act,* Revised Statues of Quebec, Chapter I-14, (1985).

9. Quebec, *An Act respecting public elementary and secondary education,* Bill 3, (1984, Chapter 39).

10. *Labour Code of Quebec, Criminal Code of Canada, Civil Code of the Province of Quebec, Canadian Charter of Rights and Freedoms.*

11. Québec, MEQ, *Regulation Number 4: Respecting the Permit and Licence to Teach* (1966); *Regulation Number 5: Respecting Criteria for Evaluating Scolarity as a Factor for Determining the Qualifications of Teaching Personnel* (1967).

12. Québec, MEQ, *Regulation respecting the Basis of Preschool and Elementary School Organization* and *Regulation Respecting the Basis of Secondary School Organization* (1981).

13. Québec, Conseil supérieur de l'Education, *Regulation of the Catholic Committee* (1974) and *Regulation of the Protestant Committe* (1975).

14. *Provisions Constituting Collective Agreements*, Binding on the one hand, each of the School Boards for Protestants contemplated by chapter 0-7.1 of the Revised Statutes of Quebec and on the other hand, each of the certified associations which, on November 29, 1982, negotiated through the Provincial Association of Protestant Teachers on behalf of Teachers in the employ of these School Boards, 1982-1985 (Amended Edition, August 1983).

15. Conseil des universités, "Bilan du Secteur de l'éducation: Sommaire," p. 10-15 and "Les programmes de formation, Volet 1" (Québec, CU, 1986); Gisèle Painchaud and others, "Crisis or Challenge: The Future of Departments and Faculties of Education," Working Paper prepared for the Association of Deans and Directors of Education of Quebec Universities, February 1984, p. 7-9. There are different definitions of "program" used in various documents; the Council of Universities uses a definition based on official enrolment data which identifies each option areas as a separate program.

16. Quebec, *Report of the Royal Commission of Inquiry on Education in the Province of Quebec*, (Quebec, 1964), Volume 2, Chapter 8, "Teacher Training," p. 264-273.

17. Ibid., p. 319-322.

18. See Note 11.

19. See Conseil des universités, "La formation des maîtres au Québec: retrospective et bilan", Annexe aux "Commentaires au ministre de l'éducation sur la formation et le perfectionnement des enseignants", (Québec: Conseil des Universités 1984).

20. Quebec, Commission d'étude sur les universités, Comité d'étude sur la formation et le perfectionnement des enseignants, *Rapport*. Louise Marcil-Lacoste, presidente (Québec: CEU, 1979).

21. Québec, MEQ, "La formation des maîtres de l'éducation préscolaire et de l'enseignement primaire – Document d'orientation(octobre 1977); "Les orientations de la formation des enseignants specialistes en adaptation scolaire – Document d'orientation ((June 1980); "La formation des enseignants de l'enseignement secondaire – Document d'orientation" (June 1980); "La formation initiale des enseignants specialistes au primaire et au secondaire (en arts, en langues secondes et en éducation physique) – Document d'orientation" (October 1980); "La formation pratique des enseignants – Document d'orientation" (October 1980).

22. Québec, MEQ. "La formation et le perfectionnement des enseignants du primaire et du secondaire: Vers des amenagements –Fiches de discussion," (June 1983); Conseil supérieur de l'éducation, *Vers des amenagements de la formation et du perfectionnement des enseignants du primaire et du secondaire: Commentaires sur un projet ministériel* (September 1984); Conseil des universités, "Commentaires au ministre de l'éducation sur la formation et le perfectionnement des enseignants" (May 1984).

23. See Conseil des universités, "Bilan du secteur de l'éducation: Sommaire," (Québec, 1986), especially p. 94 and p. 28-37 for the need of new teachers.

24. Robert Ayotte, "L'évolution du l'organisation de la rechereche québécoise," *Prospectives*, 20, 1-2 (Fev.-Avr. 1984), p. 7-16; Commission d'étude sur les universités, Comité d'étude sur la formation et le perfectionnement des enseignants, *Rapport*, Chapitre IV, "Recherche en éducation," p. 51-63.

25. Québec, Ministère de l'Education, *Rapport annuel 1985-86*, p. 32-33.

26. Conseil des universités, "Bilan du secteur de l'éducation, Volet 5: La recherche," (Québec, 1986), especially p. 23-67, 92-100.

27. Québec, *Le Québec Statistique, Edition 1985-86* (Québec, 1985), p. 476-477.

8

The Economics of Education:
Revenues and Costs

Education is a major social service in society. It is also an expensive enterprise, drawing its resources largely from public funds and distributing these funds among different sectors of the system.

In 1951, there were 638,000 elementary and secondary pupils in the public schools of Quebec, served by 27,000 teachers, one-third of whom were members of religious orders. In the Catholic sector, the average annual salary ranged from $942 for nuns to $3,000 for laymen. School boards spent $69 million on elementary and secondary education, 60% of the money coming from local property tax, 16% from Quebec government grants, and the remainder from sales tax, tuition and other sources.

In contrast, in 1981, there were about 1.2 million pupils and 67,000 teachers, few of whom were members of religious orders. Annual salaries for teachers with a bachelor's degree ranged from $20,000 to $30,000. School boards were spending $4.4 billion, 93% of this money coming from the Quebec government. Even taking into consideration the factor of inflation, this represents a dramatic change in the economics of education in Quebec between 1951 and 1981.[1]

Table 8.1 shows how educational funds were spent in Quebec, Ontario and Canada in 1982-1983.

Table 8.1
The Cost of Education: Quebec, Ontario, Canada, 1982-1983

Sector		Quebec		Ontario		Canada	
		000 000	%	000 000	%	000 000	%
Elem-Sec:	Public	4 817.5	62	6 101.2	65	17 861.3	63
	Private	302.5	4	222.0	3	668.0	2
College		944.0	12	591.3	6	2 176.1	8
University		1 436.0	18	1 969.0	21	5 581.2	20
Vocational		342.8	4	478.7	5	1 860.2	7
Total		7 842.8	100	9 362.3	100	28 146.8	100

Source: Statistics Canada, *Advance Statistics of Education, 1985-86,* Table 11, p. 28-29.

In 1982-1983, Quebec spent almost \$8 billion on education. This included federal and provincial spending on elementary and secondary schools, grants and tuition for private schools, operating and capital expenditures of colleges and universities, student aid, manpower and vocational training, federally funded language courses, and the costs of operating ministries and departments of education. It did not include a variety of education programs sponsored by social and cultural organizations and institutions, or training programs operated by business and industry. If these were all included, the cost of education in Quebec would have been over \$10 billion in 1982-1983. The major expenditures, over 60% of the total, are on public elementary and secondary education. Private education is a more important cost in Quebec than it is elsewhere, partly a result of a long Quebec tradition of private education and partly due to relatively generous support from the government; 45% of expenditures on private education in Canada are spent in Quebec. Quebec spends more on colleges and less on universities than the Canadian average because college study is compulsory in Quebec for those going on to university, while undergraduate programs are only three years.

There are some important differences between Quebec and the rest of Canada in the source of these funds for education. These are illustrated in Table 8.2.

Table 8.2
Sources of Funds for Education, Quebec, Ontario, Canada, 1982-1983

	Quebec		Ontario		Canada	
	,000	%	,000	%	,000	%
Local	181.3	2	2 683.6	29	4 316.5	15
Provincial	6 749.8	86	5 130.3	55	19 330.4	69
Federal	464.6	6	664.0	7	2 357.4	8
Other	447.1	6	884.4	9	2 142.5	8
Total	7 842.8	100	9 362.3	100	28 146.8	100

Source: Ibid., Table 13, p. 32-33.

On the average, in Canada, just under 70% of funds for all levels of education, elementary through university, come from provincial governments and 15% from local sources such as property taxes. Ontario has the most decentralized system of funding with only 55% coming from the provincial government and 29% from local sources. Quebec is at the other end of the spectrum with

86% of educational funds paid by the province and only 2% by local sources. At the same time, Quebec has a smaller proportion of funds coming from other sources such as gifts and tuition fees than is the case in Ontario and the Canadian average. Thus, Quebec has one of the most centralized systems of funding for education in Canada, and, indeed, in North America, a reflection of broader government policies of centralized control and of extending equality of educational opportunity.

Revenues and Expenditures

The major source of funds for education in Quebec is the Ministry of Education, together with the recently established Ministry of Higher Education and Science. In 1982-83, the Ministry of Education spent $6.5 billion on education from kindergarten through university. In addition, other ministries, especially Manpower and Social Affairs, also spent some funds on educational services.

These were the main expenditures of the Ministry of Education for 1982-1983.[2]

- $4 billion on grants to school boards for public elementary and secondary education, over 90% for the operation of school boards and schools and the remainder to cover capital investment and interest on loans.
- $787 million for the operation and debt charges of public colleges (CEGEPs).
- $984 million for universities, their operation (86%), capital expenditures, and debt charges.
- $250 million for aid and bursaries to post-secondary students.
- $244 million in grants to private education at the elementary, secondary and college levels.
- $81 million for the operation of the Ministry of Education, its regional offices, and its major consultative bodies – the Superior Council of Education, the Council of Universities, and the Council of Colleges.

In the same year, 1982-83, the school boards of Quebec – the organizations responsible for the operation of public elementary and secondary schools – had total revenues of $4.2 billion. This can be compared to $2.8 billion in 1976 and $4.5 billion in 1984. Of this $4.2 billion, 4% came from local taxes, 92% from the Quebec government, 0.4% from the federal government (mainly for vocational training), 0.2% from municipal governments (for the use of facilities, etc.).

The expenditures of school boards 1982-83 were of the order of $4 billion, not counting adult education. Operating expenses were divided into three main categories: educational services, $3.6 billion (88%); school transportation, $248 million (6%); and interest on long-term loans, $224 million (6%). Another $311 million was spent on capital construction (new buildings, extensions, etc). Of the total $4 billion budget of school boards, $3 billion (75%) went to the salaries and fringe benefits of staff: school board administrators, principals, teachers, other professionals, clerical and support personnel.[3]

Private elementary and secondary schools in Quebec, which received government support, had total revenues of $233 million in 1982-83, 63% of which came form government grants, 21% from tuition, and the remaining 16% from other sources. Of this total, 50% went to teachers' salaries and benefits, 25% for administration and the remaining 25% for various services.[4]

The revenues of the public colleges (CEGEPs) were almost $710 million in 1982-83, over 90% of which came from grants from the Quebec government, the remainder from fees and from other sources. Their operating expenses for the year were $698.5 million, 78% for salaries.[5]

The universities of Quebec had a total revenue of $1.357 billion in 1982-83, 73% coming from the Quebec government, 7% from the sale of products and services, and the remainder from a variety of sources including fees, endowments and gifts. About 70% of the expenditures of universities was for salaries and fringe benefits.[6]

Indicators of Education Effort

The amount of money that a society spends on education can be evaluated not only in terms of absolute dollars and cents but also in relation to its wealth and its capacity to pay, in comparison to other societies. In this regard, Quebec is usually compared with Ontario, a province of comparable size, structure, complexity, and resources.

There are two indicators of financial effort in education: the first is the per cent of the Gross Provincial Product (GPP) devoted to education, the GPP being a rough but widely used measure of the value of all the goods and services produced in a province in a given year; the second measure is the average cost of education for each person in the society, or the per capita educational expenditure.

Using the measure of the per cent of the GPP devoted to education, the education effort of Quebec is substantially greater than that of Ontario. In 1985-86, Quebec spent 8.4% of its GPP on education, compared to 6.5% for Ontario. The difference of 1.9% represents about $2 billion. The greater financial effort of Quebec is the result of higher per student costs at the elementary and secondary levels, the efforts of Quebec to "catch up" in its general level of schooling (*rattrapage*) and policies of free college education and low university fees.[7]

It is also important to look at the trends in recent years. In the decade 1972-82, Quebec's education effort increased from 9% to 9.5% while the effort of Ontario dropped from 7.5% to 6.4%. The increase was mainly due to increasing per-student costs in Quebec. In the five years between 1981 and 1986, these trends reversed: Quebec dropped from 9.5% to 8.4%, the result of severe budget cuts, while Ontario increased slightly from 6.4% to 6.5%.

This financial effort in education, as a per cent of the gross provincial product, is the result of three factors: (a) the cost per student, or the average amount of money necessary to educate a student in the system for one year, (b) the per capita GPP, the total value of all goods and services produced divided by the number of people, or the average wealth of each person, and (c) the proportion of the total population in school, or the school population divided by the total population. Effort is least when (a) and (c) are low and (b) is high; effort is greatest when (a) and (c) are high and (b) is low. Table 8.3 compares Quebec and Ontario in these factors.

In 1972, Quebec was considerably less wealthy than Ontario, its proportion of the population in school roughly the same, and its per student cost lower, a factor which compensated somewhat for its lower level of wealth. Between 1972 and 1981, Quebec's per student costs increased at a much faster rate than Ontario's (almost 300% vs. 160%), but its school population declined and its relative wealth increased, providing some relief in effort. Between 1981 and 1985, the rate of growth of student cost in Quebec dropped to under half that of Ontario; this reduced the difference in effort between the two provinces, with the other factors (wealth and per cent of population in school) having slight effect. In 1985, if the two provinces were of equal wealth, they would be making roughly the same effort to finance their respective education systems.

A second measure of overall effort is the cost per inhabitant for education, or per capita education costs. In 1972-73, the average was $389 for Quebec and $430 for Ontario, a difference for Quebec of -10%. By 1981, the average cost in Quebec had moved ahead by 20% ($1,179 vs $980), but by 1985 the gap had narrowed to 5% ($1,330 to $1,266).

The major expense in education is the cost of public elementary and secondary education, the part of the education budget administered by school boards. These costs divided by public school enrolments are the student costs for public elementary and secondary schools.

In 1972-73, Quebec school boards spent $954 and Ontario $933 for each elementary and secondary student enrolled, a difference of $39 or 4%. By 1981-82, Quebec's costs moved ahead to $3,956 and Ontario's to $3,008, making Quebec's costs almost one-third larger. Between 1981 and 1985, the rate of Quebec's growth slowed, resulting in a 10% difference in per student cost ($4,612 vs $4,186). An important question is: Why is the average cost of educating an elementary or secondary student higher in Quebec than in Ontario?

Table 8.4 shows how the per student costs of school boards are broken down in the two provinces.

Table 8.3
Comparisons Between Quebec and Ontario in Cost Per Student,
Per Capita GPP, and Per Cent of Population in School.
Elementary and Secondary Levels

	1972-73	1981-82	1985-86
Per Student Cost			
Quebec	1 358	5 361	6 170
Ontario	1 522	4 041	5 485
Difference ($)	− 164	1 320	685
Difference (%)	— 10.8%	32.7%	12.5%
Per Capita GPP			
Quebec	4 338	12 428	15 908
Ontario	5 732	15 267	19 402
Difference ($)	−1 394	− 2 839	− 3 495
Difference (%)	− 24.3%	− 18.6%	− 18.0%
% Population in School			
%Quebec	28.6%	22.0	21.5%
Ontario	28.3%	24.3%	23.1%

Source: Marius Demers, *L'effort financier en éducation: Une comparaison Quebec-Ontario 1972-1973 à 1985-1986* (Québec, 1986), Tableau 2, p. 10.

Table 8.4 suggests that salaries and benefits have been accounting for a higher proportion of per student costs in Ontario than in Quebec, but that Quebec devotes a higher proportion to pupil transportation and interest payments.

In Table 8.5, Quebec's expenditures in each of these areas are compared to those of Ontario. On the whole, Quebec was 4% below Ontario in 1972-73, 32% higher in 1981-82 and dropped to 10% above Ontario in 1985-86. Quebec expenditures in 1985-86 were substantially higher in pupil transportation and interest on loans.

The changing pattern of teacher's salaries in the two provinces is illustrated in Table 8.6. In 1972, Quebec salaries were lower but so was the number of pupils per teacher, so overall costs were comparable. By 1981, Quebec salaries had moved ahead while pupil-teacher ratios were even lower in Quebec, resulting in a substantial difference in overall cost per pupil. By 1985, Quebec salaries has once again dropped behind those of Ontario, ratios had reduced slightly so the gap in overall costs was narrowing.

The relationship between Quebec and Ontario in the category of "other"

Table 8.4
Per Cent Breakdown of Per Student Costs
Quebec and Ontario School Boards

	1972-73		1981-82		1985-86	
	Que.	Ont.	Que.	Ont.	Que.	Ont.
Teachers' Salaries	46	45	45	46	43	46
Other Salaries	22	26	25	28	24	28
Fringe Benefits	3	3	4	5	5	6
Pupil Transportation	6	4	6	5	7	5
Interest on Loans	10	10	10	4	9	3
Other Expenses	13	12	10	12	12	12
Total	100	100	100	100	100	100

Source: Adapted from Ibid, Tableau 4, p. 23.

Table 8.5
Differences in the Components of Per Student Costs
Quebec – Ontario

	1972-73	1981-82	1985-86
Teachers' Salaries	– 1%	29%	6%
Other Salaries	–17%	18%	– 6%
Fringe Benefits	–16%	10%	–13%
Pupil Transportation	50%	69%	37%
Interest on Loans	0%	202%	278%
Other Expenses	– 2%	9%	3%
Total	– 4%	32%	10%

Source: Ibid, p. 23.

salaries follows the same general pattern. This groups includes teachers on surplus and pre-retirement leaves. There was a major increase in the number of these teachers in Quebec between 1971 and 1981 and, by the latter year, there were over 2,000 surplus teachers in Quebec receiving full salary. In Ontario, surplus teachers were generally nor paid unless they were reabsorbed elsewhere in the system. The pattern again reversed between 1981 and 1985 as Quebec increases in this category (other salaries) were trimmed to 12% while Ontario's rose by 40%. Fringe benefits for teachers in the two provinces (including insurance, pension followed the same general pattern of Quebec's rapid increase followed by decline.

Table 8.6
Teachers' Salaries as a Component of Per Pupil Costs

	1972-73	1981-82	1985-86
Average Salary ($)			
Quebec	8 844	18 983	33 244
Ontario	10 270	28 672	37 960
Difference	– 1 426	311	– 4 716
Pupil-Teacher Ratio			
Quebec	20.2	16.2	16.8
Ontario	23.1	20.7	20.0
Difference	– 2.9	-4.5	–3.2
Salary Cost Per Pupil ($)			
Quebec	429	1 786	2 004
Ontario	444	1 383	1 898
Difference	– 5	403	106

Source: Ibid, Tableau 5, p. 27.

In 1971, 50% of Quebec pupils were using school buses compared to 30% of Ontario pupils; by 1984, the figures were 65% for Quebec and 40% for Ontario. Quebec relies more on school busing due to a different population distribution and declining enrolments; school closures add to the distance pupils must travel to the nearest school. Despite higher overall transportation costs in Quebec, the cost per user in 1984 was $452 in Quebec compared to $510 in Ontario.

Another important difference is in the amount of capital costs paid out of current revenues and the amount raised by borrowing. In 1972, Quebec borrowed all the money it needed for capital expenditures while Ontario only borrowed two-thirds of what it needed. By 1981, Quebec was borrowing 87% of its capital needs, but Ontario only 8%. The result has been an enormous difference between the two provinces in interest payments (debt services): in 1976, Quebec spent $88 more per pupil in interest payments than Ontario; in 1981 it was spending $286 more per pupil and in 1983, $365 more. Since that time, the difference between the two provinces has been slightly reduced.

Finally, in the area of other expenses, Quebec spent consistently less than Ontario on material and supplies, progressively more (over double the amount) during the period on services, fees, and contracts and about the same for other miscellaneous expenses.

For all these reasons, especially for the higher personnel, transportation and interest costs, the cost of educating an elementary and secondary pupil in Quebec has been substantially higher than in Ontario, though efforts have been made since the early 1980s to reduce the costs in Quebec.

A last measure of comparison between expenditures on education in Quebec and Ontario is the relationship between the cost per pupil and the per capita GPP; that is the comparison made between average educational costs and average personal wealth. In 1972-73, the per cent of the per capita GPP spent per pupil was 22% in Quebec and 17% in Ontario. By 1981, it was 32% in Quebec and 20% in Ontario, a 10% increase in Quebec compared to a 2% increase in Ontario. The per student cost rose at a faster rate during the seventies in Quebec than did the average wealth of the society. By 1985, Quebec's per cent had dropped to 29% while Ontario's had risen to 22%, following the general patterns in the other indicators used to compare the two provinces.[8]

The Financing of Universities

In addition to the problem of financing public elementary and secondary education, there has been the added problem, even a crisis, in the funding of Quebec universities.

Revenues for university education in Quebec rose from $619.4 million in 1978-79 to $991.8 million in 1986-87, an increase of 60%. However, if we take inflation into consideration, there have been a continuing series of budget cuts: -3.4% in 1978, -4.1% in 1979, -0.4% in 1980, -9.7% in 1981, -2.6% in 1982, -5.0% in 1983, -3.8% in 1984, -1.1% in 1985, and -3.4% in 1986. There were especially severe cuts in 1981 and in 1983 (in the expression of a Council of Universities Report, *coupures draconiennes*).[9]

These cuts in the funding of Quebec universities have made the per unit costs of Quebec universities the lowest in Canada. In 1978-79, there were 117,000 full-time equivalent students in Quebec universities and by 1986-87, this had risen to an estimated 159,000, an increase of 36%. Grants to universities for full-time equivalent students during the same period, in constant dollars, went from $5,295 to $3,518, a decline of 33%. The Council of Universities has appealed to the government, more than once, to end the recurrent budget cuts for universities and to provided full indexation for inflation.[10] While Quebec has been taking measures to catch up with Ontario, Ontario has increased its grants to universities in 1986 by 6%. Even though Ontario's enrolments remained stable, Quebec has cut its university budget by 3.4% even through enrolments have risen by almost 5%.[11]

The implications are clear. The operating deficits for universities have been building up, reaching $50 million in 1985, $91 million in 1986, and an estimated $129 million by 1987. A decade of budgetary constraint has led to an increase in student-teacher ratios, an aging academic staff with few openings for new professors, eroding library resources, and more limited services for students. The options are few: increase resources for universities (from private donations and contracts, for example), reallocation of resources to universities from other education sectors (not easily done in terms of existing collective agreements), increase in fees for universities (a sensitive political issue), or more efficient use of university resources (a process that has been going on for some time). The financial prospects of Quebec universities are further darkened by actual and projected declines in the level of support by the federal government for post-secondary education, a cut which may amount to as much as $6 million in the decade 1982-1992.[12]

Quebec has one of the lowest scales of university fees of any region on the continent; it also has the second highest participation rate in university education among Canadian provinces (31 full-time students per 1000 population, compared with 35/1000 in Ontario). Then too, the social expectations of Quebec for its universities, especially in an emerging information society, are increasing. This combination of high expectations, high participation, low user cost, and high government investment all suggest the need to rethink the financing of higher education in Quebec, a need recognized by the provincial government.[13]

Issues in the Financing of Education

There are a number of important question that may be asked about the general economics of education in Quebec, the level of funding provided, and the procedures by which this funding is raised, distributed, and controlled. Some of these questions are:

1. Is Quebec society making an adequate effort to pay for education and learning services in general, formal and non-formal, from daycare to post-doctoral research?

2. Is there an appropriate balance among the different sources of funds, public and private, central and local, tax-supported and user-based?

3. Are current policies for allocating funds among different sectors of education consistent with the broader social and educational policies of the society?

4. Are the operating procedures of budgeting and control appropriate, efficient, and effective?

5. Are there areas of serious financial problems that must be relieved?

6. Are there steps that can be taken to improve the fairness, economy, coherence, and effectiveness of the financing of education in Quebec?

7. Can Quebec continue to subsidize private education to the extent that it does?

8. Can Quebec continue to afford free tuition at the college (CEGEP) level?

9. Can Quebec afford to offer its young people low tuition fees for their university education?

10. Can Quebec afford its high administrative costs for its Ministries of Education and Higher Education, its school boards, CEGEPs and universities?

11. Can teachers' salaries continue to be linked to the number of years of schooling *(scolarité)?*

12. Can Quebec continue to limit local school taxation to 6%?

It should be already clear from the figures discussed in this chapter, that Quebec is making a greater effort than Ontario, in relation to its wealth, to provide funds for education. Nationally, Quebec ranked 3rd among the ten provinces, after Newfoundland and New Brunswick, in the per cent of personal income devoted to education. It ranked 5th, after the four Atlantic provinces, in the per cent of the gross provincial product (GPP) devoted to education. It ranked 2nd, after Alberta, on the per capita costs of education for each person in the labour force. Considering the general uncertainty and instability in the economic climate as well as the demands for other social services (medical, welfare, income support, care for aging, business incentives, tax relief), it is unlikely that much more money can be found to "throw into the education pot" and more likely that attempts will be made to reduce overall public expenditures devoted to education. It is naive to expect that areas of financial crisis within the education system can be healed just by "finding" more money. Since the beginning of the 1980s, there seems to have been growing acknowledgement of this fact not only among planners, but also in political, management, and union circles. Yet the practical strategies of "living with less" have still to be successfully implemented.

How we interpret the "balance" among various sources of funds – local, provincial, federal, private – depends on certain assumptions about the ideal policy of funding for education. If we subscribed to the theory of the "mixed mode" whereby different groups make proportional contributions to the costs of education – a kind of equilibrium model – then Quebec is off-balance. Nowhere in North America is the regional authority (the province or state) more powerful as a source of funds for supporting education at all levels. The consequence of this imbalance of funding is an erratic wave of generosity and constraint arising from the political and economic pressures to which the provincial government in Quebec is subjected. A more stable model would be one which balances local, regional and provincial authorities, public and private sources, and taxpayer and consumer contributions to the generation of resources. There may have to be new thoughts about how the goal of equalizing opportunity and resource allocation can be reconciled with the benefits of varied funding, personal and local economic responsibility.

Current policies of allocating resources among different education sectors – preschool, elementary and secondary, post-secondary, private education, adult learning both formal and non-formal – are largely based on historical patterns, together with ad hoc adjustments to pressure points, contractual obligations, enrolment trends and the current state of the Quebec economy. On a philosophical level, they are inspired by the twin objectives of compensation in some areas and of equality of opportunity for all. Thus, policies of allocation tend to incline in the direction of the society and of certain groups more than in the direction of market forces and individual choice. This favours a broad diffusion of resources rather than the establishment and implementation of priorities. These policies are being challenged by a number of factors: first, the population shifts from youth to adults are not being matched by shifts in resource allocation to the post-secondary and adult sectors; second, new demands of high technology, especially computers, science, technology, and career preparation are challenging resource allocation to traditional academic and cultural areas. There is a tendency to spread resources to do everything, from improving French grammar and spelling to computer programming, from ensuring broad learning programs for all to attempting to advance the talented in their competence. In a period when broad social goals are ambiguous, contradictory, and fickle in popular support, it is not surprising that educational policy in Quebec has some trouble matching resource allocation with social vision.

There is a good deal of professional discontent in Quebec about the efficiency and effectiveness of operating procedures for preparing, executing and accounting for budgets. At all levels – school boards, colleges, universities, private institutions and voluntary organizations – the centralization of funding has led to complexity of formulas, directives, procedures, approval mechanisms, categories, criteria for admissibility, deadlines and exceptions. In the mid-1980s, steps were begun to simplify and alter budget procedures for school boards for the year 1986-87, to further greater equality in allocation, more local responsibility, and simplification and lightening of the burden of budget rules. There are indications of similar initiatives for post-secondary institutions. The problem is that much of the funding comes from the provincial government and most of the expenditures are controlled by contractual obligations set at the provincial level, especially personnel salary policies. The central authority has not always found it easy to monitor in an effective way the expenditures made by various public bodies. In short, both simplification and improved accountability may be the next priorities in the evolution of financial procedures.

It is likely that most groups, institutions, and organizations involved in Quebec education believe that they are experiencing serious financial crises: school boards that are declining in size, private institutions with cash flow problems, colleges having difficulty meeting the demands of their clients, voluntary organizations whose financial life hangs on the thread of unpredictable government grants, and universities with rapidly rising deficits. There are steps that will have to be taken (some of which have already begun) to ease the economic problems of Quebec education. Some involve political leadership and considerable political courage; many imply much greater dialogue among various groups and sectors within the total system. All require greater public awareness of the costs of education, the price to be paid for the quality and diffusion of learning in Quebec society, the individual and social benefits which result, and the need for carefully thought out priorities and intelligent management. To a considerable extent, the financial problems of Quebec education are structural in nature and any medium-term solution will require some structural adjustment. The economic effort and the financial problem are clear; the political will and the professional imagination need to be mobilized.

Notes

1. Quebec, *Report of the Royal Commission of Inquiry on Education in the Province of Quebec*, (Quebec, 1964-1966), Vol. 5, p. 49, 51; Québec, *Finances scolaires, 1951-63* (Québec, 1964); Québec, *Statistiques de l'Education*, (Québec, 1985).

2. Québec, Ministère de l'Education, *Rapport annuel 1982-1983* (Québec, 1983).

3. Québec, Ministère de l'Education, *Statistiques de l'Education* (Québec, 1985), p. 48-50.

4. Ibid., p. 52.

5. Québec, *Le Québec statistique, Edition 1985-1986* (Québec, 1986), p. 452, 453.

6. Ibid., p. 451, 454.

7. This section is based on the study of Marius Demers, *L'Effort financier en éducation: Une comparaison Québec-Ontario, 1972-1973 à 1985-1986*, (Québec: MEQ, 1986).

8. Ibid., p. 50-52.

9. Conseil des universités, "La politique de financement des universités pour l'année 1986-87" (Québec, 1986), p. 5.

10. Ibid., p. 6; Conseil des universités, "Avis au Ministre de l'enseignement supérieur, de la Science et de la Technologie sur le financement du système universitaire pour l'année 1985-86" (Québec, 1985). The Minister of Higher Education acknowledged the seriousness of the problem in his defense of the credits for the Ministry of Higher Education and Science before the parliamentary commission on education, April 23, 1986.

11. Conseil des universités (1986), p. 4-5.

12. Claude Ryan, "L'avenir des universités," *Le Devoir* (27 janvier, 1987); Jean-Yves Desrosiers, "La presence féderale dans le financement de l'enseignement postsecondaire: Document de travail" (Québec, MESS, DGERU-DPD, octobre 1986), p. 2.

13. Claude Ryan, "La commission parlementaire sur les universités: Un premier bilan," texte reconstitue de l'allocution du Ministre de l'Enseignement supérieur et de la Science, à la séance de cloture des audiences de la Commission parlementaire de l'éducation sur les orientations et le financement des universités (21 octobre 1986).

Policy Issues:
Inheritance From the Past

In the discussion of Quebec education contained in the previous chapters, it is clear that there are a number of issues or themes that reoccur. Some of these themes, such as the concerns about language, religion and culture, are unique to Quebec; others are more generic in nature and, although clothed in a language and a context that are distinctive to Quebec, are to be found in a number of other jurisdictions. Indeed, insofar as these more generic themes are concerned, some of the major current issues in Quebec education, such as questions of control, choice, contraction, diversity, quality and equality, are replicated not only in other Canadian provinces but also, for example, in the United States and Britain. In this sense, and in spite of appearances that sometimes suggest the contrary, the system of education in Quebec is very much within the mainstream of educational developments elsewhere.

The overall purpose of the final two chapters is to examine some of these issues in depth. This chapter will concentrate primarily on those issues that have their roots in the past, whereas the final chapter will be concerned with those issues that will probably affect the future of Quebec.

The Question of Language

In the minds of many, the language question in Quebec was an important concern in the late 1960s and early 1970s, but is no longer a major policy issue. It was finally resolved, they would argue, with the passage of the Charter of the French Language or Bill 101 in 1977. Bill 101 eventually established the supremacy of the French language in virtually all aspects of Quebec life and, as a result, a degree of linguistic harmony has since descended on the Province. As underscored by the Superior Council of Education:

> It has been generally agreed that, if not in all its applications then at least in is basic aims, the Charter reaches a large social consensus and seems to represent a factor for social peace in Québec.[1]

Although it is only a partial truth, with some justification it can now be claimed that Quebec is as French as Ontario is English.

As far as the right of access to English schooling is concerned, Bill 101 restricted this right to native-born Quebecers with at least one parent educated in English in Quebec. Consequently all immigrants to Quebec, whether from

English speaking countries or not, are required to receive their elementary and secondary instruction in the French language. The dramatic decline of English school enrolments in recent years is, in part, an eloquent witness to the efficacity of these measures. Thus, it is claimed, the demographic survival of the French-speaking population in Quebec is assured by Bill 101.

The question of language and of survival, however, is a recurrent theme in the history of Quebec; it would be naive perhaps to believe that Bill 101, as it now stands, is the final solution to the problem. On the contrary, the language issue continues to be a major preoccupation in Quebec, from the perspectives of both the majority and minority linguistic groups. The progressive softening of some of the more contentious requirements of Bill 101, the continuing pressure from French parents for more access to quality English second language instruction, the increased pluralism in French schools, and the growth of French immersion programs in English schools, are all examples of linguistic issues that continue to be topics of importance in Quebec education. Given the somewhat emotional framework in which matters of language are often discussed, any one of these issues has the potential to erupt into a major confrontation that could well destroy the linguistic *modus operandi* that has slowly emerged during the course of the past few years.

But perhaps the most significant recent development – and possibly the one with the greatest potential for political disruption – has been the 1982 Canadian Charter of Rights and Freedoms. If it is indeed true that Bill 101 has succeeded in bringing a degree of linguistic peace to the province, the Charter has the potential to destroy that peace because its basic thrust is directly contrary to that of Bill 101. Bill 101 seeks to preserve and promote the French language in Quebec, and to this end, many of its provisions can only be accomplished at the cost of decreasing or even forbidding the use of English in Quebec. On the other hand, the education clauses of the Canadian Charter are a natural outgrowth of the Federal government's policy on bilingualism (the 1969 Official Languages Act) in which both linguistic groups in Canada have the right to services in their own language, wherever their place of residence. Official bilingualism (although not individual bilingualism) is, of course, the exact antithesis of Quebec's official policy on the French language. Whereas the Federal government is promoting the use of French (and English) throughout Canada, the Quebec government through Bill 101 is attempting to restrict the use of English in order to promote French. It remains to be seen whether the Canadian trait of compromise will overcome this fundamental dilemma.

Minority language rights are defined in section 23 of the Canadian Charter of Rights and Freedoms and guarantees the right to minority language education, whether English or French, where numbers warrant, in minority language education facilities provided out of public funds. This right is attached to parents rather than to their children; and in order to qualify for the right to have their children educated in the minority language anywhere in Canada, parents must be Canadian citizens and must meet at least one of the following three conditions:

1. The first language learned and still understood is the official minority language of the province where they reside. (This clause at present applies in all provinces *except* Quebec. It will apply in Quebec only when specifically authorized by the National Assembly or Quebec government.)

2. They received their elementary-level instruction in Canada in the official minority language of the province where they reside. (This is the so-called Canada Clause.)

3. Those parents of any child who has received in the past or is currently receiving minority language instruction have the right to have all their children educated in that language.

The first category would permit immigrants with a knowledge of English to send their children to English schools in Quebec. This would signal a return to the situation prior to Bill 22 of free choice in the language of instruction, which caused so much concern in Quebec during the period of the St. Léonard riots. It is for this reason that the Federal government included a special clause in the Charter (Clause 59) that exempts Quebec from this requirement until such time as the government of Quebec decides otherwise. The second category, the so-called Canada clause, applies in Quebec to immigrants arriving from other parts of Canada and, as such, it stands in violation of certain sections of Bill 101. The number of such immigrants is, however, relatively few and is more than counterbalanced by the number of anglophones who leave Quebec for other provinces. It is the third category that perhaps causes the greatest concern in French Quebec, not because of the danger of a massive influx of anglophones into the Province, but because of the possibility that francophone children in Quebec might thereby qualify to attend English schools.

The third category would permit the brothers and the sisters of those who have or are receiving some or all of their education in English anywhere in Canada the right of access to English schools in Quebec. Given the proximity to Quebec of Ontario, especially for example the Hull-Ottawa region, it is conceivable that a francophone parent might easily arrange for one child to receive some instruction in English outside of Quebec, or possibly in an independent school within Quebec. In any event, there is a perceived danger that the education clauses of the Charter could potentially lead to a weakening of the French language in Quebec and, as a result, there is pressure to preserve Bill 101 exactly as it is.

At the Provincial-Federal level, there is the much broader question of who should have the final jurisdiction in the matter of language and education. Education, claims Quebec, is clearly a provincial responsibility. Furthermore, it argues, the Province is in a better position to defend the French language in Quebec than is Ottawa. Bill 101 is seen by many as the logical response to the linguistic and demographic problems in Quebec and continues to receive strong support in the French-speaking community. The education clauses of the Charter are thus viewed as a direct Federal attack on Bill 101. This challenges the policy-makers, both in Ottawa and Quebec, to find a formula that will bring together the Federal concern for minority language rights and Quebec's concern for the survival of the French language.

In the past few years, there is some evidence that a solution might gradually be emerging. Bill 101 itself has strengthened the position of the French language in Quebec with the result that Quebec is less jingoistic than it was a decade ago. The Liberal government of Robert Bourassa has indicated a willingness to reach a constitutional understanding with Ottawa, and public opinion surveys[2] indicate that francophones in Quebec are now generally "more considerate of the difficulties and the legitimate demands of its official-language minority ... and are more receptive to the recognition of minority language rights than other Canadians."[3] The government has indicated that it intends to revise Bill 101 in order to remove some of its irritants. The Minister of Education, for example, has announced legislation that will grant a general amnesty to the so-called "illegal" students (Bill 58, 1986) and will amend Bill 101 in order to "reconcile it with the Canadian Charter of Rights by replacing the 'Quebec' by the 'Canada' clause."[4]

After years of emotional and heated debate on the language issue, a compromise solution on some of the major problems is perhaps now within reach, although it is unlikely that the solution will satisfy the more extreme opinions as the recent debate on bilingual signs has demonstrated. Indeed, the December 1986 Quebec Appeal Court's decision on the constitutionality of bilingual signs provoked a series of reactions (reminiscent to some of the 1970 FLQ crisis) that demonstrated how fragile the situation really is. In one respect at least, the language issue has shifted ground. Whereas a decade ago, the major issue was the survival of the French language in Quebec, an interesting issue today is the survival of the English community in Quebec. Reference has been made to the dramatic decline of enrolments in English schools, to the growth of French immersion programs and to the fact that a number of school boards have closed down English schools in order to reopen them as French schools. In addition, some 17,000 students eligible for instruction in English now receive their education in French schools. The importance of a knowledge of the French language in Quebec is obvious, particularly if young people hope to stay and find work in the Province. But, the overall impact has been to place the English-speaking community in some jeopardy, particularly in areas away from Montreal. The President of Alliance Quebec described the situation as follows:

> The English-speaking community has undergone a turbulent process of evolution over a very brief period. Our rapid population decline has had major repercussions at all levels of our community. Our educational system is being seriously eroded by a rapid decline in enrolments and our health and social service institutions face reductions in their population base.[5]

The issue of language in Quebec, whether French or English, is therefore far from dead. The French language in Quebec is now more secure and the English language less so. This *volte face* has also been accompanied by a somewhat paradoxical turn of events. As indicated earlier, Bill 101 prevents francophone from enrolling their children in English schools. The *régimes pédagogiques* also restrict the teaching of English as a second language and expressly forbid the teaching of English in French schools prior to Grade 4. On the other hand, no such restrictions apply to the teaching of French in English schools and neither does Bill 101 forbid anglophone students from attending French schools. The somewhat paradoxical result is that anglophones in Quebec are becoming increasingly bilingual, whereas francophones are effectively restricted to what has been described as a unilingual ghetto. As recently pointed out in an Advice to the Minister of Education by the Superior Council: "the fact that Francophones could eventually become the most unilingual citizens in Québec is totally unacceptable."[6]

As francophones, like anglophones, realize the advantages of personal bilingualism – particularly in terms of employment possibilities whether with the Federal civil service, in international affairs, or in business – increasing pressure from the French community has emerged in recent years in favour of better quality second language instruction. This trend is evident in the growing numbers of francophone students who have decided to pursue their college or university-level studies in English-language institutions to which, incidentally, Bill 101 does not apply. It is also evident in the fact that second language courses, particularly English, are now by far the most popular courses in the adult education sector. Whereas the English-speaking community is declining quite rapidly in numbers and in strength, the use of English in Quebec appears to be increasing. It is this realization that is responsible, perhaps, for the recent demonstrations in support of maintaining unilingual French signs and of maintaining Bill 101 exactly as it is.

At least two other educational issues concerning second language instruction deserve special mention. The first concerns the matter of the quality of such instruction. There has been strong pressure during the past twenty years to improve the quality of French as a second language within the English-speaking community. To a large extent, this has been achieved in the schools through the regular second language programs and through the various types of French immersion programs. Also, as indicated above, a significant number of English students now receive some or all of their formal education in French schools.

The English community's new attitude towards the learning of French is not difficult to appreciate:

> Whatever the future may hold, the ability of anglophone pupils to express themselves in French (as well as in English) has become the goal of most English language schools in Québec ... Life and living in Québec will only make sense and will only reach fulfillment when anglophone pupils are fluent in French.[7]

Of vital concern to parents in the English schools is that their children should graduate with sufficient competency in French so they can function comfortably both linguistically and culturally in Québec.[8]

The situation regarding the quality of the teaching of English as a second language in French schools, however, is not so clear, and is fraught with sociocultural and political difficulties. Within the context of Canada and of North America as a whole, the English language, unlike French, is relatively secure. There is therefore a natural concern in Quebec to protect, preserve and improve the quality of French. For this reason, perhaps, there has been less emphasis placed on the teaching English. On the other hand, there is a general acceptance of the fact that a knowledge of English is also of importance.

> As North Americans, Québecers recognize that fact as soon as they leave their province. Internationally, English has become the language of communication – a common language for the twentieth century. For anyone who aspires to higher education or to international openings in business, technology, the arts, the peace corps (sic) and most other fields, English becomes an invaluable tool. English is quite naturally perceived as an instrument for development, participation and equal opportunity in North America. Fluency in English represents a major asset and no attachment to the national language of Québec could justify depriving francophone youth... of such an opportunity in terms of development and advancement.[9]

The fact remains, however, that English as a second language generally is not well taught in French schools. In addition to the sociocultural and political difficulties – and in part, because of them – English instruction does not begin until Grades 4 or 5 and English immersion classes have generally, in the past, not been approved by the Ministry. The time officially allotted to English instruction is not always adhered to and appropriate teaching materials are not always available. Also, there is evidently considerable difficulty in recruiting qualified specialists to teach the subject.[10]

Many French-speaking parents are very dissatisfied with the present situation regarding the teaching of English as a second language in French schools.[11] There is increasing pressure from certain parent groups, particularly in the Montreal metropolitan area, for the Ministry to alter the *régimes pédagogiques* in order to permit the teaching of English as early as Grade 1 and for school boards to offers some English immersion classes. This pressure is countermanded, however, by other groups such as the French-language teacher unions and the *Societe'de St. Jean Baptiste,* who appear motivated by a conviction that there is already enough English in Quebec and that the major problem is the preservation of French. Because of these conflicting pressures, the Ministry of Education and some school boards find themselves in a dilemma, the final outcome of which is still unresolved. In December 1986, in the face of mounting opposition from certain elements within the French community, the Minister of Education withdrew a proposal that would have permitted some French language schools to teach English as early as Grade 1.

Finally, it is necessary to draw attention to the fact that the past twenty-five years have witnessed a gradual, but nevertheless remarkable, transformation of Quebec's education system from one which was essentially denominational in nature to one which has become both more secular and increasingly linguistic. As has been aptly pointed out: "the evidence suggests that French-Canadian education is becoming what English Protestant has been for a century: a secular body clothed in a religious garment."[12] Although the Province's school boards and certain other education structures are *de jure* confessional or denominational in nature, they are for the most part organized *de facto* on a linguistic basis. This came about primarily because of the various language laws that officially classified education institutions in terms of the language of instruction rather than in terms of their legal confessional status. This process of linguistic differentiation has been intensified particularly in the English-speaking community – a result of declining numbers and of declining resources. The emergence of Alliance Quebec as an English rights group, and the increased cooperation between the English Protestant and English Catholic teacher unions are examples of this trend towards a linguistic system. Even the Ministry of Education has officially recognized the reality of this situation by establishing a *Direction des service éducatifs aux anglophones* (1985). However, the proposal in Bill 3 to reorganize the Province's school boards on a linguistic basis was turned down in the courts as being unconstitutional. In spite of pressure from some quarters to seek a constitutional amendment, it appears that the present government does not intend to pursue this matter until such time as a stronger consensus may emerge. Nevertheless, the Minister of Education has indicated that as the major problem area appears to rest with the confessional school boards in Montreal, it may be possible to proceed with the linguistic reorganization of school boards in the remainder of the Province. In this, as in other respects, the language question is an issue that is likely to continue to be at the forefront in Quebec educational affairs for some time to come.

The Question of Religion

Religion, like language, is an issue that continues to recur periodically in Quebec's educational history. It is evident, however, that the overall influence of religion as a dominant factor in Quebec's education system and structures has generally declined in importance during the past twenty-five years. Nevertheless, the contraposition of religion and education in Quebec is quite unlike that found elsewhere in North America. Not only are school board structures organized on a confessional basis, but the teaching of religion and/or morals is a compulsory component of the elementary and secondary curriculum. These are, perhaps, the most obvious manifestations of the importance of religion in Quebec education. But the influence of religion is never far from the surface in a number of current issues and is likely to remain an important preoccupation.

During the course of the past twenty-five years, and continuing into the present, the relationship between religion and education has been undergoing a period of readjustment and realignment in which the final disposition is far from clear. From a period in which the population of the Province could be neatly divided into two religious groupings, the subsequent arrival of other religious groups and the increase in secularism, particularly in the present century, have introduced a considerable degree of pluralism into Quebec society, so that structures designed to serve the original two groups are no longer as logical as they once were. Furthermore, the Quebec Charter of Human Rights and Freedoms and the Canadian Charter of Rights and Freedoms are likely to be increasingly used to point out some of the ambiguities that currently exist.

A number of surveys conducted in Quebec indicate that public attitudes towards religion are ambivalent, sometimes contradictory, and demonstrate a wide divergency of views. Notwithstanding the fact that church attendance and religious practice have decreased overall in Quebec, the overwhelming majority of parents remain strongly in favour of religious and moral instruction for their children. Whereas many parents (and teachers) admit to wavering religious values for themselves they often acknowledge that such ideals are important for their children. It is also evident that a strong social consensus on religious matters no longer exists. There are many different religious groups in Quebec, no longer exclusively of the Judeo-Christian tradition, and there are several levels of spiritual faith, as there is also indifference and lack of faith. These characteristics are as much displayed by teachers, parents, and pupils as they are by the population at large. The school, for its part, is no longer a homogeneous institution. Instead, it is a microcosm of society and includes a wide diversity of religious beliefs and practices. Whereas this has been true of English Protestant schools for over a century, it is now becoming true of French Catholic schools because of the effects of Bill 101. Moreover, the traditional Church communities in Quebec are themselves feeling the repercussions of social evolution and of changing values; personal spiritual horizons are often fading, while the overall visibility of the Church is waning. All of these factors indicate that the role of religion is in a state of flux.

The schools, however, have been given the task (by parents and the state) of introducing and nurturing a spiritual or moral dimension in the education of all children. Even in the best of times, this is no easy task for any institution to undertake. First, there are those who believe that the teaching of religion is a matter best left to private institutions, such as the churches; and that a public social service, such as education, provided for out of public funds, should have no role in promoting religious values. Second, the school has the difficulty of resolving the differing expectations of various parent groups. Some parents expect a certain set of religious values to permeate every aspect of the curriculum and the overall ethos of the school, whereas others are content with two hours of moral instruction per week. There is also a marked difference in the specific expectations of the Catholic and non-Catholic sectors of the community. Within the Catholic sector, the general expectation regarding the religious character of the school is embedded in a specific religious tradition, both explicit and formal; within the Protestant sector, it is less rooted in a particular and precise religious tradition, and is both more general in its treatment of the

Judeo-Christian heritage and less formal as a specific area of study.

Other religious groups, now present in increasing numbers in both Catholic and Protestant schools, have similarly divergent expectations. How can a school incorporate a deep spiritual component within its educational project and at the same time respect the rights of others with diverse views? There is also the question of teachers' rights. Insofar as religious instruction is concerned, many parents and children expect high quality, coherent instruction offered by those who believe in what they teach. On the other hand, teachers have the right under the law to exempt themselves from religious instruction by reason of conscience. This arrangement works reasonably well at the secondary level where specialist teachers are employed; but at the elementary level, religious instruction is usually the job of the regular classroom teacher. Exemptions from this type of instruction at the elementary level tend to cause chaos with the timetable. This problem raises the issue of whether it is justifiable to make a declaration of religious faith a precondition for teaching courses in moral and religious instruction, or for employment within a confessional school or school board. Would not such a policy amount to discrimination on the grounds of religion and therefore be in violation of the Charter of Rights?

The issue of religion is not only linked with the search for an appropriate educational project at the level of the school, it is also intimately involved with the various proposals for the restructuring the school and school board system. The government proposal to restructure school boards along linguistic lines challenged the existence and constitutional rights of Catholic and Protestant boards. There are those in the Catholic community who argue that confessional schools cannot long survive without the support of confessional boards and there are others in non-Catholic communities who see in Protestant boards the best protection of an English-language culture, even if "Protestant" now has more of a sociological than a religious meaning. The failure of Bill 3 to survive the test of constitutionality in the courts has convinced many and reinforced the belief of others in the strength of the rights afforded to Catholics and Protestants in the 1867 Constitutional Act. Even in the face of a determined Minister of Education, the rights of Catholics and Protestants were eventually seen to carry much more weight than the powers of the Provincial government. Because of this, and perhaps more so than before, there is a renewed interest on the part of some to reinforce the confessionality of the system in order to preserve the status quo.

In conclusion, the issues related to the content and form of religious and moral instruction in the classroom may, in the long run, be far more important than those connected with structures and institutions. School boards and schools exist to further teaching and learning, and it is at this level that the issue of religious and ethical values is particularly crucial. Some people, believe that the school has no business teaching any particular set of religious and ethical values: that is has no mandate to decide what specific values are to be taught; and that any such teaching is, in fact, nothing more than unadulterated indoctrination. Others believe that pupils should be exposed to a variety of different values (values clarification) and should be taught how to make value judgements – but under no circumstances should children be taught or influenced as to what judgements to make. Others want the schools to reinforce traditional values such as respect for authority, responsibility, piety, honesty, and hard work, and they believe that it is the responsibility of the schools to inculcate these values through appropriate religious and moral instruction. Still others suggest that schools, by precept and by practice, should teach those values that are necessary for a safe and humane society: respect for the environment, the suppression of all forms of sexism and racism, the rejection of oppressive technologies and nuclear weapons, and the promotion of cooperation, a sense of community, and of voluntary simplicity.

The wide divergence of these views is indicative of the very real challenge that the education system has to face. The problem is accentuated in Quebec by the government's decision to expose all children to the same basic curriculum (the *régimes pédagogiques*), and therefore essentially to the same set of values. This is particularly true of the course in Moral Instruction, and raises the important issue of whether the state or the local community is in the best position to resolve the divergent and often conflicting views associated with the teaching of religious and moral values. The dangers associated with having only one source of moral authority are well known. If, on the other hand, these matters are left solely to local communities to determine, then there is another type of danger as pointed out in a study published by the Protestant Committee:

> The moral confusion and the sense of rootlessness created in many minds through the loss of faith in the old sources of religious authority, present a soil receptive to the lure of demagogic and authoritarian belief systems and to cheap panaceas promising security ... How can children be protected against the manipulation of demagogues or attempts at proselytization by ardent partisans unless there is some mechanism to prevent this?[13]

The question of religion – whether at the level of the classroom, the school, or the system – is therefore likely to remain a major preoccupation in Quebec education for the foreseeable future.

The Question of Power

Uncertainties about the realities of power, influence, and control in Quebec education have been one of the major characteristics of the past twenty-five years. Prior to the Quiet Revolution, the situation was relatively simple in that there were, in effect, just two agencies involved: the Church and the school boards. As the majority of school boards tended to follow the dictates of the Church, the question of power, influence, and control rarely arose as an issue; it was clear to those concerned that the Church was the ultimate moral and temporal authority in all matters related to Quebec education. But as has been explained in previous chapters, the role of the Church in Quebec education was considerably diminished during the reforms of the 1960s and, as a result, a vacuum of power was created. A simplistic view of subsequent events suggests that the government, in the form of a unified and powerful Ministry of Education, stepped into the void created and took over the responsibilities formerly exercised by the Church. It is important to realize, however, that the government is a very different type of organization to that of the Church.

In the first place, the government receives its authority from the populace at the ballot box rather than from some unquestioned and authoritative higher source and, as a result, the involvement of government in education, at least in a democratic society, also involves the participation of public opinion. Whereas the influence of public opinion in Quebec education was a relatively muted force prior to the 1960s, it has since become a major influence and one to which the government both acts and reacts. In the second place, the government is a secular rather than a religious institution. The school boards, the schools, and certain other structures, however, continue to exist within a confessional framework. This has resulted in dissonance between the legal authority for education, on the one hand, and the educational structures on the other. The past twenty-five years have witnessed a continuous re-assessment of the relationship between government and school boards. Prior to the Quiet Revolution, the relationship between the Church and school boards was straight-forward, direct, and relatively harmonious. The relationship between government and school boards is often far from harmonious and is still in process of evolution.

The government and public opinion have not been the only newcomers to to have promoted a new realignment of power. The teachers and the parents, that until the 1960s could be thought of as silent partners in the educational enterprise, have since emerged from comparative obscurity to demand what they see as their own share of power, influence and control. Whereas education in Quebec was once the exclusive preserve of the Church and the school boards and with a relatively cohesive sense of purpose, it is now a multi-dimensional activity in which several different groups compete for power.

One of the more frequently used metaphors within the Quebec education system is that of 'partnership'. In theory, at least, the three levels of the structure – the government, the school boards, and the schools – together with the teachers, and, more recently, the parents – supposedly work together in order to sustain and improve the system for the ultimate benefit of the children. Such a partnership represents an ideal about which a good deal of rhetoric is often and sometimes extravagantly expended. An alternate, more realistic, and perhaps more useful analysis to be developed below suggests that the past twenty-five years have been witness to an important power struggle between the various "partners" and that in many respects this struggle is still in the process of evolution.

The major parameters of this power struggle can be described quite briefly. Since the Quiet Revolution there has been a marked increase in the power of the provincial government, especially that of the Ministry of Education, in the whole field of education in Quebec. The powers of the Ministry to govern by regulation have left their mark on virtually every aspect of the

Quebec educational scene and have resulted in a distinct weakening of the power of school boards as well as of other intermediary bodies such as colleges and universities.

At least two major issues emerge from this state of affairs. The first concerns the logic and long-term viability of a system in which financial power and the ability to take policy and strategy decisions lie in one place (the government), whereas democratic responsibility for applying those policies and decisions lie elsewhere (the school boards and institutions). The second issue is particularly relevant at a time when there is increased concern for quality education and accountability. Is the Ministry that establishes the policies ultimately responsible for the provision of quality education and is it directly accountable for this to the public. Or are the institutions themselves responsible, although they may have little direct control over resources, staffing and programs? This is an ambiguous situation, and one in which the public is increasingly confused. Recent research evidence on the subject of "effective schooling" strongly suggests that qualitative improvements are more likely to occur at the institutional and classroom levels than through policy changes at the central level. In the light of this evidence and given the highly centralized education system in Quebec, it is questionable if the government or the Ministry is in a good position to respond effectively to widespread demands for quality education.

Insofar as the school boards are concerned, there are those who would claim that the events of the past twenty-five years can only be interpreted as a direct and deliberate attempt, on the part of successive governments in Quebec, to strip school boards of many of their traditional powers. According to this interpretation the attempt to deprive school boards of their traditional powers has been orchestrated on two distinct fronts. The first involves the gradual erosion of power by means of direct legislation: Bill 25 (1967) removed the boards traditional responsibility to negotiate salary scales and working conditions directly with their employees; Bill 57 (1975) effectively removed financial power by restricting local school taxation to 6 per cent; the excessively detailed *régimes pédagogiques* (1981) removed any pretence of local control in the matter of the curriculum; and the various proposals in the White Paper (1982) and Bill 40 (1983) attempted to remove political legitimacy from the boards by the abolition of universal suffrage.

The attempts on the second front were somewhat more subtle and concerned the various proposals to grant more power to parents and to individual schools. School and parent committees were established in every school and in every board by means of Bill 27 (1971) and Bill 71 (1972). The power of these committees was then expanded by Bill 71 in 1979 and parents were granted the right of direct representation on school boards and their executive committees by means of Bill 30 (1979). Orientation committees involving parents in decision making were legislated in 1979; and when these failed to function as planned, the government proposed a variety of structures for local control of schools in the White Paper (1982), Bill 40 (1983) and Bill 3 (1984). These measures may be interpreted as attempts to remove power from elected school boards in favour of more local control by parents which may or may not have ultimately resulted in greater decentralization of the system.

According to this interpretation of events, the past twenty-five years have been witness to a major power struggle between the school boards on the one hand, and the government on the other. Until quite recently, at least, it would be fair to state that the government was generally the winner in this struggle and the school boards the losers. However, the events surrounding the recent debate on school restructuring have tended to redress the balance somewhat. An important element in the debate was the skillful way in which many school boards were able to forge an alliance with a number of parent groups and with the public at large, so as to convince them of the importance of retaining democratically elected school boards as an essential structure strategically place between the Ministry and the schools. This debate took place at a time when a number of societies in the western world (in the United States, and in Britain, for example) were questioning the wisdom of powerful central governments, of bureaucracies and of subsequent over-regulation. The population of Quebec was not unaware or indeed unsympathetic to this trend. To some extent, and because of limited financial resources, this trend was even actively encouraged by the government. But, whatever may have been the reasons, in the ultimate confrontation in the courts between the confessional school boards and the Quebec government over Bill 57 and Bill 3, the government quite clearly lost the argument. As a result, certain school boards primarily within the French sector were frustrated by the lack of progress in terms of consolidation and restructuring. However, all school boards, and in particular the confessional school boards, are now somewhat more confident of their ability to resist the government on certain issues basic to their mission. The 1986 Estates General on the Quality of Education called primarily on the initiative of the school boards in order to bring together the various partners involved in public education in Quebec, is an example of this confidence. Another recent example is to be found in the cooperation between the government and the school boards on the methods of resource allocation and the budgetary rules, the initiative for which came from the Federation of Catholic School Commissions.[14] After almost twenty-five years of confrontation, there now appears to be a realization on the part of both the government and the school boards that a new *modus vivendi* is desirable.

The same comment can perhaps equally well be applied to another power struggle in the educational enterprise, this one involving the teachers. But in this instance, the struggle took place on two distinct fronts. The first was the well-known and periodic confrontations between the teachers' unions and the government that led to numerous strikes and back-to-work legislation; the second involves a more delicate and still largely unresolved struggle between the teachers and the parents.

One of the more important corollaries of Bill 25 (1967) was the creation of strong, centralized teacher unions, the most important of which the *Centrale de l'enseignement du Quebec* (CEQ), represented all of the teachers in the French sector. The granting to this body of negotiating powers and of the right to strike meant that it obtained a considerable amount of political power. Since its foundation it had used this power to defend and improve the salaries and working conditions of its members, but sometimes, as an important force in the political affairs of the Province. The CEQ has exhibited strong nationalistic, radical, and militant tendencies, which it has not hesitated to use in order to extract as many concessions as possible from the government. Far from being involved in a so-called "partnership", it was often distressingly clear that the teachers and the government – the employees and the ultimate employer – were involved in major power struggles with important political overtones. Until the economic crisis of the 1980s, this strategy worked remarkably well in winning for Quebec teachers salary scales and working conditions which were the envy of many teachers elsewhere. This state of affairs came to an abrupt and somewhat surprising end during a period when the *Parti Quebecois* government was in power. Faced with increasing unemployment rates and a mounting provincial debt, the government in effect turned on the teacher unions and passed legislation that reduced teachers' salaries and increased workloads. Whatever pretence of partnership that may have previously existed was finally put to rest by Bill 111 (1983).

Far from exacerbating the situation, as might perhaps have been expected, the action of the government received widespread public support and resulted in the unions undertaking a serious re-evaluation of their negotiating strategies. While continuing to be strident on a number of policy and ideological matters, the teacher unions now appear to have a more realistic attitude as to the limits of the government's financial resources. They are also aware that in a time of high unemployment, a large proportion of the public is unsympathetic to the plight of the teachers who are perceived as enjoying the benefits of reasonable salaries, long vacations, pleasant working conditions and security of employment. The teacher unions have therefore become somewhat more flexible in their positions and more realistic in their expectations. To some extent they have tended instead to turn their attention to issues concerning the quality of education and, in so doing, have attempted to seek the support of parents and of the public at large. The active participation of the teacher unions, the school boards, and the Ministry, in the Estates General on the Quality of Education (1986) is perhaps indicative of this new approach.

One of the more important groups with which the teacher unions wished to forge a stronger alliance were the parents. Organized parent groups are relative newcomers as 'partners' in the educational enterprise. Moreover, there is some question as to whether parents, as consumers rather than suppliers of education, have the right to be called 'partners' in the same sense as the others – all of whom are contractually involved (unlike the parents) in the provision of public educational services. There is no question that parent groups now have considerable influence within the system. This was made abundantly clear at the time of the debates on the White Paper and Bill 40; indeed, the Minister of Education claimed on occasion that the reforms were being promoted primarily for and on behalf of the parents. At that time, at least, the parents were viewed as partners of the government.

There are at least two areas in which the role of parent groups can be viewed as conflicting with the interests of the other partners. The first concerns the provision of educational services. At a time of declining enrolments and shrinking budgets, as in Quebec in recent years, school closures as well as cutbacks in the provision of certain educational services have occurred. Parent groups have usually opposed such actions. Sometimes their ire is directed at school boards; at other times it is directed at the government. School boards sometimes may have considerable difficulty in seeing parent groups as 'partners' when parents question the wisdom of proposed school closures and often mount substantial campaigns against what the school boards, for their part, see as unfortunate, but financially responsible decisions.

The parents are also in a strong position to bring pressure to bear on the government for new or increased services. The provision of free day-care services for all children is perhaps a classic example, as is the reduction of the age by which children can attend kindergarten, the improved teaching of second languages, or drug education, to name but a few. From the parents' point of view, these are reasonable requests; from the point of view of the government, requests for increased services have major financial implications. At a time of budgetary restraint, the government is put in the unenviable position of having to deny or officially delay many or all of these requests. Therefore, the government is increasingly reluctant to cultivate the parents as 'partners' even though there may be political advantages to so doing. Similarly, it is often difficult for the parents to think of the government as a 'partner' when its actions, or lack of actions, are interpreted as impeding the education of their children.

Finally, there is the important and still largely unresolved issue of the appropriate relationship between parents and teachers. For many years, parents were rarely directly involved in the system. Either because of a deliberate policy designed to discourage parents from becoming too actively involved in the school, or possibly because of the natural reticence of many parents to participate, the responsibility for the educational and pedagogical aspects of schooling was left entirely in the hands of the principal and teachers. Parents generally visited the school by invitation only, usually for some annual prizegiving or Christmas concert, or possibly as a result of some disciplinary infraction by the child. The question of partnership did not usually arise, except perhaps in the somewhat vague context that both parties were working independently in the best interest of the child. Today, in many schools, the situation is very different. This is partly the result of government legislation that has decreed that school committees be established in every school, but it is also the result of the fact that many parents, perhaps because they themselves are now better educated, are no longer as reticent or as reluctant to intercede in school affairs as they once were, especially when they feel that the interests of their children are at stake. Furthermore, school principals and teachers are no longer viewed as unapproachable or as the sole source of educational authority and wisdom. As a consequence of these changes, many parents now feel that they have as much right as have teachers to decide how their children should be taught and disciplined. Teachers have therefore lost some of the authority and prestige that was formerly attached to their profession; and some teachers view with alarm any proposal that would grant more control to parents. While many teachers work effectively with parents, there are others who very evidently feel threatened by them. The notion of 'partnership' is therefore a somewhat difficult one to sustain, especially when proposals to grant more power to parents are seen as diminishing the powers formerly exercised by the teaching profession.

There have been several proposals in recent years to grant more legal authority to parents within the schools; and at the same time, there has been an overall reduction of the role of teachers within the field of curriculum development as a result of the *régimes pédagogiques* developed by the Ministry. Both of these developments can be interpreted as strategies designed to reduce the influence and autonomy of teachers. In the proposals put forth in the White Paper and Bill 40, it was evident that teachers were not seen by the government as major partners within the school system – their participation on the proposed school councils, for example, was limited and not even mandatory. As a result of protests from the teacher organizations, from parent groups, and from others, the responsibilities of teachers were more fully recognized in Bill 3. The teachers, however, are in a somewhat vulnerable position in that any proposal to grant more power to parents within the schools tends to be at the expense of the powers exercised by the teachers. The situation is particularly sensitive in terms of teacher placements and classroom assignments. Many parents have very strong views on the suitability or otherwise of certain individuals to teach their children, yet teachers feel that their jobs should not depend on the personal likes and dislikes of parents. A similar situation exists with regard to teaching methods. The teachers hold that these matters should be determined on a professional basis and in the best interests of the children as a whole; not as a result of the personal intervention of a particularly vocal parent. The same thing applies in terms of acceptable classroom behaviour and discipline. It is clear that the profesional interestss of teachers and the personal interests of parents are often in opposition; and that in these circumstances, it is sometimes difficult to think in terms of partnership. Both the parents and the teachers, however, have a legitimate stake within the Quebec educational system and both groups now appear to accept the importance of the other. It is clearly in the interests of both parties to avoid conflict and to work towards a more mutually acceptable relationship.

These, then, are the basic elements of the power question. In order for the school system to function effectively, it is imperative that the various partners have a precise understanding of their own spheres of influence. Once these spheres of influence have been mutually agreed upon, and an equilibrium or balance of power established, it is then possible for the system to function effectively as a real rather than as an euphemistic partnership. At the present time in Quebec, this equilibrium or balance of power has not yet been fully achieved.

The past twenty-five years have been extremely important in terms of the power question because new groups have emerged and because of the various issues that have compelled all groups to work towards a clearer definition of their own spheres of power, influence and control. In the past year or so, there has been some evidence to suggest that the power struggle between the various partners has become somewhat less intense. As expectations have become more realistic and relationships less conflictual, there is some hope that the mid-eighties may signal the end of an era of confrontation and the beginning of a new period of cooperation.

The Quality/Equality Question

One of the more pressing concerns in education today, in Quebec as elsewhere, is the question of quality. At the same time as financial support for schools is eroding, so is the intellectual, moral, and political support for public education. Everywhere, it seems, there is mounting criticism of the quality of education and of the lack of rigorous standards. At its extreme, the critics charge that the quality of learning has declined, that pupils cannot read, write, or do simple calculations, that they have no store of common basic information about the world they live in, no intellectual or moral virtues of curiousity, responsibility, respect, or logic, and no sense of a direction or meaning in life. In the United Sates for example, the National Commission on Excellence in Education report on *A Nation at Risk* made headlines with its dramatic assertion that American public education was threatened by a "rising tide of mediocrity."[15] The report has since spawned a veritable plethora of new reports by commissions, committees, and task forces set up by State governments and national agencies all mandated to make recommendations designed to improve the quality of education in the schools. In the same year, 1983, the British government produced a White Paper entitled *Teaching Quality* which, together with the 1981 report on *The School Curriculum* and the recent White Paper on *Better Schools* (1985) have indicated a similar concern for the quality education in that country. Within Canada, *Let's Talk about Schools* in British Columbia, *New Directions* in Saskatchewan, *Pour une éducation de qualité* in Manitoba, *Secondary Education* in Alberta, *The Estates General on the Quality of Education* in Quebec, all suggest that the question of quality of education is the keynote theme of education in the 1980s.

Within Quebec, following almost two decades in which the major concerns were on quantitative matters such as additional physical facilities and improved accessibility, a remarkably broad consensus has developed in which qualitative matters are now the major priority. The question of quality and of standards, however, appears to be inextricably linked with the question of equality and egalitarianism. Quality and equality, it seems, are not mutually exclusive concepts. Briefly stated, the debate on this matter can be developed in two stages. The first states that in the name of fairness and of social justice, it is necessary to ensure that all children have equal opportunity to obtain a good education. At first glance, few would argue with this essentially democratic and egalitarian ideal. The usual corollary of this approach however is that education and schooling must therefore be essentially the same for all children, for to do otherwise would lead to charges of unfairness and elitism. The second stage of the debate is that efforts to ensure equality of educational opportunity for all children tend to produce a leveling down of standards to that of the lowest common denominator, and that this inevitably leads to mediocrity rather than the pursuit of excellence. As a result, parents and others criticize the educational system for not doing its job. There is a persistent belief that academic standards and the quality of education are not what they were in earlier generations. The schools, and especially the secondary schools, should therefore raise their standards and quality education should be restored. Such is the current state of affairs throughout much of North America.

An important element of this question, and one that is often overlooked, is that secondary education for all children on a universal basis is a relatively recent phenomena. In Quebec, in particular, access to secondary education was not universally available until the 1960s. Prior to this date, many children left school immediately after completing the elementary level or dropped out soon after. Secondary schooling was thus restricted to a minority, many of whom were among the more motivated and academically inclined. It is only quite recently, then, that the education system has had to cope with the challenge of providing secondary education for all, irrespective of motivation or of academic ability. Comparisons with the standards of earlier generations are not therefore valid.

The quality/equality question in Quebec can be examined at two distinct levels: at the policy level and at the level of the classroom. As far as policy is concerned, there can be little question that concern for quality education has always been announced as a priority in all official policy statements. For example, in the *Policy Satement and Plan of Action* (1979) concerning the elementary and secondary schools, the government stated that: "During the coming years our efforts will be concentrated on the constant improvement of the quality of education offered in our public schools."[16] It was also made clear that the quality of education was seen primarily as the ultimate responsibility of the government: "Since the school reforms of the 60's, the Government of Québec has accepted a responsibility which it does not propose to abdicate. It is that of defining the main objectives of the school system and of selecting the means whereby the quality of education throughout Québec may be ensured."[17] Notwithstanding these statements, reference has been made earlier to the question of whether the government or individual institutions are in the best position to ensure quality education.

In spite of official statements concerning quality education, it is also clear that successive governments in Quebec have regarded accessibility and the equity of resource distribution as equally important policy priorities – or even perhaps as more important. One of the consequences of this situation is that educational policy in Quebec is caught in a dilemma, resulting in a number of somewhat ambiguous situations. On the one hand, the government wishes to ensure equality of access and of opportunity for all children and yet, on the other, it has approved policies such as the *projet e'ducatif* that are designed to make schools very different one from the other. There is the fairly recent phenomenon of alternative schools, which may be viewed as a logical development of the educational project notion, and yet at the same time as a means to increase elitism and inequality (see Chapter 4). The government proposals in the White Paper and Bill 40 on local school management, for instance, were also designed to reinforce school differences. The system of public schools envisaged under these reform proposals were officially compared, in fact, to the system of private schools in Quebec – a system which is seen by many, of course, as the epitome of privilege, elitism, and inequality. The inevitable conclusion is that it is difficult, if not impossible, to ensure equality and at the same time espouse a policy deliberately designed to promote differentiation.

Another ambiguous situation concerns the *re'gimes pe'dagogiques*. In the name of improving the quality of education for all students, the *re'gimes* have led to a number of consequences that have, paradoxically, tended to reinforce the notion of a uniform minimum and, therefore, perhaps of lower standards – at least for some children. Whereas government policy exhorts the importance of individual differences and states that the main objective of education is "to enable children and young people to develop according to their own talents and their own personal resources,"[18] the *re'gimes* impose a common core curriculum for all, reduce the number of options, and abolish course differentiation and streaming. It is a moot point whether these measures will improve the overall quality of education or whether these will result in increased 'drop-outs' and lower standards.

The *re'gimes* offer the best examples of the essential difficulties inherent in attempting to ensure both equality and quality within a public system of education. In the name of providing a common basic program for all children, the majority of the courses at the secondary level are now compulsory. Included in the list of compulsory courses, for example, is a course in the physical sciences to be taken in Grade 10 (see Chapter 4). Presumably, few would disagree that some elementary knowledge of Physics or Chemistry is important for all children in the scientific-technical world of the second half of the twentieth century. The problem arises in that all children, irrespective of their interests or abilities, must pass this course in order to graduate from high school. If the standards in the course are too high, then a number of the students will presumably not achieve the pass mark of 60 per cent and, consequently, they will not be able to receive a high school leaving certificate. Some, no doubt, will then be tempted to drop out of school. If, on the other hand, and in part to avoid this problem, the standards are set so that the vast majority of students will be able to achieve the pass mark, then it can be argued that the course must, of necessity, be of a somewhat low standard. Certainly, the passing standard is unlikely to challenge the more gifted students or those thinking of further studies in the sciences. This, in a nutshell, is the essential difficulty of attempting to legislate quality and equality at the same time. Similar comments, of course, apply to all the compulsory courses in the curriculum and thus raise the question of whether or not the *régimes*, as a whole, improve or detract from the quality of education.

A somewhat similar situation exists with regard to the role of vocational education in the secondary school program (see Chapter 4). If in the name of equality of educational opportunity, the greater part of vocational education is to be delayed until all children have taken the basic secondary school curriculum, then there is a very real danger that some of the less academically inclined students might drop out of school. The Ministry of Education in Quebec is currently grappling with this problem and, after several years of discussion and indecision, has only recently produced a coherent policy statement on vocational education.[19] The question of quality versus equality in this context is evidently an issue with which the Ministry is also try is experiencing considerable difficulty.

A further potential difficulty with the *régimes* resides in the nature of the compulsory learning objectives established for each course. Simply stated, these represent the minimum objectives that all children should be able to achieve assuming reasonable effort. The abolition of streaming, however, in the name of equality, means that individual classes are now composed of children with a wide range of academic abilities. The more gifted children will, presumably, quickly attain the minimum objectives; the less gifted will require considerably longer. The teacher is expected to enrich the program for some and to spend more time with others in order to ensure that as many as possible achieve the minimum objectives. In addition to the implicit challenge of teaching several ability groups in each class, there is the distinct possibility that many teachers will tend to emphasize the basic minima. This will almost certainly take place if teachers are themselves evaluated on the basis of how many of their students are able to achieve the minimum objectives. In these circumstances, there is the potential danger that the basic 'minimum' will quickly become the basic 'maximum', eventually leading to the unpalatable conclusion that quality and excellence have been sacrificed on the altar of egalitarianism.

An extremely sensitive issue, associated with egalitarianism and the question of human rights, is the problem brought about by the government's policy on "mainstreaming". In the name of equality of access and social democracy, the government has decreed that children with learning handicaps, whether mental or physical, should as far as possible receive their schooling within the same settings and in the same circumstances as other children. The question arises as to whether this policy will result in new injustices. At the practical level and, unfortunately, as tends to happen far too often in Quebec, new policy announcements are rarely accompanied by sufficient resources to implement the policy properly. As a result, classroom teachers, many of whom have received no special training in dealing with handicapped children, are being asked to integrate these students into the regular classrooms. It remains to be seen whether these children will receive the attention that they deserve. On the other hand, if the teacher does provide the attention that they deserve, will this be at the expense of the other children in the class, resulting in a form of reverse discrimination? Does equality for some therefore mean inequality for others?

These questions apply as much to society as a whole as they do to the school system, and obviously they are not easy questions to answer. The policy, however, has been established even if the consequences have not been fully understood. There are those who question the policy, not on the grounds of its ethics, but on the grounds that the provision of special education classes for handicapped students was proving to be far too expensive. It was expedient for the government to promote mainstreaming, they argued, not necessarily because it was better but because it was cheaper.

The question of quality/equality and of the balance that should be maintained between the two, is one of the more difficult issues that policy-makers, administrators and teachers have to cope. There is no definitive solution: only compromise. It is patently clear that any policy designed to promote equality also has an impact on the question of quality. In the last resort, the question comes down to that of philosophy and ideology; it is up to society as a whole, through its elected politicians and school board commissioners, to determine its preferences.

Any informed analysis of Quebec's political and social policies in the past twenty-five years must surely conclude that social democracy, accessibility, and egalitarianism are high on the agenda of Quebec's education priorities. As suggested above, this choice has very clear implications for the system of education, especially in terms of the quality and type of programs offered in the schools. There are some other issues that stem from this set of circumstances that also have educational implications. One concerns the financing of the education system. It can be argued that the original intent of increased government control of education financing was to produce a uniform minimum for all school boards and thus ensure a degree of equity in the provision of educational services. With some adjustments for under-privileged and distant areas, this equity was largely achieved. Conversely, it can also be argued that these central government powers to control financing have been applied to generate a maximum of uniformity.

As financial support for public education continues to erode and as budget cuts continue to be imposed by the government and subsequently by the school boards, even the minimum level of services is increasingly difficult to maintain, especially within the smaller and more distant school boards. As a result, and in spite of policies designed to produce the contrary, there is a growing disparity between the facilities and choices available in the urban and rural areas of the Province. During times of budgetary restraint it seems it is increasingly difficult to ensure equality of services.

Finally there is the dilemma brought about by the increasing pluralism in Quebec. On the one hand, there are public policy statements recognizing the existence and support for various ethnic and linguistic minorities in Quebec. On the other hand, there is a tendency to view Quebec as a homogeneous entity, particularly at the political level, and with a collective and "national" purpose associated with a particular set of values. It is governmental policy that the schools be inextricably involved in the preservation and promotion of these values by means, for example, of a common education system and a common curriculum that is essentially the same for all children. As pluralism grows in Quebec and as various groups develop their own views on educational priorities, it is increasingly difficult for the government to maintain the notion of a unified and common school system.

$$* \quad * \quad * \quad *$$

These themes, quality versus equality, individual rights versus collective rights, confessional rights versus linguistic rights, and minority rights versus majority rights, are likely to dominate the educational agenda in Quebec during the remainder the 1980s. The conflicts and tensions between these alternate sets of policy priorities are already tightly drawn and only a wise man or a fool would attempt to forecast their final outcomes. It is already becoming clear, however, that because of the Charter of Rights and Freedoms, many of these issues may well eventually be resolved by judges in the courts rather than by politicians in the legislature. As experience in Quebec has demonstrated in the past, recourse to the courts has not always been in the best interests of educational progress.

Notes

1. Conseil supérieur de l'éducation, *Teaching Second Languages in Primary and Secondary Schools*, Advice to the Minister of Education, November 1, 1984 (official English version), p. 9.
2. See, for example, Commissioner of Official Languages, *Annual Report, 1985*, Ministry of Supply and Services Canada, March 1986, p. 30-31.
3. Commissioner of Official Languages, *ibid.*, p. 149.
4. Gouvernement du Québec, Le ministre de l'éducation, *Communique´de presse*, Montréal, Avril 25, 1986 (unofficial translation).
5. Michael Goldbloom, *Colloquium on Official-Language Minorities*, Ottawa, October, 1985.
6. Conseil supérieur, *Teaching Second Languages*, p. 7.
7. Ministère de l'éducation, *Consulation sur le livre vert de l'enseignement primaire et secondaire: Synthe`se des audiences anglophones*, 1978, p. 35-36.
8. Québec Federation of Home and School Associations, *A Statement to the Superior Council of Education on Second Language Teaching*, Montréal, February 15, 1984, p. 4.

9. Conseil supérieur, *Teaching Second Languages*, p. 6-7.

10. Conseil supérieur, *Teaching Second Languages*, p.28-42.

11. Fédération des comités de parents de la province de Québec, *Le Sort reservé à l'enseignement des langues secondes*, Memorandum submitted to the committee of the Conseil supérieur de l'éducation, May 1984.

12. Roger Magnuson, "The Decline of Roman Catholic Education in Quebec: Interpretations and Explorations," *Culture*, Vol. XXX, No. 3, 1969, p. 194.

13. Nathan H. Mair, *Quest for Quality in the Protestant Public Schools of Québec*, Comité protestant, Conseil supérieur de l'éducation, 1980, p. 128, 130.

14. Féderation des commission scolaires catholiques du Québec, *Enonce' des eléments d'une politique de financement appropriee aux commissions scolaires: Elément d'un nouveau modele d'allocation des ressources pour les commission scolaires*. Document de consultation, Mars, 1985.

15. National Commission on Excellence in Education, *A Nation at Risk*, U.S Department of Education, Washington D.C. 1983.

16. Gouvernement du Québec, Ministère de l'Education, *The Schools of Quebec: Policy Statement and Plan of Action*, 1979, p.12.

17. Policy Statement and Plan of Action, ibid, p. 12.

18. *Policy Statement and Plan of Action*, ibid, p.29.

19. Gouvernement du Québec, Ministère de l'Education, *La formation professionnelle au secondaire: plan d'action*, 1986.

10
Policy Issues:
Meeting the Future

The organization and processes of learning in a society are largely influenced by the inheritance which the society carries from the past to the present. Education is also influenced by how it responds to the choices which the society at present perceives to be available and how it responds to the broad social trends which are affecting the evolution of that society. In this sense, educational policy in Quebec not only reflects a social and educational past but also projects a social and educational future.

It is not surprising, then, that Quebec's preoccupation with its past is complemented by a fascination with its future. In popular journals, in serious works, and in government studies, *la prospective* is given a good deal of attention, both in terms of the projection of probable trends and in terms of possible scenarios that represent the realization of selected value assumptions.[1]

If educational policy in Quebec is to have a perspective open to the future, it must deal with three major questions: What is the array of choices open to Quebec society in the last decades of this century? What are the major social trends which are now at work shaping the future of Quebec? How can and should educational policy respond creatively to these choices and trends?

An Array of Choices

If we think of the future of Quebec as the response of a society to a series of choices, options, or possibilities – an optimistic view of the degree of control which a community may exercise over its destiny – there are nine broad areas of choice which are the subject of interest and debate in contemporary Quebec. These areas are: population, politics, economics, language, culture, society, values, work, and education.

Population choices are an ongoing source of anxiety in Quebec. Can Quebec allow the current decline in the growth rate of the population to continue? Should policies be established to increase the birth rate and are there policies that would be acceptable and effective? Should Quebec take more initiative in attracting immigrants from other countries and from other parts of Canada? Should Quebec take more initiative in encouraging Quebecers to stay in the province? Can some combination of policies encourage population growth? Is higher population growth necessarily a good thing?

Political choices open to Quebec have received a great deal of public attention in the past twenty years and the issues are by no means fully resolved. Should Quebec remain as a province of Canada and, if so, under what conditions? Should Quebec become an independent nation, and what does independence mean in practical terms? Should Quebec become part of the United States, ratifying the southward flow of electricity and tourists?

Economic choices are often less exclusive than other kinds of choices, indicating emphasis and priority rather than acceptance or rejection, and reflecting the fact that economies are increasingly interdependent. How much emphasis should Quebec place on its natural resources, especially hydro-electric power, lumber, and minerals as the basis of development? If job creation is a top priority, should more support be given to the small-business sector which is unstable, but also the main source of new jobs? How much can Quebec rely on high technology, the so-called *virage technologique*, as the source of future wealth? How much support should it give to the manufacturing industries in the face of sharp world competition, and do governments dare reduce this support? Should Quebec attract multi-national corporations and international institutions in the style of a Switzerland of the western hemisphere? Would a free trade agreement with the United States benefit Quebec? On the other hand, is it wise to avoid selecting priorities and try to follow all of these directions at once?

Linguistic choices are the most sensitive issues; they are not easily resolved once and for all time, and they touch deep emotions in everyone. Is the status of the French language in Quebec adequately protected by present legislation? Should some loosening of regulations take place to achieve a new balance of collective needs and minority rights, or will a "domino" effect set in, ultimately undermining the French language? Should Quebec become progressively bilingual or even multilingual and can French remain healthy in such an environment? Is Quebec ultimately to be dissolved in the English language bath of North America and should policies be established to ensure a smooth transition? Should Quebec recognize different linguistic regions in the province, with different policies for different realities? Is linguistic compromise the price for economic and demographic growth?

Cultural choices are closely related to linguistic ones but are broader in their implications for one's way of life. Does special protection have to be provided for the distinctive culture of Quebec, what kind of protection, how much, and at what cost? How far can Quebec go in the direction of multiculturalism, and can such trends be altered? How far can an integrated Quebec culture absorb the centrifugal forces of cultural pluralism, and does it have a choice? How can Quebec respond to the overpowering influence of the popular North American culture of fast food, designer jeans, rock videos and translated soap operas? Can Quebec foster its distinctive artistic values?

Social choices shape the central social project of the society. Should Quebec continue to support the collective values which it has traditionally espoused (social democracy, rights of the collectivity, cooperatives, wealth redistribution, government intervention and regulation)? Should it shift more in the direction of individualism, the rights and freedoms of persons and social groups within society, privatism, and diversity? Should there be less stress on equality, more on difference? Can the distance among social groups be reduced or do groups just exchange positions in an enduring pyramid? Should Quebec move in the direction of social conservation or of social reconstruction, towards preserving or challenging present institutions?

Value choices remain subjects of public discussion in Quebec, more so than in many other societies. Should traditional religious values be strengthened as an integral part of Quebec's inheritance and identity? Should religious values be replaced by a more secular humanism? Should Quebec honestly acknowledge that lifestyle and economic values have now become ethical priorities? Should more stress be given to cultural and political values? Should institutional values (professional, organizational, union) become weaker in relation to common or individualist values?

Work choices are sifted through changing patterns of employment, unemployment, career structures, part-time work, changing aspirations of women and minorities, and the impact of new technologies. Should the "work ethic" be strengthened to increase Quebec's productivity or weakened to acknowledge continuing job shortages and growing automation? Should emphasis be shifted to the importance of lifestyle, freedom, and the creative use of leisure time? Should steps be taken to reduce unemployment, with its associated dependence and loss of meaning? Should employment be reduced in order to recognize the declining importance of work in the generation of wealth, encouraging deferred entry into the job market (through extended schooling), shorter work weeks, longer holidays, job sharing, and early retirement?

Educational choices flow from the kinds of selection made in the other areas of choice. Is our present system basically sound in structure and quality and should we avoid disturbing it? Do we need to rethink our basic educational assumptions in the light of social transformations taking place? Are there key "technical" changes that can be made to improve the system without too much turmoil? Is the system too centralized or is it really out of control? Do we need more coherence or freer competition among institutions and services? Should priority in planning and resource allocation be shifted from the young to adult education and retraining? Should we seek to extend the "holding power" of the existing school system or promote a shift to a high-technology learning network? Can we reconcile quality and equality, rigor and relevance? What is the relative importance of education for a career and of education for leisure?

In one sense, this array of choices suggests a wide range of freedom in determining the future of Quebec society, and stimulates the imagination of policy makers to explore numerous possibilities. In another sense, the range of options may give a false impression of free and unrestrained choice among equal opportunities, a kind of multiple-choice policy test in which all items are equally realistic. It may also lead to the sense of "overchoice" which Toffler sees as one of the characteristics of future shock,[2] a form of paralysis in the face of too many possibilities, and to an inclination to impose closure on a single set of options in order to reduce uncertainty.

It is clear that educational policy, even one that attempts to be open-ended and forward-looking, cannot be ready for all the combinations of choice which may be possible. In their reading of the environment, policy makers in education must make assumptions about those choices that are desirable, according to some set of value assumptions, and those choices that are most likely to occur, arising from the trends that can be discerned in the present society. As a guide to educational policy, an analysis of these trends is a necessary complement to the exploration of options.

Major Trends Shaping Quebec

There are seven major trends shaping the nature of Quebec society and its future development. These trends focus our attention on certain choices available and urge us to distinguish what we consider probable from what we consider preferable. These trends are also important because they provide the major items of the social and political agenda upon which educational policy must be constructed. These trends are as follows:

1. The population is aging and its rate of growth is declining due to migration loss and a low birth rate.
2. Communication technology (computers, knowledge systems, robots) is revolutionizing Quebec's economic and social structure.
3. The role of the Quebec government is declining in importance as a result of pressures for deregulation, decentralization, and privatization.
4. Cultural and linguistic pluralism is increasing in terms of ethnicity, social values, and popular culture.
5. Economic competition is becoming sharper, among regions of Quebec, among social classes, among institutions, and between Quebec and other societies.
6. There is increasing complexity in social and individual life, resulting from the knowledge explosion, organizational interrelationships, changing life styles, and new moral issues.
7. Work, learning and leisure are merging as people move back and forth from job to education to recreation in various life patterns.

1. Population: Slowing Down, Getting Older

One of the strengths of Quebec society in the past has been its rate of growth, in some periods benefitting from waves of immigrants, but constantly supported by a high birth rate. Through the 1950s, for example, Quebec's growth rate was not much different from those of Ontario and Canada as a whole. Since the 1960s, however, the picture has changed dramatically. By 1981 the Quebec rate had slipped to 75% that of Ontario and 65% that of

Canada. Quebec government projections suggest that by 2006, Quebec's growth rate may drop to 36% of Ontario's and 40% of Canada's rate. This means Quebec's proportion of the Canadian population will slip from almost 29% in 1951 to just over 24% in 2006. This has important political implications for Quebec's influence in Canada.

The causes of this decline are not hard to find. The fertility rate in Quebec (average number of children for each woman between 15 and 49) was 3.8 in 1951, dropped to less than one-half of that (1.6) in 1981 and will vary somewhere between 1.3 and 1.8 by 2001. In the period 1951-1956, there were over 650,000 births in Quebec; in the period 2001-2006, the number of births could drop to between 46% and 66% of this level. The decline due to the birth rate is reinforced by migration patterns: in the 1950s, Quebec gained 180,000 more people than it lost through migration; in the 1970s, there was a net loss of 100,000 people. For the period 1981-2006, estimates of net migration range from –200,000 to +29,000.

Two specific trends hold special interest for educational policy makers. The first is the pattern of age distribution in the population. Young people (ages 0-14) were 22% of the population in 1981 and will drop to 17% in 2006. On the other hand, older citizens (ages 65 and over) were 9% of the population in 1981 and will rise to 14% by 2006, an increase of 71% in 25 years. The average age of Quebecers will rise from 30 years in 1981 to 40 years in 2006.

The second trend is in the pattern of the school age population. The preschool population (ages 0-4) was 540,000 in 1951, dropped to 470,000 in 1981 (–13%) and will drop even further to 390,000 (–17%) in 2001. The elementary and secondary school population (ages 5-16) was 960,000 in 1951, rose to 1,160,000 in 1981 (+20%) and will decline slightly to 1,070,000 in 2001 (–1%). The post-secondary population (ages 17-21) was 540,000 in 1951, 1,070,000 in 1981 (+98%) and will decline to 730,000 in 2001 (–32%). Thus there is a general pattern in the 1981-2001 period of a decline in the number of very young children, stability in elementary and secondary aged children, and a sharp drop in the college and university level populations.

The twin trends of a slowdown in overall population growth and of an aging population raise a question: Will the Quebec society "cool off" over the next quarter century, losing general energy, initiative, momentum and creativity, characteristics often associated with youth and vigor, and become more cautious, conservative and resistant to change? Or will it evolve into a more mature and even wiser society, becoming more compassionate and humane, experienced and reflective, characteristics often associated with age? Will the population of 2001 have different social priorities from those of 1951 and 1981?[3]

2. Technology: Heating Up

Like other developed societies, Quebec is undergoing a revolution in communication technology. This revolution is not just in ever more powerful tools and techniques: chips, microcomputers, VCRs, cable networks, lasers, fiber optics and satellites. The revolution is also in the new processes of teleconferencing, word processing, and computer-aided design and manufacturing (CAD-CAM), in the new systems of data bases, satellite networks and management systems, in the new environment of robots, electronic entertainment and electronic mail, and in the emerging epistemology of artificial intelligence, expert systems and "fifth generation" computers.

This communication revolution is not just transforming communication in Quebec; it is transforming Quebec. Its impact is being diffused through the society in jobs being lost and created, in changing work environments, in leisure and entertainment, in publishing and the media, in culture and language. It is enormously strengthening the economic importance of the knowledge-based service sector of the society and the role of knowledge industries such as research, communications, education and consulting. It is changing power relationships, making Quebec more dependent on electronic communication for social and economic life, and raising questions about the vulnerability of information and preservation of privacy. It is changing work patterns, eliminating many low and middle skilled jobs, and is leading to a new relationship among capital, resources, labor and technology as the sources of wealth. It is making the social environment more artificial as contacts are more and more mediated by technology and simulation. It is reducing the distinction between rural and urban cultures, and it is integrating the economy and culture of Quebec into a global information system.

As communication technology evolves from being a technique to becoming an environment, it is redefining Quebec's relations with the rest of the world. It is forcing it to compete with other places, especially Ontario, California, and Japan in the high-tech sweepstakes of post-industrial markets. It is immersing Quebec culture in an electronic wash of videos, data bases, networks, satellite systems and software, stimulating it with new ideas, sophisticated designs and performances, instant trends, and diverse models and standards.

It is clear that Quebec's initiation into the communication society has already taken place. But will this communication technology provide the tools to develop Quebec culture in a new way, extending opportunities for the development and influence of its distinctive imagination, or will the technology homogenize the society in a single North American popular culture, perhaps with Quebec subtitles?[4]

3. *Government: Backing Off*

Quebecers have usually sought a strong government in Quebec city, both as the central focus of power within the society and as a counterbalance to the power of the federal government in Ottawa. In the 1940s and 1950s there was Duplessis. In the 1960s and early 1970s the Liberals and later the Union Nationale parties provided strong political leadership to the social modernization and new priorities of the Quiet Revolution and, no less important, a large, competent and activist civil service provided technical and managerial leadership. Between the mid-1970s and mid-1980s, the Parti Québécois brought the leadership and power of government to the support of the French language and culture in Quebec.

Beginning in the mid-1980s, there have been signs that this trend of strong, activist and centralized government might be reversing. This was due in part to neo-conservative trends in other developed nations (especially the United States), trends to reduce the size, cost, and power of government, to cut down and simplify the presence of government in the regulation of many aspects of economic life, to shift more responsibilities to private industries and voluntary organizations, and to decentralize control of public services.

In Quebec there is also growing skepticism about the ability of government to control events and about the value of master plans of social development. Increasing criticism of many centralized services – especially health care, education, and welfare – is touching the government that is the sponsor of these services. A growing spirit of individualism is beginning to question the limits of the social democratic spirit that, until now, has generally been guiding government policy. A new middle class of urban professionals and entrepreneurs is joining with the leadership of large corporations to protest the heavy tax burden that is needed to support big government and to warn of the dangers to future economic development that this burden portends.

At the same time, other centres of power in the province are developing and becoming stronger. These include municipal, regional and local governments, business enterprises and associations, voluntary organizations, and special interest groups asserting the rights of consumers, local citizens, minorities, and cultural communities. The diversification of Quebec society into many intersecting communities is leading to increasing problems in managing Quebec as a single society, just as the diffusion of power among various organizations and regional governments is providing alternative centres for political initiative.

All this is prompting the government to rethink its position of *père de famille* or *le moteur* (depending on one's preference of metaphors) of the society, provider of all services and solver of all problems. There is talk of "deregulating" many activities of public and economic life, of "privatizing" some public institutions and services, and "decentralizing" structures to make them closer to the individuals and communities they serve. Yet there remains strong attachment to the idea of social coherence, collectivity, equalization and systems of planning. The question is: How far is the Quebec government able and willing to back off from control of the society's evolution, how far will it allow other forces to shape the future, and how can the safety net of important social services that citizens have come to expect be protected?

4. Cultures: Living with Pluralism

There has been a tendency in Quebec – and indeed in Canada – to think of culture in terms of ethnicity, to assume a biculturalism of French and English, with other cultures "fitting in," or being "added on," and to stress the intimate relationship between culture and language, at least as far as the French and English are concerned. But the cultural landscape of Quebec in the 1980s is much more diversified than this.

First, there is growing ethnic diversity in Quebec, more of a mosaic especially in the Montreal region, more vigorous attachment to ethnic identity, and more "visible" minorities. Second, both English and French languages are becoming only loosely linked to ethnic origin; many people speak French but are not "French." Third, within the French community, the traditional cultural homogeneity based on religion and geography is becoming more fragmented as American media, advanced education, alternative value systems, individualistic lifestyles, changing age patterns and the growing cultural influence of women all shatter stereotypes of "typical French culture." Finally, the growing importance of subcultures – student, professional, union, corporate, singles – is shifting the cultural attention of many people to immediate and limited issues.

Many people in Quebec have a good deal of suspicion and anxiety about the idea of multiculturalism, seeing it as a threat to the dominance of the French culture as one of the two "established" cultures of Canada, and THE established culture of Quebec. Yet as a modern society with modern aspirations, Quebec welcomes new people to increase its population and new ideas to enrich the texture of its social life. Native Quebecers are creatively building their own personal cultural synthesis. The result is that "Quebec culture" is becoming pluralist, North American, fluid, and subtle. Its cultural life flourishes yet its cultural industries remain precarious. Even the Parti Québécois, vigorously opposing any initiative to permit bilingual signs in stores or immigrant children in English schools, acknowledges that industries outside of Quebec control 98% of the films shown in Quebec, 75% of the books, 70% of the magazines, 70% of the television programs, and 85% of the records and tapes. Many people in Quebec may wonder: What is the distinctive nature of Quebec culture and can this distinctiveness be reconciled with the pressures of pluralism?[5]

5. *Competition: Staying in the Game*

The economic turbulence which has rocked every nation since the early 1970s has made it hard for Quebecers to assume the continuing progress of their material standard of living, the stability of financial institutions, the constant improvement of their system of social services, and the security of their position as a society with one of the highest standards of living in the world. Economic prospects are far from certain, prosperity far from an assured natural right.

On the contrary, Quebec finds itself in an increasingly competitive environment. Within Quebec, there is competition among different regions, especially between the Montreal region and other parts of the province; there is competition among different social groups, between traditional elites and new entrepreneurs, a competition not entirely without ethnic undertones. There is also competition among social institutions for influence and often for limited resources and, finally, there is competition among various sectors of the economy, the traditional resource and manufacturing sectors, the traditional service sector (government, education, health) and the emerging knowledge-based service industries of high technology, research, and consulting.

Quebec also finds itself competing with other societies: Ontario, the United States, Japan, and some developing nations. Economic and political influence in North America has been shifting from the north and east to the south and west, making Quebec's location less than ideal as the crossroads for the new global trade routes of the Pacific rim.

If Quebec wishes to advance or even maintain its economic and financial position, it must recognize that there are other energetic, competent, and powerful players in the game of technological development, marketing, services, and production. If the game is becoming competition for information, the stake that Quebec must build is less its resources or industries than its intelligence, imagination and skill. The question is: Just how good are its knowledge resources – and the means at its disposal for developing them?

6. *Complexity: Looking for Meaning*

As society evolves, it is becoming more complex: the number of elements in the picture is increasing, the rate of change is speeding up, the interrelationship among structures is becoming more intricate, and the choices we must make are more ambiguous in their consequences.

One source of this complexity is the changing role of knowledge in our society. The quantity of information is constantly and rapidly growing. The methods of acquiring, controlling and communicating this information are becoming more sophisticated through advances in microscopes, telescopes and computer systems. To deal with the mass of data and the interrelationship among areas of information, new knowledge systems are being developed for organizing knowledge into coherent units, for identifying relationships, and for tracing applications. Traditional knowledge paradigms of the structure of empirical science and assumptions of objectivity are being challenged by new emerging paradigms influenced by particle physics, artificial intelligence, philosophy and even mystical traditions. The speed with which knowledge is being diffused through the society is increasing and knowledge is becoming pervasive and instantaneous. The role of knowledge and knowledge industries in society is increasing in importance. The application of knowledge is transforming weapons, security systems, marketing, entertainment, health and ultimately personal and social identity.

A second source of complexity is found in the size and structure of institutions and organizations, in the elaborate hierarchies of government, business and labour, in the intricate and subtle networks, formal and informal, of individuals and groups within the society, and in the interconnectedness of organizational structures. Interlocking bureaucracies – in Quebec, in Canada, and at the international level – make it increasingly difficult to identify responsibility and often reduce the range of effective decision making available to political leaders.

A third source of complexity is the nature of the moral choices which society faces, the growing sensitivity to moral implications of issues, the difficulty of making judgments about these issues, and the problem of finding solutions to problems that do not, themselves, generate even more serious problems. There is an impetus in our society to acknowledge, and deal with, personal violence in the home and on the street, international violence of terrorism and war, threats to privacy and human dignity, stark inequality in the distribution of wealth, and new understandings of both ecology and human life.

Few of these complexities are peculiar to Quebec and they easily flow across cultural and linguistic boundaries. Yet each culture must deal with them in its own style. Traditionally, Catholic Quebec relied on a well-defined discipline and widely shared religious, philosophical, linguistic and cultural framework in which to establish meaning in personal life, to interpret issues of justice and family planning, and to "map the world." From what sources can contemporary Quebec draw the inspiration to create – or recreate – a system for dealing with the complexities and dilemmas of the post-industrial era?

7. *Work, Learning, Leisure: Merging the Patterns*

Our society is accustomed to think of work in terms of a job, learning in terms of schooling, and leisure in terms of rest, entertainment, and sports. We are also inclined to see our life in a linear way, dominated in early childhood by leisure, later childhood and adolescence by learning, our mature years by work and our period of retirement by leisure. These three kinds of activities are viewed as separate and their importance is largely defined by age. Employment, a job, is the "real" world: career defines the person, school is its preparation and retirement is its reward.

Yet these patterns have been changing in different ways. Work (in the sense of a job) is becoming a less dominant part of our lives as our working life shortens, our holidays increase, and our work week is reduced. Society is finding it increasingly difficult to find permanent, fulfilling careers for all the young people graduating from the school system. At the same time, schooling is increasing in length at the beginning of life, becoming more popular at the end of life, and intruding through various adult education and training programs through the rest of life. More and more people "work" in education; more and more learning is taking place at work and in leisure; more and more leisure is providing the meaning and satisfaction often associated with work.

It is becoming clear that the relationships among work, learning and leisure are changing, as are the very definitions of the terms. The concentration of learning in compulsory schooling for the young as a preparation for "work and life" is problematic for, in the knowledge society, the most important work is learning. The growing part of our life that is leisure is providing opportunities to "re-create" ourselves through learning and work. How can our social institutions such as cultural programs and learning institutions adapt to the changing and interpenetrating patterns of work, learning and leisure?

* * * * *

Not only is each of these major trends shaping the future of Quebec but there is a cross impact of each on the others. Technology, competition, and complexity are reinforcing pluralism and reducing government control, promoting new activities of learning, work and leisure for an aging population. And they are creating a new environment for what we call education.

Impact of the Trends on Education

These trends that are shaping the future of Quebec are also molding the future of Quebec education. The patterns of growth and the age of the population affect the size of education systems, their priorities, and the resources that will be made available to them. Communication technologies suggest new methods of stimulating learning, both within existing institutions and through new learning structures that may open access to learning to new populations, and separate learning programs from present rigidities of time and place. The changing role of government provides a new environment for the management of education, opening up decision making to new groups, requiring new skills in educational leaders, and forcing us to reexamine traditional means of allocating power and responsibility. Cultural diversity poses new challenges to the power and willingness of education to adapt to different needs and to respond in a creative way to a variety of different expectations. Competition puts a sharper edge on the importance of the quality of learning services and achievement, not only for the benefit of the individual but for the continued social and economic health of Quebec society. Complexity urges rethinking of essential matters of curriculum content and the selection and organization of learning programs to help Quebecers, young and old, live fully in the society of the 21st Century. Finally, the convergence of work, learning and leisure raises questions about the limitations and potential of our present structures, moving us in the direction of truly integrated continuing education policies for a real learning society. This is the agenda which the present and future seem to be contributing to an examination of educational policy in Quebec.

As Quebec's *population* growth slows down and its people age, we already see some of the effects on the formal system of elementary and secondary education: smaller enrolments, schools closed, older teachers and surplus teachers, limited resources. Over the next few years, different patterns of decline, stability and increase emerge in the formal education system. These are some probable trends:

1. Kindergarten enrolments (for 5 year olds) will drop 10% from 1984 to 1990.
2. Elementary enrolments will rise through the 1980s, then drop again to a 1990 level only 1% above that of 1984.
3. Secondary enrolments follow a reverse trend, dropping through the 1980s then rising by 1990 to reach the 1984 level.
4. Between 1983 and 1989, English-language enrolment on the Island of Montreal will drop 20%.
5. At the college level, enrolments will drop 9% between 1983 and 1989.
6. While university enrolments increased by 50% in the decade 1973-1983, full-time enrolments can be expected to decline over the next decade.
7. At the elementary and secondary level, the number of teaching positions will continue to decline before rising again; the number of retirements will increase slightly and then at a greater momentum; job opportunities for new teachers may be limited because they will be competing with more experienced candidates; and the average age of the profession will continue to increase.
8. In the colleges and universities, teaching staff will also decline in size and the proportion of older teachers will increase.[6]

There are other probable effects of the population shifts. As a smaller proportion of the population has immediate contact with the formal school system from kindergarten to university as parents or participants, there will likely be less overall public interest in education and thus less support for allocating resources to the system. Elementary and secondary education, especially, will likely decline in importance as interests and priorities shift within education from early education to adult learning and from the education field to other social services, especially income support, tax relief, aid to small enterprises, medicare, and care for the aged.

At the same time, the decline of the public system will pose problems of attracting and keeping competent administrators, providing adequate support and special services, and preserving the quality of service. The aging profession will make it more difficult to use and attract new teachers, assign teachers in their areas of competency, and keep the formal system flexible and capable of adapting to the challenges presented by the other trends. It is also possible, and worth serious consideration, that private education will continue to increase in popularity and that other approaches to learning – franchise schools, high-technology learning services, home study – may develop to the point where they challenge the vitality and even the viability of the public elementary and secondary system, except as extended custodial services for those unable or disinclined to avail themselves of alternative learning services.

On the other hand, the population trends invite educational policy makers to consider the learning needs of other parts of the population. Many school boards are already extending their services to childcare, adult education, and community development, though usually within the framework of existing structures and assumptions and as a supplement to their regular programs. The colleges, in particular, have been providing a wide range of services to young adults, to workers wishing to improve or transfer their skills, and to older citizens seeking cultural enrichment.

If certain population trends are causing decline in the formal system and threatening possible decay in quality, the *communication technologies* are holding promise to expand the range of learning services, to enlarge the population who may have access to these services, and to offer variety and increasing sophistication in the methods of communicating knowledge, imparting skills, and cultivating values.

At the present time, this technology is entering the education system to a limited extent: in microcomputer laboratories, courses in programming and computer literacy, accumulation of hardware and some of the educational software to accompany it, and in a general pressure to get young people ready for the computer age. Many programs in the colleges and universities are moving especially fast into computer-aided design, word-processing, robotics and other computer applications. Still, computers and the larger technology of which they are part have not substantially altered the structure and organizatrion of learning in schools; on the contrary, strenuous efforts are being made to domesticate them and absorb them into existing structures. They are rarely used to link small isolated schools or to exchange and enhance the expertise of teachers and pupils; they have not had an impact on the curriculum in terms of new skills or the pruning of old subject matter. They are not integrated into the normal learning environment of schools; data bases are not often used in the social sciences, nor is the use of information networks part of the learning skills with which schools are equipping their pupils; and even word processing is not yet a "basic." The sophistication and quality of a good deal of learning technology in education is often considerably lower than the technology found in computer games and electronic arcades.

Quebec is uncertain about the new communication technologies. They are clearly on the wave of the future, even on the wave of the present, yet they have posed political and financial obstacles in terms of choice of technology, as well as cultural and linguistic obstacles in the availability of suitable French programs. Like their counterparts in other areas, Quebec educators are also uncertain about how to respond to two rather important questions: What do we want to use computers for? What changes will they make in the education system?

If computers are to be more than electronic workbooks for skill and drill, and if the expensive technology is going to fulfill the expectations that many of its proponents hold out, then concerted, sustained and imaginative initiatives need to be taken to ensure that those who are to use the technology – especially teachers and pupils – understand and appreciate how computers, data bases, networks, and computer-based learning systems can enhance the quality, increase the quantity, and accelerate the speed of learning, as well as how they can be used to reach and teach those for whom traditional methods of instruction have been inadequate. They also need to think about how the media shape the message of what we think and how we think, and when the technology is inappropriate. This will likely require a greater investment of time and effort than university courses in LOGO and a few professional days devoted to computer literacy. It implies a more serious consideration of learning objectives, the contribution that the new technologies can make in furthering them, and the other strategies that must be used to complement them.

At a deeper level, the question is whether computers (and the technological system of which they are part) are to be integrated into the existing assumptions, structures and procedures of formal education, or whether they are truly "transforming" technologies, requiring the integration of the existing formal system into a broader learning network of institutions, people, hardware, software, links, resources and services. There are three possible scenarios: that technology will continue to play a minor part in learning services; that a fusion will take place between existing education structures and the new technology-based learning services; or that there will be two competing learning systems, the formal institution-based and the new technology-based. It is unlikely that political and economic considerations can permit Quebec to allow the first scenario to unfold and it is unlikely that schools, educators, and school boards would long survive in the third scenario. It is not yet certain, however, that the policies and strategies to develop integrated learning services are being devised.

The general movement of *government* in the direction of decentralization, deregulation and privatization of service would underline some tendencies in the governance of education. It implies new structures of management, new forms of participation, new styles of leadership and even a new reordering of traditional power relationships in the field of Quebec education.

For some years, there have been clear struggles for power in Quebec education, with the Ministry of Education retaining the dominant influence in relation to teachers' organizations, school boards, parents' associations and regions of the province. As the ministry begins to slip from pre-eminence, however, more authority will shift to school boards in setting priorities, responding to local expectations, allocating budget and being responsible for the quality of education; that is, authority will shift more in the direction of school board authority as exercised in other Canadian provinces. At the same time, individual schools will develop "educational projects" to attract students. Broad interpretation of government-set curriculum guidelines and adaptation to local needs will increase, with individual schools making their own decisions about when and how to teach second languages, the use of computers, the emphasis on different themes in the curriculum, cooperative vocational programs with the local community, and the arrangement and timing of individual courses.

The need of public schools to compete with private schools and the growing influence of private enterprise in the preparation of teaching materials and in contracts for instructional services will require public school administrators to respond imaginatively and rapidly. This will give impetus to local arrangements with teacher unions and school boards and strengthen resistance to the inertia and weight of centralized structures of decision making. Provincial leadership in the Ministry of Education, in provincial associations, and in teachers' unions will have a role to set broad guidelines and establish umbrella policies and agreements, leaving detailed planning – and the responsibility for the results – to local initiative.

It is likely that the participation of parents and adult education students in policy making will become more effective as sophisticated and demanding consumers of learning services express their needs. Educational administrators will resemble brokers of learning service, or "intrapreneurs" promoting their institutions within a loose network and providing leadership and management for the development and quality control of learning programs. The present roles of college directors-general, university rectors and private school principals in marketing programs, raising funds, and lobbying for their institutions will perhaps become the model for school board directors and school principals everywhere. In many ways the failure of Bill 40 as an attempt to redistribute and redefine authority may have been more an error of timing and tactic than a misdirected orientation.

The role that school boards will play in the process of decentralizing authority depends on how well they cultivate the support of their public and professional constituencies and how well they integrate with other public and private organizations in the community, especially social services, public administration, community development and voluntary organizations. School boards may need to change their mandate to become truly local agencies of learning services for all members of the community, from the very young to the very old, embracing daycare, occupational retraining, community development, public health, and cultural services in senior citizens' homes.

The trend away from single and centralized structures will be reinforced by the growing *cultural and linguistic pluralism* in the society, especially in the Montreal region. Planners in the Montreal Catholic School Commission, the largest French-language school board in Quebec, and the largest school board in Canada, foresee the day when fully one-half of the pupils enrolled in their schools will have a mother tongue other than French or English, a group infelicitiously referred to as "allophones." The school system, especially the Catholic sector, has not yet arrived at a sensible and sensitive means of adapting to the enormous diversity of religious and humanistic values in the community it serves, a policy that would respect both the rights of the majority and those of the minority. Added to this cultural and religious pluralism is diversity in lifestyles and expectations, demanding both open and humanistic education for some children and tough, disciplined and career-oriented training for others.

There is a tendency to see a social "problem" in diversity or the breakdown of the social consensus upon which school customarily relies for its justification, leading to social fragmentation, conflicting expectations, growing dissatisfaction and criticism, and resulting in conflict, confrontation, litigation, and pressure tactics. Such a climate is often threatening to social institutions like schools, leading them to be defensive, to resort to token involvement of groups and administrative mystification to neutralize opposition. On the other hand, it is an overriding duty of the school to prepare learners, through its program and its climate, to respect the differences of others while being proud of one's own distinctiveness. If the education system of Quebec does not learn to cherish the richness of the diversity of its population – and the lesson has yet to be learned – the cultural tensions of the society will surely impede social and economic development. Cultural groups – religious, ethnic, linguistic, social – hope to see in the learning institutions that serve them, some reflection of who they are as well as an image of what their society wishes to look like. Unless daycare centres, schools, colleges, universities and non-formal learning environments for adults acknowledge this diversity – and not just as a strategy of assimilation – New-Quebecers, women, Blacks, children of farmers, Inuit, Indians, the talented, the emotionally fragile and the unemployed will remain untouched by the institutions that the educational rhetoric of Quebec claims to be at their service.

It would be easy to trust that the social, ethnic and community security of Quebec society would support this respect for multiculturalism if we ignore the *competitive* cultural and economic environment in which Quebec's future is being forged. This is an environment of individual and societal winners and losers, with a stress on quality of performance as the only test in the "real world." In education, this competition leads to structures of control and systems of evaluation – of teachers, learners, learning, and institutions – as the necessary route to excellence. The selection and training of the best is the society's investment in the future, and school effectiveness, marketing, and the tough disciplines of language and mathematics are the touchstones of learning progress, certification and recognition.

Selection, evaluation and accountability are the pressures that competition places on the education system, moving it away from the egalitarian policy, client-based evaluation and diffused responsibility that marked Quebec education in the 1960s and 1970s. One manifestation is the "back to basics" movement. Another is the growing competition within the education sector between public and private schools and, increasingly, between school boards, Catholic and Protestant, and among individual public schools. Already there is something of a "free market" in education services in Quebec, at least in the major urban areas where public subsidization of private schools is a form of the voucher system periodically proposed in the United States. Yet this market system is not easily reconciled with the centralized structures of administration, curriculum, financing, and personnel policies such as staff engagement, salaries security and assignment. There is every indication that educational competition in Quebec will continue and intensify, complicated by the overlapping divisions of Catholic and Protestant, French and English, public and private, community school and "alternative" school. While many people argue that this competition can enhance the quality of education everywhere, it can also be argued that too much competition within a total system that is stable or declining can be detrimental to high-quality learning services. Many in the public system argue that the rules of the competitive game are inherently unfair, favoring private schools which control their own staff and enrolments and threatening to make the public system a dumping ground for those unable to enter selective schools.

A second dimension is the competition between the education system in Quebec and those in other provinces and countries, and in the international market place of careers. Bilingual, often multilingual graduates who have sound general education and advanced specialization in different scientific, technological and cultural fields should be both the goal of Quebec's education system and the challenge which it faces. It is not a goal that is realized nor a contest engaged simply by elaborate plans and structural reorganization; it requires much more attention to processes of implementation, shared values, and dynamic leadership.

The trend to increasing *complexity* is a challenge to the content of learning. It raises questions about the role of education in addressing issues of meaning, the content of a curriculum for a general education as a broad base upon which specialization can be built, and as a structure of fundamental human development. Meaning introduces the issue of values, general education the issue of concepts, and fundamentals the issue of skills.

One of the distinctive features of Quebec education in the past was the stress on general education, best represented by the curriculum tradition of the classical college. With the curriculum reforms of the 1960s, the stress moved away from general education to specialization, elective programs, credits and diversity, a fragmentation of learning programs at all levels. In the growing pluralism of the society, the teaching of common values and the imparting of a shared philosophy of meaning became problematic; in the rush to specialized competence, general concepts were reduced to compulsory courses at elementary and secondary levels and in the colleges. In the climate of change and relevance, fundamental skills were not always imparted with the patience and discipline which such skills usually demand.

In recent years, there has been a growing preoccupation with general education through the extension of compulsory courses at the secondary level, with values in both formal courses and the services which schools offer students, and with fundamental skills, especially those dealing with mastery of language, communication, learning how to learn, and habits of work and mental discipline. It was perhaps naive to expect the college level to "complete" the general education of all students and it may have been no less than tragic that universities reduced the importance or eliminated the general undergraduate programs in the humanities, social sciences, and sciences. One of the telling criticisms that may be made of the curriculum reforms of the Quiet Revolution is that, as the society became more complex in the interrelationship of its demands, the education system reduced its emphasis on those key concepts, core values and generic skills that are increasingly recognized as crucial to the survival system of all Quebecers.

As the preoccupation with these issues develops, it is likely that there will be serious efforts in the coming years to debate the elements of the repertoire of general concepts (such as balance in ecology and trade-offs in economics), core values (such as tolerance for ambiguity) and fundamental skills (creative use of information systems) and to ensure that these elements form a core of the content of learning programs at all levels.

The convergence of *work, learning and leisure* in various life patterns suggests that Quebec reconsider the fundamental assumptions of its education structures, assumptions that are built on the separation of education from other dimensions of social life (well-being, career, recreation, community participation) and on the separation of our life into discrete layers (schooling, job, retirement). The changing patterns of life make any view of education dangerously incomplete unless it is based on the idea of continuing education, of which the formal elementary-secondary system is only one part, and the formal postsecondary only a second part.

If the formal structure of education has a distinctive contribution to make to the ongoing and continuing development of both the person and the society, it is as a preparation not for life, but for living, for the balanced enjoyment of creative leisure, meaningful work and stimulating learning. This suggests the formal system must be merged in our thinking and policy making with the broader non-formal network of learning services which embrace many aspects of community life, the richness of the media and cultural resources, and services provided by the variety of voluntary organizations. This implies more than adult education programs in school boards and post-secondary institutions, and more than a program of extracurricular activities for students. It requires a broader and more holistic view of what learning is, how and where it is enhanced, and its importance as the social project of the post-industrial society which Quebec is now becoming. Finally, it implies a reconsideration of many cherished assumptions about the role of the school and school attendance, the function of the teacher in imparting knowledge, and the control of curriculum by governments, producers and experts. A Quebec that had the courage to enter into an educational revolution in the 1960s and a second examination of formal education in the 1970s and 1980s may now be ready for a broader and even more revolutionary examination of continuing learning in the 1990s.

All these trends are coming together to shape the policy agenda for the future of Quebec education. The changing pattern of the population and the merging of work, leisure and learning are redefining the clientele of education and their needs. The reduction of government, increasing competition and social pluralism are testing the power of the society to adapt and diversify. The combined impact of communication technology and of growing complexity challenge the message of learning programs and the media (electronic, institutional and personal) through which the message flows and by which it is transformed. How Quebec responds to this learning agenda will affect the success with which it deals with the different choices for the future that must be made.

Notes

1   See, for example: Jean Blouin, "Le futur du Québec," *L'Actualite*, 9,11 (novembre 1984): 49-61; Groupe québécois de prospective, *Le futur du Québec au conditionel* (Chicoutimi: Gaetan Morin, 1982); P.A. Julien, P. Lamonde, D. Latouche, *Quebec 2001: Une société refroidie* (Québec: Boreal Express, 1976); Québec, Bureau de la statistique du Québec, *L'Avenir démographique du Québec* (Québec, 1985).

2   Alvin Toffler, *Future Shock* (New York: Random House, 1970).

3   See: Louis Duchesne, "L'Evolution démographique du Québec 1980-1984," in *Le Québec statistique, Edition 1985-86* (Québec, 1986), p. 75-111; Québec, Bureau de la statistique du Québec, *L'Avenir démographique du Québec* (Québec, 1985).

4   See: Science Council of Canada, *Planning Now for an Information Society: Tomorrow Is Too Late* (Ottawa, 1982); J. Goulet, *Les répercussions culturelles de l'informatisation au Québec* (Québec: Conseil de la langue française, 1982); N. Henchey, "New Technology and the Transformation of Learning," in *Social Change and Education in Canada*, R. Ghosh and D. Ray, eds. (Don Mills, Ont.: Harcourt Brace Jovanovich, 1987) p. 42-56.

5   See, for example, Don MacPherson, "PQ stymied by English popular culture," *The Gazette* (Montreal, Thursday, October 30, 1986): B-3.

6   Conseil supérieur de l'Education, *Pour le renouvellement et le ressourcement du personnel de l'Enseignement* (Québec, 1985), especially p. 4-20; René Le Corré, *Prevision du nombre d'elèves des commissions scolaires du Québec de 1984-1985 à 1989-1990 (Québec, MEQ, 1984);* Conseil des universités, "Avis au ministre de l'Education sur le maintien et le renouvellement du personnel scientifique dans les universités québécoises" (Québec, 1984).

Afterword
Education in Quebec:
An Appraisal

After the data have been collected, the documents studied, and the patterns analyzed, the delicate yet important questions remain: What progress has been achieved? How good is education in Quebec? How would we appraise its quality? How can Quebec education be improved?

Any appraisal of a phenomenon as complex and varied as education in Quebec must rest on generalizations and impressions, on some criteria selected over others, and on the point of view of those who do the appraising. It is important, however, for those of us concerned about the quality of education in Quebec and committed to its continuous development to risk some assessment of quality. These are some points of appraisal and possible steps for further development.

1. Education in Quebec, like the society itself, is caught between its past and its future. In many ways, the Quiet Revolution of the 1960s was a rejection of the past, of Church control, of a classical tradition in education, of a paternalistic and elitist social structure, of a society out of the mainstream of modern currents. Yet the past is not so easily discarded and Quebec education remains embedded in the legal and religious structures of its past. A mentality of collective survival and vulnerability endures, even if the components and strategies differ from those of the 1950s. On the other hand, Quebec education is fascinated with the future, eager to adopt modern appearances and sophisticated in its style. It is influenced by current trends from microcomputers to mastery learning, comprehensive schools to group dynamics. There is, in Quebec education, a split personality, one that looks affectionately at the past, one that looks enthusiastically to the future, to *patrimoine* and *prospective*. It is the present with which Quebec education is having a hard time coping.

2. Since 1960, Quebec education has been truly transformed in its priorities, structures, facilities, investment of resources, the expansion of access to learning services, and its attempt to provide highly trained manpower in the crucial fields of economics, management, and technology. Few societies have changed their education system so thoroughly, so quickly, and so dramatically, and few societies have presumed to impose such high

cultural, social, and economic expectations on its education system. The legacy of this educational transformation is a structure that is in many ways unstable and tentative, with institutions often lacking in continuity and tradition, and a system burdened with ongoing criticism and enormous self-doubt, and with disappointment over visions unfulfilled.

3. The authority and decision-making system of Quebec education is the victim of the success of the educational revolution of the sixties. At that time, the fresh, young, confident and energetic Ministry of Education took charge of Quebec education and translated the Parent Report into public policy, using considerable political license to do so. After the initial phase of reform, the Ministry continued to be the dominant power, the central focus of decisions – in finance, in curriculum, in structural reform, in personnel policies, in regulations of all sorts. The balances of power were lost in the face of progressive centralization beginning in 1961 and continuing into the mid-1980s. The benefits were in coherence, consistency, standardization, and equality. The price paid was growing complexity, spiralling costs, rigidity, a great deal of dependence and a generation of ongoing conflict and power struggles among groups that in theory were supposed to be partners. In labour relations, elementary and secondary curriculum, funding policy, quality control and operational procedures, the mentality of centralization has done more than anything else to inhibit progress, discourage initiative, provoke confrontation, and deflect attention from creative action.

4. Despite this overriding commitment to structural and technical rationality, Quebec education suffers from a high degree of fragmentation. There are intersecting divisions of Catholic and Protestant, English and French, public and private, local and regional, regional and national, Montreal and the rest of the province, professional and public, employee and employer, initial training and continuing education. These have often resulted in conflict, costly duplication, rivalry, and narrow, limited positions based on particular self-interest. In a sense, legal and administrative centralization is a veneer covering confusion and disorder.

5. Between standardization and fragmentation, there is a search for some way of dealing with pluralism – among religious beliefs and lack of belief, among linguistic rights, among ethnic identities, among social groups and among the various sub-cultures of Quebec. Educational leaders recognize the increasingly pluralist nature of Quebec education, the need for mutual respect among sub-cultures, and the dangers of trying to impose "the one right way" on this environment. Yet the system has a long way to go before it sincerely subscribes to pluralism as a positive value and diversity as the only strategy subtle enough to maintain balance within Quebec. When should ideology yield to ecology as a guide for policy?

6. There is a marked tendency in Quebec education to devote extraordinary time, attention, and resources to the analysis of issues and plans and then to devote less intelligence and energy to implementation, strategies of effecting change, and getting on with practical action. There is a preoccupation with plans, working documents, studies, consultation documents, flow charts, schemas, principles, and proposals. Professionals spend a great amount of time meeting with one another. There is an almost magical belief that some change in the real world will flow naturally from a carefully phrased regulation. The Quebec documentation amassed on curriculum reform, school board reorganization, collective agreements, language rights, teacher education and the mission of the university would easily outweigh that of all the other provinces combined. A different balance in the words/actions ratio needs to be struck if Quebec's "paralysis of analysis" is to be overcome.

7. The role of the Ministries of Education and of Higher Education and Science needs to shift from control and regulation to leadership, animation, the setting of key priorities, articulation of central values, and the motivation of initiative throughout the system. If the ministries could do this, they would advance their mandate to protect the common good in education far more than through the legalism and technical detail with which they are so often preoccupied.

8. It is unlikely that the quality of public education can be preserved and enhanced unless some solution is found to the impasse of confessional school structures. Ongoing attempts to reorganize school boards have been taking place for fully twenty years. This indicates three things: a serious need to do something, sharpened by rising costs and falling enrolments; an enormous channelling, even waste, of time, talent and money away from other educational priorities; and the failure of imposed and legal strategies to resolve the dilemma. A political compromise must be struck between majority and minority rights, between Montreal and the rest of the province, between Catholics and Protestants, between English and French. Otherwise, another generation of administrative and political imagination will be sacrificed on the altar of "restructuration" proposals and legal challenges.

9. Many of the most promising and creative learning initiatives in Quebec have been outside the formal system, in daycare centres, cultural institutions, voluntary organizations, community development projects, and in print and the electronic media. Often these initiatives are fragile in their funding and short of professional expertise. Always, they lack recognition as "part of education," being considered extensions, complements, and even competition to the "real" system. Quebec is in a position to take the real leap into a comprehensive system of continuing education, integrating

learning policy for both formal and nonformal systems, sharing resources between them, using surplus elementary school teachers to work in senior citizens' homes, and taking all education as the arena for resource allocation.

10. If there has been one refrain in Quebec education from its beginning it is that the teacher is at the heart of the education system and if there has ever been an example of empty rhetoric, this is it. Individually and collectively, teachers have rarely been trusted to bring to learning the power and responsibility that engineers have brought to technology or doctors to healing. Through two decades of often bitter labour confrontation, teachers have won economic, structural and some political power; on the other hand, through the curriculum reforms of the 1980s, the effects of a declining system and through some of the provisions of standardized collective agreements, they have lost much of their authority over learning. A new conception of teaching in a changing and high-technology learning environment, new relationships among teachers, and looser collective agreements may be the only way of stopping the ongoing marginalization of teachers in the public school system.

11. One of the distinctive features of traditional Quebec education prior to 1960, at least in the French sector, was a coherent and comprehensive philosophy of curriculum. This was best illustrated in the program of the classical colleges, a learning program that assumed a common intellectual and moral cutlure. The educational reforms of the past twenty-five years have promoted specialization, discredited classical learning, reduced the importance of general education, and casually handed to the colleges the responsibility for "completing" the general education of eighteen-year-olds in two years. The reforms also sacrificed diversity of program in favor of unified curriculum structures, and promoted the accumulation of credits as the currency of progress in learning. In recent years, there has been growing concern, in Quebec as elsewhere, about the basics, fundamentals of learning, general education, communication skills and intellectual discipline. This has led to more compulsory courses in secondary school (a strategy which in itself is of limited value and not without some risk) and it may soon touch the nature of core curricula in both colleges and university undergraduate programs. Given the current social importance of general knowledge, fundamental values, and generic skills such as logic and creative thinking, more coherent humanities programs in college and new patterns leading to a general bachelor of arts or science degree may be worth some serious consideration and there appear to be some initiatives in these areas. This will require some creative dialogue about what constitutes an educated person in the Quebec of the 1990s. There are more models of general education than those found in the *Cahiers* of the CEGEPs.

12. Quebec may also find it useful to rethink the relationship between colleges and universities. There is little evidence that the colleges have been able to give reality to the idealistic vision of the Parent Commission of comprehensive, open, democratic post-secondary institutions helping students test their ambitions, round off their personal and intellectual development, and acquire democratic understanding as philosophy students sit beside students in electronic technology. Perhaps the college system should be encouraged to evolve into a diversity of institutions, some specializing in technology programs, others in adult education and community service, and others in pre-university training. Some secondary schools may be ready to add advanced programs in a sixth year to encourage direct passage of talented students to university, a possibility that was formerly a pedagogical heresy in Quebec. Perhaps some university undergraduate programs should add a fourth year to ease the transition from secondary school to university. In short, perhaps there is more than one way for a Quebec secondary school student to proceed to a university education or a career.

13. Quebec also needs to rethink its assumption that free or very inexpensive post-secondary education is the right of all young Quebecers who finish secondary school. It must also question the assumption that increasing the proportion of young people attending college and university is necessarily progressive or desirable. In its preoccupation with extending opportunities for schooling, Quebec, like many other developed societies, may have lost sight of other avenues to adulthood and personal fulfillment – like work, personal learning, and community service.

14. Finally, it is clear that learning in Quebec is being furthered with zeal and imagination by a vast number of teachers, learners, professionals, volunteers, administrators, school board members, and politicians. In the past twenty-five years, learning in Quebec has expanded dramatically in scope, sophistication, diversity, and in its avenues of access. Many organizations and institutions are providing stimulating and supportive environments for learning. And despite criticism and disappointment, a great deal of important and high-quality teaching and learning is taking place, often unrecognized in surveys, analyses and statistics. If Quebec education shares many of the limitations of education in every modern society in a turbulent age, it may also be able to build its own unique bridge between a distinctive past and a promising future.

Appendix A
Terms and Expressions

Accessibility: Rate at which a group in the population participates in the education system at different levels. The issue is sometimes discussed in terms of the relative access between groups (e.g. men and women, French and English, urban and rural) and sometimes in terms of absolute access (e.g. per cent of young people 12-18 attending secondary school).

Activist Methods: Approach to elementary school teaching advocated by the Parent Commission in the early 1960s, in Volume 2 of its report. The method was based on the psychology of Jean Piaget and it stressed progressive, child-centred techniques and pupil activities such as projects; it was a reaction to the "bookish" and teacher-centred approaches often used in Quebec schools at the time.

Alliance des Professeurs de Montréal: Major teachers' union, part of the C.E.Q., composed of teachers working in the French sector of the *Commission des Écoles Catholiques de Montreál.*

Alliance Quebec: Organization formed in 1982 to promote English rights, exchange information among various English-language organizations and act as a lobby on behalf of English-speaking interests, especially in relation to the provincial government. It maintains a network of regional organizations throughout Quebec and is active in educational, cultural, and economic fields.

Anglophone: Term for an English-speaking person or organization.

Allophone: Term sometimes used to refer to a person whose mother tongue is neither English nor French.

Alternative Schools: An institution, either private or part of the public school system, based on a defined curriculum focus (such as fine arts) or approach to learning (such as "open education"); such schools often attract pupils from beyond their local community. There are over 20 public alternative elementary schools in the French sector and over a dozen alternative secondary schools in the English sector.

Articulation: Relationship between different levels of the school system and the degree to which one level (such as the elementary school) prepares students for the next level (such as secondary school). Of special concern is the articulation between secondary and collegial levels, and between collegial and university levels.

Associate Deputy Minister: Senior officer of the Quebec Ministry of Education, under the authority of the deputy minister. There are two associate deputy ministers established in law, one for Catholic education and one for Protestant education; their responsibilities are largely restricted to issues of religion.

Availability: Status of a teacher who has been declared surplus by a school board in the light of enrolment projections and teacher needs for a given year. Teachers on "availability" continue to receive all or part of their salary and are required to be available for substitute work and other professional assignments.

Baccalaureate: (a) first degree granted by Quebec universities, usually after a three-year or 90-credit program, in such areas as arts (B.A.), science (B.Sc.), commerce (B. Comm.), engineering (B.Eng.), as well as in other fields; (b) degree (B.A., B. è Arts, Bacc.) granted by French-language universities in Quebec until the 1960s to graduates of the classical colleges.

Basics: The fundamental, core, or essential learning or subjects of study that are required of all students and usually identified with the 3 R's, stressing reading, writing, speaking, computation, and certain habits of responsibility. The movement called "Back to the Basics" includes a loose alliance of interest groups pressing for more stress on language and mathematics, fundamental skills, general knowledge, discipline, and basic values.

Bill: Proposal for a law or an amendment to an existing law, presented usually by the government in the provincial legislature. Bills are studied in three "Readings" (approval in principle, clause-by-clause examination, final approval) before being passed into law and signed by the lieutenant-governor as representative of the Queen. Sometimes a parliamentary committee is formed to hear public opinion and receive presentations concerning a bill under consideration; in a more general sense, Bill is also used in Quebec to refer to a law that has been passed (Bill 60, Bill 101).

Bill 1: (1977) First version of legislation establishing the status of the French language in Quebec; it was withdrawn and reintroduced as Bill 101, which became law as the Charter of the French Language.

Bill 3: (1984) Act reorganizing the education act and the structure of school boards along language lines, following the withdrawal of Bill 40. It was passed but subsequently declared unconstitutional by the Quebec Superior Court and so never went into effect.

Bill 21: (1967) Act establishing the legal structure for Quebec colleges (CEGEPs).

Bill 22: (1974) Act limiting the right of English schooling to those who had a sufficient knowledge of English. A testing program was established which met with opposition in the English-language community.

Bill 24: (1986) Act which modified the Education Act to protect the educational rights of religious minorities (non-Catholic, non-Protestant) to vote in school board elections and become school board members; corrected problems created by Bill 29.

Bill 25: (1967) Act forcing striking teachers to return to work. It established a single salary scale for all teachers in Quebec and created a system of labour negotiations at the provincial level between teachers' associations and school boards.

Bill 27: (1971) Act reorganizing and reducing the number of school boards in Quebec, except for the Island of Montreal.

Bill 28: (1971) Bill which attempted to reorganize school boards on the Island of Montreal, but was not passed.

Bill 29: (1985) Act which attempted to solve a constitutional problem about the rights of confessional school boards in Montreal (CECM and PSBGM) and Quebec city by restricting voting rights to Catholics and Protestants. It met with vigorous opposition from many groups.

Bill 30: (1979) Act providing for parent representatives to sit on school boards but without the right to vote and changed the date of elections for school committees from October to May.

Bill 40: (1983) Bill to reorganize school boards and change the Education Act, following a White Paper called *The Québec School: A Responsible Force in the Community*. It was withdrawn after parliamentary hearings and replaced by Bill 3.

Bill 57: (1979) Act which reduced the power of school boards to raise local taxes to

6% of operating expenses. Constitutionality challenged in the courts and as a result of a court ruling in 1984, it does not apply to the confessional school boards of Montreal and Quebec city.

Bill 57: (1984) Softened some of the provisions of Bill 101, the Charter of the French Language.

Bill 60: (1964) Two acts, one creating the Ministry of Education and the other creating the Superior Council of Education.

Bill 62: (1969) Attempt to establish integrated school boards on the Island of Montreal, not divided by language or religion. It did not pass.

Bill 63: (1969) First legislation to define language rights in education, essentially providing for freedom of choice of the language of instruction; it was passed but met with strenuous opposition in parts of the French community.

Bill 71: (1972) Act which reorganized school boards on the island of Montreal into 6 Catholic boards and 2 Protestant boards and created a School Council for the Island of Montreal.

Bill 71: (1979) Act which established the legal rights of parents to be consulted on certain policy matters and set out the framework for the rights of school committees and parent committees. It also created a framework for the formation of orientation committees in schools, defined a school and spelled out the role of the principal.

Bill 101: (1977) Act establishing the priority of the French language in law, public affairs and education, limiting the right to English schools to those who had one parent educated in an English elementary school in Quebec; parts have been declared unconstitutional (French-only text for legislation) and other parts are still the subject of court challenge (e.g. language of signs). Bill 101 is also referred to as the Charter of the French Language.

Bill 111: (1982) Act ending a teachers' strike, imposing working conditions, cutting salaries and removing the right to strike for a period of time.

British North America Act (B.N.A. Act): (1867) Now referred to as the Constitution Act (1867); the constitutional basis of Canada, together with the Constitution Act of 1982. Section 93 gives exclusive power over education to the provinces with certain guarantees for religious groups, Catholics and Protestants, in Quebec and Ontario.

Cahiers: Official programs and course guides for colleges (CEGEPs) published annually by the Ministry of Higher Education and Science; it also refers to policy documents produced by the Council of Universities in the early 1970s.

Canada Bill: (1982) Constitution Act forming, with the B.N.A. Act of 1867, the constitution of Canada.

Canada Clause: Section 23 of the Canadian Charter of Rights and Freedoms guaranteeing right of access to minority English or French schools to all Canadians with that language as mother tongue and to those whose parents were educated in that language in Canada, where numbers warrant.

Canadian Charter of Rights and Freedoms: (1982) Canada's basic charter of human rights covering legal, linguistic and educational rights.

Career Programs: College (CEGEP) programs, usually of three years' duration, leading to a diploma and the labor force. They are also referred to as technology programs and *programmes professionnels*; a minority of students go on after career programs to university studies. The major categories of career programs are biological, physical, social, administrative, and applied arts; approximately 1/2 of college enrolments are in career programs.

Catholic Committee: (a) One of two confessional committees associated with the Superior Council of Education, composed of 15 members representing educators, the Church, and parents. Its mandate is to make regulations concerning the recognition of schools as Catholic, set criteria by which a school is officially recognized as Catholic, and deal with matters of religious and moral instruction. (b) Prior to 1964, a committee composed of all Catholic bishops in Quebec and an equal number of laypersons, part of the Council of Public Instruction, which exercised authority over all aspects of Catholic education in the province.

C.E.G.E.P: (CEGEP) See College.

Centrale de L'Enseignement du Québec (C.E.Q.): Major teachers' association in Quebec, grouping teachers, education professionals, and some other workers in the Catholic French-language education sector (membership about 70,000). It is the chief bargaining unit at the provincial level and is composed of a number of local associations (syndical units).

Certificate: (a) An official document attesting that a person has successfully completed a university program equivalent to one year of study or 30 credits; normally distinguished from a degree (bachelor, master, doctorate); (b) term associated with certain programs in vocational studies offered by colleges;
(c) sometimes used loosely as synonymous with "diploma," as in a "high school leaving certificate" or a "teaching certificate"; see *Diploma.*

Charter of the French Language: *(Charte de la langue française)* Legislation in 1977, also known as Bill 101, which affirmed the legal status of the French language in Quebec, set rules for legal and business communication, limited access to English schools, restricted the use of languages other than French on public signs, and established agencies to monitor the use of the French language in Quebec. Some parts of the charter have been declared unconstitutional by the courts.

Classes d'Accueil: (literally "welcoming classes") Special classes established to aid children whose mother tongue was not French to adjust to French schools. They are now restricted to those who are recent immigrants and those required by law to attend French schools.

Classical College: *(collège classique)* Private institution, usually Church-affiliated, which, prior to the 1960s, provided the main route to university studies in the French sector. The complete program lasted 8 years, with a 4-year secondary course and a 4-year collegial course, culminating in a baccalauréat granted by one of the French-language universities. The programs were largely philosophical and literary in orientation, though during the 1950s more stress was placed on mathematics and science.

Classification: System according to which teachers are placed in categories on the basis of years of education *(scolarité)* for purposes of determining salary. There is a single system of classification for all teachers in Quebec, and the rules for recognizing study are contained in an evaluation manual.

Collective Agreement: *(Entente)* Contract signed by employers and employees' representatives covering salary, fringe benefits and working conditions for a period of time, usually from 1 to 3 years. Teachers' collective agreements are signed by the two federations of school boards and the three teachers' associations and cover all public elementary and secondary school teachers in Quebec for a 3-year period. Where the parties fail to reach agreement, the government has imposed a settlement (decree) on teachers and school boards; a similar agreement is in force for college instructors.

College: (C.E.G.E.P., *collège d'enseignement général et professionnel,* college of general and vocational studies) Post-secondary institution for all Quebec secondary school graduates wishing to proceed to university or advanced technical training in the province; some 40 public colleges offer 2-year pre-university and 3-year technical (career) programs. Tuition is free for full-time students. A number of private colleges offer a limited range of equivalent programs and charge tuition.

Commission d'Etude sur les Universités: (C.E.U.) Commission established by the government in the late 1970s to study the university system. It published a 4-volume report in 1979 covering a wide range of issues related to the university, its place in society, internal organization, and the education of teachers.

Commission des Ecoles Catholiques de Montréal (C.E.C.M., Montreal Catholic School Commission, M.C.S.C.): Largest school board in Quebec (and in Canada), covering the territory of the city of Montreal and some suburbs. The legal status is constitutionally protected as a confessional board for Catholics and a common board that may not refuse those who are other than Catholic; the board includes a significant English-language section.

Common School Board: School board that is open to all children in a territory regardless of religion even if the schools offer religious instruction. Most Quebec school boards serving the majority of the population in an area are common school boards in a legal sense.

Compulsory Schooling: Provision of the Education Act requiring all parents to send their children to school between the ages of six and fifteen or ensure that they have an equivalent education. The first compulsory education act in Quebec was passed in 1943.

Conference des Recteurs et des Principaux des Universités du Québec: (C.R.E.P.U.Q.) Association of Quebec universities which acts as a body for coordinating university activity and for exchanging information, and to represent the interests of Quebec universities.

Confessionality: Characteristic of Quebec education which divides public education along religious lines, Catholic and Protestant. The term applies to school boards and to individual schools and is rooted in constitutional and legal structures.

Confessional School Board: School board that is formally Catholic or Protestant in legal status, designed primarily to serve Catholic or Protestant pupils, and operating schools recognized as Catholic or Protestant.

Continuing Education: (*Education permanente*) Continuous or lifelong learning; a general policy of education that proposes a complete and comprehensive view of learning services and activities in a society, from early childhood to old age, of which compulsory schooling is just one part; generally the basis for programs of adult education.

Continuous Progress: System of promotion in elementary school in which pupils are advanced from one year to the next with their age group, regardless of level of achievement.

Council of Colleges: (*Conseil des collèges*) Committee established in 1979, composed of members appointed by the Minister of Higher Education and Science, with a mandate to advise the Minister on policies for collegial (CEGEP) education.

Council of Ministers: The executive branch of parliamentary government, consisting of the premier (or prime minister) and the ministers of government selected by him; more commonly called the Cabinet.

Council of Public Instruction: (*Conseil de l'instruction publique*) Before 1964, the legal authority for public education in Quebec, in the absence of a Minister of Education; composed of two largely autonomous committees, a Catholic Committee and a Protestant Committee which made regulations for their sector; administrative work for education was done by a Department of Public Instruction, headed by a Superintendent, with separate Catholic and Protestant divisions.

Council of Universities: (*Conseil des universités*) Committee established in 1968, composed of members appointed by the Minister of Higher Education and Science, with a mandate to coordinate university education, approve new programs and advise the Minister on university policy, especially university financing. it also conducts studies of specific issues.

Credit: Basic unit of a secondary, college or university course or program; most secondary programs consist of 130 credits, college programs vary between 42 and 83 credits, and undergraduate programs are normally 90 credits; a university credit equals 15 hours of lecture, or 45 hours of lectures, laboratory and personal work; 30 credits constitute the equivalent of one full year of university study.

C.S.N.: (*Confédération des syndicats nationaux*, in English the confederation of National Trade Unions or CNTU) Union representing some college instructors as well as many workers outside of education.

Cycle: Major part of a program of studies, usually 2 or 3 years in length; elementary and secondary programs are each divided into 2 cycles; at the university level, bachelor's programs are referred to as the first cycle, master's programs as second cycle, and doctoral programs as third cycle.

Decree: Order-in-council approved by the Cabinet (Council of Ministers), often referred to in relation to an imposed settlement of a labour dispute, a substitute for a collective agreement which imposes salary and working conditions for a fixed period on a certain category of workers; since 1967, there have been more decrees than collective agreements in the education sector.

Deputy Minister: Chief administrative officer and highest-ranking civil servant of a government ministry or department; there is a deputy minister of Education and a deputy minister of Higher Education and Science.

Diploma: (a) General term applying to an official attestation that a certain approved program of studies has been successfully completed; in this sense, certificates and degrees are types of diplomas; (b) official document granted by the government to those who have successfully completed secondary studies (D.E.S., *diplôme de' études secondaires*), a trade program (D.E.P., *diplôme d'études professionnels*) or collegial studies (D.E.C. *diplôme de' etudes collégiales*); sometimes used to refer to short graduate programs in university which require a first degree for admission.

Direction Générale: (Department, directorate, branch) Major department of the Ministry of Education; most important *directions générales* in the Ministry of

Education are the Direction générale de la recherche et du developpement, Direction générale des programmes, and Direction générale des regions.

Director General: Chief administrative officer of a school board, equivalent to a director of education or a school superintendent in other provinces; chief administrator of a college (CEGEP) equivalent to a principal or president; head of a *direction générale* in the Ministry of Education; term is also used in other areas such as health services and social affairs.

Dissentient School Board: School board formed by a religious minority, (Catholic or Protestant) in a territory of a common school board, to provide confessional education to the members of that religious minority; right to dissentient school boards was guaranteed by the B.N.A. Act of 1867; at the present time, there are five dissentient school boards in Quebec in the legal meaning of the term.

Education Act: Comprehensive law covering major aspects of public elementary and secondary education, regularly amended by specific Bills; this Act is the legal basis on which most of public education rests; major sections deal with the organization and administration of school boards.

Education Permanente: See Continuing Education.

Educational Project: *(Projet éducatif)* Process by which a school community, parents and educators, define the character, policy and priorities for the school, and the plan that is developed by this process; the project may deal with such matters as the religious character of the school, learning philosophy, special emphasis in the curriculum, and general procedures of operation; Bill 71 (1979) and the *Green Paper* on Primary and Secondary Education developed the concept of the educational project (sometimes called the educational plan).

Educational Workshop: *(Atelier pédagogique)* Committee of parents and teachers for a school, established in the late 1960s to encourage greater parent participation in shaping school policy. Proposed by the government, this plan met with limited success and was later replaced by school committees composed of parents.

Elementary Education: System of education for children from 6 years to 11 or 12 years of age; the program normally lasts for six years, divided into two 3-year cycles, but some children may take 5 or 7 years to complete it; children are admitted to the first year who have reached 6 years of age by October 1st and through the six years normally stay with their age group; the program is governed by the curriculum regulation *(régime pédagogique)* for pre-school and elementary education.

Eligibility: Right of access to English-language schools as determined by the provisions of the Quebec Charter of the French Language (Bill 101) and the Canadian Charter of Rights and Freedoms. In order to be admitted to an English-language school, children must obtain a certificate of eligibility. In general, children are eligible for English-language education if (a) one parent has received English elementary education in Canada, or (b) if one parent is a Canadian citizen whose mother tongue (language first learned and still understood) is English, or (c) if the parents are temporary residents of Quebec, or (d) if older children are legally attending English school, or (e) if the child needs special educational services that must be provided in English. Bill 101 is stricter than the Canada Clause of the Charter, limiting eligibility to those whose parent received elementary education in English in Quebec but the court has ruled that the Canadian Charter takes precedence.

E.N.A.P.: (Ecole nationale d'administration publique) University-level institution for training public administrators in the government, health, social services and education fields; one of the constituent institutions of the University of Quebec system.

Encadrement: (Literally "framework") Policy and procedures for organizing the activities of a school, especially the grouping of pupils, timetables, pupil services, counseling, and specific programs of study.

Enfance Inadaptée: See Special Education.

English-speaking Parents' Network: Organization grouping representatives of school and parents' committees in English-language schools.

Entente: see Collective Agreement.

Estates General: *(Etats généraux)* Special congress in 1986 of some 6,000 invited participants, organized jointly by 12 groups including the Ministry of Education and associations of parents, school boards and professional educators, to discuss the quality of education in Quebec and make recommendations; its major significance was the collaboration among traditionally opposing groups.

Evaluation: Policies, criteria and procedures for assessing the quality of pupils' learning achievement, of curriculum, of the competence of educators, and of the effectiveness of educational institutions; evaluation policy tends to stress formative evaluation (guidance for future learning) rather than summative (terminal) evaluation, and criterion-referenced procedures (degree of achievement of learning objectives) rather than norm-referenced measures (comparison to others in a group). There are official government examinations for some courses of Secondary IV and V; program effectiveness is measured by end-of-cycle tests, spot checks of a sample of schools; the evaluation of personnel, teachers and administrators is more contentious and is being given more emphasis.

Fabrique: Body of persons legally responsible for the property and material possessions of a Roman Catholic parish. *Fabrique* schools were those established by local parishes in the early 1800s.

F.C.A.R.: *(Fonds pour la formation de chercheurs et l'aide à la recherche)* Program of grants and bursaries to assist researchers, in universities and elsewhere, and to aid in the advanced training of new researchers. Funding is given in a large variety of fields and disciplines, including the study of education, and is administered by a unit in the Ministry of Higher Education and Science.

Fédération des Associations des Professeurs des Universités du Québec: *(F.A.P.U.Q.)* Major organization grouping associations and unions of academic staff in Quebec universities.

Fédération des Associations Parents-Maîtres du Québec: Federation of French-language parent-teacher associations.

Fédération des Collèges: Organization grouping Quebec colleges (CEGEPs).

Fédération des Comités de Parents de la Province de Québec: (F.C.P.P.Q.) Major provincial organization of parents, composed of members of parent committees at the school board level.

Fédération des Commissions Scolaires Catholiques du Québec: (F.C.S.C.Q.) Major provincial association of Catholic school boards and one of the bargaining agents in collective negotiations with teachers.

Federation of English-Speaking Catholic Teachers: (F.E.S.C.T.) Major teachers' union, part of the P.A.C.T., composed of teachers working in the English sector of the Montreal Catholic School Commission.

Formation: (literally, formation or training). Term applying to general education (*formation générale*), fundamental knowledge, skills and/or values (*formation fondamentale*), to vocational, technical and professional preparation (*formation professionnelle*) and to teacher education (*formation des enseignants, formation des maîtres*).

Francisation: Term referring to the policy and process of making French the official language of Quebec, especially in relation to the operation of business and to public signs.

Francophone: French-speaking; parallel to anglophone (English-speaking).

Gendron Commission: Government committee established in 1969 to study the situation of the French language in Quebec. Its report was published in 1972.

Green Paper on Primary and Secondary Education: *(Livre vert)* Document published by the Ministry of Education in 1977 to promote discussion on the curriculum and organization of elementary and secondary education in Quebec. It listed major criticisms of Quebec education, proposed changes in the curriculum and organization of elementary and secondary schools, and presented some ways in which the management of education could be decentralized. It was followed by extensive consultations and surveys of opinion, which led to the publication of a second document, *The Schools of Quebec: Policy Statement and Plan of Action.*

Illegals: Term commonly used to refer to about 1,000 pupils following elementary and secondary programs mainly in the English sector of the Montreal Catholic School Commission, but who were not legally qualified, under the provisions of Bill 101, to attend English-language schools. This program was sponsored by members of the Provincial Association of Catholic Teachers. A general "amnesty" was granted to these pupils in 1986 and they were permitted to conclude their programs and receive official recognition but no additional pupils were to be admitted in this category.

Immersion Program: Curriculum in which the second language (usually French) is taught through the use of the language as the medium of instruction for different subjects. In French immersion programs, such subjects as social studies, physical education, science, and mathematics are usually taught in French. There are various kinds of immersion programs – "early immersion" in the first years of elementary school, "late immersion" usually beginning at the end of elementary school or the beginning of secondary school, "partial immersion" where a limited number of subjects are taught in French, "complete immersion" where most subjects, except English, are in French, and "post-immersion" programs which continue immersion programs at the secondary level.

Institute: (a) general term usually referring to a specialized teaching or research institution at the post-secondary level; (b) name proposed by the Parent Commission for the new post-secondary institutions which it recommended, but the name was subsequently changed to *collège d'enseignement général et professionnel (C.E.G.E.P.)*

Institut Canadien d'Education des Adultes: (I.C.E.A.) Major French-language organization in the field of adult and continuing education.

Institut National de Recherche Scientifique: (I.N.R.S.) A major research institute established by the provincial government as part of the University of Quebec to engage in special research projects in a number of fields. For some years there was an education section (INRS-Education) but it was dissolved in 1986.

Institut Québécois de Recherche sur la Culture: (I.Q.R.C.) A research institution established by the government to engage in specialized research in the field of culture.

Integrated School Boards: Boards that offer both elementary and secondary education.

Jean Commission: Committee established in 1980 to study adult education structures and programs, officially entitled *Commission d'étude sur la formation profession-nelle et socio-culturelle des adultes*, under the chairmanship of Michèle Jean; the commission's report in 1982, **Learning: A Voluntary and Responsible Action**, contained 430 recommendations on basic policy, structures, organization and processes. Its impact on government policy has been modest.

Long Professional Program: A secondary school vocational program that continues through secondary school, leading to a diploma. These programs are being revised.

Magna Carta of Education: A body of legislation in the early 1960s which extended compulsory schooling, expanded access to public secondary education in the French sector, obliged school boards to provide secondary education, and set the framework for the creation of regional school boards for secondary education. The same expression was previously used for a set of legislation in the 19th century.

Mainstreaming: Policy of integrating children and adolescents with learning, physical or mental handicaps into regular schools and classes, to the greatest extent possible. Reversal of the previous policy stressing the identification and separation of the handicapped in special education classes.

Maternelle: Kindergarten for young children age five by October 1st.

Manuel d'Evaluation: Document which specifies the evaluation of the academic and professional qualifications of teachers (diplomas, degrees, years of schooling) and classifies them for purposes of salary.

Milieu Defavorisé: An economically "disadvantaged" district or region, one with a high degree of poverty.

Minister: *(Ministre)* Member of the National Assembly chosen by the Premier to be a member of the cabinet (or council of ministers); most ministers are in charge of government departments such as revenue, education, or social affairs.

Ministry of Education: (M.E.Q., *Ministère de l'Education du Québec)* Government department responsible for elementary and secondary education, under the authority of the Minister of Education and the deputy minister.

Ministry of Higher Education and Science: *(Ministère de l'Enseignement Supérieur et de la Science)* Government department, established in 1985, responsible for post-secondary education, colleges and universities, research grants, student loans and bursaries, and scientific research, under the authority of the Minister and the deputy minister.

Modalités: Methods or procedures, as distinct from objectives and broad policies.

Montreal Catholic School Commission: See *Commission des Ecoles Catholiques de Montreal.*

Montreal Teachers' Association: (M.T.A.) Local teachers' union within P.A.P.T., composed of teachers, French and English, employed by the Protestant School

Board of Greater Montreal.

Municipalité Régionale de Comté: (M.R.C.) Structures of regional municipal government in Quebec.

Multi-Confessional School Board: School board legally constituted to offer services to both Catholic and Protestant pupils; mainly school boards for native peoples in the north, Cree, Kativik, North Shore, Nouveau Québec.

National Assembly: *(Assemblée Nationale)* Legislature of the Province of Quebec, formerly called the Legislative Assembly, located in Quebec city.

Norms: Ratios which determine the number of teachers that may be hired by a school board or college in relation to the number of students.

October Crisis: State of emergency in October 1970 during which the War Measures Act was invoked by the Canadian government to control terrorist acts performed by the separatist group the F.L.Q.

Office de la Langue Française: Body established by Bill 101 to supervise the implementation of, and compliance with, the law regulating the use of French in signs and business and the right of access to English schools.

Official Gazette: *(Gazette officielle)* Official publication of the Government of Quebec which prints the texts of laws and regulations and, when it does so, they come into force.

Operation 55: Government-led program in the 1960s to group the large number of school boards into 55 Catholic and 9 Protestant regional school boards for purposes of offering secondary education.

Orientation Councils: (also referred to as Orientation Committees, or Ways and Means Committees) Committees provided for in Bill 71 (1979) which would bring together parents, teachers, and school administrators in a school to determine the school's policy and transform it into a kind of community school. Very few such councils were established because they depended on the participation of all three parties.

Organisation Volontaire d'Education Populaire: (O.V.E.P.) Voluntary organization offering personal, cultural, or social adult education activities. There are over 1,000 such groups many of which receive government grants.

P.A.C.T.: (Provincial Association of Catholic Teachers) Teachers' organization composed of English-speaking teachers who work for Catholic school boards, in schools where the language of instruction is English.

P.A.P.T.: (Provincial Association of Protestant Teachers) Teachers' organization composed of teachers, English and French, who work for Protestant school boards.

Parent Report: Report of the Royal Commission of Inquiry on Education in the Province of Quebec. The commission, established by the provincial government in 1961 under the chairmanship of Mgr. Alphonse Marie Parent, studied all aspects of the education system and made a series of recommendations for reform in five volumes published between 1963 and 1966. These served as the blueprint for the educational reforms of the Quiet Revolution. Volume 1 dealt with government structures, Volume 2 with educational structures, Volume 3 with various subjects of the curriculum, Volume 4 with religious and cultural pluralism, and Volume 5 with finance.

Parents' Committee: Advisory committee of parents, composed of representatives of school committees, with a mandate to advise a school board. In general, each school board has one parents' committee.

Parti Québécois: Quebec political party formed in the early 1970s under the leadership of René Lévesque, based on a platform of political independence for Quebec; formed the government of Quebec between 1976 and 1986.

Pedagogical Days: Professional days in the school calendar during which pupils do not attend school but teachers engage in various professional activities such as meetings and workshops.

Plan of Action: *(Plan d'Action, The Schools of Quebec,* the Orange Paper) Policy statement of the Ministry of Education, published in 1979, with the title *The Schools of Quebec: Policy Statement and Plan of Action.* This major government position paper followed the consultations on the **Green Paper** and led to the formulation of new curriculum regulations for elementary and secondary schools *(régimes pédagogiques).* The general thrust of the document was a return to basics, increased government control of curriculum, more systematic evaluation, and mechanisms for parent participation in school policy. In general, plan of action is used to refer to a broad plan or policy proposal.

Polyvalent: Comprehensive, term used to refer to secondary schools which include both academic and vocational programs, modelled on the American comprehensive high school.

Preschool Education: Officially approved programs for young children under 6 years of age, especially kindergarten programs for 5 year olds and some special kindergartens for 4 year olds. Daycare and nursery schools are not normally included.

Private Education Act: Law governing private schools, first enacted in 1968 and later amended on a couple of occasions. It defines categories of private schools, establishes procedures for funding some of these schools, and provides criteria for obtaining permits.

Probation: Period, normally of two years' duration, during which a teacher with a temporary teaching permit is required to demonstrate teaching competence. After successful completion of the period of probation, the teacher receives a permanent teaching diploma.

Professionnel: Term which is variously translated as vocational, technical, professional, career, or manpower, depending on the context.

Protestant Committee: (a) One of two confessional committees associated with the Superior Council of Education, composed of 15 members representing educators, parents, and various Protestant denominations. Its mandate is to make regulations concerning the recognition of schools as Protestant, set criteria for a Protestant school, and deal with matters of religious and moral instruction; (b) prior to 1964, a committee, equal in size to the number of laypersons on the parallel Catholic Committee, composed of representatives of Protestant denominations, that formed part of the Council of Public Instruction, which exercised authority over all aspects of Protestant education in the province.

Protestant School Board of greater Montreal (P.S.B.G.M.): Largest Protestant school board in Quebec, including the territory of the City of Montreal and some suburbs. It is protected under the B.N.A. act as a common and confessional school board and operates both English and French language schools.

Quebec Association for Children and Adults with Learning Disabilities: (Q.A.C.L.D.) Large, bilingual association of parents, educators and professionals concerned with services for children with various types of emotional, learning, or physical handicaps.

Quebec Association for Adult Learning (Q.A.A.L.): Association of individuals and groups interested in adult education in Quebec, primarily an English-language organization.

Quebec Association of Protestant School Boards (Q.A.P.S.B.): Major provincial association of Protestant school boards and one of the bargaining agents in collective negotiations with teachers.

Quebec Federation of Home and School Associations: Association grouping local home-and-school associations, mainly in the Protestant sector; the oldest such association in Quebec.

Quiet Revolution: Period between 1960 and about 1968 during which rapid social, political, economic, and cultural changes took place in Quebec society, including new social priorities, reorganization of social structures, especially schools, greater assertiveness in promoting French language and culture, and more emphasis on economic development.

Régimes Pédagogiques: (Curriculum Regulations) Regulations, or Orders-in-Council determining the structure of curriculum and instructional services. There are three *régimes pédagogiques*: (1) Regulation Respecting the Basis of Elementary School and Preschool Organization, 1981, (2) Regulation Respecting the Basis of Secondary School Organization, 1981, (3) Regulation Respecting the Basis of College Organization, 1984.

Regional Office: (Regional Bureau, *Direction régionale*) Unit of the Ministry of Education in each of the 11 administrative regions of the province; Lower St. Lawrence; Gaspé; Saguenay, Lac St. Jean; Quebec city; Trois-Rivières; Estrie (Eastern Townships); Montreal; Laval-Laurentides-Lanaudière (North of Montreal); Longueuil (South of Montreal); Outaouais (Ottawa Valley, Hull); Abitibi-Témiscamingue; Côte-Nord (North shore of the St. Lawrence, east to Labrador).

Regional School Board: School board composed of representatives of local elementary school boards, established to provide secondary education. There were 55 Catholic and 9 Protestant regional school boards, mainly outside of the Island of Montreal, established in the early 1960s as part of what was called Operation 55. At the present time, many local elementary school boards are becoming integrated with these boards.

Regulation: Order-in-Council, approved by the Provincial Cabinet, in virtue of some body of legislation. Regulations do not have to be approved by the National Assembly but Regulations in the field of education must, by law, be submitted to the Superior Council of Education for advice. The *régimes pédagogiques* are education regulations. Other regulations in the field of education are: Regulation No. 1 (1965), a general framework for preschool, elementary and secondary education; Regulation No. 2 (1966), on official examinations; Regulation No. 3 (1966), on the structure of colleges (CEGEPs); Regulation No. 4 (1966), on teacher training; Regulation No. 5 (1968), on the classification of teachers for salary purposes; Regulation No. 6 (1971), on the teaching of French; Regulation No. 7 (1971), on preschool, elementary and secondary education, an expansion of Regulation No. 1

and now largely incorporated into the *régimes pédagogiques*.

Reports: Official records of pupil progress sent to parents by the school. Each school must send at least 5 reports per years, one before the end of October. Reports usually include (a) an indication of the pupil's achievement in each subject, either in letters or per cent, (b) an assessment of the pupil's attitude or effort, and (c) some comparison between the pupil's result and those of the group of which he is part.

School Board: *(Commission scolaire)* Unit of educational administration, the legal body directly responsible for hiring teachers, constructing and maintaining buildings, and offering public educational services at preschool, elementary and secondary levels to children in a geographic territory. In 1986 there were 234 school boards in Quebec, 201 for Catholics, 29 for Protestants, and 4 for both Catholics and Protestants. School board members (commissioners or trustees) are elected by universal suffrage for a three-year term.

School Commission: see School Board

School Committee: Advisory committee of parents established in each elementary and secondary school, with one teacher representative and the principal **ex officio**; its mandate is to advise the school authorities on general policy and on specific topics which the committee may select, including such matters as school activities, discipline, religious and moral education, specific emphasis in the curriculum, and communication with parents. Parents are elected for a one-year term at a general meeting of parents.

School Council for the Island of Montreal: (S.C.I.M., *Conseil scolaire de l'Ile de Montreál*, C.S.I.M.) Coordinating body established by Bill 71 (1972) to set the school tax rate for school boards on the Island of Montreal, receive tax revenues and distribute them to the 6 Catholic and 2 Protestant school boards on the Island. The Council is also concerned with negotiating loans, planning, use of buildings, and special programs for the disadvantaged.

School Trustee: (a) In Canada, a member of a school board elected or appointed for a fixed term; (b) in Quebec, a member of a dissentient school board established for a religious minority in a region, with members of the majority board called commissioners.

Schools of Quebec: See Plan of Action.

Scolarité: (years of schooling) Term used in the classification of teachers for salary purposes to refer to the number of years of formal schooling or equivalent of a teacher. Categories go from 13 years of schooling or less (completion of college) to 20 years (including a doctoral degree).

Secondary Education: System of education for young people between 12 and 15 to 18 years of age; the program normally lasts 5 years, from Secondary I (7th year) to Secondary V (11th year) and is divided into Cycle One (Secondary I and II) and Cycle Two (Secondary III, IV, V). The 5-year program contains about 180 credits of study, about 150 of which are compulsory and 30 elective. There are 3 basic programs: General Education, Long Vocational Studies, and Short Vocational Studies (the vocational programs are under revision). Promotion is by subject based on a pass mark of 60%.

Secondary School Diploma: *(diplôme d'études secondaires,* high school leaving diploma) (a) General Education: 130 credits at least 20 of which are recognized as Secondary V credits, including 12 cr. (Sec. IV & V) in language of instruction, 4 cr.

(Sec. V) in French second language, (or 4 cr. (Sec. IV or V) in English second language), 4 cr. (Sec. IV) history, 2 cr. (Sec. IV or V) religious or moral education; (b) Long Vocational Studies: 130 credits with the same specifications as for General Education except for the 4-cr. history requirement and with additional credits specific to the selected vocational specialization; (c) Short Vocational Studies: minimum of 70 credits including 6 cr. (Sec. I) language of instruction, 6 cr. (Sec. I) mathematics, and 24 cr. (Sec. IV) in the chosen vocational specialization. Requirements for vocational programs are in the process of revision.

Service Régional d'Accueil et de Référence: (S.R.A.R.) Regional referral and drop-in centres for adults.

Services Educatifs aux Anglophones: (English-Language Educational Services) Unit within the Ministry of Education responsible for the coordination of Ministry activities in relation to English-language education in the province, Protestant and Catholic. It reports to an assistant deputy minister and works through the regional offices of the Ministry, especially the Montreal office. The unit includes a number of professionals and technical advisers.

Short Vocational Program: Secondary school program in an area of a trade (carpentry, electricity, construction) which usually begins in Secondary I and terminates in Secondary IV (10th year). Recent government policy has been to reduce or eliminate these programs in favor of a longer general education and more concentrated vocational programs at the Secondary V or VI level.

Special Education: General term applying to programs and services for exceptional children, the gifted and talented but mainly those with physical, emotional, intellectual or learning disabilities or handicaps. In the past the tendency was to establish special classes or schools for such pupils but at the present time the policy is one of "mainstreaming," the integration to the greatest degree possible of handicapped children into regular schools and classes.

Stage: (internship, professional practice) Period of supervised practical experience in a vocational or professional field under the control of an educational institution. Extended student teaching in school for teachers in training is an example.

Streaming: Policy of grouping elementary or secondary students into relatively homogeneous classes on the basis of ability, achievement, or interest and providing different programs. Until the new curriculum regulations of 1981, most high schools streamed students into advanced, regular and slow streams in the basic subjects of English, French, and mathematics. In practice, some streaming continues in advance mathematics and science courses but the current policy is to offer the same general program to all students, regardless of the basis on which classes are formed.

Subject Promotion: Policy of promotion at the secondary level by which a student's progress is determined by his success in each individual subject rather than by an overall average. According to this policy, a student would fail a complete year only if he failed all subjects.

Superior Council of Education: *(Conseil supérieur de l'Education)* Major advisory body to the Minister of Education and the Minister of Higher Education and Science, established in law by Bill 60 in 1964. The Council is composed of 24 members. It must be consulted before a regulation in education can come into force; it may be consulted in any matter requested by the Minister; it may initiate its own studies, and it is required to submit an annual report to the National Assembly on the state and needs of education in Quebec. Two confessional committees, the

Catholic Committee and the Protestant Committee, are formally associated with it, though they have independent powers in the area of religious and moral education.

Surplus Teacher: See Availability.

Syndical Unit: *(Syndicat)* Local unit of a teachers' association which holds a bargaining certificate under the terms of the Labour Code.

Teaching Certificate (Diploma): *(brevet d'enseignement)* Attestation of a person's legal right to teach in the elementary or secondary schools of Quebec on a permanent basis, granted by the Ministry of Education. Certificates (or diplomas) are granted to those who are Canadian citizens and who have recognized teacher training, a permit to teach, and have completed two years of probationary teaching judged satisfactory. Teaching certificates usually specify the (a) language of instruction, (b) the level, elementary or secondary, and in some cases (c) the subject area(s) in which the teacher is qualified.

Teaching Permit: *(permit d'enseigner)* A legal statement giving a person who has completed an approved teacher education program the right to teach for up to 5 years in an elementary or secondary school of Quebec. It is granted by the Ministry of Education. Permits may be converted to permanent certificates after two years of teaching judged satisfactory. Other temporary permits include "letters of eligibility" for those with acceptable qualifications but without a Quebec teaching certificate (e.g. teachers from other provinces), and "provisional teaching authorizations" for those who do not meet minimum legal requirements.

Télé–Université: Constituent institution of the University of Quebec which prepares and presents distance-education programs and university courses through television and other means.

Treasury Board: (Conseil du Trésor) Branch of the Quebec government that controls revenues and expenditures and that approves the monetary clauses of collective agreements in the public sector.

University of Québec: *(Universite'du Québec,* UQ) Public, Quebec-wide university structure established by law in 1969. Central administration is in Quebec city and there are campuses in Trois-Rivières (UQTR), Chicoutimi (UQAC), Rimouski (UQAR), Hull (UQAH), Montréal (UQAM), and Abitibi-Témiscamingue (UQAT). UQ also includes some specialized institutes such as the Institut de technologie supérieure, Télé-Université, and the Institut national d'administration publique.

U.Q.A.M.: *(Universite'du Québec à Montreal)* Largest constituent university of the University of Quebec system, established in 1969 by the integration of a classical college, a normal school, and an institute of technology. It now offers undergraduate and graduate programs in most areas except traditional professions of medicine, law, and dentistry.

Vocational Training Commission: (C.F.P., Commission de la formation professionnelle) Joint committee representing employers and employees in a region. Its role is to make agreements with educational institutions to offer apprenticeship, vocational training and retraining courses. It is under the jurisdiction of the Quebec Minister of Manpower and Income Security.

White Paper: (1982) Major policy statement of the Minister of Education, with the title *The Quebec School: A Responsible Force in the Community*, which proposed a new legal structure for individual schools, a system of parent control, a complete reorganization of school boards and other administrative measures. It was followed by Bill 40 (1983) and Bill 3 (1984) which progressively modified the proposals in the White Paper. Because Bill 3 was judged unconstitutional, the proposals of the White Paper were not put into effect.

Appendix B
Key Dates in Quebec Education

1608 – Founding of Quebec.

1635 – Establishment by the Jesuits of the first elementary school.

1655 – Establishment of the Jesuit College in Quebec City, the first classical secondary school.

1665 – Founding of the Quebec Seminary by Bishop Laval.

1670 – Founding of the first technical-trade school at St-Joachim.

1760 – Quebec became a British colony after the defeat of the French.

1763 – *Treaty of Paris* formally ceded New France to Britain.

1774 – *Quebec Act* gave legal recognition to the French language and culture and to the Catholic religion, but banned the Jesuits.

1791 – *Constitutional Act* divided Canada into Upper (Ontario) and Lower (Quebec) provinces, each with its own Legislative Assembly.

1801 – *An Act for the Establishment of Free Schools and the Advancement of Learning* created the first public school system in Quebec. It was a centralized system under the control of the governor. English Protestants established Royal schools but French Catholics were suspicious of the intent of the law and few schools were created for Catholics.

1821 – McGill College granted a Royal Charter as university.

1824 – *Fabrique Act* permitted individual parishes to establish schools under the control of the parish priest and church wardens, but little interest was shown.

1828 – Establishment of the Mechanics' Institute in Montreal.

1829 – *Legislative Assembly Schools Act* (or *Syndics Act*) was the most successfully attempt to that date to form a public school system. It provided for local bodies of school trustees elected by property owners, and for government subsidies to support local schools.

– Opening of McGill College in Montreal.

1836 – Founding of first Normal School in Montreal.

1839 – *Durham Report* issued by Lord Durham following the political unrest in 1837-38. It dealt with political and educational issues in both Upper and Lower provinces.

1841 – *Act of Union* of Canada West (Ontario) and Canada East (Quebec) included a number of educational provisions: creation of the post of Superintendent of Public Instruction, local school districts with elected commissioners, local school taxation, and common schools (but with the right of dissent for minority groups of Catholics or Protestants).

1844 – Founding of *l'Institut Canadien* in Montreal.

1845 – Legislation created a separate Superintendent of Public Instruction for Quebec.

251

1846 – Denominational school boards for Catholics and Protestants were established in Montreal and Quebec City.

1851 – Founding of Bishop's College in Eastern Townships.
  – Founding of YMCA in Montreal.
  – School Inspectorate established.

1852 – Founding of Laval University in Quebec City.

1856 – Council of Public Instruction established and the powers of the Superintendent were extended to include responsibility for teacher training and certification.

1857 – Normal Schools established for Catholics and Protestants.

1864 – Founding of Provincial Association of Protestant Teachers (PAPT).

1867 – *British North America Act* created Confederation. Section 93 granted exclusive jurisdiction in education to the provinces, but the existing legal rights of Catholic and Protestant religious minorities were protected.
  – A Ministry of Public Instruction established in Quebec.

1869 – Council of Public Instruction divided into Catholic and Protestant Committees.

1873 – Founding of *l'Ecole Polytechnique* in Montreal.
  – The elementary program in public Catholic schools officially extended to four years.

1875 – Ministry of Public Instruction was abolished and the Department of Public Instruction was headed by an appointed superintendent answerable to the Council of Public Instruction. The Catholic and Protestant Committees of the Council became autonomous for all practical purposes and all the bishops of Quebec became *ex-officio* members of the Catholic Committee. This basic structure remained unchanged until the 1960s.

1878 – A branch of Laval University established in Montreal.

1896 – Founding of Loyola College and Loyola High School for English Catholics.

1901 – Protestant Committee extended program to 11 years in Protestant schools.

1903 – Education Act provided that for educational purposes, Jews were to be regarded as Protestants.

1905 – Catholic Committee extended elementary school program to 8 years.

1907 – Founding of the *l'Ecole des Hautes Etudes Commerciales* in Montreal.
  – Founding of Macdonald College at Ste-Anne-de-Bellevue (agriculture, domestic science and teacher training) affiliated to McGill University.

1911 – First classical college established for girls.

1914 – *L'Ecole des Hautes Etues Commerciales* affiliated with Laval University.

1919 – First local Home and School Association in Quebec.

1920 – University of Montreal became independent of Laval University.

1922 – Founding of *l'Ecole des Beaux-Arts* in Montreal.

1923 – Catholic public education system extended to six years elementary plus two years *ećole complémentaire*.

1926 – Founding of Sir George Williams High School and College as part of YMCA.

1928 – Privy Council declared that Jews could not in law be classified as Protestants for educational purposes.

1929 – Catholic public education system extended to eleven years by addition of a three-year *école primaire supérieure*.

1930 – Education Act authorized a Jewish School Commission in Montreal but it never became operational.

1931 – Founding of D'Arcy McGee, first English-Catholic public high school.

1936 – First French kindergarten class.

1937 – Sir George Williams College granted first degree.

1942 – Women permitted to serve on school commissions.

1943 – Quebec's first compulsory school attendance law.

1944 – Founding of Quebec Federation of Home and School Associations.

1945 – Law guaranteed teachers a minimum salary of $600 per annum.
   – Classical course first offered in some Catholic public schools.
   – Founding of Thomas More Institute of Adult Education.

1946 – Creation of Ministry of Youth which became responsible for technical education.

1948 – Sir George Williams College awarded a university charter.

1953 – Normal Schools officially affiliated with universities.

1954 – Report of the Royal Commission of Inquiry on Constitutional Problems (The Tremblay Report), which identified public education in Quebec as a major problem.
   – Charter granted for the University of Sherbrooke.

1956 – Catholic Committee approved a new series of secondary-level programs: general, commercial, science and letters, sciences, mathematics, classical, agricultural, industrial, and domestic science. A five year *cours secondaire* replaced the higher elementary course.

1958 – Technical schools became Technical Institutes.

1959 – Death of Maurice Duplessis, leader of the Union Nationale Party.

1960 – Election of Jean Lesage and the Liberal Party.
   – Responsibility for the financial aspect of the Department of Public Instruction assigned to Paul Gérin-Lajoie, Minister of Youth.
   – – Publication of *Les Insolences du Frère Untel*, a book critical of many aspects of Quebec education.

1961 – *Magna Carta of Quebec Education* – a series of laws that abolished school fees, encouraged school boards to establish public secondary schools, increased government spending, permitted parents to vote in school board elections, and raised the age of compulsory school attendance from fourteen to fifteen years.
   – Creation of a Royal Commission of Inquiry on Education (the *Parent Commission*) to study the problems of education and to make recommendations for reform.

1962 – Founding of the Provincial Association of Catholic Teachers (PACT)

1963 – Publication of Volume 1 of the Parent Report which recommended creation of a Ministry of Education and Superior Council of Education.

- *Bill 60* tabled in Legislative Assembly.

1964 – *Bill 60* approved – established a Ministry of Education and a Superior Council of Education and two confessional committees.

Publication of Volumes 2 and 3 of the Parent Report which recommended the reorganization of structures and curriculum from pre-school to university, including the establishment of Institutes or CEGEPS.

- *Operation 55* launched by the Ministry in order to create 55 regional school boards for Catholics and 9 regional school boards for Protestants.

- Quebec's new labour code granted teachers the right to strike under certain conditions.

1965 – *Regulation 1* approved by the Government established the basic structures of elementary and secondary education.

- First French kindergarten classes organized by the Ministry.

1966 – Liberal government defeated by the Union Nationale.

- *Regulation 2* (on official examinations), *Regulation 3* (on pre-university [CEGEP] studies), and *Regulation 4* (on teacher education and certification) approved by the Government.

- School Inspectorate abolished.

- Publication by the Ministry of *The Cooperative School: Comprehensiveness and Continuous Progress* – a commentary on Regulation 1.

- Publication of Volumes 4 and 5 of the Parent Report concerning finances and school board reorganization.

1967 – *Bill 21: General and Vocational Colleges Act* created CEGEPs.

- Founding of the *Corporation des Enseignants du Quebec* (CEQ).

- Widespread strikes by teachers followed by *Bill 25* which ordered teachers back to work, imposed a single salary scale for the whole province, and set up a mechanism for collective bargaining at the provincial level.

1968 – *Regulation Number 5* concerning the classification of teachers for salary purposes.

- Report of the Royal Commission on Bilingualism and Biculturalism, Ottawa.

- *Radio-Quebec* established.

- *Bill 88* authorized the establishment of *l'Universite du Quebec.*

- *Bill 56: The Private Education Act* was approved and created a Consultative Commission on Private Education.

- The Council of Universities created.

- *Page Commission Report* recommended language boards for the Island of Montreal, but there were a number of dissensions.

- Language riots in St. Leonard, a Montreal suburb.

- Government established the *Gendron Commission* to recommend a language policy for the province.

1969 – *Bill 63* made French the working language of Quebec and guaranteed in law the right of parents to choose the language of instruction, but there was much opposition.

- Federal government enacts the Official Languages Act.

- *L'Universite du Québec* opened in Montreal, Chicoutimi, Rimouski and Trois Rivières.

— First collective agreement for teachers was signed.

— Creation of *l'Institut national de la recherche scientifique* (INRS).

— *Bill 62* proposed unified school boards on the Island of Montreal, but the Bill died in committee as a provincial election was called.

1970 — Liberals under Robert Bourassa elected to power.

— Creation of *l'Eole nationale d'administration publique* (ENAP).

— founding of *l'Institut Canadien de l'education des adultes.*

— The *October Crisis* — kidnapping of British Trade Commissioner and murder of Pierre Laporte, Quebec's Minister of Labour, led to imposition of the War Measures Act.

1971 — *Regulation 6* (on the teaching of French) and *Regulation 7* (an expansion of Regulation No. 1 dealing with the organization of elementary and secondary schools).

— *Bill 27* reduced the number of school boards outside the Island of Montreal from about 1100 to less than 250, extended the right of universal suffrage in school board elections, and created parent and school committees.

— *Bill 28* would have created unified school boards on the Island of Montreal but was withdrawn because of massive opposition.

1972 — *Bill 71* reduced the number of school boards on the Island of Montreal from 33 to 8: 6 Catholic and 2 Protestant, extended the right of universal suffrage in school board elections, and created parent and school committees. The Bill also established the School Council of the Island of Montreal to coordinate and control the budgets of its constituent boards.

— Government imposed a decreed settlement on teachers.

— Creation of *Tele-Universite'*

— The *Gendron Commission* recommended that French become the official language of Quebec.

1973 — *Corporation des Enseignants du Québec* became *La Centrale de l'enseignement du Québec*(CEQ).

1974 — *Bill 22* declared French to be the sole official language of Quebec and restricted enrolment in English schools to those with a sufficient knowledge of English. A working knowledge of French was required of Quebec's thirty-eight professions.

— Concordia University created by amalgamation of Loyola College and Sir George Williams University.

— Creation of *l'Ecole de technologie supérieure* affiliated with *l'Universite'du Quebec.*

— Publication of the Regulation of the Catholic Committee concerning the recognition of confessional educational institutions as Catholic.

1975 — Publication of the Regulation of the Protestant Committee regarding the recognition of educational institutions as Protestant.

— Creation of the *Federation des comite'des parents de la province du Québec* (FCPPQ).

— *L'Institut de microbiologie et d'hygiene de Montreal* becomes *l'Institut Armand-Frappier* and is affiliated with l'Université du Québec.

— Superior Council of Education published its Report on College Education: *Le Collège* (Nadeau Report).

1976 – René Lévesque and *Parti Quebecois* elected to power.
 – Second collective agreement is signed by the teachers.
 – Publication of the COPEX Report on *L'Education de l'enfance en difficulte' de' adaptation et d' apprentissage au Quebec.*

1977 – *Bill 101* or the *Charter of the French Language* enacted a comprehensive language policy in Quebec and restricted the right of English schooling to those with at least one parent who had received elementary schooling in English in Quebec.
 – Publication of the *Green Paper* on Primary and Secondary Education in Quebec.

1978 – Publication of a White Paper on collegial education; *Les Collèges du Quebec: Nouvelle Etape.*
 – Publication of *A Cultural Development Policy for Quebec.*

1979 – Government released *The Schools of Quebec: Policy Statement and Plan of Action.*
 – Publication of *Pour une nouvelle politique quebecoise de la recherche scientifique au Québec.*
 – Publication of Policy Statement and Plan of Action on *Children with difficulties in learning and adaptation.*
 – *Bill 24* created the Council of Colleges.
 – *Bill 30* provided for parental representation on school boards.
 – *Bill 71* provided legal definitions of the school and a school's *educational project*, defined the role of school principal, allowed for the creation of *orientation committees*, and expanded the legal rights of school and parent committees.
 – *Bill 57* restricted the right of school boards to levy school taxes to 6% of expenditures.

1980 – Government published *Adapting Schools to their Milieux*, a policy statement for schools in economically disadvantaged areas.
 – Publication by the Ministry of Education of four documents on the Educational Project and of one document on the Orientation Committee.
 – Third collective agreement signed by the teachers.
 – Publication of the Report of the *Commission d' étude sur les universités.*

1981 – Government issued two regulations (*regimes pedagogiques*), one for preschool and elementary education and the other for secondary education, dealing with educational services and curriculum organization.
 – The government announced that it intended to restructure the province's educational system.

1982 – Government issued a *White Paper* on school structures and board reorganization entitled: *The Quebec School: a responsible force in the community.*
 – Final Report of the Jean Commission on Adult Education.
 – Federal government proclaimed the *Canadian Charter of Rights and Freedoms*, Section 23 of which included minority language guarantees in education.

1983 – *Bill 40: An Act respecting public elementary and secondary education* tabled in the National Assembly and studied by the Standing Parliamentary Committee on Education. It was subsequently withdrawn.
- *Bill 111* – teachers ordered back to work and reduced salaries are imposed.
- *Manpower and vocational training Act* defined role of *Commissions de formation professionnelle.*

1984 – *Bill 3: An Act respecting public elementary and secondary education* introduced in November and passed in December.
- 6% limit on taxation in Bill 57 (1979) declared unconstitutional for confessional school boards in Montreal and Quebec.
- Superior Council of Education published a report on the teaching profession entitled *La condition enseignante.*
- Publication of Policy Statement and Plan of Action on Continuing Education.
- Revision of the law governing the colleges.
- Publication of regulations (régime pédagogique) governing College programs.
- Certain education aspects of Bill 101 modified by Bill 57 (1984).

1985 – *Bill 3* declared unconstitutional by the Quebec Superior Court and a permanent injunction was issued preventing its application.
- Government split the Ministry of Education into two: a Ministry of Education and a Ministry of Higher Education, Science and Technology (later to become a Ministry of Higher Education and Science).
- University Charter granted to *Collège Militaire Royale de St. Jean.*
- *Bill 29* recognized the taxation rights of the confessional school boards in Montreal and Quebec city, and withdraws the two confessional boards in Montreal from the budgetary control of the School Council of the Island of Montreal. Bill 29 also restricted the right to vote to those who are Catholic or Protestant.
- Parti Québécois defeated by Liberal Party in Provincial elections.

1986 – *Estates General* on the Quality of Education held in Montreal.
- *Bill 24* restored universal suffrage in confessional school board elections and arranged for all school board elections to be held on the third Sunday of November beginning in 1987.
- *Bill 58* granted amnesty to *illegal* students in English schools.
- Government published *La formation professionnelle au secondaire: plan d'action* concerning vocational education.
- *Bill 142* guaranteed some health and social services in the English language.
- Sections of Bill 101 on French-only signs declared unconstitutional by Quebec's Court of Appeal.
- *Régimes pédagogiques* modified to include a new course in physical science and new programs in vocational education to begin after age 16 years.

Appendix C

Section 93, British North America Act, 1867

93. In and for each Province the Legislature may exclusively make Laws in relation to Education, subject and according to the following Provisions:–

(1) Nothing in any such Law shall prejudicially affect any Right or Privilege with respect to Denominational Schools which any Class of Persons have by Law in the Province at the Union;

(2) All the Powers, Privileges, and Duties at the Union by Law conferred and imposed in Upper Canada on the Separate Schools and School Trustees of the Queen's Roman Catholic Subjects shall be and the same are hereby extended to the Dissentient Schools of the Queen's Protestant and Roman Catholic Subjects in Quebec;

(3) Where in any Province a System of Separate or Dissentient Schools exists by Law at the Union or is thereafter established by the Legislature of the Province, an Appeal shall lie to the Governor General in Council from any Act or Decision of any Provincial Authority affecting any Right or Privilege of the Protestant or Roman Catholic Minority of the Queen's Subjects in relation to Education;

(4) In case any such Provincial Law as from Time to Time seems to the Governor General in Council requisite for the due Execution of the Provisions of this Section is not duly executed by the proper Provincial Authority in that Behalf, then and in every such Case, and as far only as the Circumstances of each Case require, the Parliament of Canada may make remedial Laws for the due Execution of the Provisions of this Section and of any Decision of the Governor General in Council under this Section.

Appendix D
The Education Provisions of Bill 22 (1974)

40.   The language of instruction shall be in French in the schools governed by the school boards, the regional school boards and the corporations of trustees.

The school boards, regional school boards and corporations of trustees shall continue to provide instruction in English.

An existing or future school board, regional school board or corporation of trustees cannot validly decide to commence, cease, increase or reduce instruction in English unless it has received prior authorization from the Minister of Education, who shall not give it unless he considers that the number of pupils whose mother tongue is English and who are under the jurisdiction of such body warrants it; in the case of cessation or reduction of such instruction, the Minister shall also take into account, when giving his authorization, the number of pupils otherwise qualified.

Nevertheless, the School Board of New Québec may provide instruction to the Indians and Inuits in their own languages.

41.   Pupils must have a sufficient knowledge of the language of instruction to receive their instruction in that language.

Pupils who do not have a sufficient knowledge of any of the languages of instruction must receive their instruction in French.

43.   It is the function of each school board, regional school board and corporation of trustees to determine to what class, group or course any pupil may be assigned, having regard to his aptitudes in the language of instruction.

43.   The Minister of Education may however, in accordance with the regulations, set tests to ascertain that the pupils have sufficient knowledge of the language of instruction to receive their instruction in that language. He may, if need be, require a school board, regional school board or corporation of trustees to reassign the pupils on the basis of the results of those tests.

Such tests must take account of the level of instruction, including kindergarten, for which the applications for enrolment are made, and of the age and previous education of the examinees.

The regulations must provide for an appeal to the Minister, who, before deciding the matter, must obtain the advice of a supervisory committee on the language of instruction established for that purpose. His decision is final.

44.   The curricula must ensure that pupils receiving their instruction in English acquire a knowledge of spoken and written French, and the Minister of Education shall adopt the necessary measures to that effect.

The Minister of Education must also take the necessary measures to ensure instruction in English as a second language to pupils whose language of instruction is French.

261

Appendix E

The Major Education Provisions of Bill 101 (1977) As Amended by Bill 57 (1984) The Language of Instruction

72. Instruction in the kindergarten classes and in the elementary and secondary schools shall be in French, except where this chapter allows otherwise.

    This rule obtains in school bodies within the meaning of the Schedule and also applies to subsidized instruction provided by institutions declared to be of public interest or recognized for purposes of grants in virtue of the Act respecting private education (1968, chapter 67).

73. In derogation of section 72, the following children, at the request of their father and mother, may receive their instruction in English:

    (a) a child whose father or mother received elementary instruction in English in Québec, provided that that instruction constitutes the major part of the elementary instruction he or she received in Québec;

    (b) a child whose father or mother is, on 26 August 1977, domiciled in Québec and has received elementary instruction in English outside Québec, provided that that instruction constitutes the major part of the elementary instruction he or she received outside Québec.

    (c) a child who, in his last year of school in Québec before 26 August 1977, was lawfully receiving his instruction in English, in public kindergarten class or in an elementary or secondary school;

    (d) the younger brothers and sisters of a child described in paragraph c.

74. Where a child is in the custody of only one of his parents, or of a tutor, the request provided for in section 73 must be made by that parent or by the tutor.

75. The Minister of Education may empower such persons as he may designate to verify and decide on children's eligibility for instruction in English.

78.1 No person may permit or tolerate a child's receiving instruction in English if he is ineligible therefor.

79. A school body not already giving instruction in English in its schools is not required to introduce it and shall not introduce it without express and prior authorization of the Minister of Education.

80. The Gouvernement may, by regulation, prescribe the procedure to be followed where parents invoke section 73, and the elements of proof they must furnish in support of their request.

81. Children having serious learning disabilities must be exempted from the application of this chapter.

    The Gouvernement, by regulation, may define the classes of children envisaged in the preceding paragraph and determine the procedure to be followed in view of obtaining such an exemption.

    The brothers and sisters of such children may also be exempted if they are not already attending school in Québec.

84. No secondary school leaving certificate may be issued to a student who does not have the speaking and writing knowledge of French required by the curricula of the Ministère de l'éducation.

85. Persons staying in Québec temporarily or their children may be exempted by the Minister of Education from the application of this chapter to such extent as the Government may prescribe by regulation.

    The regulations shall prescribe the cases, conditions or circumstances wherein certain persons, categories of persons, or their children, may be exempted, the period for which an exemption may be granted and the formalities of application and renewal.

86. The Gouvernement may make regulations extending the scope of section 73 to include such persons as may be contemplated in any reciprocity agreement that may be concluded between the Gouvernement of Québec and another province.

86.1 The Government, by order, may, at the request of the father and mother, authorize generally the following children to receive their instruction in English:

    (a) a child whose father or mother received the greater part of his or her elementary instruction in English elsewhere in Canada and, before establishing domicile in Québec, was domiciled in a province or territory that it indicates in the order and where it considers that the services of instruction in French offered to French-speaking persons are comparable to those offered in English to English-speaking persons in Québec;

    (b) a child whose father or mother establishes domicile in Québec and who, during his last school year or from the beginning of the current school year, has received primary or secondary instruction in English in the province or territory indicated in the order;

    (c) the younger brothers and sisters of children described in sub-paragraphs a and b.

87. Nothing in this act prevents the use of an Amerindic language in providing instruction to the Amerinds, or the Inukitut in providing instruction to the Inuit.

Note: Those sections of Chapter VIII of the Act not included in this appendix, that is, sections 76, 77, 82, 83 and 88 and certain parts of sections 78, 79 and 86.1, refer primarily to administrative procedures or, in the case of section 88, to the languages of instruction for use in the Cree and Inuit communities of Québec.

Appendix F

Canada Constitution Act 1982
Charter of Rights and Freedoms
Section 23: Minority Language Educational Rights

Language of instruction

23. (1) Citizens of Canada

(a) whose first language learned and still understood is that of the English or French linguistic minority population of the province in which they reside, or

(b) who have received their primary school instruction in Canada in English or French and reside in a province where the language in which they received that instruction is the language of the English or French linguistic minority population of the province,

have the right to have their children receive primary and secondary school instruction in that language in that province.

Continuity of language instruction

(2) Citizens of Canada of whom any child has received or is receiving primary or secondary school instruction in English or French in Canada, have the right to have all their children receive primary and secondary school instruction in the same language.

Application where numbers warrant

(2) The right of citizens of Canada under subsections (1) and (2) to have their children receive primary and secondary school instruction in the language of the English or French linguistic minority population of a province

(a) applies wherever in the province the number of children of citizens who have such a right is sufficient to warrant the provision to them out of public funds of minority language instruction; and

(b) includes, where the number of those children so warrants, the right to have them receive that instruction in minority language educational facilities provided out of public funds.

Appendix G
Preamble to Bill 60 (1964)

Whereas every child is entitled to the advantage of a system of education conducive to the full development of his personality;

Whereas parents have the right to choose the institutions which, according to their convictions, ensure the greatest respect for the rights of their children;

Whereas persons and groups are entitled to establish autonomous educational institutions and, subject to the requirements of the common welfare, to avail themselves of the administrative and financial means necessary for the pursuit of their ends;

Whereas it is expedient to establish, in accordance with these principles, to collaborate with the Minister of Education, a Superior Council of Education with which shall be associated a Catholic committee, a Protestant committee, and boards to make suggestions to such Council respecting various branches of education.

Note: With the exception of the wording in the last paragraph, the text of the preamble is the same in both the Education Department Act and the Superior Council of Education Act, both of which were brought into force May 13, 1964.

Appendix H
Regulation of the Catholic Committee (1974)

Whereas every student is entitled to an education which will permit his complete development on the physical, intellectual, emotional, social, moral and religious level;

Whereas the religious dimension constitutes, for man as an individual and as a member of society, an important area field of experience and meaning;

Whereas the institution which is the Catholic confessional school must be conceived as the educational institution which openly accepts the religious dimension as an integral part of its education programme and the Christian concept of man and of life as the inspirational principle and norm of its pedagogical action;

The Catholic Committee of the Superior Council of Education, in accord with paragraphs "a", "c", and "d" of section 22 of the Superior Council of Education Act, makes the following regulation respecting the Catholic educational institutions of Quebec.

Division I Definitions

1. In this regulation:

    (a) the word "institution" means a confessional educational institution recognized as Catholic;

    (b) the words "school authority" mean every corporation of school commissioners or school trustees and every physical or moral person that is the owner of an educational institution;

    (c) the words "to be of the Catholic faith" mean to have been baptized in the Roman Catholic Church and to declare that one is of the Catholic faith.

Division II Recognition of Confessional Educational Institutions as Catholic

2. Recognition is the legal act by which the Catholic Committee of the Superior Council of Education recognizes, on its own initiative or upon request, that a confessional educational institution, public or private, is Catholic.

3. In order that recognition be maintained, an institution must
    (a) comply with the regulations of the Catholic Committee; and
    (b) follow the curricula and use the educational teaching material approved or authorized by the Catholic Committee.

4. Recognition may be revoked:
    (a) if the institution ceases to fulfill the conditions mentioned in article 3; or
    (b) if the school authority so requests.

5. The Catholic Committee may recognize as Catholic, on a temporary basis of one year, a confessional institution which does not completely fulfill the conditions mentioned in article 3.

Division III Moral and Religious Instruction

6. The institution must include in its regular schedule religious instruction which complies with the programmes approved or authorized by the Catholic Committee.

7. The institution must see to the quality of religious instruction so that the student may deepen his Christian faith and broaden his religious experience and knowledge.

8. Religious instruction must be in accord with Christian doctrine, be dispensed with intellectual rigour and be adapted to the personal development of the students' faith.

9. At the elementary level, a minimum of 120 minutes per 5-day week must be devoted to religious instruction; at the secondary level, an average of 100 minutes per 5-day week must be devoted to religious and moral instruction. In both cases, the time must be apportioned and coordinated according to the requirements of the teaching of this discipline, the needs of the students and the schedule of the institution.

10. In each grade of the elementary level, Catholic religious instruction is compulsory for all students, without prejudice to article 14.

11. In the first two years of the secondary level, Catholic religious instruction is compulsory for all students, without prejudice to articles 14 and 15.

12. In the third, fourth and fifth year of the secondary level, the institution may set up a variety of programmes of religious and moral instruction:
    (a) In the third year, the institution may offer a choice between Catholic religious instruction, which must always be offered, and moral instruction;
    (b) In the fourth and fifth years, the instruction may offer a choice between Catholic religious instruction, which must always be offered, and religious instruction of a cultural type and moral instruction.
    Without prejudice to articles 14 and 15, the student is required, in each of these three years, to choose one of the programmes offered.

13. At the post-secondary level, the institution must include in its curriculum a course in Christian thought which the student is free to choose.

14. At the elementary and secondary levels, parents or tutors may obtain exemption from courses in religious instruction for their minor children by applying in writing to the director of the institution.

15. At the secondary level, the director of the institution, after obtaining the consent of the parents or tutor, shall exempt a minor student from a course in religious instruction if the student requests it.

16. The institution must provide students exempted from religious instruction with a programme of instruction or personal research pertaining to moral formation or religious knowledge.

Division IV Pastoral Animation

17. The institution must ensure that pastoral animation is provided.

18. The pastoral animator is a member of the institution's personnel. His role consists in making the students and teachers aware of the objectives of Christian education and in promoting projects which will foster Christian faith.

19. The director of the institution must facilitate the inclusion of pastoral animation in the school programme.

20. Secondary and post-secondary level institutions must provide premises suitable for pastoral activities. They must also provide an office for the pastoral animation staff.

Division V Management and Professional Staff

21.   Every person in management, teaching and other educational services in an institution is required to respect its confessional character.

22.   The personnel of an institution must be Catholic. Should it be difficult to obtain the services of a competent Catholic person, the services of a competent non-Catholic may be retained provided such person promises to respect the confessional character of the institution.

However, Catholic religious instruction shall only be given by persons of Catholic faith.

23.   The director, in his capacity as the chief responsible officer of the institution, must ensure conditions favorable to the active participation of students and members of the teaching and non-teaching staff in the implementation of an educational programme in harmony with the Christian concept of man.

24.   It is the duty of the school authorities to take into account the particular needs and requirements of each institution when they hire and assign management staff as well as teaching and non-teaching staff.

25.   To guarantee the right of a child to religious instruction of quality, the institution must see to it that a teacher be exempted from giving such instruction:

(a) when such teacher persists in giving instruction which does not comply with the requirements mentioned in articles 7 and 8;

(b) when the freedom of conscience of the teacher so dictates.

26.   The school authorities must take the necessary measures to provide pastoral animation as well as the coordination of religious instruction and pastoral activities in institutions under their jurisdiction.

Appendix I

Regulation of the Protestant Committee (1975)

Preamble

Public education in Quebec is, and has for many years, been organized along confessional lines.

A Protestant school, from a legal viewpoint, is a group of pupils under a principal or head teacher appointed by a board elected by citizens deemed in law to be Protestant; its curricula are those laid down for Protestant schools by the Department of Education.

Schools, complying with the Regulation which follows may be recognized as Protestant, from a confessional and pedagogical point of view.

Protestant Education in Quebec has among its aims, the following:

(1) to promote excellence of educational standards open to the testing of new ideas whenever and wherever they emerge;

(2) to be aware of and have a respect for the religious convictions of parents (or guardians), whose children attend Protestant schools;

(3) to provide an education conducive to the fullest development of personality and an awareness of human worth;

(4) to ensure that moral and religious instruction is based upon sound educational principles and is related to life and experience;

(5) to transmit, as objectively as possible, the full range of its cultural heritage, including the inter-relationships of Judaeo-Christian faith, Graeco-Roman civilization and scientific and technological thought.

Ideally, Protestant Education recognizes:

(1) the freedom of the individual to interpret spiritual and moral questions according to his conscience;

(2) the importance of fostering in the minds of pupils a moral and spiritual interpretation of life;

(3) the need to encourage a sense of responsible citizenship in each child;

(4) the desirability of acquiring a knowledge of the Bible.

The following Regulation seeks to render explicit the concern of the community for the transmission of its total heritage, with complete respect for all religious and philosophical options. This approach is not dictated pragmatically by the existence of a pluralist society; it presupposes, rather, the primacy of parental responsibility in the area of one's specific religious or philosophical commitment.

The Regulation also delineates the nature of moral and religious instruction, which, when taught by competent instructors, neither proposes a specific religious or moral position, nor arbitrarily excludes from the consideration of developing young people, various approaches relating to meaning and ultimate values.

273

Division I Definitions

1. In this regulation:

    (a) the words "school authority" mean any school corporation or regional commission with the meaning of the Education Act and any person or group of persons who own an educational institution;

    (b) the word "Committee" means the Protestant Committee of the Superior Council of Education;

    (c) the word "institution" means an educational institution in the public or private sector or any section or department thereof recognized as Protestant by the Committee.

Division II Recognition of institutions as Protestant

2. Recognition is the juridical act whereby the Protestant Committee of the Superior Council of Education recognizes ex officio, or on request, that an educational institution, public or private, is Protestant.

3. Before recognizing an institution as Protestant, the Committee shall ensure that it:

    (a) observes the Regulation of the Committee;

    (b) follows the curricula and makes use of textbooks and teaching materials approved or authorized by the Committee for moral and religious instruction;

    (c) in all other disciplines follows the curricula and uses textbooks approved, from the point of view of religion and morals, by the Committee.

4. Such recognition may be revoked:

    (a) if the institution ceases to comply with the conditions mentioned in section 3; or

    (b) if the school authority so requests.

5. In the case of Paragraph (a) of section 4, the revocation may not be effected until such institution has been given written notice of the reasons for revocation and has had the opportunity of expressing its point of view within 30 days of receipt of the aforementioned notice. Within 15 days of the expiration of this delay, the Committee may revoke the recognition granted and in this case a written notice of the Committee's decision shall be given to the institution.

    6. The Committee may recognize as Protestant temporarily for one year an educational institution which does not entirely satisfy the requirements set forth in section 3.

Division III Moral and Religious Instruction and religious observance in the Institution

7. The institution shall offer to its pupils moral and religious instruction in conformity with the curricula approved or authorized by the Committee.

8. The content and the administration of moral and religious instruction shall have as their objective the growth of a moral and spiritual interpretation of life and not the indoctrination of the pupils with a denominational point of view.

9. Moral and religious instruction shall include:

    (a) courses of Bible study based on passages selected from the Old or New Testaments, or both; or

(b) courses of study dealing with world religions, philosophy or ethics, personal development, human relations and social problems;

(c) or both.

10.   The institution shall pay particular attention to the quality of moral and religious instruction in order to develop in the pupil a growing awareness of moral and religious values, the broadening of his socio-spiritual culture and experience and regard for the pupil's personal development in faith and religion.

11.   Freedom of conscience is a fundamental principle of Protestant institutions. Every pupil of such institutions shall be given an opportunity to follow courses in moral and religious instruction and to participate in activities of a religious nature; however, no student shall be required to follow such courses or participate in such activities, if, for reasons of conscience, a request to this effect is made in writing to the head of the institution by the pupil's father, mother or guardian.

In the case of pupils of the age of majority the pupil's own written request on conscientious grounds shall be accepted.

12.   The institution shall be equipped with all necessary teaching materials for moral and religious instruction.

Division IV Management and Teaching Staff

13.   It shall be the responsibility of the principal to see that moral and religious instruction is carried out with respect for the religious beliefs of parents, pupils and staff.

14.   Every teacher shall respect the nature of a Protestant school as set forth in this Regulation.

15.   Each institution shall engage competent teaching personnel necessary for the implementation of the programme of moral and religious instruction.

16.   A teacher who considers that certain provisions of the Regulations of the Committee do not respect his right to freedom of conscience may be relieved from the duty of providing moral and religious instruction or of taking part in religious activities provided that he so requests in writing at the time of engagement or reengagement, setting forth the reasons for his request.

References

Chapter One

Arnopoulos, Sheila McLeod, and Dominique Clift. *The English Fact in Quebec.* Montreal: McGill-Queen's Press, 1980.

Biouin, Jean and Jacques Dufresne. "Rapport sur l'école." *L'Actualite,* 11, 4 (avril 1986): 34-44.

Caldwell, Gary and Eric Waddell, eds. *The English of Quebec: From Majority to Minority Status.* Quebec: Institut quebecois de recherche sur la culture, 1979.

Canada, Statistics Canada. *Advance Statistics of Education, 1985-86.* Ottawa, 1985.

Canadian Education Association. *An Overview of Canadian Education.* Third edition. Toronto: CEA, 1984.

Courville, Serge. "Le développement québécois de l'ère pionnière aux conquêtes postindustrielles." In *Le Québec statistique, Édition 1985-1986.* Québec: Bureau de la Statistique, 1985, pp. 37-55.

Dion, Leon. *Quebec: The Unfinished Revolution.* Montreal: McGill-Queen's Press, 1976.

Duchesne, Louis. "L'évolution démographique du Québec 1980-1984." In *Le Québec statistique, Édition 1985-1986.* Québec: Bureau de la Statistique, 1985, pp. 75-111.

Fournier, Marcel. "L'évolution socio-culturelle du Québec de la Seconde Guerre mondiale à aujourd'hui." In *Le Québec statistique: Édition 1985-1986.* Québec: Bureau de la Statistique, 1985, pp. 113-128.

Gouin, Pierre. "L'économie du Québec au debut des années quatre-vingt." In *Le Québec statistique, Édition 1985-1986.* Québec: Bureau de la Statistique, 1985, pp. 129-142.

"Les communautes culturelles à l'école," *Le Devoir* (24 aout 1984), Cahier 3.

"Les droits des minorités," *Le Devoir* (5 mars 1985), Cahier 3.

Luetkens, W.L. "Quebec." *The Financial Times* (October 11, 1982): 21-25.

Lysons, Heather. "The Language Question and Quebec Education." In *Options: Reforms and Alternatives for Canadian Education.* Edited by Terence Morrison and Anthony Burton. Toronto: Holt, Rinehart and Winston, 1973, pp. 317-339.

MacDonald, Robert J. "Language, Education and Society in Quebec." In *Canadian Education in the 1980s.* Edited by J. Donald Wilson. Calgary: Detselig, 1981, pp. 115-132.

Mair, Nathan. *The Quest for Quality in the Protestant Public Schools of Quebec.* Québec, Comite protestant, Conseil supérieur de l'Education, 1980.

Maisonneuve, Daniel. *L'etat de scolarisation de la population quebecoise.* Québec, Ministère de l'Éduction, 1983.

McGill Journal of Education. Special Issue on Quebec Education, 7,2 (Fall 1972).

Milner, Henry. *The Long Road to Reform: Restructuring Public Education in Quebec.* Montreal: McGill-Queen's Press, 1986.

Organization for Economic Cooperation and Development. *Reviews of National Policies for Education: Canada.* Paris: OECD, 1976.

Postgate, Dale and Kenneth McRoberts. *Quebec: Social Change and Political Crisis.* Toronto: McClelland and Stewart, 1976.

Québec. *Charte de la langue française*. Québec, 1981.

_____ . *Report of the Royal Commission of Inquiry on Education in the Province of Quebec*. Alphonse Marie Parent, chairman. Quebec, 1963-1966. 5 volumes.

_____ . *Quebec's Cultural Policy on the French Language*. Quebec, 1977.

_____ . *A Cultural Development Policy for Quebec*. Quebec, 1979.

Québec, Bureau de la Statistique du Québec. *Le Québec statistique, Édition 1985-1986*. Québec, 1986.

Québec, Comité catholique, Conseil supérieur de l'Éducation. *Religion in Today's School*. 2 Vols. Québec, 1974, 1976.

_____ . *Anglo-Catholics and School Confessionality*. Quebec, 1982.

_____ . *Catholic Religious Instruction and Moral Instruction in Catholic Schools*. Quebec, 1982.

_____ . L'école publique catholique dans un système scolaire en évolution. Québec, 1982.

_____ . *L'École catholique: Situation et avenir*. Québec, 1986.

Québec, Comité protestant, Conseil supérieur de l'Éducation. *The Protestant Fact in Quebec Education*. Québec, 1977.

Québec, Conseil du Statut de la Femme. *Egalite ET independence*. Québec, 1978.

Québec, Conseil supérieur de l'Éducation. *La confessionalite scolaire*. Québec, 1981.

_____ . *Confessionality and the Schools of Quebec*. Quebec, 1981.

_____ . *Intercultural Education*. Quebec, 1983.

_____ . *Annual Report, 1984-1985* Quebec, 1986.

Québec, Ministère de l'Éducation. *Rapport annuel 1984-1985*. Québec, 1985.

_____ . *Rapport annuel 1985-1986* Québec, 1986.

_____ . *Reportoire des organismes et des etablissements d'enseignement, Édition 1984-1985*. Québec, 1984.

_____ . *Statistiques de l'éducation: Préscolaire, primaire, secondaire*. Québec, 1985.

_____ . *Indicateurs sur la situation de l'enseignement primaire et secondaire*. Québec, 1986.

Quebec, Standing Committee on Social Development. *For Quebec Families: A Working Paper on Family Policy*. Quebec, 1984.

Schachter, Susan, ed. "Working Papers on English-Language Institutions in Quebec." Montreal: Alliance Quebec, 1982.

Thompson, Dale, ed. *Quebec: Society and Politics – Views from the Inside*. Toronto: McClelland and Stewart, 1973.

Chapter Two

Audet, Louis-Philippe. "Attempts to Develop a School System for Lower Canada: 1760-1840." In *Canadian Education – A History*. Edited by J.D. Wilson, R.M. Stamp, L.P. Audet. Scarborought, Ont.: Prentice-Hall, 1970, pp. 145-167.

_____ . "Education in Canada East and Quebec: 1840-1875." In *Canadian Education – A History*. Edited by J.D. Wilson, R.M. Stamp, L.P. Audet. Scarborough Ont.: Prentice-Hall, 1970, pp. 167-189.

_____ . "Society and Education in New France." In *Canadian Education – A History.* Edited by J.D. Wilson, R.M. Stamp, L.P. Audet. Scarborough, Ont.: Prentice-Hall, 1970, pp. 70-85.

_____ . *Histoire de l'enseignement au Quebec: 1840-1971.* Montréal: Holt, Rinehart et Winston, 1971, 2 tomes.

_____ . *Le système scolaire de la province de Québec.* Québec: Les Éditions de l'Erable, 1950-1956, 6 vol.

_____ and Armand Gauthier. *Le système scolaire au Québec.* Montréal: Beauchemin, 1967.

Black, Conrad. *Duplessis.* Toronto: Macmillan and Stewart, 1977.

Burgess, Donald A. "Education and Social Change: A Quebec Case Study." Unpublished Doctoral dissertation, Harvard University, 1978.

Carter, G. Emmett. *The Catholic Public Schools of Quebec.* Toronto: Gage, 1957.

Desaulniers, O.J. "Public Education in Quebec." In *Leadership in Action.* Edited by G.E. Flower and F. Stewart. Toronto: Gage, 1958, pp. 54-65.

Desbiens, Jean-Paul (Frère Untel). *The Impertinences of Brother Anonymous.* Montreal: Harvest House, 1962.

Dion, Leon. *Le Bill 60 et la société québécoise.* Montréal: Éditions HMH, 1967.

Galarneau, Claude. *Les collèges classiques au Canada français.* Montréal: Fides, 1978.

Henchey, Norman. "Quebec Education: The Unfinished Revolution." *McGill Journal of Education,* 7,2 (Fall 1972): pp. 95-118.

Lamontagne, Jacques. "The Rise and Fall of Classical Education in Quebec: A Systemic Analysis." In *Education, Change and Society: A Sociology of Canadian Education.* Edited by Richard A. Carlton, Louise A. Colley, Neil J. MacKinnon. Toronto: Gage, 1977, pp. 140-158.

LeBlanc, Andre E. "The Educational Literature of the Quiet Revolution," *McGill Journal of Education,* 7,2 (Fall 1972): 175-188.

Lussier, Irenée. *Roman Catholic Education and French Canada.* Toronto: Gage, 1960.

MacLennan, Hugh. *Two Solitudes.* Toronto: Macmillan, 1945.

Magnuson, Roger. *A Brief History of Quebec Education: From New France to Parti Québécois.* Montreal: Harvest House, 1980.

Mair, Nathan. *The Quest for Quality in the Protestant Public Schools of Quebec.* Quebec, Comité protestant, Conseil supérieur de l'Education, 1980.

Percival, Walter P. *Across the Years: A Century of Education in the Province of Quebec.* Montreal: Gazette Printing, 1946.

_____ . *Should We All Think Alike? Differentiating Characteristics of French Canadian Education in Quebec.* Toronto: Gage, 1951.

Quebec. "Historical Sketch." In *Report of the Royal Commission of Inquiry on Education in the Province of Quebec.* Quebec, 1963. Vol. 1, pp. 1-21.

Québec, Comité catholique, Conseil supérieur de l'Éducation. *L'École catholique: Situation et avenir.* Québec, 1986.

Rexford, Elson I. *Our Educational Problem: The Jewish Population and the Protestant Schools.* Montreal: Renouf, 1924.

Rudin, Ronald. *The Forgotten Quebecers: History of English-Speaking Quebec 1759-1980.* Québec: Institut québécois de recherche sur la culture, 1985.

Tomkins, George S. *A Common Countenance: Stability and Change in the Canadian Curriculum.* Scarborough, Ont.: Prentice-Hall Canada, 1986.

Tremblay, Arthur. "Dix ans de reforme scolaire au Québec: Un bilan et un avenir." *Papers: 1969: Communications.* The Comparative and International Education Society of Canada, pp. 46-68.

Trudeau, Pierre E. *Federalism and the French Canadians.* New York: St. Martin's Press, 1968.

_____ . *The Asbestos Strike.* Translated by James Boake. Toronto: James Lewis and Samuel, 1974.

Wade, Mason. *The French-Canadian Outlook.* Toronto: McClelland and Stewart, 1964.

_____ . *The French Canadians 1760-1967.* Toronto: Macmillan, 1968, 2 vols.

Wilson, J.D., R.M. Stamp, L.P. Audet, ed. *Canadian Education: A History.* Scarborough, Ont.: Prentice-Hall, 1970.

Chapter Three

Benjamin, Claude. "Participation au Québec." *Education Canada,* 21,1 (1981): 9-15, 30.

Bouchard, Michel, Pierre Etienne, Gilles Isabelle. *Le système scolaire du Québec.* Montréal: Guérin, 1981, 1982. 2 vols.

Burgess, Donald A. "Reorganizing the School System in Quebec." *Education Canada,* 22,4 (1982): 12-16, 21.

_____ . "Quebec School Boards and the Problems of Reform." *Alternative Approaches to Determining Distribution of School Board Trustee Representation.* Toronto: Ontario Ministry of Education, 1986, Vol. 1, Chapter 5, pp. 104-133.

Gendreau, Benoit, Andre Lemieux. *Milieu scolaire québécois.* Montréal: Les Editions France-Québec, 1977.

Lessard, Claude. "The Montreal School Reorganization Process: Why and Why Not?" *Canadian and International Education,* 9 (November 1980): 33-47.

Milner, Henry. *The Long Road to Reform: Restructuring Public Education in Quebec.* Montreal: McGill-Queen's Press, 1986.

Pelletier, G. and C. Lessard. *La population québécoise face à la restructuration scolaire.* Montréal: Guérin, 1982.

Quebec. *Department of Education Act* and *Superior Council of Education Act.* (Bill 60). Quebec, 1964.

_____ . *Education Act.* R.S.Q., chapter 1-14, Updated to 1 October 1985. Quebec, 1985.

_____ . *An Act respecting private education.* (Revised) Quebec, 1983.

_____ . *An Act respecting public elementary and secondary education.* (Bill 3, 1984, chapter 39.) Quebec, 1984.

_____ . *Report of the Royal Commission of Inquiry on Education in the Province of Quebec.* "The Ministry of Education," Vol. 1, Ch. 6, pp.89-104; "The Superior

Council of Education," Vol. 1, Ch. 7, pp. 105-121; "Local School Administration," Vol. 4, Ch. 5, pp. 135-176; "Steps in the Reform of School Administration," Vol. 4, Ch. 6, pp. 177-206. Quebec, 1963-1966.

Québec, Ministère de l'Education. *Primary and Secondary Education in Quebec: Green Paper.* Québec, 1977.

_____ . *The Schools of Quebec: Policy Statement and Plan of Action.* Québec, 1979.

_____ . *The School's Educational Project.* Québec, 1981.

_____ . *The School's Orientation Committee: The What, Why and How?* Québec, 1981.

_____ . *The Quebec School: A Responsible Force in the Community.* Québec, 1982.

_____ . *Rapport annuel 1985-1986.* Québec, 1986.

_____ . Conseil supérieur de l'Education. *La restructuration scolaire: Loi sur l'enseignement primaire et secondaire publique.* Québec, 1983.

Chapter Four

Canada, Statistics Canada. *Advance Statistics of Education, 1985-86.* Ottawa, 1985.

Magnuson, Roger. "Curriculum Reform in Quebec." *Curriculum and Teaching,* 1 (1986): 69-75.

Quebec. *Report of the Royal Commission of Inquiry on Education in the Province of Quebec.* Vol. 2 and 3. Quebec, 1964.

Quebec. *An Act respecting public elementary and secondary education* (Bill 3, 1984, Chapter 39). Quebec, 1984.

Québec, Les actes des états généraux sur la qualité de l'éducation. *Objectif 100%: Exposés des personnes-ressources.* Québec, 1986.

Proceedings of the Estates General on the Quality of Education. *Objective 100%: Summary of Workshops.* Quebec, 1986.

Quebec, Ministère de l'Education. *The Cooperative School: Comprehensiveness and Continuous Progress.* Quebec, 1966.

_____ . *Programme for the Polyvalent Secondary School.* Quebec, 1967.

_____ . *L'Ecole milieu de vie: Organisation pédagogique de l'enseignement elémentarie.* 2 vol. Québec: 1971, 1976.

_____ . *L'Education de l'enfance en difficulté d'adaptation et d'apprentissage au Québec.* Rapport du comité provincial de l'enfance inadaptée (C.O.P.E.X.). Québec, 1976.

_____ . *Primary and Secondary Education in Quebec: Green Paper.* Quebec, 1977.

_____ . *Consultation sur le livre vert de l'enseignement primaire et secondaire.* Québec, 1978, 1979, 6 Vol. *Synthèse des resultats de la consultation; Synthèse des audiences nationales; Synthèse des audiences régionales; Synthèse des audiences anglophones; Resultats d'un sondage; Revue de presse sur le Livre vert de l'enseignement primaire et secondaire.*

_____ . *The Schools of Quebec: Policy Statement and Plan of Action.* Quebec, 1979.

_____ . *The Schools of Quebec: Policy Statement and Plan of Action – Children with Difficulties in Learning and Adaptation.* Quebec, 1979.

_____ . *L'Ecole s'adapte à son milieu: Enoncé de politique sur l'école en milieu economiquement faible.* Québec, 1980.

_____ . "Cadre revisé d'elaboration des programmes et des guides pédagogiques." Québec, 1980. (mimeo)

_____ . *Le projet éducatif de l'école.* Québec, 1980.

_____ . *Le projet éducatif dans quelques écoles primaires; Le projet éducatif dans quelques écoles secondaires; Reflections sur le projet éducatif de l'école.* Québec, 1980.

_____ . *General Policy for Educational Evaluation for Preschool, Elementary and Secondary Schools.* Doc. 16-7500A. Quebec, 1981.

_____ . *Regulation Respecting the Basis of Elementary School Organization (Régime pédagogique).* Quebec, 1981.

_____ . *Regulation Respecting the Basis of Secondary School Organization (Régime pédagogique).* Quebec, 1981.

_____ . "End-of-Cycle Evaluation: Information Document." Quebec, 1982.

_____ . *Technical and Vocational Education for Young People: Proposals for Revival and Renewal.* Quebec, 1982.

_____ . *L'Evaluation dans le système éducatif: Cadre géneral et perspectives de développement.* Québec, 1983.

_____ . "60% of What? Considerations on Marking, Recording and Reporting the Results of Summative Evaluation in Secondary School." Study Paper. Quebec, 1983. (16-7508A)

_____ . "L'Apprentissage, l'enseignement et les nouveaux programmes d'études." Québec, 1984.

_____ . "L'adaptation de l'enseignement." Québec, 1985.

_____ . *Statistiques de l'éducation: Préscolaire, primaire, secondaire.* Québec, 1985.

_____ . *Indicateurs sur la situation de l'enseignement primaire et secondaire.* Québec, 1986.

_____ . *Rapport annuel 1985-1986.* Québec, 1986.

_____ . *La formation professionnelle au secondaire: Plan d'action.* Québec, 1986.

Québec, Conseil supérieur de l'Education. *Draft-Regulations on Preschool Education and on the Régimes Pedagogiques of Primary and Secondary Schools.* Quebec, 1980.

_____ . *Admission Age for Preschoolers and Elementary School Pupils.* Quebec, 1982.

_____ . *Advice Concerning the Working Paper on a Sex Education Program of the Ministry of Education.* Quebec, 1982.

_____ . *Health and Social Services in the School System.* Quebec, 1982.

_____ . *The Evaluation of Learning: Does It Count?* Quebec, 1982.

_____ . *The State of the So-Called "Secondary" Subjects at the Elementary Level.* Quebec, 1982.

_____ . *La formation professionnelle des jeunes: Analyse critique des propositions ministérielles et quelques considerations complementaires.* Québec, 1983.

_____ . *La place faite aux élèves en difficulté d' adaptation et d' apprentissage et aux jeunes doués ou talentueux dans une école secondaire en quête d' excellence.* Québec, 1983.

_____ . *Le classement des élèves à l' éducation préscolaire et au primaire.* Québec, 1983.

_____ . *Le temps prescrit à l' éducation préscolaire et au primaire.* Québec 1983.

_____ . *L' Evaluation: Situation actuelle et voies de développement – Rapport 1982-1983.* Québec, 1983.

_____ . *La formation scientifique des jeunes du secondaire.* Québec, 1984.

_____ . *L' école primaire face à la violence.* Québec, 1984.

_____ . *L' enseignement des langues secondes dans les écoles primaires et secondaires.* Québec, 1984.

_____ . *Projet de règlement modifiant le règlement sur le régime pédagogique du primaire et de l' éducation préscolaire et le règlement sur le régime pédagogique du secondaire.* Québec, 1984.

_____ . *L' Enseignement des mathematiques à l' école primaire.* Québec, 1985.

_____ . *Le régime pédagogique du secondaire et la qualité de la formation de base.* Québec, 1985.

_____ . *Les diverses formes de regroupement des élèves au primaire cycle du secondaire.* Québec, 1985.

_____ . *Par-delà les écoles alternatives: La diversité et l' innovation dans le système scolaire public.* Québec, 1985.

_____ . *Réussir l' integration scolaire des élèves en difficulté.* Québec, 1985.

_____ . *Apprendre pour de vrai: Témoignages sur les enjeux et les conditions d' une formation de qualité – Rapport 1984-1985 sur l' état et les besoins de l' éducation.* Québec, 1986. Ch. 1 et 2.

_____ . *Le deuxième cycle du secondaire: Particularités, enjeux, voies d' amelioration.* Québec, 1986.

_____ . *Le deuxième cycle d' enseignement secondaire ou son equivalent: Comparaisons de sept systèmes d' éducation avec le système d' education du Québec.* Prepared by Arthur Marsolais, Jean-Louis Pare, Paul Valois. Québec, 1986.

_____ . *Projets d' amendements au régime pédagogique du primaire* and *Projets d' amendements au régime pédagogique du secondaire.* Québec, 1986.

Chapter Five

Burgess, Donald A. "The English-Language CEGEP." *McGill Journal of Education,* 6,1 (1971): 99-101.

Canada, Statistics Canada. *Universities: Enrolment and Degrees, 1984-85.* Ottawa, 1985. (81-204)

Demers, Marius. *Une analyse de l' évolution des dépenses des universités de 1972-1973 à 1983-1984.* Québec: MEQ, 1984.

Dessureault, Guy. *Recherche documentaire sur les professeurs du collégial.* 3 cols. Québec: MEQ, 1981, 1983, 1985.

Laurin, Camille. *L'Avenir des universités québécoises: Vers une politique des universités*. Québec, MEQ, 1981.

LeBlanc, A.E. "Collegial Education in Quebec – A Bibliography," *McGill Journal of Education*.

"Les Cegeps 17 ans après," Le Devoir, (27 janvier, 1984): 15-28.

Lipkin, John and Ann Denis, "Quebec's Cegeps: Promise and Reality." *McGill Journal of Education*, 7,2 (Fall 1972): 119-134.

Quebec. *Report of the Royal Commission of Inquiry on Education in the Province of Quebec*. "Pre-university and Vocational Education," Vol. 2, Ch. 6, pp. 159-194; "Higher Education," Vol. 2, Ch. 7, pp. 195-260; "The Programme of Study at the Institute Level," Vol. 3, Ch. 27, pp. 235-248. Quebec, 1964.

_____ . *Pour une politique québécoise de la recherche scientifique*. Québec, 1979.

_____ . *Un projet collectif: Énoncé d'orientations et plan d'action pour la mise en oeuvre d'une politique québécoise de la recherche scientifique*. Québec, 1980.

Quebec, Commission d'étude sur les universités. *Rapport*. 4 Vols. Québec, 1979. Vol. 1: *Comité de coordination;* Vol. 2: *Comité d'étude sur l'université et la société québécoise:* Vol. 3; *Comité d'étude sur l'organisation du système universitaire;* Vol. 4: *Comité d'étude sur la formation et le perfectionnement des enseignants.*

Québec, Conférence des recteurs et des principaux des universités du Québec. "Reflections sur l'avenir de l'université au Québec." Montréal: CREPUQ, 1985.

Québec, Conseil des collèges. *Cinquième rapport annuel 1983-1984*. Québec, 1984.

_____ . *Le cegep de demain*. Québec, 1985.

_____ . *Sixième rapport annuel 1984-1985*. Québec, 1986.

Québec, Conseil des universités. Cahier 1: *L'Évolution recente de l'enseignement supérieur au Québec,* Québec, 1972; Cahier 2: *Objectifs généraux de l'enseignement supérieur,* Québec, 1973; Cahier 3: *Les orientations de l'enseignement supérieur dans les années 70,* Québec, 1973; Cahier 4: *Perspective 1976 des orientations de l'enseignement supérieur,* Québec, 1976.

_____ . *Quinzième rapport annuel, 1983-84*. Québec, 1984.

_____ . *Seizième rapport annuel 1984-1985*. Québec, 1985.

Québec, Conseil supérieur de l'Éducation. *Le collège: Rapport sur l'état et les besoins de l'enseignement collégial.* (Rapport Nadeau). Québec, 1975.

_____ . *Les adultes dans les programmes réguliers de l'université: Des etudiants à part entière*. Québec, 1985.

_____ . *Pour le renouvellement et le ressourcement du personnel de l'enseignement*. Québec, 1985.

_____ . *Apprendre pour de vrai: Témoignages sur les enjeux et les conditions d'une formation de qualité – Rapport 1984-1985 sur l'état et les besoins de l'éducation*. Québec, 1986. Chaptre 3: "Apprendre au collège: atouts et obstacles," pp. 41-56; Chaptre 4: "Apprendre a l'université: encore un processus d'interaction," pp. 57-70.

Quebec, Ministère de l'Éducation. *College Education and the General and Vocational Colleges*. Domument Number 3. Quebec, 1968.

_____ . *Les collèges du Québec: Nouvelle étape*. Québec, 1978.

_____ . *Regulation Respecting the Basis of College Organization* Quebec, 1984.

Quebec, Ministère de l'Enseignement supérieur, de la Science et de la Technologie. *Rapport annuel 1984-1985.* Québec, 1986.

SORECOM, Inc. "Les Québécois face aux universités et aux universitaires de Québec." Montréal: SORECOM, 1982.

Young, William A. "The Ministry of Education as Policy-maker: Toward centralization in the Cegeps of Quebec." *College Canada,* 8, 5 (March 1984): 7; 9, 1 (April 1984):7-8.

Chapter Six

Blaukopf, Phyllis and Dennis McCullough. "Education and the Marketplace." *Education Canada,* 25, 2 (1985): 39-42.

Canada, National Advisory Panel on Skill Development Leave. *Learning for Life: Overcoming the Separation of Work and Learning.* Ottawa, 1984.

Canada, Secretary of State and Statistics Canada. *One in Every Five: A Survey of Adult Education in Canada.* Ottawa, 1985.

Canadian Association for Adult Education. *From the Adult's Point of View.* Toronto: CAAE, 1982.

_____ . *An Analysis of the Statistics Canada Adult Education Survey, January 1984.* Toronto: CAAE, 1985.

Morisset, Paul. "Le business de la formation." *L'Actualite'*(decembre 1985): 118.

Mouvement des Caisses populaires et d'économie Desjardins du Québec. "Memoire presenté à la Commission d'étude sur la formation professionnelle et la formation socio-culturelle des adultes." Québec, 1980.

Musée des Beaux-arts de Montréal. *Pour vous au Museé.* no date.

Provincial Organization of Continuing Education Directors – English. *A Guide to English-Language Education Services in Quebec, 1985-86.* Montreal: The Association, 1986.

Québec. *Report of the Royal Commission of Inquiry on Education in the Province of Quebec.* "Continuing Education," Vol. 3, Ch. 9, pp. 323-336. Quebec, 1964.

_____ . *A Cultural Development Policy for Quebec. (La politique québecoise du développement culturel).* Québec, 1978. 2 vols.

_____ . *On a un monde a récréer.* Livre blanc sur le loisir au Québec. Québec, 1979.

_____ . *Continuing Education program: Policy Statement and Plan of Action.* Quebec, 1984.

Québec, Commission d'étude sur la formation des adultes. *Adult Education in Quebec: Possible Solutions – Work Document.* Quebec, 1981.

_____ . *Learning: A Voluntary and Responsible Action – Summary Report; Apprendre: Une action volontaire et responsable.* Final Report and 5 volumes of Appendices: Annexe 1, *L'éducation des adultes au Québec depuis 1850: points de repere;* Annexe 2, *Sondage sur les adultes québécois et leurs activités éducatives;* Annexe 3, *Sondage sur les pratiques de formation en enterprise;* Annexe 4, *Recherche connexes de la Commission;* Annexe 5, *Bibliographie annoteé sur la formation des adultes.* Québec, 1982.

Québec, Conseil supérieur de l'Éducation. *L'avenir de l'éducation des adultes.* Québec, 1983.

_____. *Pour que les jeunes adultes puissent esperer.* Québec, 1983.

_____. *Donner la parole aux adultes.* Québec, 1984.

_____. *Les adultes dans les programmes réguliers de l'université: Des étudiants à part entière.* Québec, 1985.

_____. *La formation professionnelle de la main- d'oeuvre: Le contexte et les enjeux éducatifs des prochains accords Québec-Ottawa.* Québec, 1986.

_____. *L'Accessibilité du système d'éducation aux adultes.* (Québec, 1986).

Radio-Québec. *Radio-Quebec maintenant.* Montréal, 1985.

Société des musées québécois. *Museé et éducation: modeles didactiques d'utilisation des museés.* Actes du colloque, 30, 31 octobre et 1 novembre 1985. Montréal, 1986.

Chapter Seven

Ayotte, Robert. "L'Évolution du organisation de la recherche québécoise." *Prospectives,* 20, 1-2 (Fev.-Avr. 1984): 7-16.

Bernhard, Paulette. "Recherches en éducation faites au Canada française." *Revue des Sciences de l'Éducation,* regular feature.

Canada, Social Science Federation of Canada. *Research Activities of Professors of Education in Canadian Universities.* Ottawa: The Federation, 1986.

Cormier, Roger, Claude Lessard, Paul Valois. *Les enseignantes et enseignants du Québec: Une etude socio-pedagogique.* Québec: Ministère de l'Éducation, Service de la recherche, 1979. 9 volumes. Vol. 1: "Presentation générale, validation préliminaire et resultats bruts;" Vol. 2: "La constitution des variables dependantes;" Vol. 3: "Characteristiques démographiques, socio-culturelles et professionnelles;" Vol. 4: "Valeurs éducationnelles;" Vol. 5: "Le vecu professionnel: tache et milieu de travail;" Vol. 6: "La formation et le perfectionnement;" Vol. 7: "Le futur anticipé et desiré;" Vol. 8: "Une synthèse;" Vol. 9: "Implications pour les politiques éducationnelles."

Dispositions constituant des conventions collectives, 1983-1985. Revision du 15-10-85. Québec: MEQ, 1985.

Henchey, Norman. "Alternatives to Decay: Prospects for the Teaching Profession in the Eighties." In *Canadian Education in the 1980s.* Calgary: Detselig, 1981.

Langlois, Richard. "Les enseignantes et enseignants des commissions scolaires, une population vieillissante." Québec: Centrale des enseignants du Québec, 1984.

Lavery, Robert. "Changes in the Teaching Profession." *McGill Journal of Education,* 7, 2 (Fall 1972): 166-174.

Laurin, Camille. *The Teacher: A Professional.* Quebec: MEQ, 1981.

Le Corré, René. "Prévision du nombre d'élèves des commissions scolaires du Québec, de 1985-86 à 1990-91." Québec: MEQ, 1985.

Lesperance, André. *Une projection du nombre de retraites chez les enseignants des commissions scolaires jusqu'en 2005.* Québec: MEQ, 1985.

Provisions Constituting Collective Agreements, Binding on the one hand, each of the School Boards for Protestants contemplated by Chapter 0-7.1 of the Revised Statutes of Quebec and on the other hand, each of the certified associations which, on November 29, 1982, negotiated through the Provincial Association of Protestant Teachers on behalf of teachers in the employ of these school boards, 1982-1985.

Quebec. *Report of the Royal Commission of Inquiry on Education in the Province of Quebec.* "Teacher Training," Vol. 2, Ch. 8, pp. 261-322; "The Mission, Rights, and Responsibilities of Teachers," Vol. 5, Ch. 12, pp. 197-218.

Quebec. *Education Act.* Revised Statutes of Quebec, Chapter 1-14. Quebec 1985.

Québec, Commission d'étude sur les universités, Comité d'étude sur la formation et le perfectionnement des enseignants. *Rapport.* Québec, 1979.

Québec, Conseil des universités. "Commentaires au Ministre de l'Éducation sur la formation et le perfectionnement des enseignants." Québec, 1984.

_____ . "La formation des maîtres au Québec: Retrospective et bilan." Québec, 1984.

_____ . *Bilan du secteur de l'Éducation.* Québec, 1986. Summary and 5 volumes. Volet 1: "Les programmes de formation;" Volet 2: "Les clientèles;" Volet 3: "Besoins des diplomés en éducation;" Volet 4: "Les ressources humaines et financières;" Volet 5: "La recherche".

Québec, Conseil supérieur de l'Éducation. *La condition enseignante.* Québec, 1984.

_____ . *Vers des amenagements de la formation et du perfectionnement des enseignants du primaire et du secondaire: Commentaires sur un projet ministeriel.* Québec, 1984.

_____ . *Pour le renouvellement et le ressourcement du personnel de l'enseignement.* Québec, 1985.

Québec, Conseil supérieur de l'Éducation, Comité catholique. *Regulation of the Catholic Committee.* Québec, 1974.

Québec, Conseil Supérierur de l'Éducation, Comite protestant. *Regulation of the Protestant Committee.* Québec, 1975.

Québec, Ministère de l'Éducation. *Regulation Number Four: Respecting the Permit and Licence to Teach.* Québec, 1966.

_____ . *Regulation Number Five: Respecting Criteria for Evaluating Scolarity as a Factor for Determining the Qualifications of Teaching Personnel.* Quebec, 1968.

_____ . "La formation des maîtres de l'éducation préscolaire et de l'enseignement primaire – Document d'orientation." Québec, 1977.

_____ . "Les orientations de la formation des enseignants specialistes en adaptation scolaire – Document d'orientation." Québec, 1980.

_____ . "La formation des enseignants de l'enseignement secondaire – Document d'orientation." Québec, 1980.

_____ . "La formation initiale des enseignants specialistes au primaire et au secondaire (en arts, en langues secondes et en éducation physique) – Document d'orientation." Québec, 1980.

_____ . "La formation pratique des enseignants – Document d'orientation." Québec, 1980.

_____ . *Regulation Respecting the Basis of Preschool and Elementary School Organization.* Quebec, 1981.

_____ . *Regulation Respecting the Basis of Secondary School Organization.* Quebec, 1981.

_____ . *La formation et le perfectionnement des enseignants du primaire et du secondaire: Vers des amenagements – Fiches de discussion.* Québec, 1983.

"Seminaire sur la formation des maîtres." *Prospectives,* 16, 1-2 (Fevrier-Avril 1980): numéro special.

Chapter Eight

Bezeau, Lawrence M. "The Public Finance of Private Education in the Province of Quebec." *Canadian Journal of Education,* 4,2 (1979): 23-42.

Canada, Statistics Canada. *Advance Statistics of Education, 1985-86.* Ottawa, 1985.

Demers, Marius. *L'effort financier en éducation: Un comparaison Quebec-Ontario 1972-1973 à 1985-1986.* Québec, Ministère de l'Education, 1986.

Quebec. *Report of the Royal Commission of Inquiry on Education in the Province of Quebec.* "The Costs of Education," Vol. 5, ch. 8, pp. 1-46; "The Financing of School Commissions," Vol. 5, Ch. 9, pp. 47-112; "The financing of Institutes and Universities," Vol. 5, Ch. 10, pp. 113-156.

Québec, Assemblée Nationale. commission permanente de l'éducation, "Étude des credits du ministère de l'Éducation et du ministère de l'Enseignement supérieur et de la Science." 23 avril, 1986 – No. 3.

_____ . Bureau de la Statistique. *Finances scolaires, 1951-1963.* Québec, 1964.

_____ . *Le Quebec statistique, Édition 1985-1986.* Québec, 1986.

Québec, Conseil des universités. "Avis au ministre de l'enseignement superieur, de la Science et de la Technologie sur le financement du système universitaire pour l'année 1985-86." Québec, 1985.

_____ . "La politique de financement des université pour l'année 1986-87." Québec, 1986.

Québec, Conseil supérieur de l'Éducation. *Le nouveau mode d'allocation des ressources aux commissions scolaires et les regles budgetaires 1986-1987.* Québec, 1986.

Québec, Ministère de l'Éducation. *Rapport annuel 1982-1983.* Québec, 1983.

_____ . *Rapport annuel 1983-1984.* Québec 1984.

_____ . *Rapport annuel 1984-1985.* Quebec, 1986.

_____ . *Cadre de financement du reseau universitaire pour l'anneé 1984-1985.* Québec, 1984. (Document 37-8230).

_____ . *Statistiques de l'Éducation: Prescolaire, primaire, secondaire.* Québec, 1985.

_____ . *Regles budgetaires pour l'anneé 1986-87.* Québec, 1986. (Document 27-1873).

_____ . *Indicateurs sur la situation de l'enseignement primaire et secondaire.* Québec, 1986.

Ryan, Claude. "Le financement des universités: Un vigoureux coup de barre s'impose." *Le Devoir* (18 septembre 1986): 9.

Chapter Nine

Arnopoulos, Sheila McLeod, and Dominique Clift. *The English Fact in Quebec.* Montreal: McGill-Queen's Press, 1980.

Caldwell, Gary. "Anglophones in Quebec." *Language and Society,* 8 (Autumn 1982): 3-6.

Caldwell, Gary and Eric Waddell, ed. *The English of Quebec: From Majority to Minority Status.* Québec: Institut québécois de recherche sur la culture, 1979.

Canada, Commissionner of Official Languages. *Annual Report 1985.* Ottawa, 1986.

Charbonneau, Jean Claude. "The Lay School Movement in Quebec since 1840." Unpublished Master's thesis, McGill University, 1971.

Fédération des comités de parents de la province de Québec. "Le sort reservé à l'enseignement des langues secondes." Brief submitted to the Conseil supérieur de l'Éducation, 1984.

Keogh, Brian. "The Quebec Department of Education, Cultural Pluralism and the Anglophone Catholic Minority." Unpublished Master's thesis, McGill University, 1974.

"Les communautés culturelles à l'école," *Le Devoir.* (24 aout 1984), Cahier 3.

"Les droits des minorités," *Le Devoir* (5 mars 1985), Cahier 3.

Lysons, Heather. "The Language Question and Quebec Education." In *Options: Reforms and Alternatives for Canadian Education.* Edited by Terence Morrison and Anthony Burton. Toronto: Holt, Rinehart and Winston, 1973, pp. 317-339.

MacDonald, Robert J. "Language, Education and Society in Quebec." In *Canadian Education in the 1980s.* Edited by J. Donald Wilson. Calgary: Detselig, 1981, pp. 115-132.

Magnuson, Roger. "The Decline of Roman Catholic Education in Quebec: Interpretations and Explanations." *Culture.* 30 (September 1969): 192-198.

_____ . "Language, Education and Society in Quebec." In *Precepts, Policy and Process: Perspectives on Contemporary Canadian Education.* Edited by Hugh A. Stevenson and J. Donald Wilson. London, Ont: Alexander, Blake Associates, 1977, pp. 59-77.

_____ . "Gallicism, Anglo-Saxonism and Quebec Education." *Canadian Journal of Education,* 9 (1984): 1-13.

Mair, Nathan. *The Quest for Quality in the Protestant Public Schools of Quebec.* Québec: Comité protestant, Conseil supérieur de l'Éducation, 1980.

National Commission on Excellence in Education. *A Nation at Risk: The Imperative for Educational Reform.* Washington D.C.: U.S. Department of Education, 1983.

Québec. *Charte de la langue française.* Québec, 1981.

_____ . *Report of the Royal Commission of Inquiry on Education in the Province of Quebec.* "Confessionality and Non-Confessionality," Vol. 4, ch. 2, pp. 49-88; "Cultural Diversity in the Field of Education and the Future of Quebec," Vol. 4, Ch. 3, pp. 89-115. Quebec, 1966.

_____ . *Quebec's Cultural Policy on the French Language.* Quebec, 1977.

_____ . *A Cultural Development Policy for Quebec.* Quebec, 1979.

Québec, Comité catholique, Conseil supérieur de l'Éducation. *Religion in Today's School.* 2 Vols. Québec: 1974, 1976.

_____. *Anglo-Catholics and School Confessionality*. Quebec, 1982.

_____. *Deux questions presentes pour l'école catholique*. Québec, 1983.

_____. *Recommendations au sujet de l'enseignement religieuse au collégial*. Québec, 1983.

_____. *L'École catholique: Situation et avenir*. Québec, 1986.

Québec, Conseil du Statut de la Femme. *Egalite´ET independence*. Québec, 1978.

Québec, Conseil Supérieur de l'Éducation. *La confessionalite´ scolaire*. Québec, 1981.

_____. *Teaching Second Language in Primary and Secondary Schools*. Quebec, 1984.

_____. *Confessionality and the Schools of Quebec*. Quebec, 1981.

_____. *Intercultural Education*. Quebec, 1983.

Québec, Comité protestant, Conseil supériérur de l'Éducation. *The Protestant Fact in Quebec Education*. Québec, 1977.

Quebec, Fédération des commissions scolaires catholiques du Québec. "Énoncé des elements d'une politique de financement appropriée aux commissions scolaires: Elements d'un nouveau modèle d'allocation des ressources pour les commissions scolaires." Document de consultation, 1985.

Quebec Federation of Home and School Associations. "A Statement to the Superior Council of Education on Second Language Teaching." Montreal: The Federation, 1984.

Québec, Ministère of l'Éducation. *Consultation sur le livre vert sur l'enseignement primaire et secondaire: synthése des audiences*. Québec, 1978.

_____. *The Schools of Quebec: Policy Statement and Plan of Action*. Quebec, 1979.

Quebec, Ministre de l'Éducation. "Communique de press." (25 avril, 1986).

Rudin, Ronald. *The Forgotten Quebecers: History of English-Speaking Quebec 1759-1980*. Québec: Institut québécois de recherche sur la culture, 1985.

Schachter, Susan (Ed.) "Working Papers on English-Language Institutions in Quebec." Montreal: Alliance Quebec, 1982.

Sisson, C.B. *Church and State in Canadian Education*. Toronto: Ryerson Press, 1959.

Chapter Ten

Blouin, Jean. "Le futur du Québec." *L'Actualite´,* 9, 11, (novembre 1984): 49-61.

Canada, Science Council of Canada. *Planning Now for an Information Society: Tomorrow Is Too Late*. Ottawa, 1982.

Cetron, M. *Schools of the Future*. New York: McGraw-Hill, 1985.

Cohen, D. and K. Shannon. *The NEXT Canadian Economy*. Montreal: Eden Press, 1984.

Cordell, A. *The Uneasy Eighties: The Transition to an Information Society*. Science Council of Canada Background Study No. 53. Ottawa, 1985.

Feldman, Elliot J. and Neil Nevitte, ed. *The Future of North America, the United States, and Quebec Nationalism*. Montreal: Institute for Research in Public Policy, 1979.

Godfrey D. and D. Parkhill, ed. *Gutenberg Two: The New Electronics and Social Change.* Toronto: Press Porcépic, 1980.

Goulet, J. *Les répercussions culturelles de l'informatisation au Québec.* Québec: Conseil de la langue française, 1982.

Groupe québécois de prospective. *Le futur du Québec au conditionnel.* Chicoutimi: Gaetan Morin, 1982.

Julien, P.A., P. Lamonde, D. Latouche. *Quebec 2001: Une societe´refroidie.* Québec: Boréal Express, 1976.

Organization for Economic Cooperation and Development. *Education in Modern Society.* Paris: OECD, 1985.

Québec, Bureau de la statistique du Québec. *L'Avenir démographique du Québec.* Québec: 1985.

_____ . Ministère de l'Éducation. *Micro-informatique: Propositions de developpement.* Quebec, 1983.

Spraakman, G., T. Becher, K. Wilde, ed. *Canadian Cultural Futures: Options for Living Together.* Montreal: Canadian Association for Futures Studies, 1984.

Index